Prophecy and Diplomacy

Prophecy and Diplomacy

The Moral Doctrine of John Paul II

A JESUIT SYMPOSIUM

edited by
JOHN J. CONLEY, S.J.
and
JOSEPH W. KOTERSKI, S.J.

Fordham University Press
New York
1999

Copyright © 1999 by Fordham University Press
All rights reserved. No part of this publication may be reproduced, stored in a retrieval system, or transmitted in any form or by any means—electronic, mechanical, photocopy, recording, or any other—except for brief quotations in printed reviews, without the prior permission of the publisher.
"John Paul II as a Theologian of Culture" by Avery Dulles, S.J., was first published in *Logos: A Journal of Catholic Thought and Culture* 1 (1997): 19–33. Reprinted by permission.

Library of Congress Cataloging-in-Publication Data

Prophecy and diplomacy : the moral doctrine of John Paul II : a Jesuit symposium / edited by John J. Conley and Joseph W. Koterski. — 1st ed.
  p. cm.
Includes bibliographical references and index.
ISBN 0-8232-1975-5. — ISBN 0-8232-1976-3 (pbk.)
1. John Paul II, Pope, 1920–   —Ethics Congresses. 2. Christian ethics—Catholic authors Congresses. 3. Catholic Church—Doctrines Congresses.   I. Conley, John J.   II. Koterski, Joseph W.
BJ1249.P77   1999
241′.042′092—dc21   99-41405
                                                                                    CIP

03 02 01 00 99   5 4 3 2 1
Printed in the United States of America
First Edition

CONTENTS

Preface by Archbishop Terrence Prendergast, S.J.   ix

Abbreviations   xi

Introduction by John J. Conley, S.J.   xiii

I. Fundamental Moral Theory

1. Ethics of the Person
   Person and Society: John Paul II on Substance and Relation   3
   JAMES V. SCHALL, S.J.
   Response   21
   MARTIN X. MOLESKI, S.J.

2. Ethics and Salvation   21
   Creation, Redemption, Solidarity: Pope John Paul II's Public Theology   24
   PATRICK J. LYNCH, S.J.
   Response   37
   BENJAMIN FIORE, S.J.

3. Moral Subjectivity
   Anatomy of Conscience: A Reading of Veritatis Splendor   40
   JOHN J. CONLEY, S.J.
   Response   49
   BENJAMIN FIORE, S.J.

4. Moral Conversion
   Christological Bases for the Moral Life: Redemptor Hominis As a Key to Veritatis Splendor   52
   RONALD A. MERCIER, S.J.
   Response   74
   EDMUND W. MAJEWSKI, S.J.

5. Morality and Society
   Person, Community, Law, and Grace: Reflections on Part Three, Section One of the Catechism of the Catholic Church   82
   ARTHUR R. MADIGAN, S.J.
   Response   111
   JOSEPH W. KOTERSKI, S.J.

6. Moral Theology
   The Context of Veritatis Splendor   115
   JOHN M. MCDERMOTT, S.J.

II. Applied Moral Theory   173

7. Ethics of Culture
   Faith and Culture in the Thought of John Paul II   175
   AVERY DULLES, S.J.

8. Demographic Ethics
   John Paul II on Demographic Ethics   190
   JOHN J. CONLEY, S.J.
   Response   204
   JOHN M. MCDERMOTT, S.J.

9. Economic Ethics
   Neoclassical Economics and the Economic Encyclicals of John Paul II   211
   JOHN J. PIDERIT, S.J.

10. Marital Ethics
    The Prophetic Mission of Marriage: John Paul II's Vision of Human Sexuality   247
    MARTIN X. MOLESKI, S.J.
    Response   202
    EDMUND W. MAJEWSKI, S.J.

11. Relational Ethics
    Covenant Love: Interpersonal Person, Family, and Work in the Social Theory of John Paul II   270
    ROBERT J. SPITZER, S.J.

12. Morality and Gender
   Letter to Women *and* Ordinatio Sacerdotalis   285
   JOHN M. McDERMOTT, S.J.

13. Morality and Family Rights
   Familiaris Consortio, *Fifteen Years Since*   293
   CHRISTOPHER M. CULLEN, S.J.

14. Comprehensive Ethic of Life
   Some Observations on Evangelium Vitae   301
   ARTHUR R. MADIGAN, S.J.

III. Postscript: John Paul II's Vision   313

15. Homily   313
   STEPHEN M. FIELDS, S.J.

Contributors   319

Index   321

PREFACE

TODAY MARKS THE TWENTIETH ANNIVERSARY of the election of Pope John Paul II. To mark the occasion, newspapers have dedicated customary feature spreads and television newscasts predictable analyses of how this pontificate has elicited polar reactions in both church and world.

Along with these interpretations comes news that the papal author has no intention of letting up on his publications, as a thirteenth encyclical letter, *Fides et Ratio*, issues from the Vatican presses and is posted simultaneously on the Vatican's web site.

Despite temptations to instant analysis, the Holy Father's intellectual leadership of the Church cannot be reduced to a soundbite. Nor can his reflections on the seminal issues of our age be reduced to a limited number of column inches whenever he passes another milestone in life. Instead, profound engagement and ongoing study are called for.

This task is not an easy one, for the pope's thought is regularly clothed in the sometimes dense categories of thought common to the world of academe. Often help in engaging the texts is needed.

This is why I am so pleased that—as was done with papers from earlier assemblies—the proceedings of two recent Jesuit colloquia on the pope's thought are being made available now to a wider audience. Whatever their format—scholarly paper, summaries of papal documents, even a homily—their intent is to clarify and illuminate Pope John Paul II's thought and teaching.

The terms *prophecy* and *diplomacy* in the title are, I believe, quite apt. The prophet seeks to speak the truth from God in a particular set of circumstances for the good of God's people, often without bothering about a *captatio benevolentiae* to render listeners more receptive to the message. The diplomat, by contrast, seeks with great delicacy to establish common cause with interlocutors in order to establish a basis on which agreements may be founded.

Before and following his call to the Chair of Peter, Karol Wojtyła—whether engaged as philosopher or theologian, as ambassador or chief shepherd—has always striven to combine the clashing and complementary roles of prophet and diplomat.

I trust that engagement with the themes of these essays may encourage readers to attempt for themselves a closer reading of the pope's own writings, which are alternatively inspiring and demanding. May such study and reflection evoke, where needed, the change of hearts that prophets can only dream about and the change of minds diplomats yearn for.

TERRENCE PRENDERGAST, S.J.
Archbishop of Halifax
October 16, 1998

ABBREVIATIONS

CA	*Centesimus Annus*, 1991
EN	*Evangelii Nuntiandi*, 1975
EV	*Evangelium Vitae*, 1995
FC	*Familiaris Consortio*, 1981
GS	*Gaudium et Spes*, 1965
HV	*Humanae Vitae*, 1968
LE	*Laborem Exercens*, 1981
LF	*Letter to Families*, 1994
LPC	*Letter to President Clinton*, 1994
LR	*Love and Responsibility* (Polish, 1960; English, 1993)
LW	*Letter to Women*, 1995
MD	*Mulieris Dignitatem*, 1988
OS	*Ordinatio Sacerdotalis*, 1994
OU	*Original Unity of Man and Woman: Catechesis on the Book of Genesis* (Boston: Daughters of St. Paul, 1981)
PP	*Populorum Progressio*, 1967
RH	*Redemptor Hominis*, 1979
RM	*Redemptoris Missio*, 1990
SA	*Slavorum Apostoli*, 1985
SRS	*Sollicitudo Rei Socialis*, 1987
UUS	*Ut Unum Sint*, 1995
VS	*Veritatis Splendor*, 1993

INTRODUCTION
Prophecy and Diplomacy: The Moral Teaching of John Paul II

FOR A DECADE, the John Paul II Symposium has gathered Jesuit scholars for a biennial conference to explore the teaching of John Paul II. Interdisciplinary, the symposium features specialists from the fields of theology, philosophy, history, sociology, economics, and political science. Pluralist, the symposium fosters debate among Jesuits representing different positions on the theological and political spectrum. Jesuit, the symposium places scholarly research at the service of *sentire cum ecclesia*, the reverential "thinking with the Church" that has characterized the Society of Jesus since its origin.

The symposium has sponsored five conferences on major issues in the pontificate of John Paul II. The 1990 Loyola-Chicago conference focused on the global thought of John Paul II. The 1992 Fordham-New York conference studied his ecclesiology. The 1994 Canisius-Buffalo conference examined the pope's fundamental moral theology. The 1996 Georgetown-Washington conference analyzed his applied ethical theory. The 1998 Georgetown-Washington conference discussed millennial themes in the documents of the pope.

An earlier volume edited by John M. McDermott, S.J., *The Thought of John Paul II* (Rome: Gregorian University Press, 1993), drew primarily upon papers from the 1990 Loyola and the 1992 Fordham conferences to provide a synthetic portrait of the pope's distinctive philosophy and theology.

The current volume focuses upon the moral teaching of John Paul II. It incorporates papers, responses, and colloquia summaries from the 1994 Canisius and 1996 Georgetown conferences. Following the conference topics, the first part explores the general moral teaching of the pope, while the second part examines his ethical positions in specific areas of human action.

The decision of the symposium to concentrate upon the moral theory of John Paul II was an obvious one. The arguments of the Catholic Church on ethical issues have constituted a perennial object of scholarly debate. Several factors have created a special prominence for the moral pronouncements of this pontificate.

First, it is moral questions that most palpably divide the Catholic community, especially in the West. The polemic over contraception in the 1960s has broadened into a systematic opposition to Church doctrine on sexual conduct, family life, and human life issues. More conservative critics challenge Church positions on property rights, internationalism, and just war. Never has the Church issued so many statements on moral conduct. But the directives increasingly fall on a Catholic population more attentive to the magisterium of Oprah than to the narrow road of the gospel.

Astute observers, including many contributors to this volume, interpret the moral confusion of the Catholic community as a symptom of a deeper crisis of faith. Pastoral practice and sociological polls attest a patent erosion of belief in such basic beliefs as the divinity of Christ. Increasingly, North American Catholicism has the air of a flat deism wrapped in Christmas twinkle lights. Nevertheless, it is in the moral sphere that the anguish of the contemporary Church most powerfully manifests itself. John Paul II has constructed a veritable library of documents dealing with the most neuralgic moral controversies: sexuality (*Familiaris Consortio*, 1981); the role of women (*Mulieris Dignitatem*, 1988); economic relations (*Sollicitudo Rei Socialis*, 1987); the right to life (*Evangelium Vitae*, 1995). As his reign matures, the pope has developed a more detailed theory of the broader moral issues, such as conscience and law, shaping the surface controversies over sexuality and social justice.

Second, the moral teaching of John Paul II regularly incites political controversy. In the earlier part of his pontificate, the pope elaborated a vigorous "gospel of human rights." His writings both reflected and stimulated the Church's resistance to totalitarian and authoritarian regimes. The collapse of Communism in Eastern Europe and of militarist regimes in Latin America derived in no small part from the rights crusade engineered by the pope and his allies. In the latter part of his pontificate, with the resurgence of parliamentary democracies, the terms of the Church's ethical critique of the political order have shifted. John Paul II has increasingly criticized the tendency of contemporary democracy to deteriorate into an arbitrary rule of the majority rather than to be faithful to its rightful vocation as the defender of the rights of vulnerable minorities. Recent United Nations conferences at Cairo (1994) and Beijing (1995) provided a diplomatic background for the growing dispute between the pope and the secular West, especially as it pertains to the right to life and to the rights of the family.

Third, in the past decade the moral teaching of John Paul II has taken a decisive turn with the publication of two major encyclicals. *Veritatis Splendor* (1993) provides a detailed overview of Catholic orthodoxy in ethics, especially in the account of the moral act. It also elaborates a critique of certain contemporary tendencies, such as subjectivism and proportionalism, that have distorted moral theology. *Evangelium Vitae* (1995) offers an extensive defense of the Church's position on human life issues. The encyclical concentrates especially upon the practices of abortion and euthanasia.

These seminal documents became the focus of a renewed Church debate in general and applied ethics. These encyclicals provided the most extensive treatment to date by the pope on the moral questions tormenting the Church. They condemned certain moral theories and practices in the most solemn terms. In fact, the degree of authority of these documents became the object of its own theological dispute.

The encyclicals signaled a maturation in the method of moral analysis used by the pope. Each begins by setting moral questions in the context of biblical narrative: the dialogue between Christ and the rich young man (VS 6–27) and the conflict between Cain and Abel (EV 7–21). Each then proceeds to offer an analysis of the human act strongly influenced by neoscholasticism. *Veritatis Splendor* insists upon the moral quality of the object of the act, rather than motive or circumstance, as the key determinant of an act's moral worth (VS 78). It condemns intrinsically evil acts (VS 79). *Evangelium Vitae* condemns, as species of intrinsically evil acts, the practice of direct abortion (EV 57) and of active euthanasia (EV 65). Each encyclical elaborates a critique of contemporary society, especially of democratic institutions and mentalities that obscure the moral law. *Veritatis Splendor* concentrates upon the libertarian (VS 48–53) and utilitarian (VS 71–75) climate of current society, while *Evangelium Vitae* diagnoses the burgeoning culture of death (EV 68–77).

The encyclicals' synthesis of biblical narrative, act analysis, and social critique provides a distinctive moral rhetoric for the pope. It also presents a model for the renewed moral theology mandated by Vatican Council II (*Optatam Totius* 16).

The contributors to this volume explore the general orientations and the specific applications of the moral teaching of Pope John Paul II. In the first part of the book, the major papers place the pope's moral theory within a broader theological framework. James Schall, S.J., studies the metaphysical background for this moral theology. Patrick Lynch, S.J., places the pope's ethics within the context of the economy of salvation. John Conley, S.J., limns the concept of conscience in *Veritatis Splendor*. Ronald Mercier, S.J., studies the Christology behind the pope's ethics. Arthur Madigan, S.J., examines the social and soteriological themes in the morality section of the *Catechism of the Catholic Church*, the systematic exposition of the Catholic faith promulgated by John Paul II in 1992. These papers and responses attempt to identify the overarching philosophical and theological attitudes that shape the pope's fundamental moral perspective.

In the second part of the work, the major papers study the pope's teaching in the area of applied ethics. Avery Dulles, S.J., examines the pope's conception of culture. John Conley, S.J., analyzes the demographic ethics of John Paul II. John Piderit, S.J., critically evaluates the economic ethics of the pope. Martin Moleski, S.J., considers John Paul II's covenantal theory of marriage. Robert Spitzer, S.J., examines the sexual morality proposed by the pope. Both the major lecturers and the respondents focus upon those areas of applied ethics that have provoked the greatest tension between the magisterium and the academy, and between the Church and State in the West.

The volume also includes resumés of the group discussions at the Canisius and Georgetown conferences. These circles focused upon key ethical documents of this pontificate. They permitted Jesuits to discuss the more controverted moral texts of John Paul II and to share their divergent views on the pastoral implications of these teachings.

As a conclusion, the volume presents a homily by Stephen Fields, S.J., originally preached at the 1996 Georgetown conference. The sermon places the ethics of John Paul II within a spiritual framework of repentance and redemption. The pope's moral teaching is not an academic survey of ethical themes. Nor is it a Pelagian call to human self-regeneration. The ultimate truth concerning human conduct and moral judgment emerges only within the proclamation of God's grace.

REV. JOHN J. CONLEY, S.J.
Fordham University
New York City
6 August 1998
Transfiguration of the Lord

I.
Fundamental Moral Theory

1. ETHICS OF THE PERSON

Person and Society: John Paul II on Substance and Relation

James V. Schall, S.J.

> The human being is not a person, on the one hand, and a member of society on the other. The human being as a person is simultaneously a member of society. The concept of person is neither opposed to this membership nor places a human being beyond it. At most one could say that what is opposed to society, understood as a certain multiplicity of people, is the human individual. But this is purely quantitative opposition. And so in thinking of moral value as that through which the human being as a person is good or bad, we do not in the human being separate individuality and membership in a society, but we think them both together.[1]
>
> —Karol Wojtyła, "The Problem of the Theory of Morality" (1969)

> By community I understand not the multiplicity of subjects itself, but always the specific *unity* of this multiplicity. This unity is accidental with respect to each subject individually and to all of them together. It arises as the relation or sum of relations existing between them. These relations can be investigated as an objective reality that qualifies everyone jointly and singly in a particular multiplicity of people. We then speak of a society. . . . Only the individual people—the personal subjects—who are the members of this society are substantial sub-

---

[1] Karol Wojtyła, "The Problem of the Theory of Morality," *Person and Community: Selected Essays*, translated by T. Sandok (New York: Peter Lang, 1993), 146.

> jects (*supposita*), each of these separately, whereas the society itself is simply a set of relations, and therefore an accidental being.[2]
>
> —Karol Wojtyła, "The Person: Subject and Community" (1976)

I

In a famous essay Leo Strauss remarked that we are lucky if we are ourselves alive during the time when one or two of the great thinkers who ever lived were alive.[3] We thus have to encounter most of the great deeds and thoughts of our kind, if we are to encounter them at all, by reading books or by hearing of them through witnesses. For Strauss this meant, not the curious skepticism that we often encounter in academic deconstructionism, but the careful, accurate attention to what was said. We too, if we are persistent, can think as the writer of a given text taught us to think. At the same time we need not forget the principles of logic or philosophy itself that each of us can discover from our own given resources. These are the norms by which we ultimately test what was said or heard. These resources of intellect and nature we did not ourselves create but discover to be constitutive of the kind of rational substantial being we find ourselves to be.

I have had, I think, several quite gifted and extraordinary teachers in my day—I think of Clifford Kossel, S. J, at Gonzaga University, of Father Charles N. R. McCoy while he was at Catholic University, of Professors Heinrich Rommen and Rudolf Allers whom I had at Georgetown, and of Gertrude Himmelfarb whom I used to know at the National Endowment for the Humanities. One hardly knows what to make of those great teachers we have encountered but whom we never personally knew—I think of Plato and Aristotle, of Cicero and Augustine, and, of course, for me, of Samuel Johnson, Chesterton, and Josef Pieper. Certainly, as I have read so much of him over the years, I would consider

---

[2] Karol Wojtyła, "The Person: Subject and Community," *Person and Community*, 238.

[3] Leo Strauss, "What Is Liberal Education?" in *Liberalism: Ancient and Modern* (New York: Basic Books, 1968), 3.

John Paul II himself a great teacher whom I never met. Someone told me recently that John Paul II has already written more in his pontificate than all the other popes from Leo XIII to his time, some of whom were also quite prolific. John Paul II's academic and intellectual output both as a professor and as pontiff are of a very high order.

What strikes me in retrospect, when I recall hearing what I thought at the time to be a particularly good lecture or discussion from those whom I actually knew, was the eagerness with which I wanted also to read what I had just heard. It was fortunate that most of these men and women that I actually knew had written something or would write something that I could go back to or come across in later years. And yet the book itself, we cannot forget, is not more real than the thought it presents. One of the things that strikes me most about John Paul II is his awareness of the importance of consciousness and of that inner illumination within each of us that constitutes our own unique reality. Our inner light is grounded in our own particular being, thoughts, and actions. We are aware, furthermore, of the being and consciousness of others and seek to communicate to and receive from what is the inner self of others—these are the great realities of dialogue, debate, friendship, prayer, and communication.

Thinking in particular of those writers who lived before my time, or whom I did not know and about whom I had to read if I were to know them at all, I frequently recall C. S. Lewis's insightful remark that if we have only read a great book once, we have not read it at all. Thus it is both humility and possibility that make us aware of the vast things we shall never know. Yet, of the most important things, however difficult, we seek and should seek to know at least something—of whether God exists, of how we ought to live, of what is our final destiny. We recall those famous words of Aristotle from the last book of his *Nicomachean Ethics* (1177b30–1178a8) in which he told us that even the little we could know of the highest things is worth more than the most exhaustive knowledge of those things about which we could know almost everything.

We have all lived our lives, moreover, in a culture that has more and more presumed that knowledge of the highest things is either dangerous, utterly private, relatively impossible, or socially unimportant. It requires almost an act of bravery to maintain that tolerance, however useful at some level, is not itself the highest virtue and that, when it is made so, it is a form of theoretic skepticism. At no other point is Catholicism more countercultural or, paradoxically, more true than when it assures us that the highest things are indeed precisely worth attentive devotion. This is the sort of lifetime devotion for which the religious and philosophical lives at their best stand. And the highest things are not merely abstractions but, as we are made aware in revelation, they are realities of being that are based in the Incarnation of precisely the Word.

II

In an address he gave at the Angelicum in Rome (November 17, 1979), just after he became pope, speaking of the importance of St. Thomas, John Paul II remarked, in a lovely reflection:

> Openness is also a significant and distinctive mark of the Christian faith, whose specific mark is its catholicity. The basis and source of this openness lie in the fact that the philosophy of St. Thomas is a philosophy of being, that is, of the "act of existing" (*actus essendi*), whose transcendental value paves the most direct way to rise to the knowledge of subsisting Being and pure Act, namely to God. On account of this we can even call this philosophy: the philosophy of the proclamation of being, a chant in praise of what exists.[4]

We can detect in these moving lines a kind of impatience with systems or philosophies that do not so "directly" enable us to reach the highest things.

In addition, in these words we find a sense of awe that anything at all exists in the first place. John Paul II is not merely aware of the relation of *what is* to our own minds, which begin in openness to what is not themselves. He is also concerned, once we know "what exists," that we still have a proper human function left to complete, a completion even of ourselves, a completion we must freely choose. Yet, when we are most complete, we are also most

---

[4] John Paul II, "Perennial Philosophy of St. Thomas for the Youth of Our Times," *The Whole Truth about Man: John Paul II to University Faculties and Students*, edited by James V. Schall (Boston: St. Paul Editions, 1981), 218–19.

incomplete. So John Paul II points to a further completion, beyond ourselves, yet involving our own act—namely, the proclamation, the praise, the sense of gratitude for *what is*, the intimations of which we can already find in the *Symposium* of Plato. It is on this basis that John Paul II has a constant place for the notions of gift and gracious return to describe the good *that is*, so that we might add to existence its free acceptance by the free and rational creature.[5]

The title and subject matter of this particular reflection about person, society, substance, and relation have both an immediate and a remote origin. The immediate origin was the chance opportunity I had to review the new translation of Karol Wojtyła's philosophic essays concerning the basis of ethics, particularly in the light of my reading of *Veritatis Splendor*.[6] The remote origin goes back to an essay I published in the Italian journal *Divus Thomas* in 1980, titled "The Reality of Society according to St. Thomas."[7] Needless to say, such an apparently obscure topic was related to earlier studies, to those of Rommen, McCoy, and particularly to the work of Kossel. Kossel, in his own studies, was very much concerned with the meaning of the Aristotelian category of "relation" with its curious pertinence to the doctrine of the Trinity as well as to relational nature of human political society. The aberrations about community that came up in modern philosophy, particularly about the ultimate destiny of the human person, often related precisely to the different ways relations manifest themselves in the Trinity and in society.[8] The last time I saw

---

[5] Wojtyła, "The Personal Structure of Self-Determination," *Whole Truth about Man*, 193–94.

[6] See James V. Schall, "The Secular Meaning of *Veritatis Splendor*," *Seminarium* (Rome) 34/1 (1994): 151–62.

[7] James V. Schall, "The Reality of Society according to St. Thomas," *Divus Thomas* (Piacenza) 83/1 (1980): 13–23.

[8] See the four essays on relations by Clifford G. Kossel, S.J., in *The Modern Schoolman* (January 1946): 61–81, (November 1946): 19–30, (January 1947): 93–107, and (March 1948): 151–72. See also Kossel's essay, "Some Limits of Politics," *Essays on Christianity and Political Philosophy*, edited by George W. Carey and James V. Schall (Lanham: University Press of America, 1984), 31–40. See also Heinrich Rommen, "Organic View of the State," *The State in Catholic Thought* (St. Louis: B. Herder, 1945); Charles N. R. McCoy, *The Structure of Political Thought* (New York: McGraw-Hill, 1963); *On the Intelligibility of Political Philosophy: Essays of Charles N. R. McCoy*, edited by James V. Schall and John J.

Kossel, a couple of months ago, I remember especially the force of his voice when he warned about tampering with the doctrine of the Trinity and with the philosophical understanding necessary properly to understand, defend, and explain its meaning, as if to say that the proper understanding of the Trinity lies at the root of all sane moral and societal life, which it does.

III

"What has all of this to do with John Paul II?" we might ask. Let me begin by formulating the question in what will perhaps be a surprising manner. Nothing has more confused modern intellectual life than the rigid requirement that the only division that needs to be attended to is that between liberal and conservative, however much the boundaries between the two may shift and shake in different times and places. If we take the normal American press, at least, it will seem that, in the minds of most articulated public opinion that judges everything in its own political terms, John Paul II is said to be a conservative.

On the other hand, many perceptive conservatives worry about him rather because he seems much too liberal to them. Both are right and both are wrong; that is to say, John Paul II is something other than what is allowed by the narrow modern intellectual framework that insists such a bipolar division of philosophical, political, and moral life is a complete one. Philosophically, John Paul II identifies himself as a follower of St. Thomas and carefully seeks to relate his studies in modernity to him. This position is why both modern liberal and modern conservative thought, which often have the same intellectual roots, come under his criticism.

The collapse of Marxism and of John Paul II's special relation to this collapse, furthermore, has put something of a damper on the view that he is a conservative, however much conservatism contributed to this collapse. But if anything in retrospect seems

---

Schrems (Washington: Catholic University of America Press, 1989); and Gertrude Himmelfarb, *The New History and the Old* (Cambridge: Harvard, 1987).

clear about the death of Marxism, it is that it has made little intellectual impact on Western liberal culture, as John Paul II, along with Solzhenitsyn, suspected would be the case. Both John Paul II and Solzhenitsyn saw that the ultimate intellectual disorder behind Marxism was also, in slightly different forms, behind much of the active thought in the West. This intellectual acumen about the history and nature of contemporary culture and philosophy, I suspect, is the real reason for so much academic and political antagonism toward John Paul II. Somehow he stands for the position that, however much of value is in modern society, something of a deep and fundamental nature is wrong at its heart such that the collapse of Marxism has not and cannot lead to improvement without a clear understanding of human nature and the human relation to God and the world.

As *Centesimus Annus* in particular shows, this Marxist collapse had a tremendous effect on John Paul II himself, much more than it has apparently had on most of the intellectual elite of the West. Margaret Thatcher, in a recent address in Canada, obviously referring to *Centesimus Annus*, said this of the work of the present Holy Father:

> Now, I'm not a Roman Catholic, but the Pope, in one of his encyclicals, pointed out that the creative capacity that man has is noble. It should be respected, encouraged, and used. He said this: "In short, besides the earth, man's principal resource is man himself. His intelligence enables him to discover the earth's productive potential, of the many different ways in which human needs can be satisfied." He went on to point out they can only be satisfied in a community of effort in a vast company, and gave really the best theological justification of capitalism that we've ever known.[9]

Indeed, I think it fair to say that the most coherent and, yes, exciting alternative to Marxism or liberalism or conservatism in contemporary society is precisely located in the thought of John Paul II, a thought that uniquely is able to combine faith and politics, metaphysics, ethics, and history without forgetting the highest human destiny and the centrality of that romance of "orthodoxy" about which Chesterton so famously spoke.

---

[9] Margaret Thatcher, "The New World Order," *Fraser Forum* (June 1994): 22.

IV

In John Paul II's thought, we find both a serious endeavor to come to terms with modernity and a simultaneous effort to retain a critical stance to it in the clear light of the abiding truths of the philosophical and theological traditions represented by Aristotle and St. Thomas. What is at issue in this discussion, as I shall try to elaborate, is the position of precisely Catholicism in modernity. What John Paul II has realized, better than anyone perhaps, is precisely the widespread confusions and distortions of the meaning of Catholicism itself. His systematic efforts in works like his many encyclicals and in *The Catechism of the Catholic Church* are to be sure initially that the correct and clear statement of this teaching and practice is in fact available to those who would read and know it, whether they believed it or not.[10] Vatican II, for its part, deliberately eschewing any but the most obvious aberrations, made every effort to accommodate itself with what it perceived to be best in modernity. But Marxism and the moral dangers in contemporary democratic regimes, among other things, have made it clear that something more specific must be said about what is wrong in the modern world. Indeed, the pope notes the peculiar fascination with evil and error that seems to characterize us. "The Thomistic theory of evil is quite a revelation," John Paul II wrote,

> because it views evil as the lack of an appropriate good, and not just its opposite. Good is something ordinary and natural because it conforms to the nature of the human being and the world; evil, on the other hand, is always baffling because it conflicts with this nature. Perhaps this also explains why in literature and moral instruction more attention is paid to evil than to good. At any rate, it would be hard to deny that in the experience of morality as a distinctive and central dimension of human life moral evil tends to be more emphatic.[11]

Today, it seems, we are not so much fascinated with evil as unwilling to admit that anything that we do can be so categorized.

---

[10] See James V. Schall, *Does Catholicism Still Exist?* (Staten Island, N. Y.: Alba House, 1994).

[11] Wojtyła, "The Problem of the Theory of Morality," *Person and Community*, 137.

Much of John Paul II's philosophic work addresses itself to this claim.

It is of some importance in what I have to say that the dimensions of Catholicism in its claim to be true, even in the modern world, be understood. John Paul II, in his own philosophical studies, obviously made great efforts to understand and agree with positions in modern philosophical thought that were, in his view, capable of continuing the perennial philosophical effort that arose out of the original challenge of revelation. What I would suggest, initially, is that John Paul II has carved out a unique position, a position that could be fully described as both Thomist and also modern, without forgetting Margaret Thatcher's encomium, which would be considered by many as "conservative." It is in fact a liberal position by standards of historic liberalism, but insists in constantly adding to the idea of freedom, responsibility, truth, and common good so that liberty does not stand by itself with no justification but itself.

Let me approach the matter in this way. It is quite clear that John Paul II sees that there is a clear and dangerous tendency in modern liberalism taken not so much as the economics of a responsible capitalism but as the social policies of the modern liberal state. Moreover, there does not seem to be today, as there was during most of the eighteenth, nineteenth, and early twentieth centuries, much disagreement about the formal political institutions of the civil order, institutions that the Church in its modern documents has no trouble in accepting—parliaments, constitutions, elections, federalism, and majority rule. Unlike the nineteenth century, this area of institutional order is not where the problem of the Church with civil society lies.

The Holy Father's positions on human life and the family might thus be called "conservative" but they are radical indeed since they are the most countercultural ideas now being advocated in practice in the public order. And there is a consistent, coherent, and solidly based rationale behind them. They cannot be written off, as they so often are, as grounded only in "faith." They are grounded in reason and increasingly in the empirical record of what happens when this reasonableness is rejected. Indeed, John Paul II's position on the beginnings of human life as well as on its end is based simply in science, in truth. John Paul II teaches that human life begins "from conception" because this is the scientific fact, even though in some ways the Church seemed to know this fact before science did, and, as we now know, seems to know it even after politics has rejected its scientific truth.

V

Readers of Leo Strauss, Eric Voegelin, Russell Kirk, Paul Johnson, and many others will be aware that the intellectual structure of modern conservatism is formidable. Moreover, it is not to be identified at every point with Catholicism. What is not so clear is the relation of Roman Catholicism and the thought of John Paul II to this modern thought, conservative or liberal. In general, Voegelin and Strauss are acutely aware, as is the pope, that the disorders of modern western culture have roots that go back to the very foundations of modernity in Descartes, Machiavelli, and their immediate predecessors.[12] Strauss and Voegelin maintained in general that modernity or "gnosticism," as Voegelin preferred to call it, is a coherent series of steps designed to rid ourselves both in personal life and in the civil community of any norms or standards that do not find their complete origins in the human will, either individually or collectively. Both Strauss and Voegelin have traced this path out meticulously through classical, medieval, and modern thought. Their successors follow it into postmodernism especially through Nietzsche and Heiddeger.

Though both Strauss and Voegelin showed great respect for St. Thomas and for revelation, neither were Catholic and both dealt gingerly with Christian revelation. Strauss is almost completely silent about it. Voegelin separates himself from any definite dogmatic or definable meaning to revelation. On the other hand, both thinkers recognized a fundamental place for revelation, Jewish revelation in the case of Strauss, Christianity in the case of Voegelin.

---

[12] See Leo Strauss, *Natural Right and History* (Chicago: University of Chicago Press, 1953); Eric Voegelin, *The New Science of Politics* (Chicago: University of Chicago Press, 1952); Russell Kirk, *The Conservative Mind* (Chicago: Regnery/Gateway, 1953); Paul Johnson, *Modern Times* (New York: Harper Colophon, 1983).

In general, both recognized that some fundamental return to the Greek classics, to metaphysics and virtue, is a necessary initial step to save civilization itself from the relativist principles of modernity, which have now largely undermined all Western civil, moral, and academic institutions. St. Thomas, for instance, is looked upon by Strauss not so much for what he did with his whole system, but for his efforts to save Aristotle—that is, philosophy. Voegelin seems more open to Christianity but he is very cautious about the particulars of this revelation. He seems to have place for some sort of ongoing and multiple worldwide revelation, and he maintains that dogma as it is understood in Catholicism is something that stands between the ground or source of this revelation and the human beings who are to receive it in their own uniqueness.

In any case, both are aware that the disorders we see coming to the fore, typified by the political history of the twentieth century and by the even more explicit rejection of natural law and reason in the later part of the century, are part of a long-term decline that will remove all standards and norms by which human dignity has gradually been defined and established in the public order. From a Catholic point of view, Voegelin and Strauss are of particular importance, however, both because of their critique of modernity and because of their respect for human intelligence as such. Needless to say, this awareness is very similar to that of St. Thomas. Indeed, Strauss in particular was concerned about what happens to pious, believing Christian, Jewish, and Muslim thinkers, when they are confronted, suddenly, as they were in the Middle Ages, by the curious completeness of philosophy as represented by Plato and Aristotle who seemed to have explained everything without revelation.

The focus of John Paul II's own academic work was ethics—that is, human action. "Ethical topics are always in lively demand," John Paul II remarked in 1959; "perhaps of all philosophical disciplines, ethics is the most intriguing to people in general."[13] While this popularity is true as a matter of ordinary experience, Pope John Paul II himself did not forget that ethics

---

[13] Karol Wojtyła, "Human Nature as the Basis of Ethical Formation," *Person and Community*, 95.

needed a solid metaphysics and revelation if it were to be able to complete what it was designed to do—namely, to lead us to a life of true happiness. Again and again he returns to St. Thomas, through him to Aristotle, then to Kant and Scheler.[14] The pope distinguishes himself from modern neo-Thomism primarily because of his effort to draw something original and good from this oftentimes very intellectually dangerous modernity. What he sees in modernity is not, however, conceived as something contradictory to or even different from Aristotle or St. Thomas.

John Paul II was not arguing that there is something wrong about St. Thomas but he holds that there is needed a certain completion that centers around the idea of consciousness, a word that is very much present in Voegelin also:

> Kant's ethics of the imperative and duty met with vigorous opposition on the part of Scheler. Consciousness does not have a basically subjectivistic orientation toward some *a priori* form, from which it would then derive the whole content of its moral experience, but has a basically objectivistic orientation towards various kinds of values. . . . The good, understood as a valuable thing, stands beyond the consciousness. Scheler, however, does not concern himself with it, but throughout his philosophy and ethics deals only with values. In effect, then, just as in Kant, we again find ourselves exclusively in the realm of consciousness.[15]

Pope John Paul II in his works in theoretic ethics, sought to show the relationship of consciousness to the objective order of *what is* and in particular to the human understanding of an individual's own internal acts precisely in their reality of good or evil acts of a human person acting.

VI

What distinguishes the Holy Father then is precisely his refusal to let consciousness find its own autonomy, for that would betray both its origins and its content. What I want to do here is to

---

[14] Wojtyła, *Person and Community*, chapters I–III.
[15] Wojtyła, "In Search of the Basis of Perfectionism in Ethics," *Person and Community*, 51–52.

suggest how the pope's thought relates to that of St. Thomas and modernity. In passing, however, I might call attention to a book addressing itself to modernity in a way not unlike that of John Paul II—namely, to Hadley Arkes's *First Things: An Inquiry into the First Principles of Morals and Justice*.[16] Neither Arkes nor John Paul II are interested so much in "reconciling" Kant and St. Thomas or Aristotle. What is valuable in Kant, nonetheless, must be elaborated in the light of Aristotle and St. Thomas to be fully appreciated.

The metaphysical tradition stands as the background to human action and to the logic of morals. The uniqueness of thought that constitutes the vivid inner awareness of the human being is accounted for in the work of John Paul II not as if it were cut off from *what is*, nor as if it were some necessary response to "values" that did not pass through our judgment and will. What happens to this being when its thought and actions are not in correspondence with *what is*, moreover, becomes itself a kind of empirical evidence for the validity or invalidity of our conscious inner lives.

A passage near the end of *Veritatis Splendor* will serve, I think, to illustrate why John Paul II's reflections on person, society, relation, and substance are of such fundamental interest in the light of his own attention to consciousness and the awareness we have of our own being precisely as good or bad. "The Church's firmness in defending the universal and unchanging moral norms is . . . to serve man's true freedom . . . ," John Paul II carefully remarked.

> This service is directed to *every man*, considered in the uniqueness and singularity of his being and existence; only by obedience to universal moral norms does man find full confirmation of his personal uniqueness and the possibility of authentic moral growth. . . . This service is also directed to *all mankind*: it is not for the individual but also for the community, for society as such. These norms in fact represent the unshakable foundation and solid guarantee of a just and peaceful human coexistence, and hence of genuine democracy. . . . *When it is a matter of the moral norms prohibiting intrinsic evil, there are no privileges or exceptions for anyone*. It makes no difference

---

[16] Hadley Arkes, *First Things: An Inquiry into the First Principles of Morals and Justice* (Princeton, N.J.: Princeton University Press, 1986).

whether one is the master of the world or the "poorest of the poor" on the face of the earth. Before the demands of morality we are all absolutely equal. (VS 96)

We can meditate long and hard on such a passage.

In this reflection, we find a response to the long and controverted question in political philosophy, associated in modernity with Machiavelli, and constantly recurring, even in the works of Strauss and Voegelin, about whether there are exceptions to the prohibition of evil because of the good of the polity or of necessity. Moreover, here is found the charter for the ultimate dignity of every life, no matter what its worldly status or condition. For in its essential outlines, human worthiness begins with the rejection of intrinsic evil in all its forms. Modernity and modern politics have made increasingly strident efforts to reject this conclusion.

In John Paul II's earlier studies in the philosophy behind ethics, behind human action, he carefully went through the metaphysical side of ethics. The human being can freely act such that human actions, while not changing the substantial goodness of human being, can, even by a single act, make this being in its will and reality evil. What is of interest to the pope, if I read him correctly, is not so much to establish the validity of most of St. Thomas's analysis of the human *supposit*, the human person, of the nature of will and intellect in relation to each other, of the relation of truth to good.

John Paul II sees this effort to know and present the position of St. Thomas to be a necessary and worthy one, if we are to understand ourselves as acting persons. But in a sense, this metaphysical analysis of the being of human action is looking at its reality from the outside, even when we deal with human action and recognize that its origins are in being, intellect, will, and their operations. What interests the pope in particular is rather "how does it look from the inside?" Here is where the human individual as a mystery and the human individual as a social being meet each other. Moreover, the pope wants to know whether the elements found in revelation do in fact fit perfectly into what we know and understand in reason.

One of the Holy Father's most oft-cited phrases is that from

Vatican II, which remarked that the human being is the only creature in the universe that God willed for his own sake. In earlier essays, Pope John Paul II put this principle in this way:

> The assertion that the human being is a person has profound theoretical significance. . . . The human being holds a position superior to the whole of nature and stands above everything else in the visible world. . . . Our distinctiveness and superiority as human beings in relation to other creatures is constantly verified by each one of us. . . . The effects of human activity in various communities testify to this dignity. A being that continually transforms nature, raising it in some sense to that being's own level, must feel higher than nature—and must *be* higher than it.[17]

Each person has a transcendent end and achieves it through his or her own spiritual powers within the wholeness, body and soul, of a human *supposit*. This reflection on our being reaffirms the Aristotelian and revelational premises that the physical creation is ordered to all human beings and their own personal ends as transcending the whole of creation itself. And here, we deal not just with the collectivity of humankind but with each individual person. This is where some attention to the meaning of person, substance, relation come into John Paul II's thought.

VII

John Paul II is, in conclusion, not willing to oversimplify and he systematically wants to look at what the classical authors have said and compare their positions with modern research. He has been particularly interested in the specific nature of the will as a unique human power. He finds that many of St. Thomas's positions on the will are confirmed in recent psychological studies.[18] But it is important that neither the will nor consciousness be seen as some sort of being or reality completely independent of individual human *supposita*. "We can observe in philosophy a gradual process

---

[17] Wojtyła, "The Dignity of the Human Person," *Person and Community*, 178.
[18] Wojtyła, "The Problem of the Will in the Analysis of the Ethical Act," *Person and Community*, 3–22.

of a kind of hypostatization of consciousness," the pope remarked:

> Consciousness becomes an independent subject of activity, and indirectly of existence, occurring somehow alongside the body, which is a material structure subject to the laws of nature, to natural determinism. Against the background of such parallelism, combined with a simultaneous hypostatization of consciousness, the tendency arises to identify the person with consciousness.[19]

The attention the Holy Father has given to the notion of person, "an individual substance of a rational nature," the classical definition he constantly cites from Boethius, is precisely to counteract any temptation to make a collective innerworldly being or purpose superior to the destiny of each person. He asserts this highest destiny of each person, however, without in the least forgetting that the human being is a social animal even in regard to salvation.

We can obtain some sense of what concerns John Paul II when he distinguishes the *I-Thou* relationship from the *we* relationship. "I believe it is extremely important to distinguish the social dimension of community from the interpersonal dimension," he wrote:

> *I* and *thou* refer only indirectly to the multiplicity of persons joined by the relation (one + one), whereas directly they refer to the persons themselves. *We*, on the other hand, refers directly to the multiplicity and indirectly to the persons belonging to this multiplicity. *We* primarily signifies a set—a set, of course, made up of people, of persons. This set, which may be called a society, a group, etc., is not itself a substantial being, and yet . . . what results from accidents, from the relations between human persons, in some sense comes to the fore here, providing a basis for predication primarily with respect to all and secondarily with respect to each one in the set. This is precisely what is signified by the pronoun *we*.[20]

John Paul II has taken care specifically to point out that no "we" made up of a multiplicity of human persons is a substance but an accident under the category of relation.

This metaphysical accuracy shows, in my judgment, how aware

---

[19] Wojtyła, "Thomist Personalism," *Person and Community,* 169.

[20] Wojtyła, "The Person: Subject and Community," *Person and Community,* 246.

he has shown himself to be of the dangers that can come into social philosophy by attributing substance, not relation, to society. Any collective and independent "we" can claim a kind of independence for its own acts based on a new "substance." Likewise, by contrast, absolute individual autonomy in which every "I" transcends in end or purpose the "we" of the social or political group, as well as any transcendent purpose for itself, denies the twofold notion of human *suppositum* or purpose that John Paul II, as I pointed out in the beginning, saw as the twofold reality of the human person. First, it chooses itself with its own faculties and ends that confront the objective distinction of good and evil in almost every chosen act. Second, it chooses itself with a relation to society in which these same distinctions continue and are multiplied because of the intimate relation of everyone to everyone else.

> We can speak meaningfully of community only in the light of persons [the pope affirmed], which means only in the context of the person as the proper subject of existence and activity, both personal and communal, and only in relation to the personal subjectivity of the human being, because only this aspect allows us to grasp the essential property of human I's and their relationships, both interpersonal and social.[21]

The essential property of human I's includes its own proper understanding of its own existence and activity along with the very subjective self-awareness of what this being and its activity means objectively, as precisely good or evil.

What is remarkable about the Holy Father's thought, in the end, is not that these positions and issues need to be worked out carefully by the philosophic mind. What is remarkable is that the future Holy Father himself thought them through. Karol Wojtyła as a young academic did precisely this pondering, this thinking through, and this in a part of the world that we all thought at the time to be most obscure and totally oppressed. His "chant in the praise of what exists," as we now read through the works of this remarkable man, does reflect an astonishing openness to the "act of existing," the transcendental value of which, as we realize in

---

[21] Wojtyła, "The Person: Subject and Community," *Person and Community*, 253.

our own souls if we but listen to this chant of praise, does pave "the most direct way to rise to the knowledge of substantial Being and pure Act, namely to God."

No one else in our time, I think, teaches us these highest things in so direct a way. What characterizes us, we sometimes fear, as Allan Bloom intimated, is not that we do not possess great teachers, if we would but find them, but rather that we have "souls without longing," souls not prepared to listen to the chants of praise that are in fact all about us, as John Paul II teaches us.

Response

Martin X. Moleski, S.J.

THE LEITMOTIF OF FATHER SCHALL'S PAPER is that philosophy is a "chant in praise of what exists." For me, this focal image raises the question of how we read reality. In our day we suffer from discordant voices claiming to praise what is. For example, my heart sinks when I see men and women celebrating the new limits placed on pro-life protesters near abortion clinics. The pro-abortion choir sings in praise of the woman's right to privacy; I grieve because they seem to me to be misreading the text of God's symphony. They do not recognize the new life within the mother's womb because their philosophy limits their view of reality.

Schall is quite right that "something of a deep and fundamental nature is wrong" at the heart of our society. We need to diagnose the condition and find a prescription for what ails us. Just as a heart surgeon must persuade a patient of his fatal condition in order to win consent for heart surgery, so we must persuade our society that it is seriously ill in order to win its consent to a transformation as difficult and delicate as a heart transplant. The flaw threatening the life of society is modernism's progressive rejection of all "norms or standards" that set bounds to the individual or collective human will. Our attachment to freedom is killing us; until we surrender that freedom to its author, we shall remain in bondage to self. Schall is right that if we do not bring each other to repentance, there will be a loss of "all of the standards and norms by which human dignity has gradually been defined and established in the public order."

Schall turns to the inner life of God to cure our ailment: "The proper understanding of the Trinity lies at the root of all sane moral and societal life." For Christians, there is no higher law than the love revealed by the circumincession of the divine persons. If we take the Trinity as a model to use in public discourse, there are interesting questions to ask, which take us beyond the scope of Schall's paper: What does the doctrine of the Trinity teach us about person, society, substance, and relation?

The charge of hypostatization is, for me, one of the least interesting and most unpersuasive forms of argument in philosophy. It seems to me that we cannot speak of nonentities without sounding as if we think they are entities. Every definition of nothing makes "it" sound like a "thing." Every statement about unicorns, gold mountains, and the present King of France summons them into being, at least mentally and linguistically. It is a category error to take concretely what others meant metaphorically (and vice versa, of course, e.g., the Catholic view of "this is my body").

The charge that people hypostatize society is the crucial issue, which this essay seeks to resolve through the distinction between substance and accident. I do not find great relief arising for me from this distinction, in large measure because I do not share Schall's concern about hypostatization. The tensions and anxieties I do feel about finding the right relationship between individual and social rights are not relieved by recognizing that the person is "an individual substance of a rational nature" and that the group is an insubstantial sum of accidents "under the category of relation." I am not denying the truth or the accuracy of this distinction. I question its utility and scope. Too much emphasis on a metaphysical or ontological distinction may undercut a theological principle: God's plan is that all be one in the Son as the Son is one with the Father and the Spirit. This same reality can be approached philosophically from the reflection that the human being is an inherently social animal and that union with our fellow human beings is fundamental to our personal happiness.

From the theological point of view, it seems that *the suitable partner for a communion of persons is a communion of persons*. Human social structures may be only accidental from the point of view of metaphysics, but they seem central from the point of view of God's purposes in the divine relationship with human beings. The biblical tradition celebrates such constructs: marriage, the family, the *hakal* and the *ekklesia*, the people of God and the Body of Christ, to name just a few. The Catholic imagination provided fertile ground for the development of religious bodies within the

Body of Christ: the Benedictines, the Franciscans, the Dominicans, the Jesuits, and so forth. None of these "things" are "things" in the strict sense of the word; they all are nothing but the sum of accidents "under the category of relation." But something valuable seems to be lost by pressing the technically correct metaphysical reduction too far.

In the Scriptures, God chooses Israel and makes a covenant with her. In Hosea's prophecies against the nation, it was a curse to pass from being the People of God to being "no people"—*lo ammi*. This was the loss of a great good that God had given the people *as a people*. In Jesus, God chooses a new Israel and forms a new relation with the Body of Christ. We exist from love and for love. The purpose of the human substance is to enter into a permanent—and in heaven, endlessly ecstatic—relation with other persons. Although the Church is not a thing, nevertheless the relations that constitute the Church are the focus of God's salvific will.

I think we can espouse Schall's values without focusing on the metaphysical issues: whatever society is, its rights never surpass those of the individuals who constitute it. It is good to set bounds to the state's intervention in the life of the human person—the rights of a person are always prior to the rights of any social structure—but we need to be careful not to cut the ground from under the quasi-personal, corporate insubstantialities into which we are called. As we sing the song of what is, perhaps we can also celebrate what almost is.

2. ETHICS AND SALVATION
Creation, Redemption, Solidarity: Pope John Paul II's Public Theology

Patrick J. Lynch, S.J.

POPE JOHN PAUL II HAS WRITTEN THREE MAJOR ENCYCLICALS ON ISSUES OF SOCIAL ETHICS: *Laborem Exercens* about work, *Sollicitudo Rei Socialis* about the development of peoples, and *Centesimus Annus* to commemorate the one hundredth anniversary of the first encyclical on modern social issues, Leo XIII's *Rerum Novarum*.[1] To study John Paul II's views on capitalism, democracy, or workers' rights in these texts would indicate the public policy issues that concern him and the positions that he has taken.

The motivation for these positions, however, is the more crucial issue. At this level the theological and scriptural positions that undergird his practical teaching and policy statements on public issues emerge. Furthermore, his very reasons for making such statements come more fully to light. This public theology, as I call it, thus provides a foundation and rationale for better understanding John Paul II's current teaching and should reveal the principles for the future development of his thought.

This paper will therefore discuss the major components of John Paul II's public theology in four major sections. The first will treat John Paul II's reasons for writing (and speaking) on such topics.

---

[1] The text of *Laborem Exercens* may be found in Gregory Baum, *The Priority of Labor: A Commentary on Laborem Exercens, Encyclical Letter of Pope John Paul II* (New York: Paulist Press, 1982), 93–152; that of *Sollicitudo Rei Socialis* in Gregory Baum and Robert Ellsberg, eds., *The Logic of Solidarity: Commentaries on Pope John Paul's Encyclical on Social Concern* (Maryknoll: Orbis Books, 1989), 1–62; and *Centesimus Annus* in *Origins* 21 (May 16, 1991): 1, 3–24.

The next three will investigate the central themes of that theology, that is, his understanding of creation, redemption, and solidarity.

Why Should the Church "Speak"?

Since the nineteenth century many have questioned the propriety of religion concerning itself with public issues such as population control, the distribution of state funds, or the legalization of abortion. Any theology that claims to address such issues, therefore, must almost necessarily answer why it should "speak" about such topics. John Paul II's theology is no exception, for he discusses this issue in both *Sollicitudo* (8) and *Centesimus Annus* (5). Essentially such a task is a concrete response to the Christian love commandment to serve those in need; at a bare minimum Christianity must thus promote the cause of justice in human affairs (CA 57–58). Its evangelizing mission to proclaim in word and deed the salvation wrought by Jesus also demands that the Church address issues of public concern (CA 55).

More specifically, John Paul II considers his teachings on social questions to be the application of God's word to people's lives, life in society, and the realities connected with that life (SRS 8). By this process he seeks to enhance respect for human dignity and to promote those activities that offer hope for the coming of God's kingdom (SRS 41, 47). Offering light for the solution of problems, strength through the sacraments, and motivation actually to change one's lifestyle or the organizational structures that promote the common good are all means that John Paul II suggests in his writings to accomplish these goals (CA 55, 58, 59, 62). Furthermore, he believes that Jesus's own program to proclaim freedom for captives, recovery of sight for the blind, and release from oppression are actions especially appropriate for the laity (Luke 4:18–19; SRS 47). Volunteer work that treats humans respectfully also receives special commendation from him as a way of affirming human dignity and preparing for God's kingdom (CA 49).

In addition, John Paul II appeals to the nature of the church articulated in the opening lines of Vatican II's Dogmatic Constitution on the Church, *Lumen Gentium* (1),[2] as yet another reason for the church addressing social, political, and economic questions. Because the church is a sign and sacrament of unity with God and the whole human race, it seeks to promote the unity of all people and thus overcome the many divisions that currently separate the world into North and South or First, Second, Third, and even Fourth Worlds (SRS 14,17, 31). The Roman Catholic Church therefore offers spiritual and material help to alleviate suffering and to assist all peoples and nations in their quest for authentic development (e.g., SRS 42; CA 29).

John Paul II's reasons for addressing public issues, however, move beyond Christianity. Reflecting on his meeting with the leaders of the world's great religions at Assisi in 1986, he asserts that peace and development will depend not only upon the cooperation and prayers of people of all religions and churches but also on the involvement of all peoples of good will (SRS 47; CA 60). Such collaboration affirms and enhances human dignity and builds a more humane society.

After the above presentation on John Paul II's views for religion in general and Christianity in particular becoming involved in the public square, we can move to a consideration of those themes that comprise the substance of his public theology. The most important one—at least in the three encyclicals on which I focus—is creation, for John Paul II grounds the dignity of the human person and the rights that the person possesses in this event.

CREATION

Two assertions within the priestly creation account of the first chapter of Genesis have special importance for John Paul II—namely, that humans, male and female, are created in God's image and that God commands them to "fill the earth and subdue it" (Gen. 1:27–28; LE 4). Upon these two beliefs, John Paul II devel-

---

[2] Walter M. Abbott, S.J., *The Documents of Vatican II*, introduction by Lawrence Cardinal Shehan, translations directed by Joseph Gallagher (New York: Herder and Herder, 1966), 14–101.

ops the theological foundation for his writings on work, development, the economy, and the state.

That God created humans in God's own image is singularly significant for John Paul II's public theology since it is the essential reason for human dignity and the basis for inalienable human rights such as the right to life, the right to develop one's intelligence and freedom, and the right to religious freedom (CA 11, 47). Furthermore, this belief reveals to John Paul II that humans are ends in themselves whom God has willed for life with himself (CA 41). They thus have a capacity for the transcendent that permits them to give themselves to God and other people and therefore discover and fulfill themselves (SRS 29–30; CA 34, 41).

This capacity for the transcendent is also a fundamentally social phenomenon in John Paul II's view since "a couple, a man and a woman," share it (SRS 29). It is hence at the basis of the establishment of the family, the nation, and all parts of society and is the reason why all these institutions are subservient to the person rather than the person to them (CA 39, 49). Markets, for example, should meet the needs of people; for people, not markets, produce and consume goods (CA 39); the state, and religion too, should serve people by protecting and promoting human rights (CA 7, 22).

John Paul II's theory of the state also uses this same foundation to disclose the errors in communism, the "national security state," and the consumer society. Such ways of life deny God and spiritual values, subordinate individuals and their dignity to socioeconomic structures, and reject or try to manipulate authentic human freedom (CA 13, 19, 25).

If people are to be truly free, John Paul II holds that they must be able to know and do the truth.[3] Otherwise, evils such as the Holocaust are possible, for power, fanaticism, or self-interest may take precedence over respect for others, the acceptance of just limits, and the recognition of the truth (CA 17, 41, 46). The goal of one's life may simply be enjoyment of a series of sensations rather than a sharing in the true, the good, the beautiful, and the

---

[3] CA 17. See also John Paul II's *Veritatis Splendor, Origins* 23 (October 14, 1993): 297, 298–336, and Avery Dulles, "The Prophetic Humanism of John Paul II," *America* 169 (October 23, 1993): 7–8, for a fuller development of the interrelationship of the themes of knowledge, truth, and freedom.

communal (SRS 33; CA 36, 39). As John Paul II indicates in *Sollicitudo* (28), "having" can become more important than "being" in God's image. The importance of both freedom and truth for humans, therefore, is that they are ways in which humans share in the divine image.

Further reflection on the creation stories in Genesis, however, makes John Paul II aware that humans are not just spiritual but also corporeal (SRS 29). As a result, they have an affinity with creatures and are unable to exercise absolute control over them or their environment. In an unusual interpretation John Paul II sees this limitation as an extension of God's prohibition against eating the fruit from the tree in Genesis 2:16–17. This interpretation is also at the root of the pope's support for the modern ecological movement, for either destruction or total control of the world's resources is immoral; rather humans should cooperate with God in developing the world according to its God-given purposes (SRS 34; CA 37).

John Paul II also finds the basis for the above command in the creation stories of Genesis: in the first chapter (1:28) God commands humans to "subdue the earth"; in the second (2:15), they are to cultivate and watch over the garden (LE 4; SRS 29). This action of subduing the earth reflects God's own activity in creating the universe and therefore reveals another way in which humans are in God's image (LE 4). Furthermore, these scriptural references reveal to the pope the limited right to private property and the human responsibility to work (LE 4; 12).

Private property is thus necessary for people to express and fulfill themselves, to make a fitting home for themselves and their families, and to develop the richness of nature (LE 12; CA 6, 31, 43). As the pope points out, however, private property is not an absolute value, for God created the earth's resources for all and commanded all to "subdue" the earth and to enjoy its fruits (LE 12; CA 31). Agriculture, for example, is an excellent way of "subduing" the earth and producing crops that all can enjoy (LE 21).

In addition, John Paul II asserts that material goods are the means for all humans to develop their initiative and creativity, to meet their needs, and to open new horizons for human endeavor (LE 6, 9; SRS 29). Since a market economy at its best can achieve these goals, John Paul II gives qualified assent to a market economy for the first time in official Roman Catholic teaching.[4]

The individualism that such an economy can generate, however, does not meet with the pope's approval. Because the earth's goods are for everyone rather than just particular individuals, he holds that all peoples must work *together* to develop, produce, or harvest these goods (CA 27, 43). Furthermore, the means and results of the production process are not to control people, who have been made in God's image, but to permit them to fulfill their own calling and to advance the general welfare of society (LE 12, 26; CA 6, 13). As a now very famous phrase from *Laborem Exercens* (6) states, "Work is 'for man' [sic] and not man [sic] 'for work'."

Placing priority on the worker as a subject rather than on work is another insight that the pope attributes to his reading of the early chapters of Genesis (LE 4, 6–7). Not only are workers of infinite value because God created them in God's own image, but they are even more like God by working—an activity that God performs by creating and sustaining the world in existence (LE 4, 25). Un- or under-employment therefore cause humiliation and loss of self-respect and are unjust because they deprive humans of their right to subsistence—that is, the common use of the earth's goods (LE 18; S 18).

Workers also have rights both because of their intrinsic dignity and because of their duty to work in "subduing" the earth (LE 5, 25). In the work place, for example, people have the right to a just wage that can support themselves and their families and provide "a certain amount for savings" (LE 19; CA 15). They also have the right to organize into unions and to strike under "the proper conditions and within just limits" (LE 20; CA 7, 15).

Class struggle between workers and management, however, has no place in John Paul II's understanding, since it does not respect human dignity nor the common good, and places force above law and reason (LE 11–15; CA 14). At root he views it as a rejection of God and hence sinful (CA 14). Once again, therefore, John Paul II's thought has returned to the creation accounts in Genesis, but in this instance to their treatment of sin.

---

[4] J. Bryan Hehir, "Reordering the World: John Paul II's *Centesimus Annus*," *Commonweal* 118 (June 14, 1991): 394.

His discussion of sin, however, makes fewer direct appeals to the texts in Genesis 1–3; rather, he expands on the meaning of these texts to present his views. Sin, for example, is not only an offense against God, as Genesis 3 clearly indicates, but it also offends our neighbor and constantly draws people to evil despite the Catholic tradition's belief in their inherent goodness (SRS 36, CA 25). In addition, sin prompts nature to rebel against the humans who are to be its "masters" and makes human work difficult and burdensome (LE 9, 27; SRS 30).

What is also extremely significant in understanding sin in a social context is the importance of the sinful structures that result from personal sins (SRS 36–39; CA 38). When these structures develop and become stronger through human consent, they then spread, influence other people's behavior and prompt further sins (SRS 36). John Paul II explicitly discusses such structures in his encyclical on development, *Sollicitudo Rei Socialis* (37). Therein he writes against the "all-consuming desire for profit," the "thirst for power," and the "imperialism" especially of the former Soviet Union and the nations of the West.

To alter these structures with ones that will promote peace, development, and solidarity, John Paul II calls for a "conversion" that will change hearts of stone to those of flesh (SRS 38). This change, however, will occur only through God's intervention. John Paul II's theology must therefore move from a reflection on the meaning of creation to a study of Jesus and the meaning of the redemption that he has wrought.

REDEMPTION

By suffering and dying for all, Jesus has definitively conquered sin and evil and permitted women and men to share in his glory (SRS 31; CA 25). Although humans still have to struggle against temptation and the forces of evil, Jesus's suffering, death, and resurrection have brought a "new creation"—a "creation," however, that will not appear in its fullness until the end of time (CA 62). In the meantime Jesus guides and illumines people from within to assist them in the authentic development of themselves and their societies (SRS 31; CA 25).

As John Paul II especially indicates in his reflections on work in *Laborem Exercens* (9, 27), however, this change occurs only with difficulty, since humans have broken their covenant with God. Their present labors, however, are joined with Jesus's suffering and hence allow them to participate in the dawning of the "new age" that Jesus has brought with his victory on the Cross (LE 27; CA 25).

The pope even highlights the efficacy of suffering by connecting it with the peaceful defeat of communism in Eastern Europe in 1989 (CA 25). In this instance the suffering of those persecuted for religion inspired those seeking to fill the spiritual void created by communism. Furthermore, this nonviolent revolution was possible only because those suffering for truth and freedom united their sufferings with those of the crucified Christ and thus achieved a better world order.

John Paul II, however, has taken pains, following the lead of Vatican II in its Pastoral Constitution *Gaudium et Spes* (39),[5] to point out that such earthly achievements are not identical with the coming of God's kingdom; they are only an anticipation of that kingdom (LE 27; SRS 48; CA 25). At the close of history these glimmers of new life will be transformed into a new heaven and a new earth—that is, the full glory of God's kingdom. At present, however, John Paul II urges humans to work for a better life and world to prepare for this final coming when Jesus will give the kingdom to God who will be "everything to everyone" (SRS 31; CA 62; I Cor. 15:28).

John Paul II has also pointed out that the mystery of the Kingdom of God is in its "already but not yet" quality—a characteristic that he has particularly treated in his discussion on the importance of the Eucharist for Christian living (SRS 48). For him the Eucharist is a special locus for God's kingdom because Jesus is really present in the bread and wine and brings that kingdom with him when he enters these elements. All who receive the Eucharist therefore anticipate the coming of the kingdom in its fullness and witness to it through their faith and good deeds.

Sharing in the Eucharist also discloses the richness of the dignity that God has imparted to humans. Not only are they in the image

---

[5] See Abbott, *The Documents of Vatican II*, 199–308.

of God (as Genesis has indicated), but the divine has become human in Jesus and therefore raised humanity's value (CA 11,46). John Paul II also believes that God has granted work a special preeminence because Jesus devoted most of his life to physical work as a craftsman (LE 6, 26).

In John Paul II's public theology, therefore, the life, death, and resurrection of Jesus has added new meaning to the dignity of the person. In these events Jesus has overcome sin and offered humans the grace to follow his example even to the point of giving their lives for those in need, if necessary (SRS 26, 48; CA 25). These same events also offer hope against evil and the frailties of human nature, for through his death and resurrection Jesus began the process that will end in the coming of the fullness of God's kingdom (SRS 31; CA 25). Meanwhile God watches over us and helps us to prepare for this coming through the power of grace.

Solidarity

This ability for humans to go beyond themselves is for John Paul II not just an aspect of Christian charity but also a quality of solidarity (SRS 40). This word, which first came to prominence with the formation in 1980 of the Polish trade union Solidarity, received extensive theoretical consideration in John Paul II's 1987 "social" encyclical, *Sollicitudo Rei Socialis* (38–40). There he labeled it a virtue because of people's growing awareness of the moral consequences of their interdependence and their feelings of connection with those in distant places who suffered injustices or human rights' violations (SRS 38). Furthermore, solidarity was a Christian virtue since it was closely connected with love even of one's enemies and with a recognition of the presence of God's image in each and every person (SRS 40). John Paul II thus defined solidarity as "a *firm and persevering determination* to commit oneself to the *common good*; that is to say to the good of all and of each individual, because we are *all* really responsible *for all*" (SRS 38, italics in original).

Interest in this virtue originated according to the pope not only from a sense of interdependence but also from the need for all people to work together in shaping their common destiny (SRS

9, 26). To achieve this goal, therefore, a sense of equality and a respect for the legitimate differences among peoples needed to overcome the individualism and imperialism that resulted from an inordinate desire for power and profits (SRS 22, 39, 45). Such autonomy for both individuals and nations, however, could not be total; it would still need to sacrifice for the common good in a spirit of Christian charity if peace, justice, and unity were to become realities (SRS 39, 45).

To motivate people in this process and to provide a theological base for his understanding of solidarity, the pope offered a sophisticated rationale. His theology began with an understanding of the Trinity as "communion" and moved to an ecclesiology that considered the church to be a "sacrament", *i.e.*, in the understanding of Vatican II, a sign and instrument of unity with God and all peoples (SRS 40; LG 1).

The church expressed this sacramentality on the practical level through love of the neighbor, especially those neighbors who were poor—that is, without material goods, knowledge, or the skills necessary to earn a living (SRS 42–43; CA 33, 57). In addition, the point of this assistance was not to humiliate or to reduce the people receiving it to objects; rather, it was to affirm their dignity and to help them attain a better future for themselves, their families, and the society in which they lived (LE 25; CA 33, 49, 58).

The pope, however, did not picture these people as passive recipients of others' assistance (SRS 39). Instead, he expected them to make their needs known nonviolently to those who could help, to support those in a similar situation, and to contribute to the common good to the extent to which they were capable. He also applied the same principle to developing countries: they were to assist each other in becoming less dependent on the wealthy nations and to help the neediest nations (SRS 45). By these means John Paul II hoped that global solidarity would grow and that all would share equally in the "banquet of life" to which God invited them (SRS 39; Luke 16:19–31).

To show the way in which Christians should act in promoting solidarity, the pope pointed in *Sollicitudo* particularly to the example of Peter Claver, S.J., in assisting slaves and to his fellow countryman Maximilian Kolbe, who died for someone whom he did not know (SRS 40). Later in *Centesimus Annus* (57) he used the model of the earliest Christians sharing their goods with the poor and then subsequent generations helping those in need in their age. All of these actions were means of serving Jesus himself and furthered solidarity (Mt. 25:31–46).

John Paul II, however, had other theological reasons for encouraging the practice of this virtue. From his meditation on Genesis 1, he knew that God had created the goods of creation for all people (SRS 39). He thus urged a just distribution of these goods to ensure that all were rightfully able to meet their basic needs for subsistence and to share in creating the future with God's assistance (SRS 15; CA 35, 43).

At the same time, however, the pope recognized that humans had a dimension to their personality that enabled them through contemplation, worship, and love for others to go beyond the merely physical and their immediate awareness of the present (CA 36, 41). By giving themselves to God and other humans in love and service, they were in solidarity with each other and also preparing for Jesus's final coming in the fullness of God's kingdom (SRS 31; CA 62). Practicing solidarity, therefore, was the way which John Paul II proposed to achieve global development, greater respect for all peoples, and a readiness for accepting the arrival of God's kingdom.

Conclusions

Solidarity, however, is not the most important of the three major foci in John Paul II's public theology. Among the themes of solidarity, creation, and redemption, creation receives the most explicit attention since it provides the foundation for the dignity of the person and gives a basis for the establishment of the social institutions upon which humans depend for survival—that is, the government, the economy, and the culture. Redemption, however, is of greater value because Jesus's death and resurrection have overcome sin and death and provided the basis for John Paul II's optimistic view about the future development of humanity and its world.[6] Solidarity then applies the insights from the previous themes to the concrete situation and offers motivation for people and nations to work together to attain justice, peace, and true freedom. On the whole, therefore, John Paul II's public theology has a consistency for the positions that it takes, although one must dig to find this inner logic.[7]

What was most astonishing in doing this research, however, was John Paul II's almost total neglect of natural law reasoning in addressing "the social question." Usually the pope appealed to scriptural and theological insights on which to base his positions even when discussing such topics as human rights or the value of a democratic society. Although the natural law tradition received extensive consideration in *Veritatis Splendor* (28–83), John Paul II's approach to social questions in the three encyclicals studied in depth in this paper might actually be more helpful in a period when natural law reasoning is open to much ambiguity even among those who adopt it.[8] Furthermore, legal theorists who study the relationship of religion and politics in the U.S. now urge an ecumenical political discussion that explicitly uses religious values to shape the contemporary political consensus.[9] John Paul II's emphasis on biblical and theological themes may therefore be more helpful than using philosophical ones for participating in this dialogue. Values such as human dignity, the goodness of creation, or solidarity, for example, would be ideals upon which different religious groups might agree. These values might therefore be the basis for resolving contentious public policy issues like

---

[6] The second chapter of John Paul II's 1979 *Redemptor Hominis*, #7–12, develops this theme more fully. The text is published as a separate booklet by the United States Catholic Conference under the title *Redeemer of Man* (Washington, D.C.).

[7] My position, at least for the three encyclicals studied for this essay, challenges that of John Carmody in his March 18, 1990, Warren Lecture, "The Encyclical Theology of Pope John Paul II," 9, which was published in pamphlet form by the University of Tulsa (Tulsa, Okla.). Carmody finds a "persistent illogic" in the encyclicals as a whole.

[8] Charles E. Curran, *Directions in Fundamental Moral Theology* (Notre Dame: University of Notre Dame Press, 1985), 125–55, provides an extensive critique of natural law theory.

[9] See, for example, Michael J. Perry, *Love and Power: The Role of Religion and Morality in American Politics* (New York: Oxford University Press, 1991), 83–127, and Stephen L. Carter, *The Culture of Disbelief: How American Law and Politics Trivialize Religious Devotion* (New York: HarperCollins, 1993), 230–32.

universal health care, aid to foreign countries, and even questions of population control.[10]

Moreover, this approach may also be of great importance when entering into collaboration with other religions and Christian communities to solve the problems of peace and development. If Hans Küng is correct in asserting that world peace will occur only when there is a religious peace resulting from dialogue, then John Paul II's appeal to properly religious themes in developing positions on pressing public concerns may be more fruitful in this dialogue than discussing different philosophies.[11] In addition, creation, salvation, and the means for attaining that salvation are perennial concerns among religions. The major concerns of the pope's public theology—creation, redemption, and solidarity—are thus central to this dialogue and critical for motivating people to seek a world of justice and peace for everyone.

---

[10] Perry, 93–98.
[11] Hans Küng, *Global Responsibility: In Search of a New World Ethic* (New York: Crossroad Publ. Co., 1991), xv.

Response

Benjamin Fiore, S.J.

FATHER LYNCH HAS PROVIDED US with a useful, comprehensive summary of the principal themes of Pope John Paul II's encyclicals on public morality. His observation that, among other objectives, the pope thus seeks to promote those activities that offer hope for the coming of God's kingdom (SRS 41, 47) is important for me in that it helps to locate the Church's teaching and activity within the gospel message announced by Jesus (see Mark 1:14, "The kingdom has approached you, repent and believe"). It also ties the contemporary Church's expectations with those of the earliest Christians. I wonder whether this emphasis by the pope on the kingdom of God is not a reaction to his experience in a Poland that had announced a secular eschaton as envisioned by Marx.

Then, too, when the pope criticizes other secular political and economic ideologies, such as capitalism, the same focus on the divine plan seems to provide the basis for contrast and correction. Ironically, while the Marxist ideologues seem to have radically altered their worldview and have willingly embraced capitalism, the proponents of capitalism are some of the more outspoken and intransigent critics of papal statements that call capitalism into question.

Lynch also refers to the pope as "offering motivation actually to change one's lifestyle or the organizational structures that promote the common good." I wish his paper had followed the pope's critique of the organizations and structures in order to spell out the structural inadequacies in the world today as the pope sees these. The international banking system and the ongoing arms race are two of the aspects of global relations that reveal moral inadequacies, to say nothing of the East-West struggle that still goes on, although in a radically transformed way. While Lynch is correct to call attention to the papal recommendation of "volunteer work that treats humans respectfully," it seems that in matters of political, economic, and social justice, the pope tends to stress the deficiencies of structure in the national and international orders. I wonder if the tendency to stress the political, economic, and social organizations/organizers is not the result of his experience of a totalitarian governmental system and the resistance to it from a Church hierarchy very much regulated by the primatial bishop. The structural intervention into the Society of Jesus in the recent past and his recent stress on episcopal magisterium in addressing *Veritatis Splendor* and the *Catechism* to the bishops are other cases in point.

Lynch is right to observe in his section on creation that the creation stories, in John Paul II's view, explain why national and social institutions are subservient to the person, and not vice versa. These themes were addressed at some length in the previous John Paul II conference at Fordham. The spiritual values that reside in the human person as image of God and as divinely designated overseer and worker in the created world help the pope to clarify the errors in "communism, the 'national security state,' and the consumer society." Humans, as subjects of their work, reach personal fulfillment through it and realize their identity as workers in the image of a God who worked in creation, and in association with the Son of God who toiled in the process of the work of redemption on earth.

While Lynch is right to note that in LE, class struggle between workers and management "has no place in John Paul II's understanding," nevertheless, that encyclical was remarkable in sanctioning the protests of unions of workers against management by the leaders of the proletariat's factories and by the proletarian organizers of work—that is, the central government authorities. That encyclical also addressed the proletarianization and exploitation of the intellectuals and white-collar workers—a phenomenon widespread in the capitalistic world during the recent recession. The pope criticizes the materialistic economism behind these developments as contrary to God's will in creation. Lynch relates the thirst for power, profit, and empire to personal sin and the evolution of sinful structures.

Finally, Lynch calls attention to the spirituality of Christ's redemptive suffering, which is a common theme in Polish romanticism, national self-understanding, and popular piety. I wonder how a different experience in World War II and in a country other than in one that suffered subjugation to foreign powers for most of the last two centuries would have colored the spiritual reflections of these writings. However, as Lynch points out, there is in the pope a basic optimism about "the dignity of the human person" and "the future of human development and the world."

3. MORAL SUBJECTIVITY

Anatomy of Conscience: A Reading of *Veritatis Splendor*

John J. Conley, S.J.

THE RECEPTION OF *VERITATIS SPLENDOR* has been a curious affair. For months preceding publication of the encyclical, the popular media insisted that two issues would be prominent. First, the key topic would be contraception. Second, the pope would define the Church's doctrine on contraception as infallibly proposed. *Newsweek*'s account of the letter was typical: "The Pope intends ... an expansion of infallibility.... The Pope's goal is to demonstrate that all forms of moral reasoning theologians use to justify contraception are unacceptable."[1] When the Vatican released the document on October 5, 1993, the press was clearly perplexed. The encyclical makes no mention of infallibility. It cites contraception once, and then brusquely, in its 40,000 words. Certain journalists, such as Peter Steinfels of *The New York Times*, implausibly attempted to claim that infallibility and contraception were the hidden "subtext" of the encyclical.[2] The majority of journalists simply evinced their bafflement before the letter's opening biblical meditation and the lengthy discussion of proportionalism. The quick disappearance of the document from popular discussion indicates how thoroughly the text stumped the press, avid for a sex-and-power shoot-out.

The reception of *Veritatis Splendor* by the academy was more

---

[1] Rod Norland, "Next, A Tougher Stand on Birth Control," *Newsweek* (Aug. 23, 1993): 58.
[2] See Peter Steinfels, "A New Encyclical," *The New York Times* (Oct. 6, 1993): A1.

penetrating.[3] Academic commentators recognized the polemic that animates chapter 2, the central section of the document. The pope clearly attacks a variety of schools of moral theory that he considers deviant from orthodox tradition. In their commentaries, moral theologians rightly detected the letter's actual concern with power in the concluding section, chapter 3, where the pope charges the Church's pastors to vigilance in guaranteeing moral orthodoxy in institutions that bear the name "Catholic" (VS 114–17). This concern with the proper exercise of pastoral authority, especially in educational institutions, clarifies the anomaly of the encyclical's addressees, the bishops alone, rather than the customary audience of all members of the Church and all people of good will.

Despite its recognition of the encyclical's polemic, the overall academic reception of the letter remains superficial. Many theologians criticized the pope's censure of schools of moral theology. Richard McCormick[4] and Charles Curran[5] complained that no Catholic theologian held the extreme positions that the pope castigates. Such a critique, however, fails to recognize the critical typology that the pope employs. Such a typology detects general tendencies that distort the theses of a particular school of thought. In the controverted passages of chapter 2 (VS 90–104), the pope clearly attacks those traits of certain contemporary schools, such as proportionalism (VS 75) and fundamental option theory (VS 65), that displace the primacy of the object of moral action (VS 75) and blind the theorist to the existence of intrinsically evil actions (VS 79–81). Such a typological approach does not claim that any historic author holds precisely this position *in toto*. Moreover, the pope carefully underlines that the concept of fundamental option, if construed as "obedience of faith" (VS 66), and proportionality, if understood as a secondary moment of moral

---

[3] Among the several symposia published to discuss the encyclical, two are particularly penetrating: "Pope John Paul II's *Veritatis Splendor*," *Commonweal* (Oct. 22, 1993): 11–18, and "The Splendor of Truth: A Symposium," *First Things* (Jan. 1994): 14–29.

[4] See Richard McCormick, "*Veritatis Splendor* and Moral Theology,"*America* (Oct. 30, 1993): 8–11.

[5] See Charles E. Curran, "Pope John Paul II's *Veritatis Splendor*," *Commonweal* (Oct. 22, 1993): 14.

analysis (VS 78), can contribute to an ethical theory well within the bonds of orthodoxy.

Even more troubling is the tendency of academic commentators to study only the polemical passages of the encyclical. It is striking how frequently the critics of *Veritatis Splendor* note the beauty of the opening meditation on the rich young man (VS 6–27), yet devote little analysis to this scriptural overture. This is an odd omission, since this scriptural and Christological approach to ethics provides a model for the new method of moral theology mandated by Vatican II (VS 7; *Optatam Totius,* 16) in its clear dissatisfaction with the manualist reduction of moral theology to a set of propositions.

The focus on the battle with the proportionalists also obscures the positive restructuring of natural law ethics undertaken by the pope. John Paul II clearly states the purpose of *Veritatis Splendor* to be "to reflect on the whole of the Church's moral teaching, with the precise goal of recalling certain fundamental truths of Catholic doctrine which, in the present circumstances, risk being distorted or denied" (VS 4). As Russell Hittinger argues in his commentary, the encyclical's novelty lies precisely in its presentation of the Catholic moral tradition as an integrated whole. "More than any other encyclical, *Veritatis Splendor* presents the tradition in a complete way. It exposes the interlocking parts of the tradition and indicates why certain teachings have their respective emphasis and place within the whole."[6] Like the *Catéchisme*[7] upon which it is explicitly based (VS 5), *Veritatis Splendor* is a synthetic exposition of the general components of Catholic moral reflection rather than a commentary on a specific moral issue. It offers a retrieval of natural law ethics within the new framework of scriptural and Christological analysis and within John Paul II's distinctive method of melding philosophy and theology.[8]

Veritatis Splendor's treatment of conscience indicates the com-

---

[6] Russell Hittinger, "The Splendor of Truth," *First Things* (Jan. 1994): 17.

[7] See *Le Catéchisme Universel* (Paris: Mame/Plon, 1992), #377–80, for the analysis of conscience.

[8] For a discussion of John Paul II's debt to phenomenology, see Robert Harvanek, "The Philosophical Foundations of the Thought of John Paul II," *The Thought of John Paul II*, ed. J. Michael McDermott, S.J. (Rome: Gregoriana, 1993), 1–22.

plexity of the pope's retrieval of natural law ethics. In certain passages the document undoubtedly provides a neo-scholastic account of conscience as the exercise of practical judgment upon a specific action. In other passages, however, the encyclical proposes a more "Augustinian" anatomy of conscience, prone to self-deception and shaped by Christ, speaking through the magisterium, in the dynamic of grace and conversion. In both the philosophical and salvific registers, the pope develops an account of conscience which is clearly different from a simple retrieval of the dominant model of conscience in the Pian era.

On one level, *Veritatis Splendor* straightforwardly proposes an account of conscience familiar in neo-scholastic manuals. The pope defends the rational nature of conscience as "an act of a person's intelligence, the function of which is to apply the universal knowledge of the good in a specific situation and thus to express a judgment about the right conduct to be chosen" (VS 32). The encyclical carefully wards off possible subjectivist reductions of conscience. The reason recognizes, rather than creates, the goods to be pursued within a particular choice (VS 54). The intellect both recognizes and applies objective goods, rooted in the spiritual-somatic composite of human nature (VS 48), rather than goods fabricated by individual desire or social milieu. The encyclical also emphasizes the universal nature of the norms to be applied in specific cases. These qualifications place conscience within the proper dialectic between truth and freedom, which the encyclical designates as the key framework for authentic moral reflection (VS 34).

In defending the rational nature of conscience, the pope avoids a rationalistic reduction of conscience to a simple operation of applying universal norms to particular actions. He accomplishes this by stressing the transcendence of conscience, which discovers its origin and end in God rather than in self or nature. The conscience discovers an interior law indicating good and evil, planted by God (VS 54). The ethical dialogue of self with self "is also a dialogue of man with God, the author of the law, the primordial image and final end of man" (VS 58). Only when the search for moral truth opens to God as the supreme good and source of all finite goods can the true nature of the enterprise of conscience be adequately grasped. "Only God, the Supreme Good, constitutes the unshakeable foundation and essential condition of morality" (VS 99). This emphasis upon the transcendental trait of conscience, which recognizes God as the author of the law that it seeks to apply, reflects the more general insistence of *Veritatis Splendor* that natural law must be construed within the framework of eternal law, the divine reason reflected in all creation (VS 50).

John Paul II adds an intuitionist note to this neo-scholastic conception of conscience. The conscience not only recognizes God. The voice of God resounds within the human conscience. "Conscience is the witness of God Himself, whose voice and judgment penetrate the depths of man's soul, calling him *fortiter* and *suaviter* to obedience" (VS 58). Although this is a common catechetical image of conscience, Thomistic manualists such as Austin Fagothey[9] and Andrew Varga[10] criticized the "voice of God" theory as tainted by illuminism. *Veritatis Splendor* also refers in several passages to "the moral sense" (e.g., VS 106), another intuitionist model of conscience routinely dismissed by manualists as too reminiscent of the antirationalism of Shaftesbury and Hutcheson.[11] For John Paul II, who explicitly criticizes too syllogistic an account of conscience (VS 55), the intellect's work of deciding which action to perform or shun is ultimately an interior response to the immediate interpellation of God.

On another level, *Veritatis Splendor* undercuts this rather optimistic vision of conscience as reason's application of moral norms to specific cases. In several passages, more scriptural in tone and reference, the pope stresses the limitations of conscience. The constitutional weakness of human nature emerges. The necessity of converting the conscience through redemption in Christ is emphasized. The necessity of the magisterium of the Church to tutor the concupiscent conscience is asserted.

In sketching this more Augustinian account of conscience, the pope emphasizes the ravages of sin upon human nature. From the beginning of the encyclical, he argues that "man's capacity to know the truth is also darkened, and his will to submit to it is weakened" (VS 1). The sinful distortion of the faculties integral

---

[9] See Austin Fagothey, *Right and Reason* (St. Louis: Mosby, 1959), 207–23.
[10] See Andrew Varga, *On Being Human* (New York: Paulist, 1978), 125–32.
[11] See Fagothey, 208, and Varga, 38–39 and 125–26.

to conscience issues in a moral skepticism that repeatedly drives the individual to sever freedom from truth (VS 54). This concupiscence easily blinds individuals to the nature and depth of their moral transgressions. "Before feeling easily justified in the name of conscience, we should reflect on the words of the Psalm: 'Who can discern his errors? . . .' There are faults which we fail to see but nevertheless remain faults, because we have refused to walk towards the light" (VS 63). In its extreme form, moral concupiscence can virtually destroy the very operation of conscience by suppressing the individual's interest in—and, hence, choice of—moral truth.

One of the distinctive traits of *Veritatis Splendor*'s portrait of the distorted conscience is the pope's emphasis upon the social causes of this disorder. The deterioration of moral conscience reflects the secularization of contemporary culture. "Dechristianization, which weighs heavily upon entire peoples and communities once rich in faith and Christian life, involves not only the loss of faith or, in any event, its becoming irrelevant for everyday life, but also, and of necessity, a decline or obscuring of the moral sense" (VS 106). Not only does the practice of conscience deteriorate in such a climate of religious and ethical skepticism. Utilitarian theories of conscience and the moral act illegitimately import the instrumental logic of a technological culture. "These theories can gain a certain persuasive force from their affinity to the scientific mentality, which is rightly concerned with ordering technical and economic activities on the basis of a calculation of resources and profits, procedures, and their effects" (VS 76). While earlier moralists emphasized the role of individual ignorance and passion in fostering an erroneous conscience, the pope underlines the preeminence of social factors in eroding a conscience already weakened by sin.

This darkness of conscience is redressed only through redemption in Christ.

> People today need to turn to Christ once again in order to receive from him the answer to their questions about what is good and what is evil. Christ is the Teacher, the Risen One who has life in himself and who is always present in his Church and in the world. It is he who opens up to the faithful the book of Scriptures and, by

fully revealing the Father's will, teaches the truth about moral action (VS 8).

Christ not only reveals the fullness of the moral enterprise in clarity and integrity. He unifies the work of the moral conscience by rooting it in the transcendent movement of love (VS 13). Only through the grace of Christ is the conscience healed from its constitutional blindness (VS 23) and freed for moral perfection (VS 13). In this soteriological framework, the mature moral conscience is the "repentant" conscience (VS 104), which emerges through Christ's pedagogy of conversion.

In this pedagogy, the Church's magisterium plays a crucial role. In proclaiming Christ, the Church helps to form conscience by specifying the objective order of goods intrinsic to human nature (VS 64). The moral maturation of the believer is an internal consequence of the authentic experience of salvation. Although the Church's formation of conscience involves judgments on specific moral issues (VS 85), it is the proclamation of Christ crucified that lies at the heart of the Church's moral pedagogy. "It is in the Crucified Christ that the Church finds the answer to the question troubling so many people today: how can obedience to universal and unchanging moral norms respect the uniqueness and individuality of the person, and not represent a threat to his freedom and dignity?" (VS 85). The Church not only proclaims Christ crucified as the model of moral action. By nurturing believers capable of martyrdom (VS 90–93), the Church initiates its members into the passion of Christ itself. Paradoxically, the Church defends the goods proper to human nature (VS 50) by forming a conscience opposed to the world's wisdom and capable of embracing death over human esteem. The scriptural headings of key chapters underscore the militancy of the conscience redeemed in Christ: "Do not be conformed to this world" (Rom. 12:2 for chapter 2) and "Lest the Cross of Christ be emptied of its power" (1 Cor. 1:17 for chapter 3).

On the surface, *Veritatis Splendor*'s account of conscience is problematic. The pope appears to sketch a double-tiered theory. Conscience emerges simultaneously as an exercise of reason common to all human beings *qua* human and as a distorted faculty capable of successful operation only through redemption in Christ and communion with the Church. As Avery Dulles has noted,[12] neo-scholastic theology tended to make simultaneous claims for the power of reason to achieve detailed religio-moral knowledge and for the necessity of the magisterium to provide detailed interventions in order to acquire this knowledge. The encyclical's anatomy of conscience bears the mark of this perduring dualism.

The role of history, another problematic area in neo-scholasticism, also appears minimized in the text's account of the magisterium's role in the formation of conscience. In the list of intrinsically evil actions opposed by the magisterium (VS 80), for example, torture is prominently featured. However, the vagaries of Church teaching on this issue, which include explicit approval of torture by an ecumenical council (Vienne), popes (Clement V), and leading moralists (Thomas Aquinas, Alphonsus Liguori),[13] receive no attention.

Despite these problems, *Veritatis Splendor* reconciles the divergent philosophical and theological approaches to conscience. It is the encyclical's Christology that most successfully unifies these disparate avenues. The opening biblical meditation on Christ's encounter with the rich young man illustrates this reconciliation. At each stage of meditation on this encounter, the pope intertwines an anagogical interpretation (the relevance of the passage for all human beings in their moral quest) with a soteriological interpretation (the relevance of the passage for the Christian called to redemption).

In glossing Matthew 19:17, for example, the pope interprets the commandments as both the law of the heart common to all human beings (VS 12) and Christ's law of love, distinguished by its promise of eternal life and by the gift of grace (VS 13–15). In the encounter with Christ, the Church and the individual Christian simultaneously discover the demands of a correct human conscience—thus aligning them with all people of good will in the defense of human dignity—and the contours of conscience in the specifically Christian itinerary of redemption, conversion, and discipleship.

---

[12] See Avery Dulles, "Jesuits and Theology," *Theological Studies* 52/3 (1991): 529–32.

[13] See John Conley, "Torture as a Theological Problem," unpublished M.Th. thesis (Weston School of Theology, 1984).

Whatever traces of neo-scholastic theology it maintains, *Veritatis Splendor* does not follow the traditional neo-scholastic dualism of first specifying moral truth through the exercise of reason alone, then complementing this truth with data drawn from revelation. From its overture, *Veritatis Splendor* squarely places moral reflection in the presence of Christ. Paradoxically, the Christian's concern for the dignity of every human conscience deepens only to the extent that the Christian conscience explicitly opens itself to conversion in Christ and tutelage by the Church's magisterium. It is in the economy of salvation that the nature and norms of the right conscience surface with precision. Conversely, it is in plumbing the questions of human conscience (VS 1) that one opens oneself to the call of Christ and his Church. This paradoxical union between philosophical and theological reflection at the service of conscience reflects the reciprocity between anthropology and Christology that has typified John Paul II's thought since his inaugural encyclical, *Redemptor Hominis*.

Response

Benjamin Fiore, S.J.

FATHER CONLEY CALLS ATTENTION to the bafflement in the public media over the letter's opening biblical meditation. In the scholarly world he finds a similarly superficial analysis of the scriptural overture, even though this scriptural approach is designed to provide a model for the new method of moral theology mandated by Vatican Council II. Curiously, he also spends most of the paper treating the philosophical and moral positions in the encyclical. I would hazard a guess that the encyclical's readers will generally find the scriptural part to be merely the wind-up before the letter's pitch, which is to comment on various positions taken with regard to moral truth among contemporary theologians. The scriptural part fails to provide the expected model for postconciliar method in moral theology because, once given, the scriptural observations are not relied upon very much and are rarely referred to in the second part, where traditional sources abound. When Scripture is referred to, the references are largely to yet other passages, giving the impression that the second section was done at a different time or by someone else.

Let me focus on the scriptural content and method. In the first place, the selection of Matthew's Gospel for the paradigmatic story is appropriate, but I would have liked some consideration of the earlier version of the same story in Mark. The encyclical proceeds by referring to the Gospels and to the Pauline letters, but it would be strengthened if there were also some comment on their relationship. While the encyclical refers repeatedly to the Church's work to provide true moral teaching, the encyclical could have made the point more effectively by noting that in Matthew's Gospel this process of developing truthful moral insights from Jesus's teaching is already in evidence.

The same could be said for the reference to John's Gospel for a statement about the future work of the Spirit-Paraclete, reminding the apostles about the teaching of Jesus. The work of the Paraclete has already been done in the editing and the final preparation of the Gospel. The letter could have profited from some of the historico-critical insights of recent exegetes.

The letter does refer to both the Gospels and to Paul. In its references to Paul (primarily to Galatians 5), the encyclical finds references to objectively good and evil actions as well as to the proper use of freedom. Conley alludes to the letter's stress on the necessity of the magisterium to tutor concupiscent conscience, but one also finds in the letter a departure from the Thomistic manualists' routine dismissal of the intuitionist model of conscience when it speaks of conscience as an interior response to the immediate interpellation of God. The encyclical might well have reinforced this point with allusions to the inner promptings and guidance of the Holy Spirit, found in the often mentioned Galatians 5 passage and in many other places in the letters of Paul (Romans 8, for example) and in the Gospels as well. Once again, the philosophical bent of the pope has led him to rely on the philosophical argument and demonstration while side-stepping the evidence of Scripture.

In my view, this philosophical penchant leads the pope to emphasize truth as the counterpart to freedom. Here the pope departs from his Matthean source and relies on John. My tendency would be to elevate the place of justice, alluded to alongside truth in several places in the encyclical, as an important aim of the moral life. This is in keeping with Jesus's own proclamation of the rule or kingdom of God and its requirements. It also relates to the two tablets of the decalogue in the story of the rich young man. Moreover, given the de-christianization and secularization of contemporary society, which, Conley notes, the encyclical sees at the root of the current deteriorization of conscience, a campaign for justice might be a more acceptable starting point in the re-evangelization process. It was, after all, where Jesus began.

Finally, the crucified Christ and the call to martyrdom in the third part of the encyclical does, as Conley nicely shows, tie together obedience to universal moral norms and respect for the uniqueness and individuality of the person. I wonder, however, whether the "martyrdom" imagined by Pope John Paul II is in keeping with the Pauline and evangelical appropriation of the Cross into the Christian's identity. The scriptural discussion might have been expanded to discuss whether embracing death is actually the same as embracing the Cross. I think of Philippians 1 and 3, where Paul sees his own death as tied to the Cross but sees life under different circumstances for his followers.

In conclusion, Conley's paper clearly elucidates the encyclical's teaching on conscience and ties together the various parts of the encyclical, thus giving an excellent account of the unity of thought contained in it.

4. MORAL CONVERSION
Christological Bases for the Moral Life: *Redemptor Hominis* As a Key to *Veritatis Splendor*

Ronald A. Mercier, S.J.

SHORTLY AFTER THE RELEASE of *Veritatis Splendor*, a colleague posed a very important question. How could one hold together the Christological insights of Pope John Paul's first encyclical, *Redemptor Hominis*, with the structure of the moral life proposed in VS? The first encyclical, with all its attention to the historical and distinctively humanistic Christ "who follows the way of man," seemed profoundly different from the more static and ahistorical presentation of VS. Had the pope's perspective undergone a profound change from 1980 to 1993? The question proved fruitful, inviting attention to the Christological basis for the pope's theology, and most especially to his presentation of Christian morality.

The text of RH itself lays the groundwork for a distinctively Christological approach to morality. It notes, for example, that "Jesus Christ is the stable principle and fixed center of the mission that God himself has entrusted to man. We must all share in this mission and concentrate all our forces on it, since it is more necessary than ever for modern mankind" (par. 32).[1] The encyclical, with its dual emphasis on morality and Christology, makes explicit that the link is both necessary and consistent. Much as the dogmatic elements of the Christological presentation are of great con-

---

[1] Paragraph numbers for the text are those provided in Claudia Carlen, I.H.M., *The Papal Encyclicals, 1958–1981* (McGrath Publishing Co.), 245–74.

cern to the pope, the moral element emerges as the pope's central focus throughout the text.

Moreover, the first encyclical sets the stage for later attention to the question of "moral truth." At a critical juncture in the encyclical, the pope affirms:

> [f]or this reason the Church in our time attaches great importance to all that is stated by the Second Vatican Council in its *Declaration on Religious Freedom*, both the first and second part of the document. We perceive intimately that the truth revealed to us by God imposes on us an obligation. We have, in particular, a great sense of responsibility for this truth. By Christ's institution the Church is its guardian and teacher, having been endowed with a unique assistance of the Holy Spirit in order to guard and teach it in its most exact integrity. In fulfilling this mission, we look towards Christ himself, the first evangelizer, and also towards his apostles, martyrs and confessors. The *Declaration on Religious Freedom* shows us convincingly that, when Christ, and after him, his apostles proclaimed the truth that comes not from men but from God . . . they preserved, while acting with their full force of spirit, a deep esteem for man, for his intellect, his will, his conscience and his freedom. (34)

Indeed, it will be the contention of this essay that the heart of the teaching to be found in VS emerges directly from the same Christology found in RH, notably from its sense of the mission of Jesus, its soteriology, and its distinctive appeal to the Christological dimension of eschatology. The emphases of the first and third chapters of VS in particular flow directly from this earlier presentation.

This Christological focus in RH also provides links to the earlier thought of Pope John Paul II, both to his previous works and to subsequent encyclicals, especially regarding social morality. Indeed the structure of the argument intends a response to the challenges of totalitarianism and moral decay in the socio-cultural sphere. His doctoral thesis, *Faith according to Saint John of the Cross*, and his book *The Acting Person* provide important theological and philosophical bases upon which he builds. At the same time, the particular sense of Christ's lordship over history and the resulting moral imperative for all people ground the way in which his social teaching grows, a teaching offered as a service to authentic democracy. In a sense, we are dealing with a particularly important work, one that provides a useful point of access to VS and to the moral life generally.

This paper will explore a twofold thesis based on the centrality in RH of the redeeming work of Christ. First, the emphasis on a high Christology, coupled with a stress on the prophetic work of Christ, ground a strong sense of the normativity of the moral life, one rather categorical in form. This provides a very useful basis for a powerful and compelling social ethic. At the same time, though, especially if one takes into account recent scholarship by critics of modernity like Edith Wyschogrod,[2] this can lead to a de-emphasis of the narrative dimensions of Christology, rendering the moral message problematic in a modern context. In that light, the greater stress in VS and subsequently in *Evangelium Vitae* on providing a more meditative, narrative structure to moral argumentation takes on an important role. The question will be the ability of the encyclicals to effect the linkage between the two dimensions.

In turning to RH, one should not be surprised to find a basic "high" perspective on Christology. Significant emphasis is placed, for example, on the "entry of Christ into the world":

> As we reflect again on this stupendous text from the Council's teaching, we do not forget even for a moment that Jesus Christ, the Son of the living God, became our reconciliation with the Father. He it was, and he alone, who satisfied the Father's eternal love, that fatherhood that from the beginning found expression in creating the world, giving man all the riches of creation, and making him little less than God, "in that he was created in the image and after the likeness of God." . . . The Cross on Calvary, through which Jesus Christ—a Man, the Son of the Virgin Mary, thought to be the son of Joseph of Nazareth—"leaves" this world, is also a fresh manifestation of the eternal fatherhood of God, who in him draws near again to humanity, to each human being, giving him the thrice holy "Spirit of truth." (23)

This text, located rather early in the document, emphasizes the role of God who chooses to save us through the sacrificial atonement of the Son, shaping the subsequent structure of the docu-

---

[2] Edith Wyschogrod, *Saints and Postmodernism: Revisioning Moral Philosophy* (Chicago: University of Chicago Press, 1990).

ment. God's love is revealed in and through the Cross, revealing the judgment of God on the world, one of mercy and justice.

The emphasis is precisely on this "drawing near of God to history," a history from which God had been decisively excluded by human choice:

> The Redeemer of the world! In him has been revealed in a new and more wonderful way the fundamental truth concerning creation . . . "God saw that it was good." The good has its source in Wisdom and Love. In Jesus Christ the visible world which God created for man—the world that, when sin entered, "was subjected to futility"—recovers again its original link with the divine source of Wisdom and Love. (21)

That sense of the "futility of the world" becomes the basis for the mission of the Church into the world, and into human history. As RH points out immediately following the text cited above, the futility of the world can be seen most dramatically in the disorder found in our human treatment of the world and of one another, especially through the systems we establish in the "absence" of God. In the process, what has been lost is our sense of our dignity, a dignity rooted in the gift of God's image and likeness. We have here, in the third chapter of VS, the dogmatic roots of the strong critique of contemporary society and social structures.

The dual impact of such a high Christology, with its emphasis on the distance of God from the world wounded by original sin, a concept very much to the fore in this encyclical, cannot be overlooked. In so structuring the relationship between God and the world, the encyclical emphasizes the way in which "the good" can become virtually unknowable apart from revelation. The mission of the Son and consequently the "mystery of Redemption" take on very important and central roles in the moral life of every human person. Behind his Christological concern lies nothing less than the possibility of the moral life of the human person and hence the viability and vitality of any human community.

One finds this fundamental concern echoed in the encyclical's treatment of the sacraments of Eucharist and Reconciliation:

> The Eucharist is the most perfect sacrament of this union [with Christ]. By celebrating and also partaking of the Eucharist we unite

ourselves with Christ on earth and in heaven who intercedes for us with the Father but we always do so through the redeeming act of his sacrifice, through which he has redeemed us, so that we have been "bought with a price." The price of our redemption is likewise a further proof of the value that God himself sets on man and of our dignity in Christ. (79)

The strong emphasis on atonement for sin also shapes the eschatological presentation in the document. The resurrection stands always in the light of death, with its natural and moral dimensions. It gives us hope in the light of the threat posed by death:

> Indeed, while all this, in spite of all riches of life in time, necessarily and inevitably leads to the frontier of death and the goal of the destruction of the human body, beyond that goal we see Christ. "I am the resurrection and the life, he who believes in me . . . shall never die." In Jesus Christ, who was crucified and laid in the tomb and then rose again, "our hope of resurrection dawned . . . the bright promise of immortality . . ." (69)

In light of the fundamentally moral purpose of the text, one intending to challenge what the pope would later call the "culture of death," we see our lives in the light of the passion, death, and resurrection of the Lord, but primarily as a preparation for an encounter with the one who judges the living and the dead. Language of the "reign of God" tends to be largely absent, but this confirms his stress on the desire for a "social order conformed to the will of God" in this world. The emphasis on the struggle with the reality of sin and death overshadows the kind of eschatological reading one would find in *Gaudium et Spes*. The Cross stands very much to the fore, as it does, of course, in VS.

Of course, since Jesus is the revelation of God to us, this also shapes our sense of the nature of the Father, loving yet waiting in judgment. Scriptural texts like Matthew 25 play a critical role by emphasizing the responsibility incumbent on us, for we have seen the dignity of the human person revealed in Christ Jesus. We thereby become a "judgment" on the world, though, naturally, one that offers life to all people by existentially proclaiming the truth. The triplex of sin-atonement-judgment as a fundamental aspect of the nature of the world emerges in a consistent way.[3] This does tend to emphasize our union with God as having a distinctly moral or voluntarist cast. Again, though, the emphasis on the service the Christian life renders to society emerges as central.

This will necessarily have an implication upon the understanding of the *sequela Christi* in both RH and VS. In the first encyclical we read:

> Following Christ is not an outward imitation, since it touches man at the very depths of his being. Being a follower of Christ means becoming conformed to him who became a servant even to giving himself on the cross. (cf. Phil. 2:5–8) Christ dwells by faith in the heart of the believer (cf. Eph. 3:17) and thus the disciple is conformed to the Lord. This is the effect of grace, of the active presence of the Holy Spirit in us.

We are able, by the power of the Spirit, to live out the command *as* Christ did. This beckons us continually back to the Eucharist and to Reconciliation in a consistent process of conversion into Christ's image. We are thus enabled to keep faithfully "the moral prescriptions which God imparted in the old covenant and which attained their perfection in the new and eternal covenant in the very person of the Son of God made man" (VS, 25).

Not surprisingly, then, given the emphasis on the Cross as the revelation of Christ in his fullness, the Christian moral life always lies under the shadow of the Cross, as it were. The "form" of the moral life becomes a "martyrdom," a witness to the truth even to its fullest implications, for the sake of the world wounded by sin. RH uses not the imagery of martyrdom but that of discipleship, and being a "confessor," an unbloodied witness to the faith. (87) One finds the foundations laid for the third chapter of VS.

This sense of "confessing the truth" links the priestly work of Christ to another of his "offices," that of prophet. RH develops

---

[3] We might note the way in which this stress on the Cross, what Rahner calls the "staurological" model of salvation, tends to emphasize a somewhat "juridical" model of human life and morality. A distinctive alternative to this emerges in *Dives in Misericordia* which presents God's entry into our suffering in a way reminiscent of recapitulation. Within the moral realm, however, the critical role of judgment as a way of freedom arises in a consistent way.

powerfully Vatican II's presentation of Jesus as prophet. This prophetic work becomes the heart of the Church's faithful discipleship. The encyclical leads us directly into the critical issue of the nature of truth itself:

> In the light of the sacred teaching of the Second Vatican Council, the Church thus appears before us as the subject of responsibility for divine truth. With deep emotion we hear Christ Himself saying: "The word which you hear is not mine but the Father's who sent me." In this affirmation by our Master do we not notice responsibility for the revealed truth, which is the "property" of God himself, since even he, "the only Son," who lives "in the bosom of the Father," when transmitting the truth, as a prophet and teacher, feels the need to stress that he is acting in full fidelity to its divine source. (72)

The question of truth as a "property" of God, *ipsius Dei possessio*, one communicated to us by Christ, the bearer of truth, shouts throughout this whole section and indeed throughout the document. We are told that faith ultimately makes us "sharers in the knowledge of God" to which we must adhere in "obedience in harmony with reason," sharing in Christ's prophetic work. (72) Moreover, this truth is also a "truth about man," a phrase which recurs frequently throughout the text, a truth characterized as an "it":

> Being responsible for that truth also means loving it and seeking the most exact understanding of it, in order to bring it closer to ourselves and others in all its saving power, its splendor and its profundity joined with simplicity. (73)[4]

The "truth *about* man" certainly has real implications; it moves us into a series of propositional understandings of the moral life. A sense of a "categorical" nature of "truth about man" surfaces repeatedly; it structures both the document as a whole and the sense of the moral life.

Indeed, this categorical or propositional sense of who we are surfaces in a number of places in the document. While through-

---

[4] *Officium circa hanc veritatem assumptum etiam idem valet atque amare et curare, quo penitius cognoscatur, ita ut ad eam, cum tota vi salvifica, qua pollet, cum splendore, quo nitet, cum profunditate simul et simplicitate, quibus distinguitur, propius accedamus.* (AAS, 306)

out the document one finds constant reference to "the mystery of redemption," only twice do we have reference to "the mystery of man." Each of these in fact arises in citations of material from the Second Vatican Council, as in GS 22, cited in par. 22. The human person for the most part represents a "known quantity" within the discussion.

Within the "mystery of redemption," the human person functions far more as a datum of history, one whose identity is known in a categorical and exhaustive way.[5] For instance, one can note the way in which the encyclical approaches the question of love in human life:

> Man cannot live without love. He remains a being that is incomprehensible for himself, his life is senseless, if love is not revealed to him, if he does not encounter love. . . . This . . . is why Christ the Redeemer "fully reveals man to himself." If we may use the expression, this is the human dimension of the mystery of Redemption. (25)

With the advent of Christ, the "mystery of man" ends; Christ makes clear to us what sin had obscured, even denied. By implication, we are mystery only insofar as we lie under the shadow of sin, in the realm of death.

Christ bears that truth in a prophetic way, and the Church, impelled by the Spirit, must be faithful to that same prophetic ministry. Curiously though, especially considering the extraordinary emphasis accorded the reality of discipleship, language of Christ as the truth, of his very person as the truth, rarely surfaces. One finds it only at the beginning of the encyclical's explicit treatment of the mystery of redemption in par. 19. For the encyclical as a whole, however, Christ functions more clearly as bearer of the truth than as the truth itself.

---

[5] Here, I do not wish to go as far as Risto Saarinen in his article "Protestant Undertones, Averroist Overtones? The Concept of Nature in *Veritatis Splendor*" in Reinhard Hütter and Theodor Dieter, eds., *Ecumenical Ventures in Ethics: Protestants Engage Pope John Paul II's Moral Encyclicals* (Grand Rapids, Mich.: Eerdmans, 1998), 115–36, who sees the pope as presenting one essential nature or soul for all humans so as virtually to eliminate the reality of individuation, save by accident. Nonetheless, Saarinen is right, I think, to note the way in which Kantian aspects of the pope's thought can undermine the profoundly personalist aspect he so seeks to emphasize.

This bears key implications for "discipleship." The move is away from a relational, personal following, to a sense of a common obedience to some "truths" that transcend the relationship. This plays itself out, for example, in chapter 1 of VS. Of course, there is an abiding sense of the centrality of Jesus Christ for discipleship. Indeed, the Christian life finds its fullness only in such a relationship. The voluntarist or moral nature of the Christian life surfaces repeatedly, though, as we shall note, the growing emphasis on a more decidedly scriptural and meditative grounding for the moral life, as in the same first chapter of VS, leads us in a very different direction.

Nor should the more narrowly categorical or voluntarist reading of human life surprise one, especially given the socio-cultural agenda of the encyclicals and the need to respond to the assault on human dignity, which the pope sees as a hallmark of the contemporary era. The strong form given to the human person, the clarity of the meaning of each person, emerges in a bold way from the whole of the encyclical. This dignity as a gift from God and a ground for all reflection remains critical throughout:

> The Church, however, which has no weapons at her disposal apart from those of the Spirit, of the word and of love, cannot renounce her proclamation of the "word . . . in season and out of season." For this reason she does not cease to implore each side of the two [in any social struggle] and to beg everybody in the name of God and in the name of man: Do not kill! Do not prepare destruction and extermination of men! Think of your brothers and sisters who are suffering hunger and misery! Respect each one's dignity and freedom! (58)[6]

The pope goes on to note the way in which this revelation of God in Christ confirms the ancient commandments and, therefore, constitutes a link to Islam and to Judaism, a way of building moral dialogue in a relativist age.

The presentation of the relation of Christ to us in RH, with

---

[6] The links to the presentation in *Evangelium Vitae* are quite dramatic. Far from being a response to a request from cardinals coping with the various challenges of modern ethical life, this passage from RH reveals the focus in EV as a consistent and insistent element of the pope's thought. Indeed, one could argue that VS and EV are contained seminally within the first of the pope's major writings.

very specific interpretation of the priestly and prophetic role, leads directly to the strong emphasis on the commandments in chapter 1 of VS, notably in the meditation on Matthew 19. VS presents the decalogue as a series of truths communicated by God, a precondition to the covenant, as it were. Indeed, they are cast as the truths of human life and as such are unambiguous. Their relation to the natural law, a relation of identity, makes clear that revelation merely affirms what is knowable by reason, save for the darkening, which is the result of sin.

This gives a strongly Kantian undertone to the presentation of the commandments. One confronts an opposition between a categorical objectivity and a "relativism" that deprives one of the moral foundations for personal and social life. Need this opposition be so stark? Philosophically, of course not. Other, more nuanced presentations of "objectivity," as in the philosophy of Bernard J. F. Lonergan, S.J., would similarly refute the dangers of relativism without the Kantian structure operative in RH. They would allow also for a fuller reading of the human person as always a mystery, not simply so as a result of the ravages of sin.

Yet, the pope's concern does *not* lie in the philosophical realm. This is not to say that philosophical issues are unimportant in the discussion, but rather that the dichotomy between "the culture of life and truth" and "the culture of death and darkness" represents the heart of the moral stage presented to Christians in the contemporary era. A strongly diagnostic sense characterizes the presentation, one which does not necessarily preclude other philosophical presentations (as noted deliberately in VS), but which argues mightily for a recognition of the powerful moral struggle every age faces, though in a particularly critical way today. The secularism of the current era, however, renders the struggle even more pressing.

This sense of the centrality of Christ's "bearing the truth" to a world in shadow gives a particular cast to the recounting of the life of Jesus. In a sense, his life is telescoped into his death:

> The life of Christ speaks, also, to many who are not capable of repeating with Peter: "You are the Christ, the Son of the living God." He, the Son of the living God, speaks to people also as Man: it is his life that speaks, his humanity, his fidelity to the truth, his

all-embracing love. Furthermore, his death on the Cross speaks—
that is to say the inscrutable depth of his suffering and abandonment. (20)

We are dealing here with "natural law" in a new key, for the revelation of the human person in Jesus is "man as 'willed' by God, as 'chosen' by Him from eternity and called, destined for grace and glory." (39)

Of course, part and parcel of all this is the "concrete humanity" of Jesus, in the fullness of which he lives out the triple *munera*. Throughout the encyclical, we have a consistent repetition of various forms of the triplex found in section 10 of the encyclical:

> The Church's fundamental function in every age and particularly in ours is to direct man's gaze, to point the awareness and experience of the whole of humanity towards the mystery of God, to help all men to be familiar with the profundity of the Redemption taking place in Christ Jesus. At the same time man's deepest sphere is involved—we mean the sphere of human hearts, consciences and events. (27)

Here Jesus reveals the fullness of what a human is because he lives out absolutely the nature of the human person. His is a heart undivided by the wound of sin, and he is able, therefore, to live according to the truth of what it means to be human, according to the commandments, even to the Cross. This leads, therefore, to an ability to act freely and to shape history in conformity with the will of God. It is this which is the "full truth about human freedom"—the ability to live out one's call to follow God's will (89).[7]

This is not accidental or unimportant for the project of the encyclical. The sense of the *munus regale* found in section 21 of RH, titled "The Christian Vocation to Service and Kingship," makes the construction of human history in accordance with human dignity the morally appropriate work of all people, espe-

---

[7] *Plena igitur veritas de humana libertate in Redemptionis mysterio est alte recondita* (*AAS*, 320). In many ways, Germain Grisez has it exactly right when he notes that the moral teaching propounded here is revelation and not ultimately natural law. The strong sense of sin and its effect on us renders rather problematic our ability to know the truth. It is the exclusive domain of the magisterium with its uniquely graced charism, therefore, to teach in this area. Germain Grisez, "Revelation versus Dissent," *The Tablet* (16 October 1993): 1329–31.

cially Christians. The socio-cultural vocation surges prominently to the fore, again set against the darkness of the challenges facing us.

> [O]ne element seems to stand out in the midst of all these riches: the sharing in Christ's kingly mission, that is to say the fact of rediscovering in oneself and others the special dignity of our vocation that can be described as "kingship." This dignity is expressed in readiness to serve. (85)

The safeguarding of human rights and the reconstruction of human society in conformity with the will of God becomes the key way of sharing in the work of Christ in this world. Inevitably, of course, this means that one's fidelity to Christ exists always, and in a sense only in and through one's act of witness. It is construed not according to the disposition of the heart nor even according to one's knowledge or intent, but according to the act itself in the light of its objective truth *because* it is in this way that it will be experienced as witness by the world. This aspect of human activity cannot be stressed highly enough in such a context. The encyclical, moreover, roots this in a primary way in the evangelical witness of Christ.

One finds an almost exact repetition of this sense of our "moral work" in VS 38. The text notes that our authentic dominion is over our action in the world, though always for the sake of the world. Freedom exists with respect to objects in the world; transcendental freedom is "control over the self," again picking up the theme of "obedience even to the Cross." The middle term in Rahner's theology of freedom—the awareness of the mystery of oneself in the growing encounter with the mystery of God—finds no echo here, though, of course, it is not denied. In many ways, and we shall return to this later, that more symbolic, as distinct from categorical, approach to the human person and creation, remains as yet undeveloped, precisely because of the sociocultural mission set out in the text.

In this case, the union between us and Christ is rooted in action and in will, as noted in RH's affirmation that "[o]ur sharing in Christ's kingly mission—his 'kingly function' (*munus*)—is closely linked with every sphere of both Christian and human morality" (85). We are then pointed back toward the commands that evoke an obedience to "objective truth," along previously developed lines. What we have yet to see, however, and what will begin to develop in VS and EV, is a stress on the narrative structure of Christ's life or on the broader implications of the humanity assumed by the Lord. That would await a more distinctly narrative reading in the light of VS and EV, in which the "mystery" of the human person emerges much more emphatically.

The emphasis on the action-based union between us and Christ finds its echo in RH's presentation of the mission of the Spirit, "the mystery of the divine economy." The Spirit of Jesus, who plays such a dramatic role within the presentation of RH, acts so as to order the human person correctly on an interior level, allowing reason to operate correctly and to affirm the revealed truths:

> This invocation addressed to the Spirit to obtain the Spirit is really a constant self-insertion into the full magnitude of the mystery of the Redemption, in which Christ, united with the Father and with each man, continually communicates to us the Spirit who places within us the sentiments of the Son and directs us towards the Father. (71)

The Spirit is the reconciler, healing the disorder that results from sin, the disorder that clouds our human reason; we can thus be conformed like Christ to the will of the Father.

The work of the Spirit creates a union, as the text notes, but the union stressed here is primarily extrinsic. We follow the path of Jesus, are freed to do so, and our moral life is judged according to his pattern. Yet, the "new creation" represents more of a return to the original innocence of creation. The "new life" described in section 18, for example, calls one to "the search for truth, the insatiable need for the good, hunger for freedom, nostalgia for the beautiful and the voice of conscience." (70). This filiation by the Spirit finds its form and content in the moral realm, which is not surprising given the intense attention given in this encyclical to the importance of witness in a world of darkness.

Also important here would be the sense of Christ as "lord of the Church and lord of our history." (92) This carries through the conception of the role of the triple *munera* in the life of Christ and of the Christian. Christ by his work restores authentic humanity and thus enables the construction of a world in conformity with the will of God. One has, therefore, a strong sense of the *social* imperative of Christian morality, which shapes our communities in the light of God's desires. Christ commands us to create a Church and a history in conformity with the fundamental rules of created human nature. This has an impact on all Christian vocations, but one particular example calls married couples to live their vows as a vocation for the sake of the world (86–87).[8]

This emphasis on action in accord with the truth of human nature as the heart of the Christian vocation constitutes a key aspect of the encyclical and the mind of its author. George Huntston Williams noted in his analysis of the work of Karol Wojtyła a real link between this sense of vocation and his own philosophical corpus:

> The crucial facts in Wojtyła's theory of acting are as follows: "man-acts" are a narrow class of experience, and are only able to be performed freely through the use of self-determination; they are performed in reference to an objective truth, an absolute; they fulfil or do not fulfil the person's human potential, according to whether they are or are not true to a perennially valid ethical norm, thus making the person good or bad. The freedom or self-determination of a person thus depends ultimately upon his free choice of (the revealed) truth as to the good.[9]

While acts can cover a variety of realities, including contemplation, prayer, thought, or interior activity, their conformity to a norm that fundamentally is extrinsic remains important. As a number of authors have pointed out, it makes the question of individuation rather a difficult one.

A similar presentation emerges in one of the earliest writings of Karol Wojtyła, his dissertation on John of the Cross. Two aspects in particular come to the fore, both of which find their echo in the image of the obedient, prophetic work of Jesus. First, the definition of "soul," one very much in keeping with the dominant imagery of the time, comes through very clearly:

---

[8] Interestingly, the one appeal to the evangelical counsels deals with the clerical and religious states, both of which are called to a higher path in conformity with Christ in a different way. The emerging stress on "martyrdom" in VS will, however, nuance this quite significantly.

[9] George Huntston Williams, *The Mind of John Paul II: Origins of His Thought and Action* (New York: Seabury Press, 1981), 207.

We have before us the complete works of St. John of the Cross. ... These works provide the basic material for our investigation. The time of their composition is not known for certain, but they contain an explicit teaching on the virtue of faith as the means of union of the soul (*that is, the intellect*) with God.[10]

He goes on to stress that intellect should really be read as *ratio*, requiring the "obedience of the intellect," which he affirms in the text. Faith becomes the assent to "revealed truths" accepted only thanks to God's gift of the Spirit. A second dimension of faith, "ontological faith," allows the intellect to move away from a purely natural way of knowing to a supernatural one that accepts revealed truths. Yet, here again, truths are plural and categorical in form.[11] As he noted in *The Acting Person*, we are essentially dealing with "thinking and comprehending."[12] Truth applies in the first place to categorical statements. Christ bears to us the revelation of truths through a life lived prophetically, royally, and as priest, offering a sacrifice worthy to God and effective to us.

A second element enters here. Both Wojtyła's early works and *Redemptor Hominis* reject as problematic two understandings of "knowing." These surface in the doctoral thesis and in *The Acting Person*. First, Wojtyła points to an ongoing challenge from "illuminationism" since the human person cannot attain to such a knowledge of God. One must act through the intellect lest one come to perceive oneself as the arbiter of truth.[13] Second, though, he rejects all forms of "psychologism," which would effectively remove God from the process of knowing and render truth meaningless. Williams makes this point clearly, noting in the process the way in which the young Wojtyła sought systematically to distance himself from what he perceived as Kantian relativism.[14]

The "obedience of faith" exists, therefore, between two poles: the first an immediate sense of the truth, the second a pure empiricism. These poles, nonetheless, represent real challenges to our

---

[10] Karol Wojtyła, *Faith According to Saint John of the Cross* (San Francisco: Ignatius Press, 1981), 22–23. Emphasis in the original.

[11] Ibid., 238–49.

[12] Cardinal Karol Wojtyła, *The Acting Person* (Boston: D. Reidel Publishing Co., 1969), 158. *Analecta Husserliana*, X. Trans. Andrzej Potocki.

[13] Wojtyła, *Faith*, 15–16, for example.

[14] Williams, *The Mind of John Paul II*, 156–59.

receiving and holding the truth in the modern world. They represent the source of much of the darkness we experience in our lives. Healing comes from above; the meeting of "the Word" and the obedient human intellect in Christ provides a clear alternative to any such impoverishment of "the truth." In the same way, the perception of truth in VS represents a real response to these same challenges of relativism and empiricism in our age, found especially in proportionalism and utilitarianism. Such alternatives are rightly rejected.

This helps clarify what the pope intends in sections 13 and 14, two critical sections of RH, which initially seem at odds with the presentation in VS. In section 13 the pope speaks of "man" as the key to the mystery of redemption:

> Accordingly, what is in question here is man in all his truth, in his full magnitude. We are not dealing with the "abstract" man, but the real, "concrete," "historical" man. We are dealing with "each" man, for each one is included in the mystery of the Redemption and with each one Christ has united Himself for ever through this mystery. (39)

The implications of this address to the human person surface in the next section:

> This man is the way for the Church—a way that, in a sense, is the basis of all the other ways that the Church must walk—because man—every man without any exception whatever—has been redeemed by Christ, and because with man—with each man without any exception whatever—Christ is in a way united, even when man is unaware of it. (42)

The human person here may well seem at first to be constituted by the historical situation or to exist in a condition still to be discovered as Christ seeks us out. Yet, we deal here with a phenomenological presentation of the person, one that claims an ability through an analysis of the phenomena of human life to capture in a morally determinative way the essence of the human person. Such an essence provides a sure foundation for all people who are recapitulated definitively and categorically in the person of Jesus. The particularities of situations present no problem to an exact knowledge of the moral call.

This conforms, of course, to a long tradition within Catholic moral philosophy and theology. In particular, one can see parallel concerns concerning illuminationism and "psychologism" in the works of numerous moralists in the late 1950s and 1960s. Josef Fuchs's critique of Rahner's theology is a case in point. At the same time, however, especially in the light of development in transcendental and postmodern philosophy and theology, one has to ask whether this represents a sufficient account of the "human act" and of the moral life. While it does serve a very important function in setting firm limits that safeguard the dignity of the human person against the various assaults experienced in contemporary society, does it provide a positive vision that is open to development as well as to defense? In many ways, precisely this same question arises in VS in terms of the positive meaning of the personal relationship with Jesus Christ constitutive of the moral challenge of discipleship.

In a sense, we move to a second aspect of a key virtue of RH and of all the pope's encyclicals—namely, justice and right relationships, especially among persons in society. In a sense, the move made by the pope in RH provides a warrant for a major development in the Church's social teaching. The moral teaching, forged in the light of the struggle with totalitarianism, an issue that provides a constant echo in RH, VS, and EV, provides a strong basis for moral dialogue with contemporary society. The phenomenological cast of the argument provides, moreover, a warrant for attention to the concrete condition of every human person, but more notably those whose dignity faces the more severe assault.

In rooting the social teaching of the Church not in a "structure of society," not in questions of utility or function, not even in "rights," but in the very person of Jesus and the revelation he bears or is, the pope re-centers social ethics, giving it a fresh importance. By comparison with earlier encyclicals, the teaching of RH adds an urgency and a theological warrant to the imperative for action in the world, making it both new and compelling. Linking the issue of social and political activity directly to the person and work of Jesus makes such questions the equal of all other aspects of moral teaching. The issue of "dominion" over the world and over history as a clear sign of fidelity opens up rather dramatically the sense of "examination of conscience," both by continuing the development from Paul VI and affirming a bold new initiative.

At the same time, questions of rights, when linked directly to questions of revelation, again take on a more profound and sharper importance than even that found in the groundbreaking works of John XXIII and Paul VI. Rights do not exist in some Kantian sense as the discovered prerequisites for social peace nor even simply as a person's "due," they emerge from the very will of God for the world revealed in the life and work of Jesus. Certainly one can find parallels in earlier works, notably in Paul VI's *Populorum Progressio*, but the force provided by the explicitly theological warrants in RH and VS demand clear attention and immediate response. The Christological context provided in RH lays the theological groundwork for the explicit affirmations and extensions of human rights found in *Laborem Exercens, Centesimus Annus*, and *Sollicitudo Rei Socialis*. Without the clear and compelling groundwork in RH, the other presentations would hang rather loosely.

RH goes a step further, of course, in dealing with the importance of morality to life as a whole. The revelation of Jesus becomes essentially a moral one. Through his person and teaching, and especially his fidelity even to the Cross, he links in a forceful manner the life of faith and the response of a moral life. This provides a clear context for the rejection of any distinction of the life of faith and the moral life, as noted in VS's critique of "fundamental option."[15] We have a radical affirmation of the normativity of the moral life rooted deliberately in the life and witness of the Lord.

As noted above, one would not wish to lose such a strong foundation of the moral life, especially in the realm of social ethics. Nevertheless, questions arise about ways in which this model provides a possible extension of the proposed model, one that would *both* prevent a relativistic reading of morality and develop more fully the meaning of the "call to holiness" which the pope so emphasizes. Not surprisingly, given the strong emphasis placed upon the cross as the full measure of Jesus's revelation of the

---

[15] VS 65–68. See the critical questions raised by Joseph Fuchs in his "Good acts and good persons," *The Tablet* (6 November 1993): 1444–45.

meaning of human life, we read in RH, and a fortiori in VS and EV, of the holiness of a life unto martyrdom. This radical call for a fidelity that witnesses to the Cross as a service to one's contemporaries rings boldly from the text.

Yet another aspect that lies relatively undeveloped in RH surfaces tantalizingly in VS's affirmation of the moral life; though negative norms provide critical limits to reflection, they necessarily open profoundly to the limitless quality of the positive norms, or in a Christological sense, to the following of Christ.[16] In essence, this flows directly from the meditative quality of the introductions to RH and EV. In a way it expands the basis of the discussion, without losing the desired foundational firmness. Indeed, one could say that the concern of RH and VS to respond to the fundamental problems of our age, notably the lack of clear moral norms and the rejection of authority, requires something more than the categorical reading in much of the encyclical.

A number of scholars critical of the contemporary era and its worship of the narrow rationality that grounds relativism and moral doubt point to an overly categorical or pragmatic philosophy as itself part of the problem.[17] John Ralston Saul certainly points to the lack of modesty regarding the claims of reason as in part the source of the relativism and totalitarianism that the pope rightly rejects.[18] Similarly, Edith Wyschogrod points to a critical lack in moral reasoning today—namely, that of context or narrative, notably the attentiveness to holiness, a key concern for Pope John Paul II. Wyschogrod notes the following:

> Heidegger shows that the notion of theory derives from a particular ontology, that of modern science. . . . But the description of truth conditions laid down by the science of logic cannot be self-grounding. . . . [L]ogic is the product of a tradition that cannot justify or account for itself. A second difficulty that attaches to the notion of

---

[16] See VS 13, "The commandments thus represent the basic condition for love of neighbour; at the same time they are the proof of that love. They are the *first necessary step on the journey towards freedom*, its starting-point."

[17] A parallel concern emerges, of course, in *Fides et Ratio* (1998), which in many ways endorses a return to a much more deliberate attention to wisdom as a context for philosophical and theological reflection; see especially no. 9–11.

[18] John Ralston Saul, *Voltaire's Bastards: The Dictatorship of Reason in the West* (New York: Vintage, 1993).

theory . . . is that . . . nature is regarded on the one hand as made up of calculable homogeneous units that can be manipulated at will and as comprehensible in terms of causal laws. Human beings are construed as part of nature and, as such, open to the same mode of interpretation as other entities.[19]

This is not to say, of course, that the pope argues for the manipulation of humans nor that he would view the human person as ultimately empirically determined. I would wonder, rather, whether the form of argumentation designed to counteract the ravages of overzealous reason might not have the inverse effect of playing to the same assumptions as our contemporary "myths."

Wyschogrod and others note that our contemporary culture has become "narrative-less," without a community of shared values or vision, without a "community of saints." In the process, morality dies not because of philosophical skepticism nor even because of rampant relativism, but because of a lived poverty of human meaning; such meaning arises primarily in relational, not categorical, terms. The emphasis on limits works well only in the context of the radical affirmation of a vision that gives meaning to the limits.

Ironically, however, this need not be the case, given the wide scope of the pope's writings. The staurological emphasis in RH and VS certainly represents critical elements in any moral presentation. Yet, alone, such an emphasis is insufficient for dealing with the moral project facing us today. Too narrow a focus on limits can reduce the moral scope of the pope's project of building a "culture of life"; indeed, the "meditations" at the beginning of VS and EV replicate the emphasis on limits to moral action, a point noted by several scholars who stress the broader implications of the texts upon which the meditations reflect.

The more narrowly construed "revelation of the mystery of the human person" needs to be expanded into an attentiveness to the impact of the grace loosed by the resurrection on the human person and on the world. The result would be an expanded vision and would ground a deeper moral appeal in our age. It would retrieve the critical moral moment of discernment of call as a complement to decision concerning the particular act to be done.

---

[19] Wyschogrod, *Saints and Postmodernism*, 160–61.

It would contextualize the normative aspects of morality. It would build on the call to service, worship, and celebration in the final section of EV, which is perhaps the most critical aspect of a response to the moral loss of bearings in our culture.[20]

In essence, this pneumatological dimension would pick up on the pope's emphasis on humans as ones who share in the creative work of God. By the Spirit we move toward sharing in the redemptive work of Christ as we build a culture of life. While the stress on limits provides a precondition for such a move, it would broaden the emphasis to include not simply the knowledge of what is revealed in Jesus of Nazareth, but also the way in which the person of Jesus is discovered in persons of faith by the power of the Holy Spirit, a "hagiographic" extension of the work of the encyclicals.

This would tend to re-center slightly the way in which Christ "reveals the mystery of the human person." Our modern temptation is to reduce the human to that which is "known about," with a consequent stress on a voluntarist model. The work of Walter Kasper[21] and Ewert Cousins[22] points to our need to retrieve the relational dimension of personhood in the face of our move to categorization. Both ground their perception in the Trinity, but they approach it through the humanity of Jesus, the economic Trinity, and in so doing stress the mystery of Jesus's humanity as a starting point, one perpetually deepening and never exhausted. The fidelity of Jesus throughout his life, his growth in grace and wisdom, and his ever-deepening sense of ministry, reveal the totality of the involvement of the person in the quest for God, placing *intellectus* in a wider, relational, context.

Here the emphasis would fall on the narrative quality of Jesus's life in its totality, moving us into what Ricoeur would call the "narrative path," which could ground and give a compelling

---

[20] Stanley Hauerwas, "Abortion: Why the Arguments Fail," in his *A Community of Character: Toward a Constructive Christian Social Ethic* (Notre Dame: University of Notre Dame Press, 1981), 212–29, stressed quite rightly how the role of Christians as "confessors," witnesses to the positive implications of the moral life, provides the most convincing response to the moral decay of modernity.

[21] Walter Kasper, *The God of Jesus Christ* (NewYork: Crossroad Publishing Co., 1984).

[22] Ewert Cousins, "A Theology of Interpersonal Relations," *Thought* (1970): 56–82.

quality to the "grammar of categorical norms." Such a model is found, not surprisingly, in the Marian encyclical *Redemptoris Mater*, which ironically provides a much more compelling ground to the moral life. It would ask of people the discipline of reading their own lives narratively, notably in terms of purpose and meaning, as an eschatological completion to the earlier stress on our limitations. It would also provide an important *telos* for the subjective dimension of morality so rightly emphasized in *Laborem Exercens*. Such a vision of self- and culture-creation as the pope provides in LE and EV requires more than the emphasis on limit; it requires a point of entry into discernment of the moral good or of the call of God in the concrete circumstances of one's life, as in the choice of a way of life. It would recognize the important contemporary insight of the moral role of spirituality as informing conscience and as grounding a positive witness to our culture, a compelling one rather than a "convincing" one.

In sum, the work of Pope John Paul II in stressing the Christological bases for the moral life provides a rich point of entry for reflection: a beginning, not an end. It forces us to come to terms with the richness of the Christ event in all its meaning to us, and as a foundation for building a culture of life and reversing the decay into death. In the process, though, the explicit call to discipleship in RH and VS requires from us deeper attention to forming conscience, both personally and communally, in a positive way, in imitation of the one who in his relationship with Father and with the faith of Israel, in his fidelity to the Scriptures, exemplifies to us the life of holiness, and who, by the loosing of his Spirit bids us find that same call to discovery of the mystery of God in our lives and in our world.

Response

Edmund W. Majewski, S.J.

FATHER MERCIER'S PRESENTATION on *Veritatis Splendor* provides us with numerous points for discussion. I will respond to some of his observations and questions and then offer some observations of my own.

The encyclical stresses the importance of linking morality to the person of Christ. Pope John Paul II insists that "we must first of all show the inviting splendor of that truth which is Jesus Christ himself. In him who is the truth man can understand fully and live perfectly, through his good actions, his vocation to freedom in obedience to the divine law summarized in the commandment of the love of God and the love of neighbor" (VS 83). Morality is situated in the splendor of truth that shines forth in creation and in the human being. It is related to the ultimate human good and supreme goal and to the deepest truths about what it means to be authentically human and a creature called by God to eternal life.

Veritatis Splendor, of course, is related to *Redemptor Hominis*. But I think that it would be unfair to say that the first provides us with a more static view, while the second gives us a more historical and humanistic view of Christ. Jesus Christ is both the universal and the concrete particular at the same time. As the center of the universe, he draws us to follow him to the Father. The commandments are absolute and immutable, but the manner in which each person fulfills them is unique and calls into existence freedom and creativity.

Mercier is correct that we follow Christ primarily not by outward imitation but through an interior imitation that involves us in an ongoing process of conversion. The Christian is called to take a radical stance for Christ and his values. I am reminded of von Balthasar's understanding of the Christian state of life as involving the taking of a stand in faith before Christ. The "where" (or basic orientation) of the Son is totally in the Father; the "where" of the Christian is totally in Christ, not as external imitation or in the achievement of an ideal, but primarily as a new and personal orientation of one's entire existence. To a degree the stand of the Christian is also influenced by the stand of Mary, who is more contemplative because she must first wait and be receptive to the will of God and then grow into an awareness of her basic "yes" to the will of God. Furthermore, just as it was impossible for Jesus to stand in a position of neutrality between the Father and the world in order to mediate between these two realms, so too the Christian cannot take a neutral stand but must live from the basic decision of faith.[23] Both Pope John Paul II and von Balthasar insist that the Christian state of life is a radical vocation to a new life in Christ that makes serious demands on all, not just on the clergy or religious, but on the laity as well.

The pope goes beyond a perspective that conceives of morality merely as a set of objective norms that must be observed, at least to some minimal degree. In this sense, I would say that the pope includes but also transcends a more static vision of morality: "This is not a matter only of disposing onself to hear a teaching and obediently accepting a commandment. More radically, it involves holding fast to the very person of Jesus, partaking of his life and his destiny, sharing in his free and loving obedience to the will of the Father" (VS 19). The Italian theologian Angelo Scola notes that for John Paul II "morality appears primarily as a participation in the unfolding of Christ's complete giving, that of the good teacher who loved us to the end (see VS 20)." The moral life is our free response to the person and event of Christ, and hence is seen as a journey in which we walk with Jesus and in Jesus toward the ultimate good and truth and life. The Holy Father approaches morality not so much as a burden but as an act of freedom that allows us to participate in the life of Christ himself and so to attain eternal life. Mercier notes that chapter 3 of *Veritatis Splendor* sees the moral life as a sharing in Christ's death, as a martyrdom, in contrast to *Redemptor Hominis*, which uses the image of a confes-

---

[23] See Hans Urs von Balthasar, *The Christian State of Life* (San Francisco: Ignatius, 1983), 183–249.

sor. The two images may be less opposed than it appears. In a secular society whose supreme virtue is tolerance of all moral positions, Christians who uphold the sanctity of life from the moment of conception will probably not undergo a martyrdom of death, but a martyrdom of alienation: society will treat them as if they do not exist and will regard their opinions as having no relevance to societal issues.

The encyclical also stresses the importance of truth in an objective sense and emphasizes the universality and immutability of the moral law as expressed in the commandments. It rejects relativism, proportionalism, and utilitarianism. My own experience of teaching theology to students at the collegiate level brings me to the conclusion that most are relativists. They often deny that truth and moral values exist in any objective sense. Instead, they claim that all truths and values are relative and that what one person considers wrong may not be wrong for everyone or for society as a whole: "I have my morality and you are entitled to your own morality." Truth is reduced to opinion. The Church is frequently criticized by them for being too judgmental. When we raise the issues of rape, the Holocaust, and other evils in class discussions, students are often at a loss about how to deal with these evils from a moral perspective that goes beyond the subjective level and the level of feelings. Yet it is only with great reluctance that they admit that there might be moral absolutes that transcend the feelings of particular individuals.

Mercier mentioned that the pope's own moral teaching was forged in the light of his struggle with the major totalitarian regime of the twentieth century. This is true. Hence, the pope insists upon the objectivity and absoluteness of moral norms. Otherwise, morality becomes subservient to ideologies and the moral person becomes the one who has power to enforce his or her own subjective vision of good and evil. We are invited to follow the call of Christ who is king, prophet, and priest. However, it is essential to remember that the true king does not create values but submits to the truth. He remains free and a king because he rules over himself. The stress on the content of the commandments brings out the truth that all is not relative, that everyone from the lords of the world to the humblest of the poor must submit to the moral norms.

Mercier also notes the Christological context of the encyclical. The revelation of Jesus is a revelation of the moral order and of the dignity of human persons. At the same time the pope also links the natural law with revelation. Theologians and philosophers need to study the question of how revelation and natural law are connected and what role each should play in moral theology today. But I would emphasize that the approach of the Holy Father to morality is truly original. Of how many books and articles dealing with moral theology can we honestly say that the work is inspiring? And yet this is the case with *Veritatis Splendor*. Its first chapter contains a stroke of rhetorical genius when the pope is commenting on the encounter of the rich young man with Jesus. "What must I do to be saved? What good must I do to have eternal life?" The young man serves as a metaphor for the universal quest for meaning, for fulfillment, for how we ought to live—questions that arise from the hearts of all men and women, believers and nonbelievers.

Furthermore, the pope links the moral life with the person of Christ and with following him. The good is attractive to the young man precisely because of its rightness and beauty. Christian moral norms are attractive to us not simply because these norms can be presented in an attractive manner, but because Christ himself is the norm for the Christian. Our moral life is a call to holiness and perfection, which corresponds to our call by Christ to become sons and daughters of the Father. Therefore, we must ask what images of Christ are important for us, according to the Holy Father, for our following of Christ in his way to the Father, to God who alone is good. Is there not something supremely attractive about Christ, which caused the multitudes as well as this rich young man to follow him? This narrative element in the encyclical allows the Christian to enter into the realm of the moral by first entering into the question of the mystery of human existence and the meaning of Christian discipleship.

Of course, for a free person morality requires the exercise of conscience in order to apply moral principles to diverse situations creatively. One has to deal with the formation of conscience on the theoretical and categorical level. A great misunderstanding of the role of conscience exists among many Catholics and even among some theologians today. I must follow my conscience, but my conscience must be properly formed. Furthermore, my conscience does not create the moral norms nor is my conscience just the sum of my feelings. For the pope, moral conscience seems to be the scene of one's encounter with the call of the living God. It is "the voice of God," "the place in which no other man can enter, where man is alone with himself, and you are alone with God." Nevertheless, although one encounters God in solitude, the individual person always exists in community with and for others. This is very important for John Paul's personalist understanding of the human person. Although conscience begins with the individual, it leads one beyond oneself. In order not to be deceived, the individual must live in a continual dialogue with others regarding the good, the true, the just, and the beautiful. Thus, the authentic subject is never identical with the so-called isolated individual of modern philosophy, but a person who becomes himself only in and for community. Therefore, this authentic exercise of conscience is a form of ecclesial listening, a form of discernment of moral judgment, in which one's subjective experience and reason are informed by the objectivity of the voice of the Spirit speaking in and through the whole Church.

Authentic formation of conscience first recognizes the objectivity of truth prior to the judgment of conscience: conscience does not subjectively establish its own moral norms; rather, its judgments must conform to the truth, the truth about man himself and about his ultimate good and happiness. It also includes the interiority of the call of morality: we must make free and personal choices regarding the good. Finally, it includes an openness to our teachers on the way to morality, and especially to the teachings of Scripture and the magisterium. The moral theologian Livio Melina notes that Christian conscience is a call to assume an internal, ecclesial conformity with a Marian disponability to the Spirit.[24]

Of course, it might be objected that the formation of conscience involves the formation of a reality that remains personal and free. A set of moral rules can never replace the role of con-

---

[24] Livio Melina, "Moral Conscience and Communio: Toward a Response to the Challenge of Ethical Pluralism," *Communio* 22/4 (winter 1994): 673–86 at 685.

science. Livio Melina sheds light on the relationship between an individual's conscience and the Spirit speaking through the Church:

> As von Balthasar puts it: "Charisms are not conferred to individuals through the mediation of the Church, but are rather given by God, by the glorified Christ, in view of the Church. An individual receives the absolute singularity of God and Christ as a gift, a singularity which cannot be deduced from the community, nor conjectured in it, even though the community can count on this singularity as something that enriches it and has been thought out for it. Therefore, the individual, as someone entrusted by God with a special gift, is inserted into the community at his depths and is bound to it by a greater generosity. In this sense, the Church can never bypass personal conscience, nor can it ever substitute for it. Individual ecclesial communities, far from being able to dispense with conscience in the name of obedience, must rather conceive of themselves as a pedagogy for the growth of conscience and as a mystagogy to the personal and irreplaceable link of the person with the Spirit who speaks to it from within. The ideal to aim for will be not so much an outward conformity with precepts as the formation of mature personalities who know how to express themselves visibly in works, and in the unity of faith and charity in the dynamics of communion.[25]

Perhaps this would fill in the narrative that some might find lacking in *Redemptor Hominis* and *Veritatis Splendor*. My own view is that both encyclicals do make use of the narrative and the Scriptures. After all, the call to the young man symbolizes the existential confrontation between Jesus Christ and every human being who encounters him. Narrative community does have a role in shaping morality. But we must ask, *what* community and *whose* narrative? Clearly, a special place is given to those who teach in the name of Christ and also to the saints. All voices do not deserve to be heard as having the same authority. On the other hand, there are some Catholics who do find some elements of Church teaching difficult. Some wonder whether an over-rigorist interpretation of moral teaching may impose serious burdens upon individuals. This is an issue that must be faced.

---

[25] Ibid. 685–86.

Perhaps we should make a distinction between absolute norms that are universally binding and ideals for which we ought to strive but which we do not always attain. For example, the Church teaches nations to avoid war and violence, yet it has developed the just war theory to deal with situations where the use of force may sometimes be necessary. This does not mean that the Church has abandoned its ideals. On the contrary, recent official teaching and theological reflection make it clear that certain types of war may never be legitimate. The Church has tried to work for peace and justice in numerous ways, but reluctantly permits war under certain circumstances. This approach might be useful in some other areas of moral theology, as long as we do not undermine respect for moral norms in general.

Some see the encyclical's emphasis on the reality of sin more as a call for the correction of sin than as an invitation to divinization. I would raise a few notes of caution here. First, our own century has revealed how powerful the reality of sin is and how great our tendencies to sin are, despite the prevailing sentiment that no one really sins, that we only make mistakes. Therefore I think that the approach of the pope is badly needed. Second, the call to holiness involves a long process of conversion and growth. True, we live in the resurrection, but we never leave behind the mystery of sin and the Cross. The moral life remains a struggle, even for those who are advanced in the spiritual life. Hence, a greater emphasis on divinization is needed, but we must not lose sight of the truth that this is not an easy process. It involves conforming to the divine life, not to the values of this world. Third, we are called to work for the kingdom of God, but Vatican II was most reluctant to equate the Church or any particular society with the fullness of the kingdom of God, which remains an eschatological reality. Finally, I agree that we do need to retrieve the more relational dimensions of personhood, a task that is occurring in contemporary trinitarian theology. Furthermore, morality is fundamentally relational, since we are called to seek the good in relation to the good of others. A more explicit Marian element is also needed in moral theology. I would argue that the Marian element would bring out the attitude of receptivity and contemplation before the truth: we do not create truth but must open ourselves to it and submit to it. Of course, this submission to the good is not mechanistic, but free and creative. Morality does leave room for creativity on the part of human actors. There is a need for reflection on creativity in the application of moral norms; at times, a variety of legitimate responses may be necessary. For example, all Catholics who are committed to the sanctity of life from the womb may not agree on all strategies carried out by various pro-life groups trying to protect human life and to prevent abortion. It could even be argued that some strategies do not further the pro-life cause but only strengthen the resolve of those who uphold the right to legal abortions. Of course, the disagreement about practical strategy does not mean that committed Catholics should do nothing about abortion until all pro-life groups come to a unanimous agreement about their strategy.

In conclusion, I hope that our discussions of *Veritatis Splendor* will continue and deepen. This remarkable document sees morality as essentially a call to holiness that is universal. It also moves beyond seeing morality as a set of rules, not in the sense that Catholic morality is devoid of content, but rather in the sense that it involves a personal journey of seeking and doing the good. Above all, it presents the good as linked to the true and the beautiful. Indeed, I would argue that the pope's originality lies in emphasizing the attractiveness of the good in his treatment of the encounter of Christ with the young man. Catholic moral theology will be renewed only when it is presented as attractive to Christians. The saints became saints not by obeying rules, but by following Christ and transforming their lives into something beautiful for God and the Church. This means that the Church and moral theologians must do more to present Catholic moral and social teaching as well as teaching on human sexuality and marriage from a more positive perspective, demonstrating how such teaching leads to the fulfillment of human persons, the family, and society.

5. MORALITY AND SOCIETY

Person, Community, Law, and Grace: Reflections on Part Three, Section One of the *Catechism of the Catholic Church*

Arthur R. Madigan, S.J.

IN SECTION 5 OF THE ENCYCLICAL *Veritatis Splendor*, we read: "If this encyclical, so long awaited, is being published only now, one of the reasons is that it seemed fitting for it to be preceded by the *Catechism of the Catholic Church*, which contains a complete and systematic exposition of Christian moral teaching." As it happens, the encyclical came out in English before the *Catechism*, but in any case the "complete and systematic exposition" to be found in the *Catechism* and the exploration of "certain fundamental questions regard the Church's moral teaching" to be found in the encyclical are complementary. I hope, then, that these reflections on the basic moral teaching of the new *Catechism* may be appropriate to a meeting concerned with the thought of Pope John Paul II. I say "reflections." I have not studied the sources or the redaction of the new *Catechism* with the thoroughness or the skill of a professional theologian, for I am not a professional theologian, moral or otherwise.

A word about the structure of the *Catechism*. Like its predecessor, the *Roman Catechism* or the *Catechism of the Council of Trent*, the new *Catechism* has four parts, corresponding to the Apostles'

Creed, the seven sacraments, the ten commandments, and the Our Father. But the new *Catechism* divides each part into two sections, and the first section of each part is new in concept, presenting basic material that one should assimilate in order to understand rightly the details in the second section. Thus part one opens with a general discussion of Christian faith, revelation, and Scripture, and then goes on to the articles of the Apostles' Creed. Part two opens with a discussion of Christian sacramentality, and then proceeds to the seven sacraments. Part three opens with a general discussion of the moral life, human and Christian, and then discusses the content of the moral life, following the Ten Commandments. Part four begins with a general discussion of prayer, and then goes through the Our Father, petition by petition.

Now a few words about the genre of the *Catechism*. One might suppose that, to borrow from Gertrude Stein, a catechism is a catechism is a catechism. But this *Catechism* is offered to two distinct audiences: primarily to the bishops and religious educators, but also to the faithful in general (*Fidei Depositum* 11–12). It is intended as a reference text for the catechisms or compendia to be composed in different countries (FD 11), a resource for bishops to help them to draw up new local catechisms that will take account of diverse cultures and situations. As a reference work for bishops and catechists, it bears comparison with the briefer and more schematic *General Catechetical Directory* of 1971.[1] But to judge by the stacks of the *Catechism* to be found in bookstores, there is also an expectation that great numbers of ordinary people will buy and read, or at least consult, the *Catechism*. I have been trying to read the *Catechism* not only for my own benefit but also as a catechist might read it, asking how I would put this or that part of it across, what parts the people I meet most need to hear, what parts would give them the most encouragement, what parts would give them the most difficulty, how I would try to handle their difficulties. These are the points on which I will try to focus.

---

[1] Sacred Congregation for the Clergy, *General Catechetical Directory* (Washington, D.C.: U.S. Catholic Conference, 1971). While not a substitute for the *Catechism*, the *Directory* can still be of use, especially for its remarks on catechetical method.

Person: The Philosophical and Theological Anthropology of Chapter One

The introduction to part three of the *Catechism* begins with a citation from Leo the Great: "Christian, recognize your dignity. . . ." Part three is theological throughout. There is no question of beginning with a general philosophical consideration of human moral life and then at some point adding a biblical or Christian dimension. This is not to say, however, that the theological anthropology is without philosophical presuppositions.

The layout of section one is straightforward. Chapter 1 provides a philosophical and theological anthropology that touches on human dignity, beatitude, freedom, the morality of acts, the morality of passions, conscience, the virtues, and sin. Chapter 2 develops this anthropology on a social and political level. Chapter 3 takes up the moral law, grace, justification, and the Church's authority in the moral life.

Chapter 1: The Dignity of the Human Person

"Dignity" is a crucial term in the *Catechism*.[2] This is an opportunity for the catechist to tap into an important and attractive discourse in contemporary life. At the same time, the catechist will face the task of making clear what genuine human dignity really means. Dignity as the *Catechism* understands it is grounded in the human being as the image of God and as called to beatitude. It is manifested in human freedom, deliberate action, and action according to conscience. This is in contrast to any dignity that would belong to human beings in isolation from God or from one another. To the extent that contemporary notions of dignity presuppose self-responsible freedom, they are talking about something else.[3] Dignity is an attractive term; but the task for the cate-

---

[2] The subject index to the French edition of the *Catechism* gives forty references under the entry "Dignité." I have not found any corresponding entry in the index of Denzinger-Schönmetzer. The subject index to the English edition seems to have been drawn up on different principles and contains no entry for "Dignity."

[3] I borrow the term "self-responsible freedom" from Charles Taylor, *The Sources of the Self* (Cambridge: Harvard University Press, 1989).

chist, or perhaps I should say for the apologist, is to put across a notion of dignity rather different from that which the audience may already have.

Article 1. Man: the Image of God This article draws heavily on the anthropology of Vatican II's Constitution on the Church in the Modern World, *Gaudium et Spes*.[4] Its key elements are: the human being is created in the image and likeness of God, has a spiritual and immortal soul, has spiritual powers of intellect and will, has been seduced by the Evil One since the beginning of history, is aware in conscience of the difference between good and evil, has misused freedom by doing evil, is internally divided by the conflict between good and evil, and is offered restoration in Christ. A catechist would be well advised to go back over the full text of *Gaudium et Spes*.

Article 2. Our Vocation to Beatitude: I. The Beatitudes; II. The Desire for Happiness; III. Christian Beatitude Article 2 links the human desire for happiness (*bonheur*) or beatitude (*béatitude*) with the beatitudes of Matthew's Sermon on the Mount. It indicates that the beatitudes should have a prominent place in the Christian life and a fundamental place in catechesis. Article 2 construes the beatitudes in several ways: as the heart of the preaching of Jesus (1716), as the completion of the promise to Israel, moving beyond the promise of an earthly land to the promise of the kingdom of heaven (apparently in the sense of the kingdom located in heaven) (1716); as a depiction of the countenance (perhaps in the sense of personality) and love of Jesus Christ (1717); as a statement of the actions and attitudes characteristic of Christian life (1717). The beatitudes answer the natural desire for happiness, a desire of divine origin (1718); they disclose that God is calling human beings to share in divine beatitude (1719). On the other hand, Christian beatitude, entrance into the glory of Christ and into the life of the Trinity, is supernatural, surpassing human intelligence and human power to achieve it, only taking place by the grace of God (1721– 22). The beatitude of heaven determines the criteria of discern-

---

[4] Also in chapter 1, art. 6; chapter 2, art. 1, 2, and 3; and chapter 3, art. 1.

ment in the use of earthly goods in conformity with the Law of God (1729).[5]

Article 3. Human Freedom: I. Freedom and Responsibility; II. Human Freedom in the Economy of Salvation The key assertions are familiar: that God has given human beings the dignity of initiating action, of being the masters of their acts; that this liberty brings with it responsibility, answerability for one's acts; that various factors can affect the voluntariness and imputability of actions. Obviously these assertions oppose any form of determinism—genetic, psychological, economic, or other.

In this article, the *Catechism* spells out what it means by human dignity, using the vocabulary of freedom and of natural right. Number 1738 asserts the natural right of each human person to be recognized as a free and responsible being (the right to respect). The right to exercise one's freedom, in particular in moral and religious matters, is inseparable from the dignity of the human person. Of course, the point is not that you can do anything you want (see 1740) but that you have a right to be recognized and treated as a certain kind of being. Article 3 invites the catechist to make use of the very attractive rhetoric of freedom and of rights, but the catechist will also have the task of spelling out what may seem an unusual notion of freedom and an unfamiliar conception of human rights.

Article 4. The Morality of Human Acts: I. The Sources of Morality; II. Good Acts and Evil Acts It is no surprise to read in article 4 that morality depends on what is chosen, on why, and on circumstances. There is not a great deal of detail in this article, and only two footnotes, one to Matthew 6:2–4, to point out how a bad intention can make an action that was good in itself be bad, the other to Aquinas (*Collationes in decem praeceptis* 6), to the effect

---

[5] A contrast with Aquinas may be illuminating. In *Summa theologiae* I-II, q.3, Aquinas makes use of the Aristotelian position that human happiness consists in intellectual vision or contemplation, and extends it and transposes it beyond the bounds of this present life, arguing that human happiness must consist in seeing God. Instead of using contemplation as its principal or privileged description of the happiness that human beings naturally desire, article 2 uses the beatitudes of the Sermon on the Mount.

that a good intention does not justify a bad action. The key assertions are that the end does not justify the means, that circumstances are secondary elements in a moral act, and that they cannot change the basic evil of an evil act. There are concrete behaviors—for example, fornication—which it is always erroneous to choose, because the choice of them entails a disorder of the will—that is to say, a moral evil (1755). The evil of certain kinds of acts, such as blasphemy, perjury, murder, and adultery, can be specified independently of changing circumstances (1756). Article 4 does not use the expression "intrinsically evil acts," but it speaks of acts that are "always gravely illicit by reason of their object" (1756). Likewise, article 4 does not use the terms "situationalism," "consequentialism," or "proportionalism,"[6] but it leaves no doubt that circumstances are strictly secondary factors in moral assessment and that certain kinds of action are always and everywhere wrong. While article 4 is not polemical, it is to be understood in the light of the critical presentation of consequentialism and proportionalism in *Veritatis Splendor*.

For the moment I am going to pass over article 5 on the passions and proceed directly to article 6 on conscience.[7]

Article 6. Moral Conscience: I. The Judgment of Conscience; II. The Formation of Conscience; III. To Choose in accord with Conscience; IV. Erroneous Judgment Article 6 leads off with a citation of *Gaudium et Spes* on conscience as awareness of law, obligation, a law inscribed by God on the human heart. Conscience is the most intimate human center, the sanctuary where one is alone with God and where God's voice lets itself be heard. To hear and follow conscience one needs a certain interiority, self-presence, or reflectiveness, which is often threatened in contemporary life

---

[6] Neither the French edition nor the English edition of the subject index has entries for "Consequentialism," "Proportionalism," or "Situationalism."

[7] There is a discrepancy between number 1700 of the *Catechism*, which previews the eight articles of chapter 1, and the actual text of chapter 1. The actual text discusses the morality of acts (art. 4), the morality of passions (art. 5), conscience (art. 6), and virtue (art. 7). Number 1700, however, indicates a different order: the morality of acts (art. 4), conscience (art 5.), the sensible life and the spiritual life as means of human growth (art. 6), and virtue (art. 7). This discrepancy concerning articles 5 and 6 is found in the French and is faithfully transmitted in the German and English versions.

(1779). The education of conscience goes on throughout a person's whole life. This education of conscience should counter egoism, pride, and complacency, but also fear and what the English translation calls "resentment arising from guilt."[8] Education of conscience guarantees freedom (1784). Situations may arise that make moral judgment less assured and decision difficult (1787). One should attempt to interpret the data of experience and the signs of the time with the help of prudence, the counsel of competent people (*personnes avisées*), and the help of the Holy Spirit and his gifts (1788). There are some general rules: the rule not to do evil that good may result, the Golden Rule, and the rule not to scandalize or harm the conscience of others (1789). One has to follow one's conscience, even if it happens to be in error, but conscience *can* be in error (1790; see VS 62).

Article 6 suggests at least three lines of reflection. The catechist might well explore further than the *Catechism* does the relation between the intellectual or judgmental dimension of conscience and the affective dimension of conscience. The catechist may need to consider the topic of moral development, for example, or the pros and cons of the work of such authors as Lawrence Kohlberg[9] and Robert Coles.[10] Finally, the catechist may need to identify those factors in social life that militate against the maturation of conscience and to devise strategies to counter these factors. Now, back to the passions.

Article 5. The Morality of the Passions: I. The Passions; II. Passions and Moral Life The phrase of number 1700 ("they make their whole sentient and spiritual[11] lives into means of this growth")

---

[8] The French is *ressentiments de la culpabilité*. A more accurate translation would be "guilt feelings." It is noteworthy that the *Catechism* not only does not confuse conscience with psychological guilt feelings, but it construes the education of conscience as involving the prevention or the healing of such feelings. The German translation is *Schuldgefühlen*, but the German adds the adjective *falschen*, so that the target is not guilt feelings as such, but rather erroneous or mistaken guilt feelings.

[9] *Essays on Moral Development I: The Philosophy of Moral Development* (San Francisco: Harper & Row, 1981); *II: The Psychology of Moral Development* (San Francisco: Harper & Row, 1984).

[10] *The Moral Life of Children* (Boston: Atlantic Monthly Press, 1986).

[11] The French is *spirituelle*, which can mean "intellectual" as well as "spiritual." The German is *Geistesleben*. At 1764 the English renders *la vie de l'esprit* as "the life of the mind."

seems to be the rubric for the discussion of the passions in article 5. The description of the passions is rather more positive than I would have expected. The passions are what assures the connection between sensible life and the life of the spirit or mind (*esprit*) (1764). They are the inexhaustible reservoir of images and affections where the moral life is expressed (1768). Moral perfection involves a person's being moved to the good not only by will but also by sensible appetite (1770). But passions do not determine the morality of acts or the sanctity of persons (1768). Article 5 is saying that passions are good in their place, but that they should be secondary to intellect and will.

The philosophical anthropology of article 5 has three features that deserve to be noted. The first is the use of the term "passions" as a catchall term for all sorts of feelings, emotions, and impulses. The challenge is to find a better way of speaking about the dimension of passion, feeling, and emotion in human moral action. Is a passion the same as a feeling? Is "passion" an adequate term or even an accurate term to cover feeling and emotion?

The second feature is the fairly sharp distinction between intellect and will on the one hand, and the passions on the other. Here the issue is whether this traditional philosophical anthropology with its sharp distinction between intellect and will on the one side and passion on the other gives an adequate base from which to understand human moral activity.[12]

The third feature is the superiority of intellect and will over the passions, and the desirability of their being controlled by intellect and will. How should we respond to the notion that the most important kinds of moral knowledge are either feelings or at least inextricably bound up with feelings? How should we reply to the modern or the contemporary exaltation of feeling as superior to intellect, and this precisely in moral matters? This issue has lately received attention in the context of feminism, in particular by the suggestion that there are distinctively masculine and feminine ways of apprehending moral reality.[13] But the issue goes back be-

---

[12] It is worth pointing out that the sharp distinction between intellect and will on the one hand and passions on the other does not entail an extreme dualism of soul and body. The rejection of such a dualism is prominent in VS 48–50.

[13] See Carol Gilligan, *In a Different Voice: Psychological Theory and Women's Development* (Cambridge: Harvard University Press, 1982); Eve Browning Cole, *Philosophy and Feminist Criticism* (New York: Paragon, 1993), 73–119.

fore the rise of feminism. It goes back at least as far as the Pascalian dictum that the heart has its reasons, reasons that reason does not know. Is that just a rhetorical flourish, or is there something in it of which we must take account?[14]

Article 7. The Virtues: I. The Human Virtues; II. The Theological Virtues; III. The Gifts and Fruits of the Holy Spirit Virtue is defined as a habitual and firm disposition to do what is good (1803). Article 7 speaks of the moral virtues, notably prudence, justice, fortitude, and temperance, both as humanly acquired (1804) and as purified and elevated by divine grace (1810). They make it easy and enjoyable for a person to do what is good (1810). The theological virtues (*vertus théologales*) of faith, hope, and charity are infused in human beings by God to enable them to act as God's children and to merit eternal life (1813).

One of the most interesting developments in recent Anglo-American philosophy has been an increased attention to the concept of virtue and to particular virtues.[15] This has been a welcome development, at least in contrast to earlier debates about moral skepticism, relativism, and emotivism. Does article 7 invite the catechist to expound what is sometimes called a virtue ethics? Yes and no. Yes, in the sense that one could expand on this section, develop the individual virtues in detail, working out, for instance, a detailed theory of prudence or practical wisdom and its relations with conscience and feeling. (Here, I would suggest, Aristotle still has something to contribute.) But if a virtue ethics means an ethical theory in which virtue displaces law as the central ethical category, a theory that focuses on fundamental stances or attitudes that characterize persons rather than on laws that characterize types of actions, then there is nothing in article 7 to indicate sympathy with such a virtue ethics; and it would seem to fall under the

---

[14] I have found John Macmurray, *Reason and Emotion* (New York: Barnes & Noble, 1962) helpful in this area. Macmurray's central thesis in this book is that intellect and emotion are two distinct modes of reason and that each is capable in the best case of objectivity.

[15] I am thinking of the work of Philippa Foot, Iris Murdoch, and, in a rather different sense, of the work of Alasdair MacIntyre and others who have revived Aristotelian ethics.

censure of *Veritatis Splendor* 47 and 55. The virtues have an ancillary status.[16]

Article 8. Sin: I. Mercy and Sin; II. The Definition of Sin; III. The Different Kinds of Sins; IV. The Gravity of Sin: Mortal and Venial Sins; V. The Proliferation of Sin Article 8 on sin is not the place to look for surprises, but some of its nuances are worth noticing (e.g., 1846–47). The mercy of God can only be understood if we admit the reality of sin and of ourselves as sinners; 1848: conversion to God *"requires the disclosure of sin"*[17] (citing with emphasis *Dominum et Vivificantem* 31); and 1851: sin manifests its violence and multiplicity in the passion of Jesus.

What things are sins? Part three, section two of the *Catechism* will discuss in detail violations of the Ten Commandments, but article 8 focuses on the Pauline sin lists, quoting Galatians 5:19–21 and referring to Romans 1:28–32, 1 Corinthians 6:9–10, Ephesians 5:3–5, and Colossians 3:5–8 (1852).

The *Catechism* maintains the distinction between mortal and venial sins. Mortal sin requires grave matter, full awareness or knowledge, and deliberate intention or full consent (slightly different terms are used in 1857 and 1859). If one asks, "knowledge of what?" the answer is "knowledge of the sinful character of the act, of its opposition to the law of God" (1859). This suggests that one would not have to know the intrinsic malice of the act or what made it wrong, but only that God had prohibited it.[18]

---

[16] According to Archbishop Jean Honoré, the drafters of the *Catechism* received criticisms to the effect that the chapter on the virtues was too short, as well as suggestions that the moral section of the *Catechism* should be structured by the beatitudes and the virtues rather than by the Decalogue. See his "Catechism presents morality as a lived experience of faith in Christ" in *Reflections on the Catechism of the Catholic Church*, ed. J.P. Socias (Chicago: Midwest Theological Forum, 1993), 140.

[17] The English translation, which here follows the official translation of *Dominum et Vivificantem* (Washington, D.C.: U.S. Catholic Conference, 1986), 55, reads: "requires convincing of sin." The Latin in AAS 78 (1986): 843 is *conversio enim postulat persuasionem de peccato*, perhaps better "requires being convinced of sin." The French is *requiert la mise en lumière du péché* ("requires that sin be brought into the light"). The German is similar: *dass die Sünde ans Licht gebracht wird*.

[18] This does not imply what philosophers call a divine command theory of evil, but it would be compatible with a divine command theory of evil.

Like love itself, mortal sin is "a radical possibility of human freedom" (1861). The question here is what is meant or implied by the term "radical." Our freedom "has the power to make choices forever (*pour toujours*)" (1861), and that ultimacy seems to be what the term "radical" connotes. This raises the question of the theory of fundamental option—the view that distinguishes between the level of radical choice for or against God and the choices, even sinful choices, which we make in ordinary everyday life. On this view a genuinely mortal or hell-deserving sin would occur, if it were to occur, at the deepest level of a human person, even at what might be called a transcendental or pre-predicamental level.[19] One way of expressing this theory is to say that genuinely mortal sin takes place at a level of a person's "fundamental option" rather than in discrete, identifiable, individual actions. The *Catechism* does not join this issue, but *Veritatis Splendor* 65–70 strenuously opposes such a theory.

The question for the catechist, it seems to me, is whether to drop fundamental option theory entirely or to try to make something of it within the terms of the *Catechism* and of *Veritatis Splendor*. Here the catechist may want to weigh the pros and cons of fundamental option theory. The weakness of the theory is that it tends to a trivialization of individual human acts and, in the extreme, to a denial of human freedom or human self-determination. Still, the theory has the merit of emphasizing the continuity of human moral life and of resisting what I would call an angelist construal of human freedom. It offers a way of affirming human freedom without having to affirm that people are regularly faced with decisions about making 180° turns in their moral lives.

It may be appropriate to recall that the introduction to part three highlights the biblical and traditional image of the two ways that a person may take, the way of life and the way of perdition (Matthew 7:13, Deuteronomy 30:15–20, *Didache* 1.1) (1696). This is the closest, so far as I can see, that the *Catechism* comes to the notion of a fundamental option as a category for understanding the Christian moral life; and perhaps it offers a way to present

---

[19] See Karl Rahner, "The Fundamental Option" in *Theological Investigations* VI (London: Darton, Longman & Todd, 1974), 181–88; also in *A Rahner Reader*, ed. Gerald A. McCool (New York: Seabury, 1975), 255–62; see also Louis Monden, *Sin, Liberty, and Law* (New York: Sheed & Ward, 1965), 30–44.

a sort of fundamental option theory within the framework of the *Catechism*.

Number 1864 offers an interesting interpretation of the unforgivable sin of blaspheming against the Holy Spirit (Mark 3:29 and parallels in Matthew 12:32, Luke 12:10). The unpardonable blasphemy against the Holy Spirit is a deliberate refusal to accept the mercy of God by repenting one's sins. In effect, this is to take Mark 3:29 as addressing not so much opposition encountered by Jesus in his ministry as the contemporary tendency to dismiss sin as something unreal, at least something that does not figure in one's own life.[20]

The subsection on the proliferation of sin is something of a grab bag: effects of sin leading to vice, obscuring of conscience (1865); capital sins (1866); sins crying to heaven (1867); various forms of cooperation in sin (1868). Perhaps most noteworthy is 1869, which speaks of the reign of concupiscence, violence, and injustice among humankind, with ramifications for social situations and institutions. "Structures of sin" (the quotation marks are in the original) are the expression and effect of personal sins. One can speak of "social sin" in an analogous sense (there is a reference to *Reconciliatio et Paenitentia* 16). The intention here seems to be to admit the reality of "sinful structures" and of "social sin," but without a great deal of specification and without taking away from the primacy of deliberate sinful acts on the part of individual human agents.

We have noted the prominence of citations from *Gaudium et Spes* in articles 1 and 6. The tone of article 8 is somewhat different. Perhaps a clue to the difference can be found in the citations,

---

[20] E. J. Mally (*Jerome Biblical Commentary* on Mark 3:29) interprets the blasphemy against the Holy Spirit as "that which ascribes Jesus's works to the power of one other than God's Holy Spirit manifest in Jesus's victory over the demons." Similarly, D.J. Harrington (*New Jerome Biblical Commentary* on Mark 3:29) writes: "In the Marcan context, the unforgivable sin is attributing the work of the Holy Spirit in Jesus's healings to the power of Satan. J. A. Fitzmyer (*The Gospel according to Luke*, II.964, on Luke 12:10) takes it somewhat more generally: "the unforgivable sin is not to be understood merely as the rejection of Christian preaching or the gospel, but the persistence in consummate and obdurate opposition to the influence of the Spirit which animates that preaching; it involves a mentality which obstinately sets the mind against the Spirit of God, and as long as that obstinate mindset perdures, God's forgiveness cannot be accorded to such a person."

notably in the citations of the Pauline lists of sins and vices and the four citations from Augustine (1847, 1849, 1850, 1863). Catechists might well go back over the Pauline sin lists and consider how to present them, and they might well renew their acquaintance with Augustine.

COMMUNITY: THE PERSON AND SOCIETY ACCORDING TO CHAPTER 2

Chapter 2: The Human Community

Article 1. The Person and Society: I. The Communal Character of the Human Vocation; II. Conversion and Society This chapter is largely based on *Gaudium et Spes* and on a series of papal documents, notably *Centesimus Annus* and *Sollicitudo Rei Socialis*, then *Mater et Magistra* and *Pacem in Terris*, and then, further back, the addresses of Pope Pius XII.[21]

There is nothing very surprising in subsection I. Human beings need social life (1879). Society is defined as a group of persons bound together in an organic way by a principle of unity that transcends each of them (1880). The family and the city are particularly natural forms of society (1882). "Socialization"—participation in a wide variety of societies—is a good thing (1882).[22] Yet socialization has its dangers: excessive state intervention is a threat to individual freedom and initiative; the remedy is the observance of the traditional doctrine of subsidiarity (1883), which is opposed to all forms of collectivism, a term that so far as I can see is left undefined (1885).

The basic point of subsection II is that the physical and instinc-

---

[21] Archbishop Jean Honoré reports that chapter 2 was drafted in response to the criticism of many bishops that the text as it then stood ignored the social and community dimension of human beings. See his "Catechism presents morality as a lived experience of faith in Christ," 140–41.

[22] This offers a point of contact with the emphasis of Peter Berger and others on the importance of "mediating structures" and the so-called third sector. See P. Berger, R. J. Neuhaus, *Empowering People: The Role of Mediating Structures in Public Policy* (Washington: American Enterprise Institute, 1977); Ann McKinstry Micou, Birgit Lindsnaes, *The Role of Voluntary Organizations in Emerging Democracies* (Danish Center for Human Rights/Institute of International Education, 1993).

tive dimensions of social life should be subordinate to the interior and spiritual dimensions. Social life is something spiritual, not just something physical (1886). The elevation of mere means into ends and the treatment of persons as mere means to ends lead to unjust social structures, which makes the Christian life difficult and practically impossible (1887, citing Pius XII's address of 1 June 1941). If social life calls upon personal interior conversion, that is not to say that everything is left to personal conversion; conditions should be arranged to favor it (1888).

Article 2. Participation in Social Life: I. Authority; II. The Common Good; III. Responsibility and Participation Subsection I speaks of the legitimacy of authority, the duty of obedience, and respect to authority (1897–1900, with references to Romans 13:1–2, 1 Peter 2:13–17, 1 Timothy 2:1–2, 1 Clement 61.1–2, the Letter of Barnabas 4.10). Authority itself comes from God, but the selection of a form of government and of officials should be up to the citizens (1901). Authority does not draw its legitimacy from itself (1902). The only legitimate exercise of authority is for the common good. An authority that goes against the moral law can lose its claim on the consciences of its subjects and degenerate into oppression (1903, citing *Pacem in Terris* 51). Number 1904 cites *Centesimus Annus* 44 in support of a government by law and in favor of a governmental system with checks and balances.[23]

Subsection II discusses the common good, which has three elements: respect for the person as such (1907); social well-being and the development of the group (1908); peace—continuance and security of just order (1909). As above, the order of things should be subordinated to the order of persons (1912, citing *Gaudium et Spes* 26.3).

Subsection III affirms that participation—the taking of respon-

---

[23] Here Americans may perhaps feel a pat on the back. And yet there is a problem to be faced in the system of limited government with checks and balances. It fosters—indeed has to foster—a mentality in which the good of process takes priority over other goods. This mentality is well expressed by Alexander M. Bickel, *The Morality of Consent* (New Haven: Yale University Press, 1975), 123: "The highest morality is almost always the morality of process." This esteem for process is, it seems to me, neglected in much of current Catholic discussion about public policy on abortion.

sibilities for self, family, and society—is good (1913–15). To escape from provisions of law and to shirk one's social duty is bad (1916). Authorities ought "to strengthen the values which attract the confidence of members of the group and [which] encourage them to put themselves at the service of others" (1917).

Article 3. Social Justice: I. Respect for the Human Person; II. Equality and Differences Among Men; III. Human Solidarity The central assertion of subsection I is that the only way to social justice is respect for the transcendent dignity of humankind. The person is the ultimate goal of society (1929). This implies respect for the rights that flow from humankind's dignity as created beings; these rights are prior to society and impose themselves on society (1930). We should consider other people as other selves, even those who think or act differently than we do (1931–33). This suggests a degree of openness to a pluralistic society, without attempting to define the limits on this pluralism.

Subsection II says that *equality* among human beings bears on personal dignity and the rights that flow from it. There is to be no discrimination touching the fundamental rights of the person (1935). Equality among human beings does not imply the end of differences among persons and cultures; there are positive benefits to be derived from the differences among people and among cultures (1937, citing Catherine of Siena). Certain economic and social *inequalities* are iniquitous (1938).

Subsection III deals with solidarity. Solidarity has been expressed as friendship and as social charity, but it is obligatory, a direct exigence of human and Christian fraternity. Human solidarity and charity constitute a law that stems from original community, from the equality of rational nature among human beings, and from the redemption of humanity by Christ (1939, citing Pius XII, *Summi Pontificatus*). Solidarity is a matter of sharing goods, spiritual as well as material (1940, 1942; cf. 1948). The resolution of socioeconomic problems requires different kinds and levels of solidarity (1941).

Chapter 2 has been written so as to apply to a worldwide variety of societies and political systems. It does not go into detail in a way that would be immediately applicable to any given society or political system. The core imperatives are few and simple: respect human dignity, respect equal human rights, shun collectivism, promote the common good, foster participation and solidarity. The task of the catechist will be to flesh out these imperatives in the context of our own society and political system. Here it seems to me that the catechist will have to face two issues.

First, at least in our current context, politics is inseparable from economics. And so the catechist will have to have at least a general idea of how the imperatives of chapter 2 can mesh with the economy of a highly developed nation such as the United States.[24] More fundamentally, the contemporary American catechist may wish to critique the tendency to view society in economic terms, as a sort of engine to generate prosperity, so that individuals can then pursue whatever they choose to pursue in their private lives.

Second, there is the whole problem of the way that we speak about rights in contemporary American society. In her book *Rights Talk*,[25] Mary Ann Glendon contends that the discourse about rights in contemporary American society has become debased. What is the catechist to do about the fact that people in our society think largely of property rights, privacy rights, sheer freedom of action? More practically, how do you lead someone to recognize a right that he or she does not recognize? How do you get someone to give up the idea that he or she has a right to this or that? Can we put across a message about human dignity and common good in terms of rights? Or is the language of rights bound to distort this message?[26]

It seems that the rhetoric of human rights can be enlisted in ways that are profoundly disrespectful of human dignity—think of some applications of the right to privacy—and that the rhetoric

---

[24] *The Ethical Foundations of Economics* (Washington, D.C.: Georgetown University Press, 1993) by John Piderit, S.J., is an example of the kind of work that needs to be done in this area.

[25] Mary Ann Glendon, *Rights Talk* (New York: Macmillan/Free Press, 1991).

[26] To take an example, David R. Carlin, Jr., contends ("Americanizing the Anti-Abortion Argument," *America* [October 6, 1990]: 214–17, esp. 217) that the pro-life side of the abortion debate needs to be framed in terms of rights if it is to have any impact on discussion in America today. Joseph Flanagan, S.J., contends, on the other hand, that the insight that has to be gotten across is that life—my life or anyone's life—is a gift, and that talk of a right to life effectively blocks the insight that life is a gift. Here I am drawing on private conversation, and it is possible that I am making Father Flanagan say more than he said or meant.

of human rights can be set in opposition to the forms of solidarity of which chapter 2 speaks. It is at least a good question whether rights talk tends to drive out solidarity talk, and vice versa. Yet, at the same time it is arguable that the rhetoric of rights taps into the most humane elements of American consciousness. Perhaps our task is to clean up rights talk in our society—that is, to promote a kind of rights talk that supports and reinforces the various forms of solidarity rather than weakening or undermining them.[27]

LAW AND GRACE: THE HUMAN SITUATION ACCORDING TO CHAPTER 3

Chapter 3: God's Salvation: Law and Grace

Article 1. The Moral Law: I. The Natural Moral Law; II. The Old Law; III. The New Law or the Law of the Gospel Article 1 of chapter 3 is a presentation of three types of law, or, perhaps better, three faces of one and the same law: the natural moral law, the old law of the Old Testament, and what the *Catechism* calls the new law or the law of the Gospel (*la loi évangélique*). All three are grounded in the eternal law (1951). The natural law is inscribed in the hearts of all people and is binding on all (1954, 1956, with reference to Cicero, *De re publica* 3.22.33). The application of the natural law varies widely according to circumstances (1957), and

---

[27] There is more than a little philosophical controversy going on about rights—not just about what rights human beings have or ought to have, but about the status of rights as such. Are rights things that hold independently of what anyone may think, or are they social constructs? The question may seem a simple one, but think of the difficulty that some people have distinguishing between natural moral rights and legal or constitutional rights. Are rights somehow deducible or derivable from the essence of a human being? Does the objectivity of morality stand or fall with the objectivity of human rights, or are these independent matters? To put it mildly, there is a great deal of difficulty about what is to count as evidence in discussions of rights. Alasdair MacIntyre, one of the great defenders of the objectivity of morality in our time, concludes that belief in natural human rights is on the same level of rationality as belief in witches and unicorns. See *After Virtue*, 2nd ed. (Notre Dame: University of Notre Dame Press, 1984), 69. A catechist working with sophisticated people should at least have a look at MacIntyre and see how much he or she really wants to invest in the theory of natural human rights, and whether he or she can find another way—some alternative to the language of rights—to express the sacredness and dignity of human beings.

yet it remains basically unchanged through history (1958). Natural law is the basis of civil law (1959). Even though the natural law is binding on all people, not everyone perceives its precepts clearly. In the de facto situation, sinful human beings need grace and revelation to perceive the precepts of the natural law (1960). Hence God gave Israel the old law, which "expresses numerous truths naturally accessible to reason" (1961).

The functions of the old law are to manifest the fact of sin (1963) and to prepare for the Gospel (1964). The new law is the perfection, at least on this earth, of the divine law, both natural and revealed; it is identical with the interior law of charity engraved on hearts by the Holy Spirit (1965). It is summed up in the Golden Rule (1970) and it coincides with the new commandment of John 15.12, to love one another (1971). The most particular expression of the new law is to be found in the Sermon on the Mount (1965; see 1968). But the sermon is to be taken together with such moral catecheses as Romans 12–15, 1 Corinthians 12–13, Colossians 3–4, and Ephesians 4–5 (1971). The new law is a law of love, grace, and freedom (1972). The new law includes the evangelical counsels (1973), but this is not to say that all are obliged to the counsels (1974).

Here it seems to me that the catechist has to face two sets of issues. The first revolves around the philosophical conception of natural law. The second concerns the biblical conceptions of law. In the United States in recent years, natural law has had little or no press outside the Catholic community, and a fair amount of bad press within that community. Much of this bad press has to do with the application of natural law argument in matters of sexual conduct. (The dismissal of natural law in this area sometimes coincides, perhaps not entirely consistently, with a readiness to affirm natural rights in other areas.) The catechist will have to determine whether to bite the bullet and to present natural law as such, or whether to try to transpose what is said in the language of natural law into some other linguistic or conceptual framework, whether a personalist framework or a framework of value theory or a framework of virtue ethics. There is a real question, however, whether such a transposition can avoid the errors of subjectivism and relativism stigmatized in *Veritatis Splendor* 43–53.

Supposing, then, that the catechist decides to bite the bullet and to present the natural law, there is a question of what understanding of natural law to present. For this itself is a controverted matter, more controverted than the text of the *Catechism* would suggest.[28] Even among thinkers who would identify themselves as natural law theorists, there is considerable diversity of understanding about what natural law means, and currently there is a fairly hot debate about what has come to be called the "new natural law theory" advanced by Germain Grisez, John Finnis, Joseph Boyle, and others.[29] The new natural law theory would seem immune to the accusation of physicalism that was one of the standard criticisms of the older natural law theory. At the same time, however, critics such as Ralph McInerny and Russell Hittinger

---

[28] For a history of the different conceptions of natural law, see M. B. Crowe, *The Changing Profile of the Natural Law* (The Hague: Martinus Nijhoff, 1977).

[29] I owe the phrase to the title of Russell Hittinger's book, *A Critique of the New Natural Law Theory* (Notre Dame: University of Notre Dame Press, 1987). If I may oversimplify: the basic divide is between those who ground morality in an observation of the workings of human *nature* and those who ground morality in the demands of practical *reason*. Consider this example of the older approach, taken from Thomas J. Higgins, S.J., *Man as Man: The Science and Art of Ethics* (Milwaukee: Bruce, 1956), 410: "To use an important faculty so as to prevent it from its natural end is intrinsically wrong. But in positive contraception one uses the important faculty of sex so as to prevent it from its natural end. Therefore positive contraception is intrinsically wrong." Exponents of the new natural law theory such as Germain Grisez and John Finnis are sensitive to the charge of physicalism—that is, to the charge that natural law theory simply and crudely infers from the way in which a human faculty usually or ordinarily operates that this is the way in which that human faculty ought to operate. The core of the new natural law theory is the recognition of certain basic values and of certain requirements of practical reasonableness. In Finnis's version (*Natural Law and Natural Rights*, 59–99) the basic values are life, knowledge, play, aesthetic experience, sociability, practical reasonableness, and religion. He lists eight requirements for practical reasonableness (100–33): having a coherent plan of life, no arbitrary preferences among values, no arbitrary preferences among persons, detachment from one's specific and limited projects, not lightly abandoning one's commitments, recognition of the limited relevance of consequences, respect for every basic value in every act, and fostering the common good. Why, on this new theory, is contraception wrong? The following argument is given by John Finnis, Germain Grisez, Joseph Boyle, and William E. May, " 'Every Marital Act Ought to be Open to New Life': Toward a Clearer Understanding," in *The Teaching of Humanae Vitae: A Defense* (San Francisco: Ignatius, 1988), 43: "Since contraception must be defined by its intention that a prospective new life not begin, every contraceptive act is necessarily contralife." To put the argument in Finnis's terms, contraception is wrong because it involves acting against the basic good of life and thus contravenes practical reasonableness.

have raised doubts about the new natural law theory.[30] So far as I can see, the *Catechism* does not take sides between the "old" and "new" schools of natural law theory.[31] The catechist who decides to employ the language of natural law, however, had better clarify his or her understanding of that law and, in particular, how he or she intends to handle the charge of physicalism. One exercise that Jesuits in particular may find rewarding is to read or reread the chapters on natural law in John Courtney Murray's *We Hold These Truths*.

The second set of issues revolves around the *Catechism*'s treatment of the biblical conceptions of law and, in particular, around its construal of the teaching of Jesus, especially in the Sermon on the Mount, precisely as a new law. Questions might be raised from an historical-critical point of view about the relation between the preaching of the historical Jesus and the Sermon on the Mount as we have it in Matthew 5–7, but let us bracket these for a moment. The *Catechism* adopts what we might call a Matthean perspective—a perspective that places great stress on the continuity between Israel and the Christian community and, in particular, between the law and the moral code of the Christian community. This continuity is not affected by the abrogation of certain ritual and juridical precepts (1972).

---

[30] See Ralph McInerny, "The Principles of Natural Law," *American Journal of Jurisprudence* 25 (1980):1–15, and the reply by John Finnis and Germain Grisez, "The Basic Principles of Natural Law: A Reply to Ralph McInerny," *American Journal of Jurisprudence* 26 (1981):21–31. See also Russell Hittinger, *A Critique of the New Natural Law Theory*, and the reply by Germain Grisez, "Critique of Russell Hittinger's Book, A Critique of the New Natural Law Theory," *New Scholasticism* 62 (1988):438–64, as well as Hittinger's reply, 465. Also, Germain Grisez, Joseph Boyle, and John Finnis, "Practical Principles, Moral Truth, and Ultimate Ends," *American Journal of Jurisprudence* 32 (1987):99–151.

[31] At any rate, not explicitly. But consider the language of #1755: "There are some concrete acts—such as fornication—that it is always wrong to choose, because choosing them entails a disorder of the will, that is, a moral evil (*comporte un désordre de la volonté, c'est-à-dire un mal moral*)." #1761 reads similarly. The wrongness of the act is grounded in the disorder of the will that would be involved in the will's choosing the act. This is at least akin to the type of argumentation that characterizes the new natural law theory. Contrast any approach that would *first* prove the act to be evil, and only *then* conclude that it would be wrong for the will to choose the act. *Veritatis Splendor* 48 defends the natural law against the charges of physicalism and biologism, and the end of *Veritatis Splendor* 50 says that the natural law does not admit a split between freedom and nature.

Here it may be worthwhile to read #574–98, which discuss the relations between Jesus and Israel. The overall tendency of the exposition is to stress the continuity of Jesus's mission with the old covenant. Jesus is the one who observes the law in its fullness (578–79). He is the only one who can do so, being divine (580). Jesus has come to be the ultimate interpreter of the law (581). The difference between Jesus and the scribes and pharisees is that Jesus is the ultimate interpreter of the law, but not, so far as I can see from the *Catechism*, that Jesus speaks independently of the law.

Does the catechist want to place his or her catechesis squarely within this Matthean perspective, or does he or she want to situate the Matthean perspective alongside other New Testament perspectives? There is New Testament support for speaking of the Christian life in terms of adherence to a law, support not only in Matthew and James (1.25; 2.2), but also in such texts as Galatians 6.2 (the law of Christ), Romans 3.27 (the law of faith), and Romans 8.2 (the law of the spirit of life in Christ). But it would be possible, without fostering an antinomian attitude, to incorporate in catechesis a range of Pauline and Johannine texts that underline the radical newness of the Christian life. And it would also be possible to incorporate an element from the synoptic Gospels that receives short shrift in this section of the *Catechism*—namely, the polemic against the abuse of law and tradition that has come to be known as Pharisaism. It is remarkable how little of this polemic survives in the *Catechism*, even in the sections referred to under the subject index entry "Pharisees."[32] Here the catechist is confronted with the issue of whether to consider the scriptural polemic against Pharisaism as something of merely antiquarian interest, or as something to be minimized for the sake of ecumenical relations, or whether to regard the polemic against Pharisaism as perennially relevant to the situation of the Christian community itself.

Article 2: Grace and Justification: I. Justification; II. Grace; III. Merit; IV. Christian Holiness   Article 2 draws heavily on the Council of

---

[32] The subject index of the French text, under "Pharisiens": 447, 535, 574ff, 595, 993, 1481, 2054, 2286, 2613. The Pharisees come off well—better, I am tempted to say, than in Matthew, Mark, and Luke. I have been unable to locate a corresponding entry in the subject indexes to the English and German versions.

Trent's decree on justification. That decree accepts and elaborates the Pauline doctrine that justification is by faith, placing this doctrine in the broader context of the New Testament taken as a whole. It thus vindicates the need to prepare onself for justification, the need for the justified to observe the commandments, and the possibility of the justified person's meriting salvation, while rejecting exaggerated and erroneous notions of what it means for a person to have faith.

Article 2 raises two issues for the catechist. The first is the *place* of justification by faith within the Christian life as a whole. Protestants, I take it, tend to see justification by faith as the core of the Christian gospel, as the *articulus stantis aut cadentis ecclesiae*, the article on which the church stands or falls. My own recollection of my years in theology is that there was considerable sympathy for some form of this position.[33] My sense is that the *Catechism*, however, treats justification by faith as a point of real but secondary importance. If I may use the language of *context* to express the difference: where Protestants would regard the doctrine of justification by faith as the context within which they would interpret the Decalogue or the Sermon on the Mount, the *Catechism* seems to take the natural law, the Decalogue, and the Sermon on the Mount as the context within which to interpret justification by faith.[34]

The second issue has to do with the possibility of an experience of grace, or of grace's being in any sense an experiential category. The first sentence of *Catechism* #2005 says: "Since it belongs to the supernatural order, grace *escapes our experience* [the emphasis is in the original] and cannot be known except by faith. We cannot therefore rely on our feelings or our works to conclude that we are justified and saved." Is section 2005 ruling out any experiential dimension to grace in general, or to sanctifying grace in particular? The overall point of 2005 seems to be that no one should

---

[33] Emblematic of this sympathy are the dying words of George Bernanos's country curé, so given to self-examination and self-reproach: "Qu'est-ce-que cela fait? Tout est grâce." "What does that matter? All is grace."

[34] Archbishop Jean Honoré says that the discussion of justification was inserted at this point (rather than back in part one as some had wished) precisely to counter a certain Pelagian, moralistic, or casuistic tone in the text as it then stood. See his "Catechism presents morality as a lived experience of faith in Christ," 141–42.

claim to know whether he or she is actually justified, actually in the state of grace or not.

The second sentence of 2005 refers to DS 1533–34, chapter 9 of Trent's decree on justification. The concluding story from the trial of Joan of Arc makes the same point. But the assertion of 2005 that graces escapes our experience and cannot be known except by faith goes a step or two beyond the text of Trent to which it refers.[35] At any rate, section 2005 invites us to reflect on the place of the experience of grace, the experience of God, in our catechesis. I have to admit that I find the tone of 2005 to be somewhat anti-experiential or counter-experiential. Yet I also wonder whether I have been sufficiently critical of my own experience, whether I have been at times a bit to quick to claim to know what the movements of grace have been in my life, and whether #2005 is saying something that I need to hear.[36]

This discussion may seem to be straying from the topic of basic moral theology, and yet there is some relation between the notion that grace is not something experienced and the emphatic affirmation in article 3 of the need for the Church's magisterium as a guide in moral matters. The contemporary debate about the place of the magisterium in moral matters has been framed in part as a conflict between magisterial pronouncement and personal experi-

---

[35] Chapter 9 of Trent's decree on justification is directed at two errors: that of boasting of one's confidence or certitude about the remission of one's sins, and resting content with that alone (DS 1533, cf. canon 12, DS 1562), and that of insisting that absolute confidence in the remission of one's sins is a necessary condition for their being remitted (DS 1534, cf. canons 13, DS 1563, and 14, DS 1564). Note that at the end of chapter 9 the Council says: ". . . *cum nullus scire valeat certitudine fidei, cui non potest subesse falsum, se gratiam Dei esse consecutum*" ("since no one can know with the certitude of faith, into which falsity cannot enter, that he has obtained the grace of God"). The Fathers at Trent expended considerable effort drafting and re-drafting the chapter and canons on certitude about the state of grace, and their intention was to rule out certain heretical errors—that certitude of being justified was necessary for justification and that certitude of being justified was sufficient for justification—but to leave open the Scotist position, that a person could conceivably have a *moral* certitude of being in the state of grace. Here I am relying on Hubert Jedin, *A History of the Council of Trent*, tr. E. Graf, O.S.B. (London and New York: Thomas Nelson, 1961) II.247–53, 285–90.

[36] I have also wondered whether something in our Ignatian spirituality, or in our contemporary versions of Ignatian spirituality, has led us to be insufficiently critical of experience, too certain of how God is acting in our lives and the lives of others.

ence, even an experience that understands itself as an experience of grace.[37] I am not saying that #2005 was inserted with the conscious intention of ruling out that sort of appeal, but that it is at least one of its implications. If we do not experience the movements of grace in our lives, then our personal experience is not really a guide to how we are doing in the Christian life, and we must rely on authority. But would that be a case of *qui nimis probat*? At any rate, the catechist is going to have to figure out what to say about the relationship between grace and experience. And sooner or later that is going to turn into the question about the relationship between faith and experience, and the possibility of an experience of God.[38]

Article 3. The Church, Mother and Teacher: I. Moral Life and the Magisterium of the Church; II. The Precepts of the Church; III. Moral Life and Missionary Witness #2031, in the introduction to article 3, says that the moral life is a form of spiritual worship. This idea deserves further development, and I can think of two directions. First, it suggests the possibility of integrating moral theology and moral experience with liturgical theory or sacramental experience. Second, it suggests a criterion that could be used in moral judgment: is this course of action something that makes sense as a form of worship? Is this action an action that somehow honors God?

Subsection II is a brief statement of the five main commandments of the Church. Subsection III places the moral life of Christians in the context of the Church's tasks of attracting people to God and of hastening the coming of the kingdom.

Subsection I, which will doubtless attract the most attention, is concerned with the place of the Church's magisterium in the

---

[37] A simple example: "My spouse and I know the Church's teaching on birth control; but we have also prayed over the matter and made our decision, and we find that God blesses us in our decision."

[38] It is one thing to construe the official church as having the role of checking, disciplining, enlightening our limited and fallible experience of God, and another thing to construe the official church as making up for a deficit of experience of God. On the relation between experience and authority, I have been influenced by Rosemary Haughton's reflections on what she terms "formation" and "transformation" in *The Transformation of Man* (Springfield: Templegate, 1980), 7–12, 242–80.

moral life of Christians. I have no illusions about settling all the issues that arise in this connection, but here are the principal assertions. #2034 (citing *Lumen Gentium* 25) affirms the ordinary magisterium of the pope and the bishops in matters of faith and morals. #2035 affirms the charism of infallibility as extending both to the deposit of revelation (again citing *Lumen Gentium* 25) and "to all those elements of doctrine, including morals, without which the saving truths of the faith cannot be preserved, explained, or observed." The point is repeated at 2051 in slightly different language: "The infallibility of the Magisterium of the Pastors extends to all the elements of doctrine, including moral doctrine, without which the saving truths of the faith cannot be preserved, expounded, or observed."[39] The footnote to #2035 refers to *Lumen Gentium* 25 and to the declaration of the Congregation for the Doctrine of the Faith *Mysterium Ecclesiae* 3.[40] In fact, #2035 and #2051 go a step beyond the language of *Mysterium Ecclesiae* 3. That declaration speaks of the application of infallibility to matters *"sine quibus hoc depositum rite nequit custodiri et exponi"* ("without which this deposit [of faith] cannot be duly preserved and explained").[41] #2035 and #2051 add "or observed." My surmise is that the addition of "or observed" betokens some broadening of the scope of the so-called indirect magisterium to include matters required for the observance of the truths of faith; but I am not certain of what is and what is not meant by "observed" in this context, and so I cannot say what exactly these matters would be.[42]

To return to the text, 2036 (citing *Dignitatis Humanae* 14) says that the authority of the magisterium extends to the specific precepts of the natural law because observance of them is necessary for salvation. When the magisterium issues a reminder about the

---

[39] In the French text of 2035 and 2051, the three words are the same: *gardées, exposées, observées*.

[40] The French gives two footnotes, one to *Lumen Gentium* 25 for the point that infallibility extends as far as revelation, the other to *Mysterium Ecclesiae* 3 for the application of infallibility to matters connected with revelation. These footnotes have been combined in the English version.

[41] *AAS* 65 (1973): 401.

[42] On the matter of indirect magisterium I have been helped by F. A. Sullivan, S.J., *Magisterium: Teaching Authority in the Catholic Church* (New York and Ramsey: Paulist Press, 1983), 119–52.

prescriptions of the natural law, it is exercising its prophetic office, recalling to all people what they are in truth and what they ought to be. #2037 says that the faithful have both the right to proper instruction in the divine saving precepts and the duty to observe Church ordinances, even if these are disciplinary. #2039 speaks against a merely individual approach to conscience (*une considération individuelle*),[43] and against any attempt to oppose personal conscience and reason to the moral law or to the magisterium.

Concluding Remarks

Part three, section one of the *Catechism* is a remarkable synthesis of the basics of human and Christian moral life. When I suggest that there are some problems about this synthesis, what I mean is not that we should pass a judgment on the *Catechism* and then go our merry ways, but rather that as catechists (or preachers or counselors) we have our work cut out for us. I am thinking in particular of work in three areas: the use of Scripture, the history and development of moral teaching, and the place of experience.

There is a certain innocence in the way that part three, section one of the *Catechism* uses Scripture. It prescinds from historico-critical issues. For example, it does not ask how much of the Sermon on the Mount Jesus actually preached, or in what respects Jesus's preaching might have been restated or modified to address concerns in the community for whom Matthew wrote. Rather, the *Catechism* interprets the Sermon on the Mount with the help of Irenaeus, Augustine, and Aquinas.[44] I am not saying that this is a bad thing, and I can see good reasons why the drafters should not have inserted the revisable views of Scripture experts into the *Catechism*. I am aware that people can use an historico-critical approach to place such a distance between themselves and the

---

[43] The English reads: "conscience . . . should avoid confining itself to individualistic considerations."

[44] Part one, chapter 1, article 3 (101–41) speaks of the Scriptures. It seems to me that #111 of the *Catechism* contrasts the work of exegetes and the work of the magisterium rather more sharply than does the constitution *Dei Verbum* of Vatican II. And #115–18 of the *Catechism* affirm (in small print, to be sure) the validity of the allegorical, moral, and anagogical senses of Scripture; so far as I can see, *Dei Verbum* left these senses unmentioned.

Scripture, or between the Scripture and Jesus, that they strip the scriptural word of its power to challenge and heal. Newman began the *Grammar of Assent* by citing Ambrose's dictum that God did not decide to save people by way of dialectic, and I am not about to say that God decided, instead, to save people by way of the historico-critical method. But apart from this or that historico-critical issue, this section of the *Catechism* prescinds from what is sometimes called the hermeneutic question—granted what a text meant in its original context or to its original audience, what should it mean to people in a different context today? Now, I do not want to make the hermeneutic question into the thirteenth article of the Apostles' Creed. But if the historically conditioned character of Scripture and the legitimacy of the hermeneutic question are things that you take for granted, or if you are presenting the *Catechism* to someone who takes them for granted, you have your work cut out for you.[45]

Part three, section one of the *Catechism* is long on the continuity of moral teaching but short on the development of moral teaching. When I say "long on continuity," I refer to the identification of the biblical ten commandments with the main precepts of the natural law, to the interpretation of the Christian moral life as the following of a new law that is a fulfilment, not a replacement, of the old law (and which still includes the natural law, which remains essentially the same in every time and place), and to the contemporary magisterium's authoritative understanding of natural law, old law, and new law.

When I say that part three, section one is "short on development," what I mean is that it says very little about how the understanding of God's will for us, as expressed in nature and revelation, has developed over time. I am not saying here that the drafters of the *Catechism* ought to have included a section on development of moral teaching, and I am aware that people can use historical development as an excuse to relativize and disregard the whole tradition of moral teaching. If, however, you are trying to present part three of the *Catechism* to someone who knows

---

[45] For a different way of using Scripture in moral matters, see Lisa Sowle Cahill, *Between the Sexes: Foundations for a Christian Ethics of Sexuality* (Philadelphia: Fortress; Ramsey: Paulist, 1985), esp. 15–44.

something about the history of ethics, or even to someone whose overall outlook on things is historical, or if you yourself are such a person, you have your work cut out for you.[46]

As regards experience, I just want to remind the reader of what I said above about the *Catechism*'s assertion (2005) that grace, being of a supernatural order, goes beyond our experience and can only be known by faith. Some of the pages of the *Catechism* are appealing, precisely as some of the pages of Pope John Paul II's writings are appealing, precisely because they make contact with human experience, clarify it, challenge it, and call it to growth and conversion. Still, if we are presenting the moral teaching of the *Catechism* to people who tend to test ideas by how well or ill these ideas square with their experience (and my sense is that this description fits a fair number of American Catholics), we are going to have to present the moral implications of God's creation and self-revelation in as experiential a way as possible. And this is as good a place as any to make the point that Christian moral instruction both presupposes and communicates an image of the Christian God.

I suggest that these three areas of concern (Scripture, development, experience) are connected. Like *Veritatis Splendor*, the *Catechism* is concerned to safeguard the reality of good and evil, the objectivity of moral norms. Like *Veritatis Splendor*, the *Catechism* does not base itself on historico-critical study of Scripture, or on historical scrutiny of moral teaching, or on personal experience. It rests its case on a tradition of interpretation and on the authority of the Church's magisterium. As a good twentieth-century academic, I bristle at the suggestion that I might need the help of authority. But I am reminded of some thoughts of Christopher Dawson on the early Church's struggle with gnosticism and syncretism, and on the importance of Church authority in this struggle:

> If Christianity had been merely one among the oriental sects and mystery religions of the Roman Empire, it must inevitably have

---

[46] On the awareness of historical development, see John W. O'Malley, S.J., *Tradition and Transition: Historical Perspectives on Vatican II* (Wilmington: Michael Glazier, 1989), esp. 44–81, and "Reform, Historical Consciousness, and Vatican II's Aggiornameno," which appeared originally in *Theological Studies* 32 (1971): 573–601.

been drawn into this oriental syncretism. It survived because it possessed a system of ecclesiastical organization and a principle of social authority that distinguished it from all the other religious bodies of the age.[47]

The errors of our own day have more than a little in common with gnosticism, and if the invocation of Church authority was essential to combat gnosticism, so it may be essential to combat the errors of our own day. Yet, as Dawson well knew, the Church's encounter with Greco-Roman culture went far beyond the conflict with gnosticism and syncretism, and for this encounter to bear fruit, more was required than ecclesiastical authority and discipline. If the *Catechism* is telling us not to let biblical criticism and hermeneutics, historical study or appeals to personal experience, get in the way of our recognizing certain basic truths and living by them, this caution is well taken. But I allow myself to hope that these very truths may be appreciated more adequately in the light of biblical criticism and hermeneutics and historical research, and practiced more fully in the light of personal experience; and that to these ends what we here present may have something to contribute.

---

[47] Christopher Dawson, *The Making of Europe* (Cleveland and New York: Meridian, 1965), 47. See 48: "The doctrine of St. Clement is characteristically Roman in its insistence on social order and moral discipline, but it has much in common with the teaching of the Pastoral Epistles, and there can be no doubt that it represents the traditional spirit of the primitive Church. It was this spirit that saved Christianity from sinking in the morass of oriental syncretism."

Response

Joseph W. Koterski, S.J.

FATHER MADIGAN'S REMARKS rightly put emphasis on the propaedeutic character of the first section of part three of the new *Catechism of the Catholic Church*. Like the initial sections of the other three parts, it offers a general discussion in order to orient our reading of the more detailed second section—in this case we have an introduction to morality before being given a treatment of the content of the moral life, organized by a consideration of each of the Ten Commandments. In the orientation thus provided we can see the distinctive hand of Pope John Paul II, who insists throughout his ethical writings that there can be no ethics without an adequate theocentric anthropology, and no anthropology without an adequate personalist metaphysics. Madigan has given a thoroughgoing review of the material and has noted some special concerns for the catechist. His reminders about the strengths and the limits of virtue ethics and his cautions in the area of "the felt knowledge of grace" are especially prudent and timely. Let me turn my attention here to some points he has raised about the pope's philosophical presuppositions.

The *Catechism*'s reminders about the need to recognize human dignity borrow the linchpin characteristic of all John Paul II's ethical analyses. The universality and objectivity of ethics stems from the reality of our common human nature, as the tradition of natural law thinking has always held, but in placing so much emphasis on the person, the pope's standard manner of arguing takes a path more often associated with personalist and idealist traditions. Unlike any other created nature, human nature is essentially personal because made in the image and likeness of God and called to beatitude. The personal character of human nature introduces an element so different from all other created natures that it almost stands in contradiction to the idea of nature—namely, the subjective, individual dimension. As a result, human nature is a nature that is only "given" in part; it must also be generated by the living person, for through every choice and act we become the sort of person who does the specific sort of thing—whatever it is—that we are now doing. Through all the daily decisions of living, one crafts the person one is. This occurs not just when one consciously sets out to be one sort of person rather than another, but whenever one acts.

In one respect or another, by our various choices we either respect or disrespect the basic dignity that comes from having a nature made in the image of God. As Madigan puts it, the dignity referred to here is centered on the right to respect, to be recognized as a free and responsible being, the right to exercise our freedom, especially in moral and religious matters. It is not a right to do as we please but to be treated as a certain kind of being. Even if these might not be the aspects of human dignity emphasized in the usual discourse of freedom and human rights, they can be intelligibly expressed in a secular rhetoric, without reference to God. Yet they are frequently denied in human rights violations, abused in ways disrespectful of human dignity (for example, the use made of the idea of "privacy" in certain contexts), and given the variety of ways available in law and philosophy to define "person," recourse to the concept of "person" fails to settle many ethical disputes. This situation forces us to return to the ground of their normativity, the divine creation of the human being in God's own image.

Without this biblical basis there is an antinomy here that can perplex thinkers in both the natural law and the personalist traditions by the interminability of ethical disputes. Natural law thinkers have readily appreciated freedom as the aspect of human existence that places us in the sphere of morality but have been loathe to regard the subjectivity as in any way constitutive for morality; they would prefer to take freedom as a necessary condition for morality. Personalists are more comfortable with the idea of working out one's morality by distinguishing authentic and inauthentic uses of freedom, but they have traditionally been suspicious of the category of nature as alienating. Even if they subtly use nature as a silent partner in their arguments, the necessary condition for personal continuity over time, it is not constitutive in morality. John Paul II's moral theory is committed to explain ethics in terms of both person and nature.

Now, the desire to balance subjectivity and objectivity in one's ethics is a fine intention, but to achieve this balance in practice can easily elude us. The section on morality in the *Catechism*—more than many an academic treatise on ethics—has special reason for trying to find a way to do this in practice, for catechisms are intended to give practical advice for living, even this one, which intends to be a master-catechism from which others can be constructed. How does it do so? By locating the source of human dignity ultimately in being the image of God. It may be that this is part of the reason that the *Catechism* focuses again and again, as Madigan shows us, on human dignity—not the dignity that would belong to human beings in isolation from God or from one another, but "the dignity grounded in man's being the image of God and being called to beatitude, manifested in freedom, deliberate action, action according to conscience." The term suggests both something ontological and something ethical: there is an inalienable dignity that comes from being human, and this is an objective value that ought to be reverenced by others, an ethical given rooted in a claim about nature as found in reality. But there is also a dignity which a subject must live up to, one's human vocation, so to speak, that doesn't depend on honor or office, but on authentic use of one's natural powers of intellect and will, one's body and emotions. It is a point often made in the encyclicals, for instance, in *Laborem Exercens*, which tries to show how work worthy of a human being lets one live in properly human dignity.

This approach is also a practical answer to those who ask what is specifically distinctive about Christian ethics, who seek to identify points that all people of good will could agree upon as fundamental ethics, and then seek to know what Scripture and tradition add to the demands or to the resources of morality. It seems to me that John Paul II could praise what is good and useful in any ethics that lacks a Christian turn and yet still enhances human dignity, but would find that the full truth about humankind comes only with Christ, for Christ is the source of the human dignity being praised.

One could argue, I presume, that since antiquity moralists have found reason and will to be a source of dignity, for they permit one to commit oneself for or against the good; similarly, one finds this argument in Marxist writings such as *Natural Law and Human Dignity*[48] by Ernst Bloch. But believers add a substantive claim about this dignity when they insist that reason and will also make each human being the image of their creator. In more speculative writings like the encyclicals from the beginning of his pontificate, John Paul II meditated on what the truth is that really sets us free. In so doing he used the language of freedom and human rights, not in a way many secular currents would speak of them, but in a way that makes clear that Christ alone is that truth. So too here in a document that is attempting to be very practical. The thoroughly Christological cast of this entire section of the *Catechism*, and especially chapter 3, which is entitled "God's Salvation: Law and Grace," makes an extremely strong connection between morality and soteriology—not that we are saved simply by being moral, but that there is only one way to be saved—through Christ—and that the reason for living morally flows from making the response due to Christ. Or, to take up another piece of evidence, Madigan rightly noted that the *Catechism* does not focus on intellectual vision or contemplation as a privileged description of the happiness that human beings naturally desire, but offers the Beatitudes as the picture of human happiness. It is not just our picture of the means that requires the inclusion of Christ, but our picture of the end.

---

[48] Ernst Block, *Naturrecht und menschliche Würde* (Frankfurt: Suhrkamp Verlag, 1961), tr. by Dennis J. Schmidt as *Natural Law and Human Dignity* (Cambridge: MIT Press, 1986).

6. MORAL THEOLOGY
The Context of *Veritatis Splendor*

John M. McDermott, S.J.

PAPAL ENCYCLICALS are not issued into a void. They respond to various needs of the Church. *Veritatis Splendor* certainly has its own context. Through his various teachings and the *Catechism,* Pope John Paul II has been redefining the traditional faith of the Church in personalist terms for the new millennium. Closely tied to questions of dogmatic belief and formulation are questions about morality. When Vatican Council I defined that in speaking *ex cathedra* the pope enjoys infallible divine assistance in defining doctrine about faith and morals (DS 3073f.), the Fathers of the council were only recognizing the deep connection between faith and morals that characterizes Christian revelation. Scripture presents moral norms as well as the object of faith. This connection is to be expected. If God is ultimately love (1 John 4:8,16), faith must presume in the believer an experience of love. Otherwise the object of faith cannot be recognized and affirmed. Lest faith be deprived of meaning, love, however imperfect, must respond to love. Not surprisingly, in a time when many of the tenets of Christian faith have been placed in question, there have also been attacks upon the Church's traditional moral teachings. These attacks have come from within the Church as well as from without. Consequently the pope saw as his duty the reaffirmation of traditional Catholic morality.

Dissent from traditional morality within the Church stems from the same Vatican Council II to which Pope John Paul II appeals for inspiration and confirmation. Without doubt, that council marked a change in theological emphasis from the era that preceded it. The meaning and depth of that change depend upon the interpretation given to its documents. Prima facie one would expect that the pope, who participated in all the sessions and contributed to the final formulation of the council's decrees, understand them better than the theologians who were on the outside looking in. Nonetheless, many of the latter appeal to other theologians who were present and influential at the council, in order to support their interpretation. Sometimes this involves an invocation of the "spirit" rather than the "letter" of the council. This appeal beyond and sometimes against the letter, however suspicious, should not be disqualified a priori. For the interpretation of any document depends upon the theoretical and practical presuppositions that authors and readers bring to it.

It is the purpose of this essay to examine the divergent philosophical and theological presuppositions that animate the current debate about morality in the Catholic Church and grant a perspective about the intent and success of *Veritatis Splendor*. Given the importance of St. Thomas in Catholic theology, a brief consideration of his vision precedes a discussion of his various interpreters. The main distinction of import for the current crisis in moral theology lies between the *conceptualist* and *transcendental* interpretations of Thomas's thought. After their basic philosophical and theological oppositions are recounted, the application of each system of thought to moral theology is analyzed. Against that background the significance of *Veritatis Splendor* can be appreciated. Not only does the encyclical respond to the needs of the Church but it also invites theologians to undertake, with the pope, a new interpretation of St. Thomas that centers on freedom and understands natures only in function of freedom.

The Role of St. Thomas

St. Thomas Aquinas has played a preeminent role in Catholic theology. Probably the world's greatest speculative mind, he laid down the parameters for much of the subsequent debate in Catholic theology. Since Leo XIII's encyclical *Aeterni Patris* (1879) recommended the Angelic Doctor most strongly to the study of all Catholic thinkers and encouraged his teaching as the basis of seminary education, St. Thomas's doctrine has served as the field of battle for diverse theological schools. The very balance and depth of his thought has permitted the proliferation of interpretations. Pope Leo XIII rightly saw that St. Thomas could respond to the philosophical babble of modernity, for in handling the perennial problems of thought, he provided the sound basis for trenchant clarifications of many difficulties. But the novelties of modernity, unforeseen by Thomas, in turn permitted new interpretations of his thought. Because his own vision transcends the rationalism that has marked modern philosophy, its very balance could lend itself to distortions at the hands of disciples who concentrate upon one aspect to the neglect of the whole and attempt to deduce logical, but erroneous, conclusions from a truncated system of thought.

In order to be faithful to reality Thomas knew that he had to balance various philosophical and theological emphases in a unified synthesis.[1] As faith is different from reason, so the supernatural order of revelation transcends the natural order known by reason. Insofar as the one God is the source of the truths of both faith and reason, these truths cannot contradict each other. Indeed, they also find a unity in the human subject who is called to affirm them. Though the supernatural transcends the natural, it also presupposes it. It would be meaningless to consider something "beyond-nature" unless "nature" has some recognizable meaning. It stands as a basic axiom of Catholic theology that grace presupposes, heals, and perfects, but does not destroy nature (see ST I,1,8 ad 2; 2,2 ad 1; II-II, 171, 2 ad 3). Correspondingly faith presupposes reason. For without some understanding of faith, it is impossible to understand what God is revealing and people are affirming.

Despite the references of faith to reason and of the supernatural to the natural, there remain difficulties in establishing their exact correspondence. If the natural order does not make sense of itself, there is no way of understanding the faith announced in the words of human speech and no basis for humankind's free cooperation in their response to faith. Without basic intelligibility,

---

[1] Our basic understanding of St. Thomas is spelled out in "The Analogy of Knowing in the *Prima Pars*" in *Gregorianum* 77 (1996): 261–86, 501–25. Of a similar opinion is W. Hankey, *God in Himself* (Oxford University Press, 1987).

people have no reason for any choice, and their "choices" are reduced to instinctive reactions to stimuli, as occur among the brute beasts. Inversely, if the natural order does make sense, offering some knowledge of God and God's will as well as grounding the possibility of intelligent, free choice, revelation is in danger of being seen as an unwarranted intrusion upon human nature. If people possess natural knowledge of both God and the moral law, as well as enjoying freedom to follow that law, it would seem unjust of God to condemn to hell anyone who has fulfilled that law. For people would have accomplished everything required of them by their nature. An additional demand could be seen as unnatural and beyond the order of justice established in nature.[2]

---

[2] The traditional scholastic response to this exaggeration has been either to point to humankind's weakened nature and say that, unlike a perfectly healthy nature, it is incapable of fulfilling the entire natural law (see E. Hugon, O.P., *Tractatus Dogmatici*, II, 10th ed. [Paris: Lethielleux, 1935], 101f.) or, more deeply, to distinguish moral from physical—that is, natural capacity. Although human nature is wounded by original sin, it retains its physical capacity to choose the good; nonetheless, though the unbaptized may accomplish individual acts that are morally good, due to the wounds of original sin and the pressures of life, which prevent adequate reflection, people will over time inevitably fall into sin. Thus humankind is physically capable but morally incapable of continuously fulfilling all the duties of the natural law. See C. Boyer, S.J., *Tractatus de gratia divina*, 3rd ed. (Rome: Gregoriana, 1952), 48f., 52–57; B. Lonergan, S.J., *Grace and Freedom*, ed. J. Burns (New York: Herder and Herder, 1970), 48–52. However psychologically accurate such a description of fallen human nature may be, it lacks any ontological foundation. In Catholic theology, moral obligation derives from nature and its inherent natural law. What is physically possible should be morally possible since freedom pertains to the natural will, which is oriented to the good. Moreover, if an individual's distraction is such that he or she is not aware of the seriousness of his or her action and all its implications, the lack of sufficient knowledge would diminish the guilt involved. Finally, the more good works an individual performs, the more she or he develops good habits that render virtuous actions more facile; hence over time the performance of good works is more deeply ingrained in the individual's nature; this strengthens a weakened nature. Moreover, the performance of a good action should demand less reflection as the habit overcomes distraction.

St. Thomas is much more cautious in his treatment of the problem in ST I-II, 109, 8c. He argues that in the state of corrupt nature a person cannot without grace avoid venial sin (which does not entail the loss of God's friendship) and that human reason, touched by mortal sin, can resist individual mortal sins without grace's healing. He avoids the consideration whether in the state of corrupt nature a person can avoid all mortal sins without grace.

The imperviousness of this conundrum to a solution derives from theology's inability to determine the exact meaning of original sin; for theology, both Catholic and Protestant, has traditionally started with "nature" and natural faculties

Yet faith, which goes beyond nature and reason, is apparently demanded of a person for his or her salvation (Mark 16:15f.; Acts 4:12; DS 75f., 2021, 2104). Hence fulfillment of the natural moral law does not suffice for salvation; nature cannot provide the basis of final human happiness.

To avoid both extremes, Thomas, following the lead of Pseudo-Dionysius, postulated the "natural desire" of seeing the essence of God, the First Cause (see SCG III, 50; *Comp. Theol.* 104; ST I, 12, 1c; I-II, 2,5,3; 3,8c.; but compare I-II, 2, 8c; 5,8c.3). Though God's existence can be known naturally from created effects, this knowledge does not satisfy the human desire to know. Knowing that God exists, one naturally desires to know what God is. This involves seeing God in himself, and such knowledge touches God's inner, trinitarian life, a supernatural mystery known only by revelation.[3] The intuition of the infinite God that terminates this desire is supernatural insofar as it transcends humankind's natural way of knowing through forms abstracted from material singulars. The finite intellect intuits God's essence, which takes the place of an abstracted form, substituting what the Scholastics called the *species impressa* and rendering the subsequent concept, or *species expressa*, superfluous.

To explain how the finite could be elevated to intuit the infinite God, Thomas postulated a supernatural "light of glory" (*lumen gloriae*), that strengthens the natural force of the intellect while being added to the intellect. For a human being has to see God with a created intellect, even though the beatific vision surpasses the natural intellect. Throughout his doctrine Thomas maintained a delicate balance between nature and grace. On the one hand, the desire for the beatific vision is natural and the human intellect enjoys the beatific vision; thus the natural order is presupposed and preserved in its integrity. Yet what nature desires is supernatural, the intuitive vision. The natural order is pre-

---

such as the will, in which freedom has been located, instead of with freedom, which belongs primarily to the person.

[3] For the relation of the conceptualist philosophy to theology, see J. McDermott, S.J., "Faithful and Critical Intelligence in Theology" in *Excellence in Seminary Education*, ed. S. Minkiel et al. (Erie: Committee on Priestly Formation, ACPA), 68–74; "The Methodological Shift in Twentieth Century Thomism" in *Seminarium* 31 (1991): 245–53.

vented from being closed in upon itself, impervious to the demands of revelation. Indeed, only by accepting revelation and grace does the individual realize himself or herself fully.

Within the natural order itself Thomas also effected a very delicate balancing act between essential and existential orders. Thomas saw clearly that not only is God pure, infinite existence, but also created realities are composed of essence and existence. What things are, essences, exist, and their existence is different from their essence; only God, whose essence is infinite existence, surpasses the contingency that characterizes all creatures who do not give themselves existence. A basically Aristotelian essential order, in which essences are known through formal abstractions, guarantees the finite intelligibility of reality.

To that order Thomas added a more neoplatonic (or Dionysian), dynamic existential order in which all finite essences participate for their existence in God's infinite act of existence. Whereas the formal intelligibility of essences are grasped in concepts, the existential reference of a dynamic judgment opens up the existential order to human knowledge. Since essences cannot be known apart from an abstractive process beginning with actually existing material singulars, the essential order presupposes an existential order. Moreover, no judgment is possible without a concept; hence the existential order also presupposes an essential order. This mutual inclusion of essential and existential orders, concept and judgment, provides St. Thomas with very flexible instruments for analyzing reality. There is unity amid diversity, as well as diversity within unity. Thomas can appeal to either aspect in order to maintain the proper balance between finite intelligibility and its grounding in the infinite God who surpasses the grasp of every finite intellect.

Thomas's Cajetanian Disciples

A balanced vision is delicate, difficult to maintain. As Thomas's disciples were faced with new problems and had to deal with the rationalizing tendencies of late medieval philosophy and the new Galilean physics, the majority tended to emphasize the more conceptual, essential emphases of Thomas's thought. The great Cajetan, who had encountered the new physics during early studies at Padua, formulated a Thomistic synthesis that stressed heavily rational consistency. Though he acknowledged the real distinction between essence and existence and appealed to the existential order to resolve difficulties that might emerge from a purely essentialist viewpoint, he tended toward a conceptual rationalism. In his developed theory of abstraction, the mind reaches reality—that is, being—at various levels of scientific knowledge by abstracting from individuating, sensible matter (physics), from sensible matter (mathematics), and from all matter (metaphysics). The metaphysical concept of being is analogous, with the widest extension. It not only grasps being as abstracted from all individual instances and limitations but also contains those instances and limitations themselves insofar as they are "being." However vague and analogous this concept of being might be, it well serves its purpose in guaranteeing philosophy's rational foundation. For if being can be conceptualized, all of reality can be grasped in concepts.

This conceptualist philosophy also served the Cajetan interpretation in their conflict with Protestants. Against the latter's nominalistic heritage, which stressed the uniqueness of individuals whose inmost reality is known only to God, Cajetanian Thomists might insist on the intelligibility of nature—to abstract is not to lie—and point to nominalism's irrationalism, which also destroys theology insofar as the human intellect must think in order to understand and receive revelation. Likewise, by guaranteeing the meaning of reality, they afford one reason for the free choice of revelation. Before the proclamation of the Gospel, a person might step back, understand, and decide whether or not to accept that revelation. Since the human mind knows reality through concepts, supernatural knowledge or revelation is communicated in conceptual propositions. These propositions transcend the ability of the human mind to grasp their inherent intelligibility insofar as they are supernatural. Yet one must have a reason for accepting and affirming their truth lest one's rational freedom, the cooperation with grace, be excluded from the act of faith. The reasons for faith must accordingly be extraneous to the content of faith but sufficiently strong to move a person to a free assent. Hence appeal is made to the trustworthiness of the divine messenger,

Jesus Christ, who announced those truths. His trustworthiness was guaranteed by God insofar as Jesus fulfilled Old Testament prophecies and worked miracles, performances beyond human power that God in such important matters regarding human salvation would never let a deceiver accomplish.

Thus the revealed propositions proclaimed by Christ are to be accepted in faith on his authority. In this way the theological foundations of authority are established. In order to preach, preserve, and interpret correctly his message, Jesus established a Church, vesting his authority in the twelve apostles and their episcopal successors. Their task includes proclaiming the dogmatic truths of the faith and interpreting Christ's moral law, defining them when necessary in times of crisis. Theologians serve the Church by defending its teachings from attack, searching the sources of revelation, Scripture and tradition, to determine the content of faith, deducing implicit truths from revealed truths, and explaining the truths of faith through analogy with other revealed truths, between natural and supernatural truths, and in correspondence to humanity's final end. So strong is the objective emphasis of this vision that it easily accepts the Anselmian notion of redemption whereby an infringement of an objective order by sin demands in justice a restitution of God's honor; only God can make reparation for an infinite offense, yet the satisfaction has to be accomplished by a human individual who presents to God a free sacrifice. The solution is found in the God-man offering himself on Calvary.[4]

Other Interpretations of St. Thomas

Although the Cajetanian tradition long held sway in the Dominican order and produced many great speculative minds from John of St. Thomas to Jacques Maritain, it was not the only interpretation of St. Thomas. In the Jesuit order a diverse understanding of freedom and human cooperation with grace led to a substantially

---

[4] For an overview of the historical development of neo-Thomism, see G. McCool, S.J., *Catholic Theology in the Nineteenth Century* (New York: Seabury, 1977) and *From Unity to Pluralism* (New York: Fordham Univ. Press, 1989).

different approach to philosophy and theology. Linked to such names as D. Molina and F. Suarez, a strong alternative to Cajetanian Thomism developed. Whereas the Dominicans professed to maintain a strict fidelity to St. Thomas, Suarez and his disciples admitted to adapting St. Thomas to new problems and clarifying certain points of his thought. Suarez even denied the essence-existence distinction, considered by Thomists to be fundamental to Thomas's vision, and attributed intelligibility to the singular as such.

Suarezianism dominated the Jesuit order even after Leo XIII's *Aeterni Patris*, but the immense authority of the papacy and the revival of interest in the original texts of Thomas led many Jesuits to abandon Suarez in favor of Thomas. Theirs, however, was a Thomism with a difference. The Jesuit cardinal Louis Billot accepted the essence-existence distinction but introduced many Suarezian elements, especially regarding freedom, into a brilliant theological synthesis that attracted many disciples in the first half of the twentieth century. But with Cajetanian Thomists and Suarezians, he regarded as central to philosophy and theology the analogous concept of being.[5] The primacy of that concept would, however, be placed into question by many of the young Thomists of his own order.

Through his historical studies E. Gilson concluded that the Cajetanian interpretation was erroneous. Not the concept, but the existential judgment gives access to reality. Gilson's reinterpretation may have been instigated by the early winds of existentialism stirring at French universities, but his emphasis on the objective, hierarchical vision of Thomas's universe and his consequent determination to maintain a strong essential order with clear distinctions among beings prevented him from accepting a totally existentialist position.[6]

More radical were the transcendental Thomists who arose in the Jesuit order. Wishing to fulfill the desire of Leo XIII to rein-

---

[5] An excellent study of Billot, showing the synthetic unity of his thought, has recently been defended at the Gregorian University by A. Cozzi, *La Conoscenza e la Libertà di Gesù Cristo nel Sistema Teologico di L. Billot*. It should be published soon.

[6] See E. Gilson, *Le Thomisme*, 5th ed. (Paris; Vrin, 1944); *Being and Some Philosophers*, 2nd ed. (Toronto: Pontifical Institute of Medieval Studies, 1952).

troduce Catholicism as a formative cultural element in the modern world, they undertook a dialogue with modern philosophy, especially with Kant and his successors. While accepting modern subjectivity as their starting point, they hoped to overcome Kantian agnosticism in religion without falling into idealism by relying on the existential judgment and the dynamism that it reveals.

The judgment's primordial reference to the phantasm or material singular excludes idealism, while its natural dynamism propels the individual subject beyond oneself to the dynamism's fulfillment. Since the concept is only a part of the judgment that attains truth and reality, the concept alone cannot claim to reach reality. The affirmation of truth goes beyond the abstract concept toward being. Insofar as every finite presentation, be it concept or phantasm, can be placed into question through the movement of mind transcending every limitation, nothing short of God, infinite being, can satisfy the natural longing of the intellect for truth. Lest human knowing be deprived of all intellectual foundations, God must be implicitly affirmed in every judgment. All conceptual knowledge of God is transcended toward an intuitive vision of God. In this way transcendental Thomists revivified Thomas's "paradoxical" doctrine of the natural desire for the supernatural and joined most closely natural and supernatural orders: the human being cannot achieve self-perfection unless in supernatural union with God.[7]

Whereas concepts, by the very clarity of their formal abstractions, stress the divergences among the realities conceived, the dynamism basic to transcendental Thomism tends to dissolve distinctions in view of a greater unity. These unities are to be attained at ever higher levels of synthesis until the ultimate union of God and the human person is achieved in the beatific vision. Along with the natural-supernatural distinction, the intellect-will distinction is overcome. This distinction had been established in

---

[7] For the recurrence of the central paradox, see the texts cited by J. McDermott, S.J., in "The Theology of John Paul II: A Response" in *The Thought of Pope John Paul II*, ed. J. McDermott (Rome: Gregoriana, 1993), 631f., n. 36. For some major thinkers in transcendental Thomism, see J. McDermott, S.J., "Pierre Rousselot," *Storia della Teologia*, III, ed. R. Fisichella (Rome: Dehoniane, 1996), 663–73; "Karl Rahner," ibid., 735–47; "Bernard Lonergan," ibid., 751–62; "De Lubac and Rousselot," *Gregorianum* 73 (1997): 735–59.

conceptualist Thomism on the basis of the diversity of the spiritual faculties' formal objects, the true specifying the intellect and the good specifying the will. But in transcendental Thomism the distinction is transcended insofar as the dynamic intellect seeks the true as its fulfilling good. The affirmation of the deepest truths can be said to be most free since will and intellect contribute to every judgment and choice. Similarly the distinction between matter and form, or spirit, is transcended because knowledge occurs primarily in the existential judgment, which refers a form to its unity with the material singular (phantasm) from which it was abstracted. No abstracted form exists without an implicit reference to materiality. In a dynamic view, matter is also united to spirit in view of their single origin and goal in the God who created both. Matter can therefore be considered "frozen spirit." Thus there is a certain intelligibility in the material singular, even if it is grounded in the infinite mystery of God. On another point the distinction between object and subject is overcome insofar as knowledge of reality is attained only in a judgment, which is an act of the subject. There is no objectivity unless over subjectivity.

Given the primordial unity between object and subject, K. Rahner could even hold that being is self-consciousness (*Sein ist bei-sich-Sein*). Thereby metaphysics, the science of being, is identified with rational psychology as well as with epistemology, the study of knowing and its conditions. Finally, since being is attained only in the subject's existential judgment, there is no way of speaking about God, infinite being, without some reference to the subject and the world. Rejecting a simplistic theism, which opposes God to the world, Rahner wrote that the unity (*Einheit*) of human transcendence and its goal, God, is "the first and ultimate reality [*das Erste und das Letzte*]."[8]

The application of such a philosophy to theology not only is inevitable, given the flexibility of the nature-grace distinction, but also entails a radical revision of theological method and a profound reinterpretation of ecclesial doctrine.[9] The act of faith is no longer referred to revealed propositions but to the revealing God

---

[8] K. Rahner, S.J., *Grundkurs des Glaubens* (Freiburg: Herder, 1976), 67; J. McDermott, S.J., "Rahner on Two Infinities: God and Matter," *International Philosophical Quarterly* 28 (1988): 439–57.

[9] McDermott, "Faithful," 75–81; "Methodological Shift," 253–65.

beyond them. Since God intends to save all people and grace fulfills nature's dynamism, grace can be seen as offered from the beginning and always to everyone with natural existence, even apart from ecclesial preaching. Given the equivalence of objectivity and self-consciousness, God's gift of self as uncreated grace can be understood as self-revelation. Jesus Christ is seen not as one entering the world from without in order to restore a fallen order but as the culmination and goal of God's one salvific plan intended from the beginning of creation. Insofar as the beatific vision is the goal of all human striving and constitutes an essential moment of the hypostatic union, Rahner claimed that in Christ's human nature is an active obediential potency or natural desire for the hypostatic union.[10] Furthermore, since grace and revelation are offered to all, the Church is seen as the most explicit expression, the basic sacrament, of the grace offered to all. In matters of doctrine it does not so much introduce novel doctrines from without as help its audience to formulate more clearly their experience of grace. Insofar as the infinite mystery experienced in grace transcends all conceptual formulations, no dogmatic statement can claim to exhaust the mystery. Indeed, in order to be understood properly, each dogma must be referred back to its originating mystery. Dogmatic statements are not absolute in themselves but involve an implicit reference to the believing subject as well as to the revealing God. Hence it is incumbent upon the theologian not to repeat propositions from the past but to reformulate the truths contained therein in ways more intelligible to contemporaries. If the theologian comes into conflict with the magisterium, he or she should attempt to preserve the ecclesial link, aware that any decision of the magisterium always requires further interpretation and application to the concrete circumstances of the case. Thus, willingness to dialogue is essential to theology in an epoch of pluralism when no one theologian can hope to master all the subordinate disciplines required to attain a total theological viewpoint. Unlike the conceptualist theology, wherein pluralism consists in the diverse explanations offered for

---

[10] K. Rahner, S.J., "Jesus Christus," *Sacramentum Mundi*, ed. K. Rahner and A. Darlap (Freiburg: Herder, 1967–69), II, 930, 944; see J. McDermott, S.J., "The Christologies of Karl Rahner," *Gregorianum* 67 (1986): 104–23, 297–327.

the dogmatic formulations, the pluralism of transcendental theology, which is proclaimed insuperable due to the human epistemological concupiscence, consists in the diverse formulations of the dogmas themselves.

Clearly the finite intelligibility of the abstract concept is seriously imperilled by the ongoing movement of mind revealed in the judgment, and with that formulated dogmas and ecclesial mediations are relativized. Surely the most astute transcendental Thomists like Rousselot, Maréchal, de Lubac, Rahner, and Lonergan sought to preserve and shore up the value of conceptual knowledge.[11] Like the best of the conceptualist thinkers, they recognized that a balance has to be maintained between essential and existential orders, the formal intelligibility of concepts and the dynamic existential referent of judgment. But as the conceptualist thinkers tended to absolutize the finite intelligibility of the essential order, so the transcendental Thomists were drawn by their fundamental judgmental dynamism to relativize all finite mediations of intelligibility, revelation, and grace. Where the greater thinkers strove to maintain Thomas's delicate balance, the less astute disciples unfortunately fell into extreme positions. This thesis can be relatively easily illustrated through the comparison of conceptualist and transcendental moral theologies.

Some attention is also given to spirituality insofar as transcendental theology subsumes the conceptualist spirituality into moral theology.

MORAL THEOLOGY

Christian morality developed from the injunctions of Old and New Testaments, decisions of Church councils, and the teachings

---

[11] For their attempts at balance, see J. McDermott, S.J., *Love and Understanding* (Rome: Gregorian, 1983); "Tensions in Lonergan's Theory of Conversion" in *Gregorianum* 74 (1993): 101–40; "Dialectical Analogy: The Oscillating Center of Rahner's Thought" in *Gregorianum* 75 (1994): 675–703; "The Analogy of Knowing in Karl Rahner" in *International Philosophical Quarterly* 36 (1996): 201–16; "Sheehan, Rousselot, and Theological Method" in *Gregorianum* 68 (1987): 705–17; "De Lubac and Rousselot," 741–58. Although J. Aleu, *De Kant à Maréchal* (Barcelona: Herder, 1970) is quite good, the definitive study on Maréchal, tracing his development, has not yet been written.

of the Fathers of the Church.[12] Insofar as Christian morality corresponded with the morality of their environment, neither St. Paul nor the Fathers hesitated to borrow catalogues of virtues, norms, and arguments from pagan philosophers, even while rejecting other heathen practices as immoral. While referring to their Christian faith as the norm of discernment, they clearly employed reason in applying revelation and elaborating its implications. As the Middle Ages progressed, the science of canon law flourished. Church law included many moral prescriptions culled from Scripture and councils, and theologians also tried to explain systematically the Church's moral teaching. None succeeded so well as St. Thomas in the *Secunda Pars* of his *Summa Theologiae*, where he explicated Christian living and its metaphysical foundations in a profound study of the virtues. His successors expanded various aspects of that comprehensive treatment.

From the seventeenth century until recently, the emphasis upon confession as an instrument to overcome sin and to foster the growth of holiness encouraged the wide dissemination of manuals for confessors. Since moral theology was taught principally in seminaries to prepare future priests to be good confessors, skilled at recognizing sin and directing souls to virtue, the manuals tended to concentrate on concrete issues rather than entertain speculative questions and establish the link between dogmatic and moral theology. After a brief inculcation of basic principles the manuals analyzed many "cases" (*casus*) so that the confessor might recognize the correct application of principles to complicated concrete instances. Such a method of study fitted easily into the conceptualist mentality with its clear distinctions and emphasis upon objective norms. But its validity would be severely questioned when the transcendental interpretation of Thomism gained the theological ascendancy.

Conceptualist Morality

If thought governs action as well as reflects reality, the practical consequences of the conceptualist viewpoint are not difficult to

---

[12] For an overview of moral theology's development, see A. Lemkuhl, S.J.,

follow. Obligation flows from being as free rational creatures are called to live according to the laws of their nature, and their nature is what is grasped in conceptual abstraction. One might recognize that materiality and the consequences of sin render difficult the adequate comprehension of human nature, but none dare deny that human nature can be grasped in a concept. Otherwise, the whole natural basis of Catholic philosophy and the moral law would be radically put into question.[13]

Moral manuals generally start with an analysis of the specifically human act—that is, a free act posed with rational deliberation, and then study what inhibits it: ignorance, violence, concupiscence, fear, and various other impediments.[14] While recognizing that the subjective intent of the agent ultimately defines the morality of an act and that one is bound to follow the sure dictates of conscience, even if erroneous, this subjective emphasis is more than balanced by the axiom that an act is specified by its object.[15] Hence, what one chooses, not the sincerity of the choosing, defines the morality of an act and of the agent. One has the obligation of forming one's conscience according to right reason, which perceives the structures of reality. All reality is subject to law, whether necessarily, as in the case of irrational natures, or freely, as in the case of the human being. The ultimate basis of law is the eternal law, which is identical with God's immutable essence.

"Theology: Moral Theology," *The Catholic Encyclopedia*, ed. C. Herbermann et al., XIV (New York: Appleton, 1912), 601–11, and the articles on "Moral Theology" by F. Murphy, L. Vereecke, and J. Farraher in *New Catholic Encyclopedia*, ed. W. McDonald et al., IX (New York: McGraw-Hill, 1967), 1117–23.

[13] The struggle of J. Maritain, the greatest of this century's conceptualist thinkers, to preserve the concept as the basis of a moral system is given in "Moral Systems: Maritain and Schüller Compared," *Divus Thomas* 88 (1985): 3–11.

[14] Merkelbach, O.P., *Summa Theologiae Moralis* (Paris: Desclée de Brouwer, 1931), I:55–98; A. Vermeersch, S.J., *Theologiae Moralis*, 2nd ed. (Rome: Gregoriana, 1926), I:49–101; A. Sabetti, *Compendium Theologiae Moralis*, 33rd ed., ed. T. Barrett (New York: Pustet, 1931), 9–27; T. Slater, S.J., *A Manual of Moral Theology*, 5th ed. (New York: Benziger, 1931), I:1–18; H. Davis, S.J., *Moral and Pastoral Theology*, 7th ed., ed. L. Giddes (London: Sheed and Ward, 1958), I:11–33; H. Noldin, S.J., *Summa Theologiae Moralis*, ed. G. Heinzel (Innsbruck: Rauch, 1956), I:41–66 (Noldin is different from the others in that he begins with a consideration of the human being's final end).

[15] Merkelbach, pp. 104–6, 133–36, 141f., 146–60, 184–200; Vermeersch, pp. 102f., 107–13, 317–22; Sabetti, pp. 28f., 31f., 35–39; Slater, pp. 18–25, 29–33; Davis, pp. 34–44, 56–58; Noldin, pp. 67–69, 72f., 197–202.

Human participation in this highest law is called the natural law, which a person perceives by means of reason, that serves as the proximate, subjective norm of morality.[16] Since the norm of reason is understood as attaining natures by abstraction from matter, *i.e.*, from time and space, there is a strong tendency to emphasize the immutability and universality of the natural law's precepts.[17] Because these laws are absolutes, when they define an act as intrinsically evil, circumstances may at most mitigate the subjective guilt involved, but they in no way change the moral evaluation of the illicit act itself.[18]

Conceptualist moralists are certainly aware that many acts, considered in abstraction, are "indifferent." But most consider that in the concrete all human acts are morally good or evil insofar as a reference to a chosen end is involved. The end qualifies the means, otherwise indifferent, as good or bad. Not that the end justifies the means. No end, however noble, can justify the choice of an intrinsically evil means; one should not choose evil in order that a good result.[19] Moralists also recognize that besides the immutable, universal first principles of the moral law and what immediately derives from them, other principles are dependent upon circumstances in their application.[20] Though justice, for example, prohibits theft, a starving man might steal to preserve his own life and sustain his family; the duty to preserve life precedes the obligation to respect property ownership. There is always need for prudence in applying properly the general rule to concrete circumstances.

The complexity of reality, which can be analyzed in so many different ways, demands careful, sharp distinctions in argument.

---

[16] Merkelbach, 113–18, 128f., 218–33; Vermeersch, 102, 141f., 228–34; Sabetti, 102f.; Slater, 55, 59, 73f.; Davis, 123–32; Noldin, 111–16.

[17] Merkelbach, 109–12, 116f., 133, 135, 157, 221, 223f., 229, 231–33; Vermeersch, 156, 177–79, 228–33; Sabetti, 29, 102; Slater, 22, 33, 65, 73f.; Davis, 123f., 125, 126–28; Noldin, 72f., 113–16. Vermeersch is not so insistent as the others on this and similar points; he is more aware of the role of the subject and the relativity of many norms.

[18] Merkelbach, 133–40, 143–53, 160f.; Vermeersch, 114–16, Sabetti, 29f., 703–6; Slater, 25f.; Davis, 60–63; Noldin, 73–75.

[19] Merkelbach, 149, 153; Vermeersch, 103f., 112f., 116, 389; Sabetti, 28–30, 32f.; Slater, 20f., 22–25, 65; Davis, 39f., 57–63; Noldin, 75–79.

[20] Merkelbach, 231f., 237f., 239f.; Vermeersch, 230f.; Sabetti, p. 29; Slater, p. 21; Davis, 128f.; Noldin, 113f.

This "casuistry" is no empty exercise in academic acuity but a sincere attempt to harmonize the absoluteness of the moral law based on reason with the concrete demands of living. Formal, universal abstractions, if applied rigorously to all circumstances, might result in real harm. Moralists know how to gain flexibility in the application of laws. A higher law can abrogate a lower. It is only a question of determining the higher law and identifying the cases in which it supersedes the lower. In particularly difficult cases moralists invoke the principle of double effect. This principle relies heavily on the intention of the agent, who, for a proportionately grave reason, posits a cause with two effects, of which one is immediately good but the other, not directly willed, unavoidably results in an evil. For example, the surgical removal of a diseased uterus to save a woman's life may also result in a fetus's death but is morally permissible, provided that the former aim alone be directly willed.[21] In this way finality, introduced through the subject of action, plays a role alongside formal causality with its heavily "objectivistic" emphasis.

An appeal to the existential order might also loosen up certain absolutes, as when Maritain simultaneously proclaims every person's absolute right to life but allows that the exercise of this right—exercise referring to the concrete, existential order—can be prevented by the state for serious reasons as it implements the death penalty.[22] Finally, God is recognized as the author of the natural law who can permit and even command certain exceptions to the natural law, as in the sacrifice of Isaac.[23]

Despite these real recognitions of subjective intentionality, existential interruptions, and divine exceptions, the whole tendency

---

[21] Merkelbach, 162–168; Vermeersch, 121–23; Sabetti, 11–15; Slater, 7f.; Davis, 13f.; Noldin, 83–85. For the flexibility gained traditionally in Catholic moral theology by appealing to finality rather than to a formal ethic, see B. Schüller, S.J., "Zur Problematik allgemein verbindlicher ethischer Grundsätze," *Theologie und Philosophie* 45 (1970): 1–23; "Typen ethischer Argumentation in der katholischen Moraltheologie," ibid., 526–50; "Neuere Beiträge zum Thema 'Begründung sittlicher Normen,' " *Theologische Berichte*, IV, ed. F. Furger and J. Pfammatter (Zürich: Benziger, 1974): 109–81.

[22] J. Maritain, *Man and the State* (Chicago: University of Chicago Press, 1951), 101f., 104; *Neuf leçons sur les notions premières de la philosophie morale* (Paris: Tequi, 1950), p. 167.

[23] Vermeersch, 108, 231f.; Slater, p. 21; Davis, 56, 129; Noldin, 115f.; see, to the contrary, Merkelbach, 109–12, 236–39.

of conceptualist moral theology is to stress objective, universal absolutes, especially when dealing with the sixth and ninth commandments where no light matter in impurity is recognized.[24]

It is easy to find the main provisions of the natural law epitomized in the universal prohibitions and commands of the Decalogue. To overcome the difficulty of proper abstraction subsequent to the soul's encasement in a body and the effects of original sin, the supernatural order, which builds on nature, adds a certain stability and clarity to moral demands.[25] However harsh these demands might seem, revelation gives people the power to acknowledge more readily their absoluteness and their own sinfulness, for grounding the law is a God of mercy, forgiveness, and love.[26] Indeed, the authority of Christ's Church, guided by the Spirit, has the obligation of accurately interpreting the moral law and promulgating it as binding on consciences. Moreover, the divine positive law, even though parts of the Old Testament were abrogated by Christ, continues by Christ's command in the New Testament. These laws are likewise intended for all people and are incumbent upon the Church for preaching.[27] The notion of divine positive law flows from the conceptualist understanding of revelation as supernatural propositions. The explicit revelations of God touch morality and are accepted on authority alone since they surpass the human insight that can discover the natural law.

After such a view of the natural law and positive divine law, it is to be expected that the Church's positive law strive for universal application. Christ's Church is for all people, and uniformity of legislation makes religious laxity, based on exceptions, difficult to justify. Lest excessive harshness reign, and in order to ensure the proper application of laws, however, room is usually made for dispensations from positive law and for privileges or favors granted by the lawgiver and communicated to subjects either di-

---

[24] Vermeersch, 390; Sabetti, 288; Slater, 210; Davis, 224; II, 205–13; Noldin, 274; Merkelbach, II (1932), 928–31 (but see 947).

[25] J. Maritain, *Science et sagesse* (Paris: Labergerie, 1935), 82f., 139f., 241, 244–55, 289–92, 298, 305, 332f.

[26] J. Maritain, *Moral Philosophy*, trans. M. Suther et al. (New York: C. Scribner's and Sons, 1964), 83f., 87–90.

[27] Merkelbach, I:277–82; Sabetti, 103f.; Davis, I, 132–34; Noldin, 116–20; Vermeersch, 234f., and Slater, 74f., limit the positive divine law to faith and sacraments; they allow also that Christ gave approval for later ecclesiastical law.

rectly or through the clergy and religious superiors.[28] Furthermore, *epikeia* allows exceptions from the letter of positive law. It involves an equitable interpretation of the law in extraordinary circumstances unforeseen by the legislator who, it might be validly surmised, did not intend to bind subjects in cases that harm the common good or bring great hardships to individuals.[29] A Church based on authority and trusting in the validity of concepts can develop a finely chiseled legal system, as the Code of Canon Law promulgated in 1917 more than adequately testifies. Juridical clarity of thought, carefulness in action, and respect for ecclesiastical authority mark the Catholic conscience.

Moral teachings are not intended as pie-in-the-sky ideals. They have to be lived in the concrete. Because moral doctrine is expressed in abstractions and not even the most meticulous casuistry can foresee every conceivable case of conscience, moral teachings are never divorced from a spirituality that likewise derives from conceptualist principles. Spirituality not only channels the energy to live according to the universal law but also accounts for different individual callings within the universal Christian vocation.

The sharp, metaphysical distinction between universal form, attained by abstraction, and matter, which resists the penetration of the human intellect, influences the conception of Christian spirituality. For the soul, the formal human element, is entrusted with the task of conquering the lower passions and subjugating them to proper moral habits. Thus the universal is to be interiorized. This process of spiritualization is admittedly a struggle. Good habits of action are to be inculcated, and purity of intention is the ideal to be striven after. For not only does matter resist spirit, but also original sin has deprived humankind of its original integrity and causes disorder in its own members. Henceforth a person is obligated to the combat against the world, the flesh, and the devil. To control the sensual instincts by good habits, their mortification

---

[28] *Codex Juris Canonici* (Rome: Vaticana, 1917), canons 15, 63–86, etc.; Merkelbach, 324–27; Vermeersch, 220–26; Sabetti, 97–100, 121–23; Slater, 70–71, 80–82; Noldin, 170–82; Davis, 177–84; L. Bouscaren, S.J., A. Ellis, S.J., F. Korth, S.J., *Canon Law: A Text and Commentary*, 4th. ed. (Milwaukee: Bruce, 1963), 65–74.

[29] Merkelbach, 319f.; Vermeersch, 200f.; Sabetti, 95; Slater, 63f., Noldin, 152f.; Davis, 187–89; Bouscaren-Ellis-Korth, 34.

has to be accomplished by strict ascetical practices.[30] Although pleasure is not condemned, one is often warned against the dangers of seeking it for its own sake.[31]

Original sin not only destroyed the harmony between spirit and body, it also introduced rebellion against God within the soul, a rebellion that can only be overcome by Christ's grace submitting the soul to its supernatural calling, to the obedience of faith in the Church and, ultimately, to the beatific vision. On the pilgrimage through life in the Church one passes along the purgative, illuminative, and unitive ways toward the vision of God. Though conceptualists conceive the final fruitive vision primarily in terms of the intellect's fulfillment, they recognize that the will also enjoys the possession of God. Indeed, on earth the will enjoys a primacy over the intellect insofar as love of God, not knowledge of God, carries a person to his or her beatifying goal. People are called to love God above all for God's own sake and their neighbors for God's sake.

This distinction and primacy of the love of God from and over love of neighbor accords well not only with the natural-supernatural distinction insofar as the neighbor is on the natural plane while supernatural truth and life, necessary for salvation, come from God, but also with the proof for God's existence from motion as employed in conceptualist thought. This proof arrives at the one who fulfills all the potentiality of the individual nature. The individual does not go to God over love for his or her neighbors; rather love for them is subsumed into the dominant, primordial love for God who fulfills the individual's natural love of his

---

[30] A. Tanquerey, S.S., *The Spiritual Life*, trans. H. Branderis (Tournai: Desclee, 1930), 29–39, 42–44, 101, 119, 163–69, 175f., 362–92; A. Royo, O.P., and J. Aumann, O.P., *The Theology of Christian Perfection* (Dubuque: Priory, 1962), 238–342; M. Smith, *Practical Ascetics* (St. Louis: Herder, 1928), 1–18, 27–39, 152f.

[31] Tanquerey, 371f.; Royo-Aumann, 263–71; Vermeersch, 110–12; Slater, 25; Davis, I:40. Sabetti, 31, considers the seeking of pleasure alone to be a venial sin; Merkelbach, I:150f., considers an act done for pleasure alone evil. The difference between the stricter Dominican position and the less rigorous Jesuit one may be due to their respective understandings of grace and freedom. The former sees the good accomplished by God with the human will refraining from posing an obstacle, the latter saw free human will choosing in circumstances foreseen and arranged by God. In the latter case the natural use of a faculty attaining its end always involves pleasure; thus doing God's will and pleasure are compatible.

or her own perfection. Thus a well-ordered love embraces first God, then one's own spiritual good, then the neighbor.[32]

Since the demands of the Christian life in this vale of tears are strenuous, failure always threatens. Fortunately the sacraments strengthen us with grace along our pilgrimage to the goal. A sacramental awareness encourages a strong sense of personal sin insofar as the transgressions of the universal law can be absolved and a real conversion effected in the sacrament of penance. Yet membership in the Body of Christ also emphasizes the social implications of personal sin, and the celestial hierarchy intercedes for the imperfect members of the Church militant.[33] A spirituality centered on the Mass encourages Catholics to support the sacrifices entailed in the Christian life. Difficulty in following the moral norms is to be expected. Christ, after all, felt repugnance before the sacrifice of Calvary, and the Mass daily makes present that sacrifice on the Church's altars. One does not twist God's dictates to one's own needs; rather one adapts oneself to God as found in the Church. There is no question of the Mass's relevancy; it is efficacious *ex opere operato*. Moreover a sacrifice is not supposed to be entertaining, yet sacrifice is an unavoidable part of life, and the Mass illuminates its meaning by letting us share in Christ's redemptive suffering.[34]

Beyond the commandments of God and the Church are the counsels of our Lord for leading a more perfect life. All Christians are obliged to seek a greater perfection. This does not mean accepting all the counsels, which are only means for increasing supernatural charity. Yet one cannot contemn them without sin, and one is expected to attempt to follow at least some of them.[35] Of primary importance are the evangelical counsels of poverty, chastity, and obedience. All are called to live according to the spirit of these counsels, and some are called to the religious life, a state of perfection, where the life of the counsels, combatting the

---

[32] J. de Guibert, S.J., *The Theology of the Spiritual Life*, trans. D. Barrett (New York: Sheed and Ward, 1953), 56–58; Tanquerey, 578f.; Royo-Aumann, 131f.; Smith, 109–13.

[33] Tanquerey, 81–99, 130–38; Royo-Aumann, 211–14, 345–63; Smith, 126–31.

[34] For the significance of our sufferings as redemptive see Tanquerey, 71f., 77f., 239, 465; Royo-Aumann, 271–79.

[35] Tanquerey, 169–71, 233–36; de Guibert, 61–72; Royo-Aumann, 137–54.

spirit of riches, fleshly pleasures, and self-will, is lived more intensely. Not that all religious are holier than lay people—God's graces are given to all—but the state itself commits religious to an exemplary pursuit of perfection and the conditions of the religious life render that pursuit easier.[36] Considered in the abstract—a way of consideration congenial to a conceptualist theology—the religious state of celibacy is better and more blessed than the married, lay state. So it had been defined by the Council of Trent (DS 1810).

Whether the individual is called in the concrete to this or that state can be discovered by attending to God and exercising the charism of discernment or, more often, following the rules for the discernment of spirits. This discernment is employed in testing the origin of any interior motion that urges one to go beyond the universal commands and prohibitions incumbent upon all good Catholics. A sure test of a motion's divine origin is its conformity to the theological and moral doctrines of the Church and the recipient's obedient attitude to ecclesial authority.[37] Not surprisingly, in all this theology and spirituality of supernatural authority, after the theological virtues of faith, hope, and charity, the greatest emphasis is placed on the virtues of humility and obedience; even blind obedience is praised.[38] Supernatural reality is beyond natural insight. The ways of God might not be the ways of humankind, but people are expected to accept God's will. Moreover, given the hostility to the Church in many parts of the world, only a rash warrior disobeys orders in the struggle for survival.

The Fall of Conceptualist Morality

Though the conceptualist theology has been described in the present tense, its heyday passed with Vatican Council II. The

---

[36] Tanquerey, 170f., 183–86; de Guibert, 70f.

[37] De Guibert, 135–44; Finlay, 138f., saw the lack of vowed religious as a sign of lower standards of holiness in non-Catholic, Christian communities.

[38] Tanquerey, 314f., 391, 521–24, 530–45, 641 (humility); 185f., 236, 268, 360, 497–506 (obedience); de Guibert, 66, 71, 139f., 278–82; Royo-Aumann, passim, esp. 455–59, 490–94; Smith, 53–62, 68–72.

council actually forged a compromise between the conceptualist and transcendental theologies. That the compromise came about, however, meant that there were various problems with the conceptualist theology. The proliferation of theological opinions within that theology indicated its incapacity to resolve all problems. Major disputes about grace and freedom, sacramental causality, the meaning of person, and the analysis of faith's act marked irresolvable conundrums. Yet because they were admittedly dealing with supernatural mysteries, theologians were willing to bear a great deal of tension. The supernatural utterly transcended the natural. Nonetheless the clear division between natural and supernatural provided almost insuperable difficulties when the problem of development of dogma had to be faced. Theological tensions had already arisen when the use of natural reason to deduce new doctrines from previously defined dogmas had to be justified.

How might natural reason validly make deductions from supernatural propositions whose truth transcends the grasp of the natural human intellect?[39] But the problem was intensified with the solemn definition of the corporeal assumption of the Blessed Virgin Mary into heaven by Pius XII in 1950 (DS 3903). Scripture mentions nothing about Mary's assumption nor is there any written reference to it before the fifth century. While it is imaginable that the doctrine was preserved in the oral tradition of the Church from the first century, the improbability of its explicit transmission without written record led many theologians to seek other ways of explaining the development of dogma. Not the logical deduction of one proposition from another but the explicitation of a

---

[39] The validity of using natural reason to draw theological conclusions from revealed truths, which utterly surpass the insight of the human mind, leads to a great division among theologians on what can be considered virtually revealed. See A. Gardeil, O.P., *Le Donné révélé et la théologie* (Paris: Lecoffre, 1910), 163–86, 227–51; "Introduction à théologie," *Revue des sciences philosophiques et théologiques* 13 (194): 576–90; F. Marin-Sola, O.P., *Evolution homogène du Dogme catholique* (Fribourg: St. Paul, 1924), 52–60, 134–340, 423–54; R. Garrigou-Lagrange, *Reality*, tr. P. Cummins (St. Louis: Herder, 1950), 66–68; *The One God*, tr. B. Rose (St. Louis: Herder, 1946), 49–56, 67–71, 85; S. Cartechini, S.J., *Dall'Opinione al Domma* (Rome: Civiltà Cattolica, 1953), 108–24; G. Van Noort, *Christ's Church*, tr. and rev. J. Castelot and W. Murphy (Westminster: Newman, 1961), 111f.; Y. Congar, *A History of Theology*, tr. and ed., H. Guthrie (Garden City: Doubleday, 1968), 242–60.

more vague "personal" experience seemed to serve better as a model of dogmatic development.[40]

The Vatican II constitution *Dei Verbum* managed to maintain a balance between a propositional and a personalist notion of revelation. Clearly the council Fathers were not overthrowing the propositional faith that they had learned in the seminaries and that undergirded their apostolic authority. Nonetheless, it was not immediately apparent how the two understandings of revelation could be reconciled, and the novelty was exploited by younger theologians who pushed into the limelight after the council. Analogously, the constitutions on the Church, *Lumen Gentium*, and on the Church in the modern world, *Gaudium et Spes*, went beyond the conceptualist understanding of the Church as an institution founded by Christ to proclaim his message and administer the sacraments. The Church was seen also more organically and dynamically as the Body of Christ, a center of supernatural life, and as the universal sacrament of salvation, the manifestation of that interior life to the world. Thus the interior life of grace received a pre-eminence, and it was easy to interpret the external institutional structure as secondary to the interior life. Moreover, once the Church was understood as the pilgrim people of God, its insufficiencies were more openly recognized. With the traditional theoretical underpinning of Church authority somewhat relativized, it took only *Humanae Vitae* to reveal the extent of the crisis facing the Church in its modern context.

After the invention of the birth control pill, which regulates the fertility cycle without being so intrusive as earlier methods of birth control, some moralists asked if the Church's prohibition against artificial birth control, expressed so clearly in Pius XI's encyclical *Casti Connubii* (1930), applied to the pill. Paul VI took the matter under advisement and established a committee to study the issue and report back to him. The Vatican Council, though presenting a more personalist understanding of marriage, deliber-

---

[40] B. Altaner, "Zur Frage der Definibilität der Assumptio B.V.M.," *Theologische Revue* 44 (1948): 129–40; M. Schmaus, *Katholische Dogmatik*, V (Munich: Huebner, 1955), 232–36. For new attempts at justifying the dogma, see H. Rondet, S.J., "La Definibilité de l'Assumption," *Etudes Mariales* 6 (1949): 59–95; J. Filograssi, S.J., "Tradizione Divino-Apostolica e Magistero della Chiesa," *Lo Sviluppo del Dogma* (Rome: Gregoriana, 1953), 450–53, 457–89.

ately left the decision on birth control to the pope. Some theologians interpreted the establishment of a committee as a sign that the Church's doctrine was not clear on the issue, and on the principle that a dubious law does not bind, some confessors began to permit their penitents to use the pill. When the committee report was finally submitted to the pope, the majority declared themselves in favor of opening the way to the legitimate use of the pill. But after further deliberation and prayer, Paul VI sided with the minority and reiterated that the use of the pill and all forms of artificial birth control are contrary to the natural moral law. He saw clearly that if the connection between sexual intercourse and procreation were broken, the way would be open to the destruction of traditional Catholic sexual morality.

Unfortunately, the time of apparent indecision had permitted people to develop the habit of using the pill, encouraged the notion that moral laws could be changed, and let theologians become hardened in opinions contrary to traditional morality. So a wail of protest from theologians, clergy, religious, and articulate laity alike arose in opposition to *Humanae Vitae*.[41] The old morality was condemned as abstract, showing no concern for concrete issues and problems, as biological, ignoring the realm of love and personal encounter, and as spiritualistic, overlooking the role of the body in the expression of love.[42] The authority of the Church in moral matters was also questioned. Theologians pointed out that the magisterium could and did err in noninfallible pronouncements.[43] Others were more radical in their criticism. Even

---

[41] See A. Valsecchi, *Controversy*, trans. D. White (Washington: Corpus, 1968), 163–204; M. Zalba, S.J., "Num Concilium Vaticanum II hierachiam finium matrimonii ignoraverit, immo et transmutaverit," *Periodica* 68 (1979) 613–35; M. Moore, *Death of a Dogma* (Chicago: Community and Family Study Center, 1973), 10–20, 56–74; G. Wills, *Bare Ruined Choirs* (Garden City: Doubleday, 1972), 159–87.

[42] See, for example, J. Pleasants, "A Biologist Asks Some Questions" in *The Catholic Case for Contraception*, ed. D. Callahan (London: Collier-Macmillan, 1969), 30–40; S. Callahan, "Procreation and Control," ibid., 41–64; "Theologians's Statement," ibid., 67–70; M. Novak, "Frequent, Even Daily, Communion," ibid., 92–102; M. and J. Ryan, "Have You Thought It Out All the Way?" ibid., 103–27; C. Curran, *Christian Morality Today* (Notre Dame: Fides, 1966), 79–85.

[43] B. Schüller, S.J., "Bemerkungen zur authentischen Verkündigung des kirchlichen Lehramts," *Theologie und Philosophie* 42 (1967): 534–51; K. Rahner,

before the encyclical, ecclesiastical office had been condemned as authoritarian, little open to dialogue with the modern world, as clericalist, employing clerics to decide sexual and marital questions of which they had little or no experience, and as juristic, more concerned with conformity than with encouraging diversity in the gifts of the Spirit. Some rejected the Church as hindering humankind's approach to God and falsely substituting human institutions and traditions for an encounter with the living God.[44]

Transcendental Morality

The wide wave of protest that washed over the Church in the wake of *Humanae Vitae* did not mark just a blind opposition to ecclesial authority. It had been prepared and supported by a changing view of Thomistic theology and philosophy. Though the better theologians strove to maintain a balance between the existential judgment and the finite intelligibility of concepts, their disciples often stressed the former to the neglect of the latter. We first present the new emphases of transcendental morality before indicating the obvious excesses that called forth *Veritatis Splendor*.

If transcendental theology's dynamic approach to reality tends to overcome the various conceptual distinctions worked out by conceptualist thinkers, the realm of moral theology will not remain untouched by its worldview. Moral theology becomes integrated into dogmatics. Since faith involves more than the intellectual affirmation of propositions, but the commitment of the entire human being to God's self-revelation, moral conduct is intimately involved in faith's very acceptance and interpretation. For God's self-giving in grace becomes the principle of human salvific action, thereby making "moral theology in its material thematic an interior element of dogmatic theology." And the grace of faith, however unthematic, is offered to all.[45] The appli-

---

S.J., "Zur Enzyklika 'Humanae Vitae,'" *Schriften zur Theologie* IX:276–301; G. Baum, "The Right to Dissent," *Catholic Case*, 71–76.

[44] C. Davis, *A Question of Conscience* (New York: Harper and Row, 1967); J. Kavanaugh, *A Modern Priest Looks at His Outdated Church* (New York: Trident, 1967); W. Dubay, *The Human Church* (Garden City: Doubleday, 1966).

[45] K. Rahner, "Dogmatik, *Sacramentum Mundi,* ed. K. Rahner and A. Darlap (Freiburg: Herder, 1967–69) I:917–23; "Glaubenszugang," ibid., II:414–18; see

cation of transcendental theology to moral doctrine has far-reaching consequences.

First, the clear distinction between love of God and love of neighbor in conceptualist theology is to be surpassed. The same dynamic movement of knowing and loving joins the categorical object to the transcendental, humanity to God. J. Mouroux accentuates the primacy of supernatural love of God, but it no longer stands alongside and above love of neighbor. "To spend oneself for one's brother is to rejoin and serve one's God. . . . there is but one love which never separates men from Him in whom they are called, nor Christ from those He bears within Himself."[46] If the two loves are joined into one, it does not matter essentially whether one starts with God or with humanity. K. Rahner so clearly affirms the formal identity of God and love of neighbor that "the categorical-explicit love of neighbor is the primary act of love of God."[47] For any particular act of love of neighbor is carried by the unthematic, transcendental horizon that is the God of grace.

That somewhat startling conclusion results from both the blurring of the natural-supernatural distinction in a world called to a single destiny and the fundamental dynamism of the spirit that unites intellect and will in affirming the finite reality of this world while transcending it. As finite and infinite are joined in the spirit's basic affirmation, as the spirit comes thereby to spiritual self-possession, so a person knows God only in and through the finite,

---

also E. Schillebeeckx, O.P., "What Is Theology?" in *Revelation and Theology*, tr. N. Smith, I (New York: Sheed and Ward, 1967) 93f., 152–54; and "Scholasticism and Theology," ibid., 247–52, 257f. Though Schillebeeckx is not a transcendental Thomist in the strict sense, he has many points in common with them.

[46] Mouroux, *The Meaning of Man*, tr. A. Downes (Garden City: Doubleday, 1961) 227–30; see also Mouroux, *Le Mystère du Temps* (Paris: Aubier, 1962), 147–50.

[47] K. Rahner, S.J., "Über die Einheit von Nächsten- und Gottesliebe," *Schriften*, VI:284–96, esp. 295; "Heilsauftrag der Kirche und Humanisation der Welt," *Schriften*, X:556–62; B. Schüller, S.J., *Gesetz und Freiheit* (Düsseldorf: Patmos, 1966), 14, 32, 110; "La théologie morale peut-elle se passer du droit naturel?" *Nouvelle Revue Théologique* 88 (1966): 460. For a more detailed study of Schüller's position see McDermott, "Moral Systems," 11–23. J. Fuchs, S.J., *Personal Responsibility and Christian Morality*, trans. W. Cleves et al. (Washington: Georgetown, 1983), 28–31; P. Teilhard de Chardin, S.J., *Le Milieu Divin*, trans. B. Wall et al. (London: Collins, 1964), 101.

the personalized environment constituted by his or her neighbors; since this basic knowledge involves love, love of God cannot be attained without love of neighbor.

Second, with the relativization of the concept and the change of emphasis from formal to final causality, the universal validity of many moral laws, especially in sexual matters, is questioned. Arguing that the intellect's synthetic activity, *synderesis*, joins the value-content (*Wertgehalt*) and significance (*Bedeutsamkeit*) to form a concrete moral demand (*Sollensatz*), B. Schüller concludes, "God's will is mediated to us through the specific situation, which we are in our given historical circumstances."[48] As the judgment joins categorical and transcendental in one affirmation of intelligibility, so, in the transition from metaphysics to morality, which flows from the unity of intellect and will, the subject's moral direction to the Good involves a concrete insight into categorical circumstances.

Henceforth the concrete milieu provides the locus of moral choice and the intuition into the concrete situation provides the starting point for moral reflection: "There is only one source of ethical norms—namely, the historical reality of the value of the inviolable human person with all its bodily and social implications. That is why we cannot attribute validity to abstract norms as such."[49] The conclusion to such a premise follows easily: "God's law is in its material content man himself, as he is entrusted to himself by God, not only in his belonging to a public community [with its universal laws] but also in other many-faceted, human relations, and not least in his irreplaceable individuality. God's law therefore also demands from man that he be himself."[50]

Insofar as the human being is a dynamically open being on the way to fulfillment, moral science, like every other science, is conceived now not as a system of abstract universals nor as "a ready-made achievement," but as "an ongoing process" in which

---

[48] Schüller, *Gesetz*, 38.

[49] E. Schillebeeckx, O.P., *God the Future of Man*, trans. N. Smith (New York: Sheed & Ward, 1968), 148–52; Schüller, "La théologie morale," 464, 471; *Gesetz*, 14, 38, 66f.; J. Glazer, S.J., "Transitions between Grace and Sin: Fresh Perspectives," *Theological Studies* 29 (1968): 260–74.

[50] Schüller, *Gesetz*, 66f.

"at the moment of existential crisis . . . we have to decide for ourselves what we by our own choices and decisions are to make of ourselves."[51]

The turn to the subject effected in epistemology and metaphysics results, in moral theology, in the primacy of the fundamental option for the determination of moral goodness or evil. The moral qualification of any act depends not so much upon the finite objects of the individual choices as upon the general moral stance and the basic orientation of the free subject toward God or selfishness in his life. "God's commandments are moral demands only because they demand of man not this or that, but himself in the substance of his being; they are only expansions and organic parts [*Ausgliederungen*] of the one divine law: Thou shalt love God with thy whole heart."[52]

The primacy accorded to charity, the love of God and neighbor, in a world called to a single supernatural destiny, not only replaces formal abstractions of natures as the basis of the natural law but also abrogates the need and possibility of a divine positive law. For love is the supreme command applying equally to all, and before its demands, which are known by reason, all moral action has to be justified. There is no specifically Christian content in morality. "The moral demand as a whole has its ground in God's creative act, not in His redemptive act in Jesus Christ." So

---

[51] B. Lonergan, "Dimensions of Meaning," *Collection*, ed. F. Crowe (New York: Herder and Herder, 1967), 262, 264. In the reference within note 49, Schillebeeckx made the distinction between the concrete moral claim and the later abstract, scientific universalization and defense of it. Though "science" is understood differently in both cases, there is underlying agreement. Schillebeeckx saw moral science as incapable of justifying fully any moral choice, but Lonergan and others just directed moral science to the concrete and its conditions of possibility.

[52] Schüller, *Gesetz*, 89, 32–41, 61f., 75, 87–97, 196, 108f, 114f., 131, 140–42; "Das irrige Gewissen," *Theologische Akademie* II, ed. K. Rahner and O. Semmelroth (Frankfurt: Knecht, 1965), 10, 12–16; "Bedenken gegen die ethischen Kategorien des Rates und des überschüssigen guten Werkes," *Testimonium Veritati* (Festschrift Kempt), ed. H. Wolter (Frankfurt: Knecht, 1971), 204; J. Fuchs, S.J., *Christian Ethics in a Secular Arena* (Washington: Georgetown, 1984), 34–41; C. Curran, *A New Look at Christian Morality* (London: Sheed & Ward, 1969), 73–115 (esp. 110–12), 235–45; J. Fuchs, S.J., *Human Values and Christian Morality*, trans. M. Heelan (Dublin: Gill and Macmillan, 1970), 92–111; B. Lonergan, "*Existenz* and *Aggiornamento*," *Collection*, 242; *The Philosophy of God and Theology* (London: Darton, Longman, & Todd), 1973), 43.

Schüller holds that both the *lex Christi* and the *lex naturae* "have an identical material content" while the former presupposes the latter and deepens it.⁵³

Attempting to delineate more clearly the relation of the *Christianum* to the *Humanum,* J. Fuchs distinguishes the categorical content of morality from the transcendental attitude, or intentionality. The former remains in principle open to everyone's insight and argument in establishing concrete norms, and the motivating power of the latter increases through the Christians' explicit awareness of the Absolute as Father and the significance of Christ's Cross. While the *Humanum* is dynamically open to the *Christianum,* the categorical component of Christian morality consists in the "morality of genuine being human." Yet, in view of God's universal salvific will and the fact that the profound moral decision of the free subject "tends to escape thematic reflection," Fuchs assumes that God is also present unthematically to the intentionality of the non-Christian humanist.⁵⁴

With the turn to the subject and the interiorization of grace and in view of the decreasing role of ecclesiastical authority, tremendous emphasis is laid on the importance of having individuals form their own consciences and of their obligation to follow it. Recognizing the dialectical relation between the community with its laws, to which the individual is bound, and the internal law of conscience, in which God addresses him or her, Schüller writes, "Every moral obligation is grounded only in the *lex interna,* in which man is brought before God, his Creator, without human mediation [*ohne Vermittlung durch eine menschliche Instanz*]." Seeing then conscience as "fundamentally the call to a decision for salvation," he concludes, "insofar as it does that, conscience is correct in every case, is infallibly true, reveals to man the truth of his existence, and constitutes him as a moral being." Consequently

---

⁵³ B. Schüller, S.J., "Christliche Ethik-autonome Ethik?" in *Christliches Gesellschaftsdenken in Umbruch,* ed. S. Szyczik (Regensburg: Pustet, 1977), 286; "La théologie morale," 472f.; "Zur Diskussion über das Proprium einer christlichen Ethik," *Theologie und Philosophie* 51 (1976): 330f., 339–43; J. Fuchs, S.J., "Is There a Christian Morality?" in *Moral Theology No. 2: The Distinctiveness of Christian Ethics,* ed. C. Curran and R. McCormick (New York: Paulist, 1980), 3–18; D. Tettamanzi, "Is There a Christian Ethic?" ibid., 20–57; C. Curran, "Is There a Catholic and/or Christian Ethic?" ibid., 60–85.

⁵⁴ Fuchs, "Is There," 8, 7, 18.

he defends the obligations of following even an erroneous conscience and of respecting such a conscience in others.[55]

With the recognition of the uniqueness of so many moral circumstances, the norm for the formation of one's conscience changes from the formal qualification of the act to the consequences resulting from the choice made. "Ontic," or "premoral," evil can even be chosen directly if the overall, resultant good outweighs the evil involved.[56] To a certain degree the conceptual theology leaves the door open to such a change of perspective in holding the principle of double effect. For insofar as the intention of the agent for a good purpose justifies the letting occur of what would otherwise be considered a morally evil act but is, even if foreseen, not directly willed, certain actions, otherwise considered evil in themselves, are permitted—that is, relativized in view of the proportionately greater good directly willed.[57] Thus final causality, or intentionality, takes a primacy over formal causality in the evaluation of moral actions.

The conceptualist morality with its stress on abstract, formal absolutes restricts the application of the principle of double effect

---

[55] Schüller, "Das irrige Gewissen," 13, 15, 17f.; "Religionsfreiheit und Toleranz," *Theologische Akademie*, II:99f.; "Direkte Tötung—indirekte Tötung," *Theologie und Philosophie* 47 (1972): 342–45; "Bedenken," 206; J. Glazer, S.J., "Authority, Connatural Knowledge and the Spontaneous Judgment of the Faithful," *Theological Studies* 29 (1963): 742–51; Fuchs, *Christian Ethics*, 71–76; *Personal Responsibility*, 44–48, 216–27; C. Curran, *A New Look*, 127–37, 223–26.

[56] Schüller, "Direkte Tötung," 342f., 345–47, 349, 353; "Typen ethischer Argumentation in der katholischen Moraltheologie," *Theologie und Philosophie* 45 (1970): 528–30, 532–37; "Die Personwürde des Menschen als Beweisgrund in der normativen Ethik," *Theologie und Philosophie* 52 (1978): 551–54; *Die Begründung sittlicher Urteile*, 2nd ed. (Düsseldorf: Patmos, 1980), 73–78, 150, 173; Fuchs, *Christian Ethics*, 71–86; L. Janssens, "Ontic Evil and Moral Evil," in *Readings in Moral Theology No. 1: Moral Norms and Catholic Tradition*, ed. C. Curran and R. McCormick (New York: Paulist, 1979), 40–93; R. McCormick, S.J., *Ambiguity in Moral Choice* (Milwaukee: Marquette, 1973), 53–106; M. Nolan, "The Principle of Totality in Moral Theology" in *Absolutes in Moral Theology?* ed. C. Curran (Washington: Corpus, 1968), 232–48; G. Milhaven, S.J., "Towards an Epistemology of Ethics," *Theological Studies* 27 (1966): 228–41.

[57] P. Knauer, S.J., "The Hermeneutical Function of the Principle of Double Effect," in *Readings*, 1–39. Although Knauer cannot rightly be considered a transcendental Thomist (see his *Der Glaube Kommt von Hören*, 6th ed. (Cologne: Verl. Styria, 1978), his position on morality fits in well with their argument and has been adopted by many of them.

to a few, difficult cases where the need for flexibility is obvious, but as the transcendental theology accentuates the uniqueness of individual decisions, the principle of double effect soon finds itself applied to every finite act, which stands in relation to other acts as well as to the ultimate horizon of intelligibility and love affirmed, at least implicitly, in every choice. So not a single act in isolation, but the whole existential context of every act has to be judged. Then, insofar as every choice of a value involves the denial of another value, "every human act brings evil effects with it," and the "moral good" can be redefined as "the best possible realization of any particular value envisaged in its entirety."[58]

L. Janssens, by defining "ontic evil" as "a lack of perfection which impedes the fulfillment of a human subject" or "a deficiency which frustrates our inclinations," can look on human limitation as a natural cause of suffering: though limitation itself is not an evil, "each concrete act implicates ontic evil because we are temporal and spatial, live together with others in the same material world, are involved and act in a common sinful situation." In short, "ontic evil is always present in our concrete activity." Nonetheless, people are called upon not only not to will ontic evil for itself but also to reduce it as much as possible. Humankind's very protest against moral evil reveals that we are living from a future utopia of ideal norms.[59] Hence where the conceptualist restrains the principle of double effect from applying to the direct willing of an evil means to attain a good end, the proportionalist argues that a mere physical evil does not necessarily determine a morally evil will. Instead the physical evil has to be evaluated in the entire existential context of any decision. As long as a commensurate proportion between the end ultimately willed and the limited means, however "physically evil," is maintained,

---

[58] Knauer, "Hermeneutical Function," 16, 17; see also Schüller, "Typen," 528–530, 532f.; "Zur Problematik allgemein verbindlicher ethischer Grundsätze," *Theologie und Philosophie* 45 (1970): 7–9.

[59] Janssens, 67, 69, 66, 60, 69, 79, 84–87. Some tension exists in Janssens's position insofar as he seems to presuppose a universal, necessary, absolute, disinterested reason to which the will should be ordered (71f.). For not only does the transcendental position affirm a basic unity of intellect and will but also Janssens's own understanding of an essentially dynamic human nature oriented to an end would seem to subordinate all intellectual activity to the good of self-realization (see 67, 69, 81f., 85).

the "physical evil" can be accepted and willed as a mere means.[60] Within such a teleological perspective the conceptualist distinction between licitly permitting an evil and immorally willing a bad (nonmoral) means to a good end are barely distinguishable.[61]

In conceptualist morality prudence entails a special insight into particular cases in order that the proper principle be applied to them. Connatural moral knowledge results from the impregnation of the sensible faculties by the habits enjoined by the moral principles. Insofar as in transcendental thought the direct point of reference in morality transcends concepts, connaturality concerns the straight appetite mediating directly between the God of grace and the concrete case to be decided, and prudence involves taking all the circumstances into account. The virtues, as traditionally understood, are habitual inclinations to good acts, but for transcendental thought authentic morality is located in the existential profundity of freedom. At most, free acts can use abstract norms as guides, but only insofar as they are truly appropriated by the subject and judged applicable or not in actual circumstances.[62]

When Janssens identifies the objective norm of morality with a

[60] Knauer, 18–20; Janssens, 71f., 78f.; Schüller, "Direkte Tötung," 348; "Typen," 530–33; "Die Personwürde," 551–54.

[61] B. Schüller, S.J., "The Double Effect in Catholic Thought: A Re-evaluation" in *Doing Evil to Achieve Good*, ed. R. McCormick and P. Ramsey (Chicago: Loyola University, 1978), 173–76, 182–92. Although R. McCormick, S.J., *Ambiguity in Moral Choice* (Milwaukee: Marquette University Press, 1973), 53–65, 67, sympathetically, but critically, presented Schüller's argument, in his later "Commentary on the Commentaries" in *Doing Evil*, 254–65, he took back his criticisms and agreed almost totally with Schüller.

[62] Schüller, *Gesetz*, 83–110; "Todsünde—Sünde zum Tode?" *Theologie und Philosophie* 42 (1967): 335–40; Fuchs, *Personal Responsibility*, 130f., 143–46, 222–27. In "Zu den Schwierigkeiten, die Tugend zu rehabilitieren," *Theologie und Philosophie* 58 (1983): 535–55, Schüller unfortunately avoids the real problem of "rehabilitating virtue": how does one find a value for habit (sometimes too easily dismissed as "bourgeois") when the whole movement of modern philosophy since Kant has been to locate freedom in the interiority of the subject who makes particular free decisions? (See esp. 551–53.) If every free act resists determination, habit seems only to inhibit real freedom and authentic morality. Clearly a rethinking of the relation of freedom to habit is needed. The tendency of transcendental Thomists to consider freedom primarily, if not exclusively, as Augustinian, or liberated, freedom (see Rahner, *Grundkurs*, 46–50, 61, 101–03, 119, 124f., 134f., 174f.), leads to many problems. See J. McDermott, S.J., "Metaphysical Conundrums at the Root of Moral Disagreement," *Gregorianum* 71 (1990): 713–26.

future utopia, he probably stands under the influence of Teilhard de Chardin and the utopian optimism of the 60s. In such a context it is easy to reinterpret God's transcendence as the transcendence of the eschatological future to which the world is "horizontally" oriented ("God, the future of man") instead of the more traditional vertical, eternally present, divine transcendence. This utopian juncture of God and humanity at the end of history, the eschatological kingdom of God in which God is to establish justice, peace, and equality, clearly borrows much from neo-Marxist thought, indeed, from Kant's vision of the kingdom of heaven in which happiness is proportionate to morality. In view of this ideal future, Janssens and Schillebeeckx see moral action arising not so much out of acquired habits and connatural knowledge as from a "contrast-experience." Even though utopia, the "humanly desirable," cannot be fully articulated, some awareness of it is implicitly given in a felt protest against current evil in the world. "The moral imperative is first discovered in its immediate, concrete, *inner* meaning, before it can be made the object of a science and then reduced to a generally valid principle."[63] Thus the universals of the conceptualist theology are relativized in terms of both the present, existential conditions of decision and the indefinite future ideal of action.

Within this "new morality" the role of the ecclesiastical hierarchy is redefined. In the face of present novelty and the in-breaking future, from which humankind principally receives meaning, the hierarchy should no longer limit itself to repeating traditional formulas. In common with all other Christians, it receives the Holy Spirit and has to be open to the call of the Spirit inside and outside the Church. The Church as a whole is understood as engaged in dialogue—that is, listening to the world and learning from the world "in which she recognizes the familiar voice of God." For God's grace summons all people to realize the kingdom, whether they are explicitly conscious of this call to "utopia" or not. Without doubt not all morality can be reduced to or deduced from abstract, universal norms. Room has to be left for pluralism within and outside the Church. Furthermore, instead

---

[63] Schillebeeckx, *God the Future*, 153–55, 190–92; Janssens, 85–87; Teilhard de Chardin, *The Divine Milieu*, esp. 56–62.

of merely promulgating juridically formulated prohibitions, the hierarchy is called upon, while acknowledging its limitations, to act prophetically, to encourage free initiative and responsibility, and to criticize by word and example the backslidings of a worldly society too ready to absolutize a finite vision and too dilatory in striving for the world's culminating union with God, its absolute future.[64]

The universal view of God's salvific plan involves the Church and the Christian in new moral obligations. God's attraction of all creation, unified in spirit and matter, toward himself in Christ leads to the interpretation of the world as somehow sacral, "the history of God" or "the divine milieu."[65] But this sacralization of the world can be inverted. Insofar as nature is distinguishable from the supernatural and the world possesses its proper autonomy, the secularization of the world can be encouraged. Hence Christians should dedicate themselves to the world's development, ready to criticize any limitation of the world to the merely human or manipulatable, prepared to develop the human in fraternal solidarity and love within the single evolutionary dynamism heading, consciously or not, to the meeting with God at the end of history. "Grace perfects the true worldliness of the world."[66]

---

[64] Schillebeeckx, *God the Future*, 153, 125–28, 143–64, 196f., 201–03; D. Maguire, "Morality and Magisterium" in *Readings in Moral Theology No. 3: The Magisterium and Morality*, ed. C. Curran and R. McCormick (New York: Paulist, 1982), 34–66; C. Butler, O.S.B., "Authority and the Christian Conscience," ibid., 171–87; J. Boyle, "The Natural Law and the Magisterium," ibid., 442–53; Curran, *A New Look*, 226–31; J. Fuchs, *Personal Responsibility*, 206–8; K. Rahner, S.J., "Über die Frage einer formalen Existenzethik," *Schriften*, II (Einsiedeln: Benziger, 1955), 236–42, 244–46; "Theologische Reflexionen zur Säkularisation," *Schriften*, VIII: 637–66; "Heilsauftrag der Kirche und Humanisierung der Welt," *Schriften* X, 556–67; "Die Frage nach der Zukunft," *Schriften*, IX: 536–40; R. Faricy, S.J., *All Things in Christ* (London: Collins, 1981), 55–62; J. Metz, *Theology of the World* (New York: Seabury, 1969), 93–97, 115–24.

[65] Teilhard de Chardin, *Le Milieu Divin*, esp. 56–62, 105–28; K. Rahner, S.J., "Jesus Christus," *Lexikon für Theologie und Kirche* V (Freiburg: Herder, 1960): 957f.

[66] Metz, *Theology of the World*, 49, esp. 19f., 25–34, 41–55, 63–77, 141–55; Rahner, "Theologische Reflexionen," 637–55; R. Faricy, S.J., *Building God's World* (Denville: Dimension, 1976), 126–40; *All Things*, 32–43, 555–58; in *La Secularisation: fin ou chance du Chrétianisme*, ed. C. Troisfontaines (Gembloux: Duclot, 1970) see the articles by F. Crespi, H. Schlette, C. Pinto de Oliveira, and J. Gonzales-Ruiz; Schillebeeckx, *God the Future*, 68, 76–79, 132f., 157–64, 189–99; A. Auer, *Christsein in Beruf* (Düsseldorf: Patmos, 1966), 213–29, 238–

Both interpretations, sacralization or secularization of the world, are possible since the continuity of nature and grace in transcendental theology allows the interpreter to start at either end. Starting with supernatural completion, one can interpret every preliminary state as occurring under the influence of grace; starting with the foundational nature, one can interpret the culmination of the process as completion of the natural striving. In either case a unity of interpretation is attained and the consequences are the same. As J. B. Metz writes, " 'To Christianize the world' means fundamentally 'to secularize it.' " The world as a whole serves as the field in which God brings the single salvific plan to fulfillment, and the Church loses its unique role as a means of grace vis-à-vis a sinful world. The Church is still recognized as a sacrament of salvation and unity for the world, but, given a new understanding of sacrament, *sacramentum mundi*, it is only the intensification or thematic acceptance of the grace everywhere operative. Within the process of progress, the Church, as humanity's *avant-garde* or evolution's *phylum* in which eschatological grace has come to its thematic manifestation, shows the way as the humble servant of humankind's forward striving toward greater freedom by criticizing false absolutes and the oppression of freedom as well as by offering the motivating vision to overcome the anxieties of the merely human. " 'Church' is not a reality besides or over this societal reality; rather it is an institution *within* it, criticizing it, having a critical liberating task in regard to it." Thereby, in referring to humankind's superhuman goal, the Church contributes to the construction of a new world, a cooperation with God's creation, the realization of the world's potentialities. As the postconciliar Schillebeeckx writes: "The message which Christianity brings to the world is this—humanity is possible! . . . humanity is possible through the resources of man himself, but that means through the resources of redeemed man with his 'new heart.' "[67]

50, 260f., 277–93, manages to combine the relative autonomy of the human with a Teilhardian vision of the sacral permeating all of reality.

[67] Metz, *Theology of the World*, 49f., 115–24, 134–36; Schillebeeckx, *God the Future*, 193, 109, 112, 129–38, 157, 191; Teilhard de Chardin, *The Phenomenon of Man*, tr. B. Wall (New York: Harper, 1959), 291–98; E. Binns, "The Very Quick of the Life of the Church Today," *The Teilhard Review* 6 (1971–72): 86, 88–91; Faricy, *Building*, 150–71; see also H. Mühlen, *Entsakralisierung* (Paderborn: Schöningh, 1971), 91f., 119–24, 149–76.

Just as the Church is no longer seen as a supernatural institution planted in a foreign soil from on high, neither is the Christian encouraged to flee the world unless this abandonment is understood as a flight beyond the present state of the world toward the eschatological future or insofar as it creates indifference and allows one to gain the distance necessary for a more intelligent and dedicated commitment to the world: "Christianity does not imply any neglect of the secular task, but, on the contrary, gives Christians a more intensive stimulus to carry it out. Their eschatological expectation urges Christians to work for a better world for all people." R. Faricy adds: "God is served and adored actively through creatures, in and through earthly activity itself . . . heaven is attainable only through the completion of the world."[68]

Clearly the principal point of reference for the believer is no longer a Church endowed with a special supernatural knowledge that transcends human insight and enables its guardians, the hierarchy, to judge the world. Instead, believers face the world without any special thematic knowledge, and the bishops of the Church are on the same level before God's unthematic revelation. The implications of such a shift of perspective are immense. One more readily understands how the relation of service and humility has changed in the wake of Vatican II. Before the council, Catholics manifested humble obedience to the hierarchy, to whom salvific knowledge had been entrusted, and criticized the world for not having converted to the Church; after the council, Catholics serve humbly the world and criticize the hierarchy for not adapting to the needs of the time. That in itself could prove perilous for any central religious authority, but in issuing *Veritatis Splendor* the pope was not concerned merely with defending the authority of the Petrine and episcopal offices but primarily with preventing deformation of Catholic morality. Though more profound theologians in the school of transcendental Thomism managed to hold the balance between essential and existential orders, concept and judgment, nature and grace, the system itself can easily lead to exaggerations. That may be indicated in three areas that are ad-

---

[68] Schillebeeckx, *God the Future*, 102; Faricy, *All Things*, 56–58; Rahner, "Die ignatianische Mystik," 342–48; Fuchs, *Human Values*, 178–85, 200–203; Teilhard de Chardin, *Le Milieu Divin*, 95–104; Metz, *Theology of the World*, 93–97.

dressed in the encyclical: the role of the magisterium, the fundamental option, and the validity of universal moral norms.

Magisterium

Claiming to apply consistently what he had learned from K. Rahner and other theologians and taking the doctrine of *Humanae Vitae* as a clear illustration of his argument, H. Küng rejected papal infallibility. But the pope had not claimed to be defining *ex cathedra* the immorality of artificial birth control. Küng was obviously exaggerating papal claims in order to appeal to a circle of Catholics dissenting on *Humanae Vitae*. The foundation of his denial was the proposition that no human statement can attain definitive truth. K. Rahner strongly attacked Küng's position by pointing out that it would lead as well to the rejection of an ecumenical council's infallibility and of the definitiveness of Scripture.[69] But Küng broached the issue. More recently the role of the magisterium, especially in moral matters, is put into question in more subtle ways.

Though A. Dulles has always distanced himself from transcendental Thomism on account of its relativization of historical meaning in favor of the transcendental experience, he too has stressed the Church from below. He conceives the hierarchy primarily as servants of God's word. Within such a perspective theologians might likewise be considered a "magisterium" since they too engage in teaching God's word to the people and so "should have a voice in doctrinal decisions."[70] Where Dulles's proposal for including theologians in the decision process about dogma consists in relatively moderate and vague suggestions, some broaden the notion of "magisterium" further. Arguing for the laity's "authority in the expression of faith," C. Duquoc writes:

---

[69] H. Küng, *Infallible? An Inquiry* (London: Collins, 1971); K. Rahner, "Kritik an Hans Küng," *Stimmen der Zeit* 186 (1970): 363; "Replik auf Hans Küng," ibid. 187 (1971): 157f.

[70] A. Dulles, S.J., *The Resilient Church* (Garden City: Doubleday, 1977), 104–6; see F. Sullivan, S.J., *Magisterium* (New York: Paulist, 1984), 174–218, esp. 203f., to the contrary, even though he shares many presuppositions of the "personalist position."

All have received the Spirit, as the Pentecost story shows, and this reception by all creates the distinctive character of the Church. True, it does not destroy office, but the office has no status except in relation to this primary gift. The authority of believers is thus linked with baptism as the sacrament which confers the Spirit and incorporates into the Church. It follows that what has to be worked out is the role of the hierarchy, not the other way around. There is one mediator, Christ who gives the Spirit. The hierarchy is not a mediator in the sense of determining the gift of the Spirit.[71]

H. Fries likewise argues for "a discovery of truth from below." "The sense of the faith of the faithful enjoys a function of discovering and bearing witness to the truth. In no way does it rely solely on derivation from another source." The ecclesiastical *magisterium*'s role is accordingly described as serving communication, keeping dialogue open, and acting as an information communication center. "The normal and due element in the Church must be the collective discovery of truth in a condition of dialogue."[72] Unfortunately, without clear norms for distinguishing truth from falsehood, the process of dialogue tends to become open-ended and, as such, frustrating. As long as the content of an ineffable transcendental experience serves as the content of faith, it seems impossible to limit it definitively to any clearly expressed proposition.

The theology that postulates an unending quest for truth also undermines the magisterium's role in matters of morality. The primacy of concrete act of decision, fundamental option, over abstract universals, leads to a type of nominalism denying the validity of universal principles and to the refusal of the magisterium's ability infallibly to define moral laws. A simple opposition is drawn between the universal principles and norms regarding classes of acts defined by the magisterium and actual moral decisions that concern concrete, unique cases enmeshed in a complex

---

[71] C. Duquoc, "An Active Role for the People of God in Defining the Church's Faith," *Concilium* 180 (1985): 81; see the other articles in the same journal by E. Schillebeeckx, H. Waldenfels, and H. Fries, which go in the same direction.

[72] H. Fries, "Is there a *Magisterium* of the Faithful?" *Concilium* 180 (1985): 89f. Fries attributes these positions, with which he agrees, to W. Kasper, but the references he gives are erroneous.

net of innumerable circumstances and consequences. Insofar as all of the latter complexity contributes to a judgment about an act's moral goodness, a rational attempt by the magisterium to define the irreformable norms of action is deemed a priori impossible and meaningless. "Moral principles of their very nature cannot be irreformable . . . with regard to their *content*."[73] More simply V. Rush writes:

> Infallibility does not descend to concrete cases. . . . So, while Church authority may speak out in moral generalities in interpreting revelation and in trying to help us understand what the revelation of God is, such authority can never speak out infallibly and tell us what to do about a particular case in our own life. So there is no possible conflict of conscience with an infallible teaching authority. The burden for deciding about particular cases always remains our own.[74]

A more complex, and at first glance less radical, reduction of the magisterium reaches a similar conclusion. It starts from two premises: first, there is no separate region of Christian morality apart from the natural law morality, which is in principle grounded in human nature as knowable to human intelligence; second, there is a distinction between categorical and transcendent ethical grounding, or the rightness of acts and the moral goodness of the subject, or secular ethic and salvific ethic. The latter component of each pair refers to the absoluteness of the moral demand grounded in God to whom the subject's intention responds. Faith deals with the maintenance of a proper intention in this realm.

---

[73] G. Hughes, S.J., "Infallibility in Morals," *Theological Studies* 34 (1973): 421–26. He naively exempts truths of faith from his nominalistic position, considering them capable of being timeless since received by revelation on authority, 416, 417, 420f., 426, 427f. See also T. O'Connell, *Principles for a Catholic Morality* (New York: Seabury, 1978), 95f. Hughes's position is repeated in his *Authority in Morals* (London: Heythrop, 1978), esp. 91–110. See B. Tierney, "Infallibility in Morals: A Response," *Theological Studies* 35 (1974): 507–17, who claimed that to be consistent Hughes would have to join him and Küng in a denial of papal infallibility. For the nominalism at the root of this "new morality" see J. McDermott, S.J., "Metaphysical Conundrums at the Root of Moral Disagreement," *Gregorianum* 71 (1990): 713–742.

[74] V. Rush, *The Responsible Christian* (Chicago: Loyola University Press, 1984), 236; see also J. Hanigan, *As I Have Loved You* (New York: Paulist, 1986), 141f.

The former component concerns the area of concrete action in this world in which the goodness or badness of actions is judged within the whole context of their conditions and consequences. This is the realm of natural reason where theologians, respecting the plurality of opinions and the results of the human sciences, seek to win an insight into proper moral conduct. "Moral norms of comportment are not mysteries of faith. Their content must be 'positively open to reason (*einsehbar*) and clearly definable.' " Since the latter field of activity is subject to natural human insight, the magisterium, argues J. Schuster, can claim here no exclusive privilege in divining good and evil. Instead, its infallibility extends only to questions regarding the final grounding in faith of the moral order and the proper determination of the subject's moral intentionality. Though the magisterium may pronounce on innerworldly moral issues, it is not infallible but subject to criticism and revision.[75] Hence infallibility in moral matters has been restricted in practice to affirming what is a tautology in theological morality. All the magisterium is allowed to say in its infallible moral definitions is what the believer already believes—namely, that moral intentionality has ultimately to do with God. Elsewhere the magisterium cannot claim any binding authority or special insight in concrete decisions regarding Christian behavior. In Schuster's view, since ecclesiastical structures are intended to serve the communion of believers, the teaching office's main role, besides motivating virtue, seems to consist in keeping the lines of communication open among the various local Churches to preserve their unity.[76]

By no means do all transcendental Thomists agree with this exaggerated position. K. Rahner, for example, seeks to maintain the analogy between infinite horizon and finite intelligibility in moral matters. Even while proposing an existential ethics to cover individual matters of moral decision, he argues for the Church's

---

[75] J. Schuster, S.J., *Ethos und kirchliches Lehramt* (Frankfurt: Knecht, 1984), 164–89, 288–94, 317–30, 380–84; see also J. Glaser, S.J., "Authority, Connatural Knowledge, and the Spontaneous Judgment of the Faithful," *Theological Studies* 29 (1963): 743. Schuster, 289–94, follows Hughes in distinguishing moral statements from irreformable statements of faith.

[76] Schuster, 327–29, 383–85.

capacity to proscribe universally certain acts, like abortion, as immoral.[77] Schüller, whom Schuster quotes, holds that because the Church lives under the guidance of the Holy Spirit, it is less prone to error than individuals, who should remain open to its pronouncements in forming their conscience. Indeed, there can be no final discrepancy between the demands of conscience and the infallible pronouncements of the Church. "For the one who believes in the Church as Christ's Church, there can be simply no conflict between the command of his conscience and the command of the Church insofar as she speaks in the power of her highest teaching authority."[78]

The Fundamental Option

At the basis of the confusion about the magisterium's role in moral matters stands the doctrine of the fundamental option, whereby what ultimately determines the moral quality of the acting subject, sin or virtue, is not the act regarded objectively in isolation, but the intention of the judging subject, who must reach a decision in view of one's own unique circumstances. But this theory leads to other difficulties. Rahner identifies concupiscence as the resistance offered by nature to the person's free act. After Adam's loss of integrity, this means that "the person never retrieves his nature entirely."

Aware of the difficulty of objectively identifying the subjective profundity of existential commitment in any choice and even of describing the freedom that "gives itself over always to the entirety of the one and whole act of freedom of the one and whole, temporal-finite life," Rahner holds that the fundamental option,

---

[77] K. Rahner, S.J., "The Individual in the Church," *Nature and Grace*, tr. D. Wharton (London: Sheed and Ward, 1963), 51–83, esp. 51–64, 74f.; "The Appeal to Conscience," ibid., 84–111, esp. 99–103, 106; "Über die Frage einer Existentialethik," *Schriften*, II:227–46; "Der Anspruch Gottes und der Einzelner," *Schriften*, IV:521–36.

[78] B. Schüller, S.J., "Das irrige Gewissen," in *Theologische Akademie*, II, ed. K. Rahner and O. Semmelroth (Frankfurt: Knecht, 1965), 25f., 19f., 27f.; "Bemerkungen zur authentischen Verkündigung des kirchlichen Lehramts," *Theologie und Philosophie* 42 (1967): 537–39; "Zur theologischen Diskussion über die *lex naturalis*," *Theologie und Philosophie* 41 (1966): 501.

while using for its realization the individual, temporally and spatially objectifiable acts and their motivations, "cannot be identified simply in objective reflection with one such act nor represent the mere moral sum total resulting from such individual acts nor be simply identified with the moral quality of the last of these free individual acts realized (before death)."[79] Because bodiliness joined the human being to the material world, a person is also to a certain degree removed from his or her own control: "the free subject is always already present to itself in its freedom and simultaneously distanced from itself through the objective reality through which it must necessarily mediate itself to itself." That alienation is only overcome when death dissolves the tension between body and soul. The moment of death marks the definitiveness of a person's free response to grace. Rahner writes, "Freedom in its original essence aims at the original, simple entirety of a being's existential realization, and therefore it is first definitively accomplished when it offers itself through the deed of life into the absolute weakness of death."[80]

Building on such statements as well as Rahner's position that grace is constantly offered to people as their supernatural existential, P. Schoonenberg stresses human limitations in knowing and willing as well as the incompleteness of all possibilities of choice in this ongoing world. He then draws the conclusion that no rejection of God previous to a hypothetical, all-inclusive decision made in the moment of death about the significance of life is really ultimate: "The first and only act in which the person disposes of his whole nature occurs at the moment of transition from time to eternity; it is the act by which man chooses his eternal attitude, thus definitively and irrevocably deciding his direction. This is, in the fullest sense of the word, the act of love unto life or sin unto death." As a result, Schoonenberg distinguishes both venial and moral sins from the sin unto death, which alone he considers a definitive rejection of grace: "It is not enough to commit a mortal sin in order to be punished with hell; man must also afterwards continue to reject the grace of conversion . . . the

---

[79] K. Rahner, S.J., "Zum theologischen Begriff der Konkupiscenz," *Schriften*, I:393; "Zur Theologie der Freiheit," *Schriften*, VI:224.

[80] Rahner, *Grundkurs*, 104, 111; see also "Erlösung," *Sacramentum Mundi*, I:1172.

'basic moral acts' and the mortal sins prepare us for the last good or evil choice in death and for its prefigurations during this life."[81]

Taking this position, Schoonenberg ignores a half of Rahner's dialectical oscillation: the subject, as we saw in the citation from Rahner, is "simultaneously" present to self and distanced from self. In *Grundkurs* it is possible to line up parallel series of quotations stressing, on the one hand, how the human person is entrusted to himself or herself, capable of taking a position with regard to self as a whole and to all reality and, on the other hand, how people in their freedom are interiorly determined by their situations.[82] Rahner never explicitly denies the possibility of mortal sin in this life. He even writes of the human rejection of grace "in the concrete order": "Through a NO to divine love of that kind, man of himself can no longer reckon on the continuance of that love, especially as it is the love of the absolutely holy and just God who is the absolute contradiction of such a refusal."[83]

B. Schüller strongly opposes Schoonenberg's interpretation, defending the traditional doctrine about the possibility of mortal sin as a definitive rejection of God in this life, which a person alone cannot reverse; every decision is not immanently provisional.[84] The Catholic tradition has long held the sinner cannot presume upon the grace of conversion (DS 310), especially if it is supposed to occur in a hypothetical all-embracing decision at the moment of death. Were people incapable of rejecting God, they would be equally incapable of loving God definitively in this life, and the meaning of human freedom in this life would be radically relativized: at most, preparations for a final act—which act, however, is entirely free, not determined by its predecessors. Salvation becomes otherworldly. Furthermore, it is not clear how the moment of death overcomes the limitations of human knowing and willing. Short of the beatific vision, a finite person cannot know adequately the infinite God and realize fully what rejection of God entails. The human perspective remains partial, and the de-

---

[81] P. Schoonenberg, S.J., *Man and Sin*, tr. J. Donceel (Notre Dame: University of Notre Dame Press, 1965), 34 (also 32), 39.

[82] Rahner, *Grundkurs*: see 41f., 46, 48f., 101 with 113–17, 119.

[83] K. Rahner, S.J., "Salvation," *Sacramentum Mundi* (London: Burns & Oates, 1970) V:426.

[84] B. Schüller, S.J., "Todsünde—Sünde zum Tode?" *Theologie und Philosophie* 42 (1967): 321–40.

sire to know God continues unfulfilled until the beatific vision. Hence the excuse of imperfect knowledge about God always offers itself to maintain the provisional character of any finite decision. Yet the full knowledge of God in the intuitive vision perfects freedom by removing any possibility of rejecting the Supreme Good.

If Schoonenberg's position relativizes finite decisions by emphasizing the distinction between finite and infinite in the fundamental judgment that is also a voluntary commitment of love, the juncture of finite and infinite in the same judgment can, inversely, deny the very possibility of a fundamental option. If, as Rahner writes, "in every knowledge and deed man affirms absolute Being as their real ground and affirms it as mystery,"[85] how is it possible to reject God in favor of some finite reality? Even in the choice of self, insofar as one's own being participates in God's being, one implicitly chooses God. Given the unity of intellect and will, just as an atheist affirms God unthematically in every judgment, the egoist apparently loves God in every choice of self. An infinite God cannot be juxtaposed to the world without resulting in what Rahner considers a false, irreligious dualism.[86]

Rahner is doubtless aware of the conundrum involved in the fundamental option theory. He recognizes that the possibility of rejecting the infinite horizon, which is the condition of possibility for every choice and is implicitly affirmed in every choice, involves a "real absolute contradiction." So he affirms that human freedom can actually effect such a contradiction. Clearly Rahner is caught in the conundrum of evil, which has no positive reality of its own and cannot be explained. Yet the need to affirm a contradiction should warn against hastily drawing from the premises of transcendental Thomism conclusions contrary to Church doctrine.[87]

Norms of Moral Behavior

If the fundamental option theory manifests theoretical difficulties about the subject's capacity to reject God, the need of conversion

---

[85] Rahner, *Grundkurs*, 85.
[86] Ibid., 72.
[87] Ibid., 104–08; "Theologie der Freiheit," 216–20.

becomes all the more difficult to convey; acts once considered sinful are seen to be justifiable and proper in certain circumstances. Excessive emphasis on subjective intention, the complexity of circumstances, conflict situations, the alleged need of compromising between principles and reality, and the necessity of foreseeing the consequences of an action to judge its moral quality leads to moral chaos. Relativizing an abstract, universal concept of nature results in a moral nominalism, or situation ethics, where general norms are readily put aside.[88] Some so relativize the universal concept before the uniqueness of circumstances and the primacy of individual conscience that they not only allow exceptions to Church teachings but also admit that sometimes "morally responsible" exceptions cannot be gathered together under any rule since "human moral existence as we know it, live it and often suffer it, can be impregnable to human efforts to render it coherent."[89] Such an irrational conclusion was already implicit in the nominalism which Rousselot acknowledged to be at the basis of transcendental Thomism and that is repeated in other transcendental Thomists, though its more astute proponents take measures to restrict it and justify universal concepts.[90]

---

[88] See B. Kiely, S.J., "The Impracticality of Consequentialism," *Gregorianum* 66 (1985): 655–86; McDermott, "Metaphysical Conundrums," 734–42.

[89] L. Cahill, *Between the Sexes* (Philadelphia: Fortress, 1985), 149. Her judgment in favor of exception and denying universal natures is prepared for in 73–77, 107f., 143–48. Overall, her appeal to the Church as the community of discernment is very vague because it is not clear what Church she is talking about; her view of the Church seems to be "from below," and the necessity and role of institutional structures are never really explained. Her method of grounding morality seems to be a very subjective, if not arbitrary, amalgamation of present experience, selected texts from Scripture, and a vague notion of tradition. How her constant insistence on the equality of the sexes can be maintained without a universal nature would be a further interesting question.

[90] P. Rousselot, S.J., *L'Intellectualisme de St. Thomas*, 2nd ed. (Paris: Beauchesne, 1924), 95. The citation from Rousselot's later letter, given in n. 2 on 106f., was added by L. de Grandmaison, S.J. Unfortunately, in his desire to defend Rousselot, he distorted the letter's meaning by omitting essential words. See P. Tiberghien, "A propos d'un texte du Père Rousselot," *Mélanges de Science Religieuse* 10 (1953): 99–106; J. McDermott, S.J., *Love and Understanding* (Rome: Gregorian, 1983), 27–33, 230; on Rousselot's attempts to counterbalance nominalism see ibid., 55–71, 115–139, 154–166, 240–278. For Rahner's nominalism see McDermott, "Rahner on Two Infinities," 443–454; on his attempts to counterbalance it see McDermott, "Dialectical Analogy," esp. 680–86. For Lonergan's nominalism see, for example, *Verbum*, ed. D. Burrell (Notre Dame: University

Nominalism is implicit also in J. Fuch's restriction of universality to the fundamental first principle of the natural law *bonum faciendum, malum vitandum*. After distinguishing between the personal goodness of the subject and the rightness of acts, he limits absoluteness to the former since there the moral absolute, ultimately rooted in God, is experienced emotionally and intellectually prior to reflection. This foundational conscience perceiving the absolute is oriented to ethical objectivity whereas the situational conscience, aware of all the diverse circumstances of each individual case, applies the foundational conscience for the discovery of more specific norms through the creative use of practical reason. Since the application presupposes knowledge of the human person and that individual's complete world, which is subject to change, and since the moral law is not apprehended outside the individual conscience, the magisterium, whose task is to protect revelation, should not issue commands. Instead, offering norms, it should invite the believer in a dialogue of mutual openness to form his conscience responsibly.[91] Though Fuchs distinguishes foundational and situational consciences, he also postulates their continuity insofar as the latter applies the former. Yet their continuity cannot be intellectually identified because not only does the perception of the absolute involve emotions beyond a reflexive intellectual act but also the constant change of concrete circumstances prevents an adequate abstraction.

Between the infinity of God, the absolute, and the material infinity of the concrete there is not much room for discursive,

---

of Notre Dame Press, 1967), 87, 154; and McDermott, "Tensions," 114–117; he balances that by his insistence on the necessity of the first act of understanding, responding to the question *quid sit*. Maréchal always resisted nominalism and insisted on the unintelligibility of matter. Nonetheless, diverse aspects of his thought, shared with other transcendetal Thomists, tend to relativize the validity of his concepts. They can be found in *Le Point de Départ de la Métaphysique*, V, 2nd ed. (Brussels: L'Edition Universelle, 1949): for example, the natural desire for the beatific vision, 419–425, 447–450, 464–468; the fundamental unity of intellect and will, 310–314, 464f.; the subject as immediately self-conscious, 61f., 102, 110–113, 116, 119–124, 478, 533; the concept as a synthetic unity of an indeterminate supposite and a formal determination, 132f., 216–219; the abstract *species* as dynamically in relation, 215–219, 313f., 440–443; concepts as implicit judgments, 455, 459; the dynamic intellect going beyond form, or concept, to reality, 257–259, 360, 401, 443–447, 452–455, 458f., 472, 477f., 519.

[91] J. Fuchs, S.J., "The Absolute in Morality and the Christian Conscience," *Gregorianum* 71 (1990): 697–711.

finite reason and ethical argumentation. No wonder that the magisterium's attempts to defend the intelligibility and universal application of the moral law are rejected. But such an interpretation of morality has come a long way from the initial debate over *Humanae Vitae* when B. Schüller claimed that the magisterium's interpretation of the moral law must prove itself by arguments accessible to all.[92] Now apparently some theologians not only admit that moral choices are ultimately impervious to discursive reason but also demand that the magisterium be secondary to the authority of the individual conscience, however rationally incoherent.

The nominalism at the basis of the fundamental option theory renders impossible the magisterium's claim to interpret moral norms, even if the doctrine is not explicitly denied. For example, although R. McCormick agrees with the Vatican's argument that the connection between sexual union and procreation is essential to the symbol of corporeal love between man and woman, he disagrees with its conclusion banning all *in vitro* fertilization with the question, "But in all situations, in every act?"[93] By raising such a question, he excludes all rational responses a priori. For once the priority of the singular over the abstract is presupposed, no abstract argument can cover all possible cases. But by disqualifying in advance all responses, McCormick destroys the rational bases of his own thought. If it is impossible on his presupposition to justify an exceptionless norm, it is equally impossible to justify rationally any exception. Of course, other theologians, as already indicated, explicitly state that the magisterium cannot definitively define concrete moral norms.

Relying on the majority of current moral theologians, F. Sullivan concludes that, given both the complexity of problems facing people today and the impossiblity of an "irreversible determination" of an infallibly true norm in the flux of history and of human nature itself, the definition of Vatican I about papal infalli-

---

[92] Schüller, "Bemerkungen," 536; "Sittliche Forderung und Erkenntnis Gottes," *Gregorianum* 59 (1978): 30.

[93] R. McCormick, S.J., "The Shape of Moral Evasion in Catholicism," *America* 159 (1988): 185.

bility in matters of faith and morals does not really apply to "particular norms of natural law" beyond its basic principles.[94]

The extent of the relativization of moral norms is illustrated by the book *Human Sexuality*, commissioned by the Catholic Theological Society of America. Redefining a priori the purpose of sexual activity as "creative and integrative" instead of the traditional "procreative and unitive," arguing that the basis of a moral judgment comprises the whole action with its circumstances and moral intention, and urging all to remain open to further evidence and research while considering each case on its own merits, the authors find reasons to proclaim legitimate exceptions to Church prohibitions in matters of artificial birth control, artificial insemination, preceremonial and extramarital sex, and homosexuality.[95] Other theologians, appealing to the same principles, can

---

[94] F. Sullivan, *Magisterium* (Dublin: Gill and Macmillan, 1983), 138–52, esp. 148–52. There is a serious tension in Sullivan's position insofar as he accepts a conceptualist distinction between revealed propositions and the "virtually revealed," that is, what can be deduced from revealed propositions, in order to maintain that the particular norms of the natural law cannot be deduced from revealed propositions (135–38). But elsewhere (129–31) he denies that the deposit of faith should be limited to "a certain number of revealed truths"; instead it is to be understood in terms of insights of "ecclesial contemplation" which "can bring to light truths where are really contained in the total Christ-event, and therefore really contained in the Gospel, even though they are not found explicitly in Scripture or in the early records of explicit Christian belief." This change of perspective on revelation lets him adopt the transcendental Thomist view, which is also accepted by the "authoritative" theologians he cites in denying the ability of the Church to define particular norms of the natural law. But, if dogmatic truths can be brought out from the Christ-event infallibly defined by the magisterium, why are moral norms denied the possibility of being defined by the magisterium and instead reduced to the straitjacket of the conceptualist theology? Like Hughes and Schuster, Sullivan overlooks the connection between relativizing moral norms and relativizing dogmas. It should also be noted that there existed a deep and unresolved debate among conceptualist theologians whether an affirmation of the virtually revealed can also be demanded as of divine faith. At stake is the role of reason in dealing with supernatural propositions. *Cf. supra* n. 39.

[95] A. Kosnik et al., *Human Sexuality* (New York: Paulist, 1977), 86–98 (method), 114–28 (artificial contraception), 133–36 (sterilization), 138f. (artificial insemination), 148f., 178f. (extra-marital sexual relations), 150–52 (open to exceptions), 160f., 165–69 (preceremonial sexual relations), 189f., 202–6, 208f., 214–16 (homosexuality), 220, 225–28 (masturbation). See also C. Curran, "Personal Reflections on Birth Control," *Christian Morality Today* (Notre Dame: Fides, 1966), 67–76; "Sexuality and Sin: A Current Appraisal," *Contemporary*

justify abortion "to save human life or for other values that are commensurate with human life."[96] D. Maguire even considers suicide a morally valid alternative:

> Suicide may at times be moral. Even then, like war, it will be tragic; but it can like war be moral. Generally, I judge, persons perform suicide because they have been stripped of the essential ingredients of human life—hope and love. It would be naive to think that human perfidy is not capable of depriving some of its members of these ingredients so that they can do no more and must depart. There may be cases where all of the disvalues of suicide can be outweighed by ineffable pain and loneliness. In those cases, it is the survivors who are to be morally indicted, not the victim, who seizes the only remaining relief.[97]

Thus is guilt removed from the individual and attributed to others, often members of the grieving family. Indeed Maguire's argu-

---

Problems in Moral Theology (Notre Dame: Fides, 1970), 175f., 176f., 179f.; "Catholic Moral Theology Today," *New Perspectives in Moral Theology* (Notre Dame: Fides, 1974), 41f.; "Dialogue with the Homophile Movement: The Morality of Homosexuality," *Catholic Moral Theology in Dialogue* (Notre Dame: Fides, 1972), 209–19. See to the contrary J. Dolan, S.J., " 'Humanae Vitae' and Nature," *Thought* 44 (1969): esp. 369–73, where, echoing *Humanae Vitae*, he points out very early how the rejection of the encyclical's position leads to the rejection of other traditional norms in sexual morality.

[96] C. Curran, *Politics, Medicine, and Christian Ethics* (Philadelphia: Fortress, 1978), 131; *Contemporary Problems in Moral Theology* (Notre Dame: Fides, 1970), 143–45; "Abortion: Its Legal and Moral Aspects," *New Perspectives*, 178–93. Most other dissenters are somewhat more restrictive, allowing aborting before "individualization" of the zygote and appealing thereby to proportionalist reasons: see, for example, A. Wolter and T. Shannon, "Reflections on the Moral Status of the Pre-Embryo," *Theological Studies* 51 (1990): 603–26. A long debate between Shannon and M. Johnson followed, most recently displayed in "Quaestio Disputata: Delayed Hominization," ibid. 58 (1997): 708–17. In the whole debate one should exercise caution before identifying the reality with the current state of scientific knowledge. That a zygote may split within the first fourteen days need not imply that individuation has not occurred previously; it just means that the basis for the individuation in the zygote cannot be determined by current science. Unless a scientist would rely on chance or arbitrariness, there must be a physical cause within the zygote of the individuation that manifests itself at twinning. The final stage of development occurs due to the influence of the final cause, which is effective by already informing the reality in process toward it. So there would be two distinct formal principles at work in a zygote that later twins, whereas in a zygote that does not twin there is only one formal principle of activity.

[97] D. Maguire, *Death by Choice* (1973; rpt. New York: Schocken, 1975), esp.

ment seems to deny any freedom to the suicide "victim" insofar as one is confronted with "musts" and forced to seek "the only remaining relief." Human transcendence, which opens up so many possibilities and relativizes moral "absolutes," has suddenly shrunk drastically. Paradoxically, if Francis of Assisi were granted the fulfillment of his prayer "to love rather than to be loved," he might be considered the most justified candidate for suicide—being deprived of all friends, just as Jesus was abandoned on the Cross. But after denying freedom to the suicide victim, Maguire concludes almost immediately thereafter that "there are times when the ending of life is the best that life offers. Moral man will see this, and then, more than ever, he will know the full price of his freedom." It is a strange freedom that destroys itself and then casts the guilt on others.

With the relativization of "objective" norms and transcendental Thomism's turn to the subject, the traditional notion that following of the natural law results in one's fulfillment and happiness can be interpreted so as to render the individual subject the norm of morality. In seeing "holiness as self-realization," G. Baum rejects the asceticism and legalism of the past because it encouraged self-hatred, guilt, and love of death. "True humanity is not found, according to the New Testament, by seeking conformity to fixed moral and cultural categories: true humanity is found precisely by breaking through these categories when they limit man on his way to growth and reconciliation." Though the necessity of the cross is acknowledged, this "conversion" is said to consist in self-knowledge. Since God's Word allegedly initiates the process, "entry into self-knowledge *is* divine revelation." Finally "self-realization in our context means man's entry into his destiny, his humanization."[98]

The conceptualist spirituality has in many ways been assumed into transcendental morality, which is principally concerned with the full realization of God's will in the concrete circumstances to which universal norms do not apply but discernment must be applied. Lacking, of course, are the universal norms and the guid-

---

221, 85f., 199–202, 216–21; "The Freedom to Die," *Commonweal* 46 (1972): 425–27.

[98] G. Baum, *Man Becoming* (New York: Herder and Herder, 1970), 139, 141f., 157, 159.

ance of ecclesial authority. These are not so necessary in view of the immediacy of each subject to God's self-revelation. But then it is easy to turn the traditional spirituality upside-down. One need only emphasize the unity of body and spirit before denying the link between sexual intercourse and procreation.

G. Milhaven notices that the mere stressing of love without procreation does not distinguish marital love from other types of love or friendship. This leads him to the positive evaluation of eros, or sensible pleasure, as a moral goal to be achieved or heightened even if it involves a surrender to irrational drives. "The very fact that the involuntary violence to which one must abandon oneself comes from one's unconscious depths and anonymous animal nature contributes to one's distinctively human life." With such an erotic perspective on marriage, the self-sacrificial element of marital love is not enough. "One needs and wants to be wanted . . . Nothing is more depressing than sacrificial accommodation." Furthermore, self-sacrificial love often turns out to be too much: "Setting selfless love as one's ideal is often a redoubtable defense against probing by self or others, of one's real motives. It easily leads to unnecessary guilt feelings, for one cannot come close to the ideal . . . the Christian ideal of selfless love and total self-giving has been one of the most effective instruments of the oppression of women." Instead of stressing self-sacrifice, sexual morality should be "centered and based on the value of happiness (*Glück*), one's own and others'."[99] Unfortunately the erotic distinction, discovered to distinguish married love from friendship, does not differentiate marriage from other heterosexual or homosexual relations. Moreover, pleasure cloys and, due to original sin, strongly tends to keep the subject's attention riveted to the self and one's own "self-fulfillment"; if not corrected, this quickly destroys relationships. Thus withers the joy that accompanies or follows gently the sacrificial forgetfulness of self before the beloved. In short, it is easy to see how the adaptation of moral theology to the hedonistic standards of modern society corrupts Christianity and destroys people. Against this false adaptation to the world *Veritatis Splendor* is directed.

---

[99] J. Milhaven, "Conjugal Sexual Love and Contemporary Moral Theology," *Theological Studies* 35 (1974): 707f., 709 (quoting S. Callahan), 705; see also Kosnik, 95.

The Encyclical

Given the context of moral theology at the time of the encyclical's publication, the reader must note how it refuses to let itself be subsumed under the conceptualist or the transcendental theology. Each theology has strong points that balance the weaknesses of the other. In many ways the encyclical repeats emphases of the transcendental theology. Its opening meditation on the call of the rich young man is striking insofar as the example is applied to all Christians as revealing the norm for the moral life. The conceptualist theology is inclined to distinguish the universal norms of the natural law from the evangelical counsels, like the call to total poverty illustrated in this Gospel story. Whereas the former are binding on all, the latter, precisely because of its individual calling in unique circumstances, cannot be applied to all. Yet the pope employs this Gospel text, traditionally interpreted as a counsel of greater perfection, to all Christians as fundamental to the moral life. Moreover, he does not distinguish natural law from Christian morality. Morality is understood as the following of Christ without reserve, and Christ does not exclude anyone from his call. The fulfillment of the moral law occurs only as a gift from God in Christ. Indeed, love of God and love of neighbor are considered an "inseparable unity" in Christ's mission. For the law is not just a series of commands, but Christ, the law's fulfillment, is a "living and personal law." For the law is fulfilled in love, and "all are united to realize their freedom under grace by following Christ" (6–24).[100]

Going beyond the first chapter of *Veritatis Splendor*, the pope also accentuates many points that accord with the theory of transcendental Thomism. The human person is a unity, body and soul (48–50, 67). Love is the foundation of the natural law (87), and conscience is engaged in a dialogue with God (58f). Ultimately, the natural law is grounded in God, the supreme Good (18f., 99). Since faith cannot be separated from morality (88f, 107) and all are called to follow Christ wholeheartedly, this choice is interpreted as a fundamental option (65–67). Human freedom has to be set free in truth by love for love (86f.).

---

[100] The numbers in parentheses refer to the paragraphs of the encyclical. References to *Evangelium Vitae* (below) are made similarly.

Despite these emphases shared with transcendental Thomism, the pope is careful not to adopt its exaggerations.[101] He takes them clearly into his sights when they refuse the validity of the immutable natural law's universal norms and attack the magisterium's obligation to interpret the moral law definitively (4, 32, 51–53, 64–69, 74–79, 82, 90, 103). Repeatedly he insists on the absoluteness of negative moral norms, which apply to all circumstances and allow no exception. As the traditional conceptualist morality insists and the pope repeats, there are some acts that are "intrinsically evil," that is, always and per se wrong; they can never be ordered to God (78, 80–82, 95, 115). Whereas positive moral precepts, though immutable, cannot be applied a priori to all possible circumstances but allow ever new, higher realizations, the negative moral prohibitions should never be transgressed, even if death has to be preferred to performing an evil action (52f.). Circumstances or a good intention may diminish subjective guilt (62f., 81), but they do not alter the *species* of an evil act; the act itself can never be justified or transformed into a good act (77f., 80f.). Mortal sin marks a definitive break of communion between the sinner and God, which can only be repaired by the new initiative of God's redemptive grace. Thus the fundamental option for or against God takes place in this life through the use of human freedom with regard to serious moral matters (67–70).

With the affirmation of universal negative prohibitions and the identification of the fundamental option with particular acts, the pope likewise preserves the traditional role of the magisterium in defining moral questions, refusing to consign theological dialogue and decisions to theologians caught up in ethical pluralism. For he affirms that morality pertains to the essence of the Christian message and the responsibility of the magisterium to interpret that aspect of Christ's teaching (2–5, 7, 29f., 36f., 49, 56f., 95f., 109f., 114–117). He lists certain acts which are always and per se seriously wrong by reason of their object (80). In his subsequent encyclical, *Evangelium Vitae* (1995), appealing to natural law, Scripture, Church tradition and the Petrine authority conferred

---

[101] G. McCool, S.J., "The Theology of John Paul II" in *The Thought of Pope John Paul II*, 29–53, points out many similarities between the pope and transcendental Thomists. Our "Response," 55–68, indicates various points on which the pope distinguishes himself from transcendental Thomism.

by Christ, the pope identifies certain acts as grave moral disorders and violations of God's law (57, 62, 65).

In arguing for his position, the pope adopts neither the tenets and axioms of the older conceptualist theology nor the presuppositions of the more moderate transcendental theologians. Clearly he does not consider the magisterium bound to any one theological system. Instead, he relies on appeal to Church tradition and the need of communion within the Church (3, 29f., 51f., 86, 96f., 101). The denial of moral absolutes—especially universal negative prohibitions—not only goes contrary to the whole Catholic tradition but also destroys intelligible moral discourse within the Church. If, for example, the father of several nubile young daughters considers fornication, adultery, and homosexual activity to be contrary to Christ's will but the person in the pew behind them sees nothing wrong but much commendable in "liberating" those daughters to such activity, the bands uniting those Christians in love and the kiss of peace will be very much strained. A community that imagines that it can live with such moral confusion is doomed to extinction.

Because the language of moral behavior, which is necessarily universal, can allegedly never be applied a priori to all circumstances, the meaning of words will be placed in question. In concrete cases of decision and policy there will be no way of arriving at a consensus, for ecclesial authority has been judged incapable of giving universal moral norms for concrete cases and an ethical pluralism has become ensconced in magisterial chairs. Without clarity in concrete decisions, the meaning of moral conversion will become very vague and evaporate. Surely in innerworldly decisions that allegedly involve the weighing up of various ontic, or premoral, goods before coming to a moral decision, the greater the force of any temptation—that is, the stronger to appeal of any apparent good—the more reasons a person will find for yielding to temptation. Thus, exactly in the moment of temptation, when a person has the greatest need of principles, he or she will be deprived of their assistance for moral action.

The pope's position in *Veritatis Splendor* involves, it seems, a fidelity to the Catholic tradition and an enlightened common sense, which is not bound by the ideological constrictions of any intellectual fad or transitory system of thought. He is doubtless very aware of the internal contradictions of such a system as transcendental Thomism.[102] But his refusal to bow to the constrictions of any theological interpretation does not imply that he lacks a theoretical basis for his position. One suspects rather that his own rethinking of Thomism is more profound than either conceptualist or transcendental Thomism. Both these systems started with nature—that is, the necessary principle of activity to which the necessary laws of human thought are supposed to correspond. Philosophers have always sought a necessity in external reality to ground the laws that govern thought. For thought without necessity seems to lack coherence; it threatens to become arbitrary. At least since Plato and Aristotle the external necessity was located in "natures." Conceptualist Thomism understands the human primarily in terms of an essence, or nature, abstracted from individuating matter. That nature displays universal traits revealing an ideal way of acting and offering the basis of the natural moral law. Transcendental Thomism in contrast understands human nature primarily as an existential intellectual dynamism, revealed in the necessary structure of judgment, which transcends the limitations of concepts and the natures allegedly grasped by concepts. But in both, the necessity of natures seems to be in opposition to human freedom, to which the historical revelation of Christianity appeals. In *The Acting Person,* K. Wojtyła, after noting that traditional philosophy starts with nature, stresses the need to rethink philosophy primarily in terms of freedom and the person.[103] As if to reiterate that point, *Veritatis Splendor* identifies the question of freedom as "the crucial issue" in the whole debate about morality (31–34, 84–87).

Though not stressing freedom, Plato and Aristotle made room for it insofar as the unintelligibility of (prime) matter impedes the absolute rational necessity of human thought and the natures to which thought corresponds. St. Thomas achieved greater room

---

[102] See McDermott, *Love and Understanding,* 291–301; "Christologies," 308–26; "Karl Rahner," 746f.; "Tensions," 132–39. And many other contradictions can be pointed out. What else can be expected of a "system" that exalts and defends theoretical pluralism? If pluralism is justified, no system can claim to have definitive truth, and any system's claim to justify pluralism is thereby undermined.

[103] K. Wojtyła, *The Acting Person,* tr. A. Potocki (Dordrecht: Reidel, 1970), 267–71.

for freedom in his Christian synthesis insofar as he introduced an existential order beyond the Aristotelian essential order. The former provides the contingency of the essential order, which need not be, and this contingency relativizes the necessity of natures. By the intelligent balancing of both orders, Thomas was able to assure the intelligibility necessity for reason while leaving room for God's supernatural intervention into the world and the human response to grace.

In his major philosophical work, *The Acting Person*, K. Wojtyła sets himself the task of analyzing the structure of free action. He sees clearly that freedom itself involves a structure. Though in one sense people make themselves, they have also to accept themselves as given and act in a given world that itself manifests structure. Freedom is not arbitrariness but is grounded in truth. Thus, people have reasons for their choices. And this finite structure of intelligibility is open to God, who addresses humankind, made in God's own image, in the appeal to human freedom through innerworldly realities. Ultimately, a person is the being of freedom called to sacrifice self for God and others, a being called to respond to the God of love in love. Precisely because K. Wojtyła lays such stress on freedom, his reflections on sexual morality published in *Love and Responsibility* justify the Church's traditional morality not in terms of nature and natural processes, but in terms of love as an act and process of self-sacrificial commitment to another person.

By taking such a stance, the pope shows himself as anything but naive and unaware of the current problems of moral theology.[104] If anything, his critics are much more limited than he, being unaware of the limitations of their own intellectual frameworks, however "progressive" they may imagine themselves. At

---

[104] R. McCormick, S.J., "Veritatis Splendor and Moral Theology," *America* 169 (Oct. 30, 1993): 9–12, claims that the positions criticized by the pope are not held by the proportionalist theologians. W. May, "Theologians and Theologies in the Encyclical," *Anthropotes* 10 (1994): 39–59, however, has identified in the writings of proportionalist theologians citations of positions rejected by *Veritatis Splendor*. Other theologians under attack have responded by attacking the doctrine of the encyclical. See *The Splendor of Accuracy*, ed., J. Selling and J. Jans (Kampen: Kok Pharos, 1994), *Moraltheologie im Abseits?*, ed. D. Mieth (Freiburg: Herder, 1994), and *Veritatis Splendor: American Responses*, ed., M. Allsopp and J. O'Keefe (Kansas City: Sheed and Ward, 1995).

the basis of their system, if they are transcendental Thomists, is a nominalism that is usually left unaddressed. The pope, by contrast, in returning to St. Thomas and the Catholic tradition, has revitalized a structure of thought that can deal with freedom by maintaining the proper balance of essential and existential orders, finite intelligibility, and the mystery of the infinite God who knows individuals in creating them so that God might call them, despite sin's wounding of nature, to a share in everlasting life through Jesus Christ.

II.
Applied Moral Theory

7. ETHICS OF CULTURE
Faith and Culture in the Thought of John Paul II

Avery Dulles, S.J.

IN ONE WAY OR ANOTHER the relationship between faith and culture has always been a concern of the Society of Jesus. Since its first charter of approval, the Jesuit order has understood the defense and propagation of the faith to be at the heart of its apostolate. Education, a major involvement of our Society, is a means of imparting culture, and Christian education seeks to impart culture consonant with the Gospel. As Jesuits, therefore, we have good reason to welcome the attention given to the theme of faith and culture since Vatican Council II and especially in the teaching of the present pope. This new interest is reflected in the documents of the 34th General Congregation, which in 1995 spoke of "the faith that evangelizes culture" and which treated the Gospel and culture as one of the three main aspects of the Jesuit mission today.[1]

The relationship between faith and culture first emerged as a major theme in official Catholic teaching, at Vatican II, which touched on the question in many documents, including the Constitution on the Liturgy, the Declaration on Christian Education, the Decree on the Lay Apostolate, and the Decree on the Church's Missionary Activity. The theme permeates the entire text of the Pastoral Constitution on the Church in the Modern World, *Gaudium et Spes*, which devoted the second chapter of part two to the specific topic of promoting the proper advance-

---

[1] See Decree 2 and Decree 4 of *Documents of the Thirty-Fourth General Congregation of the Society of Jesus* (St. Louis: Institute of Jesuit Sources, 1995), esp. 38 and 49–65.

ment of culture.[2] The other chapters in part two deal with marriage and the family (chapter 1), socioeconomic life (chapter 3), political life (chapter 4), and peace and international relations (chapter 5). Chapter 2 did not attempt any rigorous definition of culture, but it indicated that culture was a socially constituted environment in which certain ideas, attitudes, values, and modes of behavior are transmitted to new generations. Contemporary culture, as perceived by Vatican II, was profoundly affected by science and technology, both of which were contributing to rapid social change and were bringing about closer contacts among cultures that had hitherto been relatively isolated.

In its chapter on culture *Gaudium et Spes* asserted that "the human person . . . can attain to real and full humanity only through culture" (53). It stated also that "in revealing himself . . . God has spoken in terms of the culture peculiar to different ages" (58); that culture can provide conditions either congenial or uncongenial to the reception of the Gospel (57), and that culture should always be directed to the total perfection of the human person and the general good of the community (59).

In the same context the Pastoral Constitution recognized that we stand at the dawn of a new age in human history, in which humanity has a new consciousness of its ability to determine the future and a deeper sense of its responsibility for that future (54–55). While acknowledging that contemporary culture tends to be agnostic and immanentistic, thus presenting obstacles to Christian faith (57), *Gaudium et Spes* encouraged Christians to live in close contact with the people of their own time and to be confident that valid discoveries in the human sciences could contribute to a better understanding of the Gospel (62).

The relationship between faith and culture was further explored by Paul VI in his apostolic exhortation "On Evangelization in the Modern World" (*Evangelii Nuntiandi*, 1975). He

---

[2] Donald R. Campion, commenting on *Gaudium et Spes* for Walter M. Abbott's edition of *The Documents of Vatican II* (New York: America Press, 1966), calls the section on the development of culture "the Constitution's most novel venture in theological exploration" (190). For additional commentary see Roberto Tucci, "Culture" in John H. Miller, ed., *Vatican II: An Interfaith Appraisal* (Notre Dame: University of Notre Dame Press, 1966), 453–77; Hervé Carrier, "The Contribution of the Council to Culture" in René Latourelle, ed., *Vatican II: Assessment and Perspectives* 3 (New York: Paulist, 1989), 442–65.

adverted to the gravity of the present split between the Gospel and culture and to the need to evangelize cultures, regenerating them by contact with the Gospel. The Gospel, he maintained, is always embodied in forms borrowed from human cultures, but it nevertheless transcends every particular culture. It permeates them all without becoming subject to any one of them (EN 20). In later sections of the same exhortation Paul VI observed that the universal Church is present in individual churches having distinct cultural patrimonies (62), and that culture should always be directed to the total perfection of the human person and the general good of the community (59).

Karol Wojtyła, as a poet, dramatist, and philosophy professor in a Communist country with a deeply rooted Catholic heritage, developed a keen interest in the relations between faith and culture. As a young bishop he took an active part in the composition of *Gaudium et Spes*, and submitted a written intervention proposing about a dozen emendations to the draft of the chapter on the Church and culture.[3] He played a prominent role in the Synod of Bishops in 1974, which supplied the materials for *Evangelii Nuntiandi*. As a cardinal he lectured at various places, including the Catholic University of the Sacred Heart in Milan, on "The Problem of the Constitution of Culture through Human Praxis."[4] Elected pope in 1978, he set up a Pontifical Council for Culture in 1982. In the letter establishing this council he wrote: "Since the beginning of my pontificate I have considered the Church's dialogue with the cultures of our time to be a vital area, one in which the destiny of the world at the end of the twentieth century is at stake."[5]

In what follows I shall try to synthesize the teaching of John Paul II on the relationship between faith and culture, which is found scattered through innumerable encyclicals, apostolic ex-

---

[3] *Acta Synodalia* (Vatican City: Typis polyglottis, 1977) IV/3: 349–50.

[4] "Il problema del costituirsi della cultura attraverso la *praxis* umana" in *Rivista di Filosofia neoscolastica* 69 (1977): 513–24; English translation, "The Problem of the Constitution of Culture through Human Praxis" in Karol Wojtyla, *Person and Community: Selected Essays* (New York: Peter Lang, 1993), 263–75; hereafter abbreviated "Problem."

[5] Letter to Cardinal Agostino Casaroli, May 20, 1982, establishing the Pontifical Council for Culture, *Osservatore Romano* (Eng.), 28 June 1982: 19–20 at 19.

hortations, letters, addresses, and homilies, as well as books and articles composed before he assumed the papal office.[6] I have gathered up his thinking under seven headings that are my own.

1. *Theological Anthropology.* Behind all of the pope's thinking about culture stands the theological anthropology that is concisely expressed in Vatican II's Pastoral Constitution, *Gaudium et Spes,* and is amplified in books such as John Paul II's *Catechesis on the Book of Genesis.*[7] Central to this teaching is the idea that every human person is created in the image of God (GS 12), and is therefore endowed with inalienable freedom and personal dignity. As Vatican II had already said, the human being is the only creature on earth that exists for its own sake (GS 24). The Gospel reveals the deepest truth about humankind (GS 41), including the truth that in Jesus Christ, God has in some way self-united with every human being (GS 22). In his inaugural encyclical, *Redemptor Hominis,* the pope drew the consequence that because everyone is included in the mystery of redemption, all are entrusted to the solicitude of the Church. "The object of her care is man in his unique unrepeatable human reality, which keeps intact the image and likeness of God himself" (RH 13). For this reason the Church professes a universal humanism: no individual or group is beyond its motherly solicitude.

According to Holy Scripture, God created the human being not as an isolated individual but as a social being, destined to live in communion with others. The first community was marked by a difference of gender: "male and female he created them" (Gen 1:27). Although called to exercise dominion over the rest of creation, human beings were not given arbitrary dominative power. They were obliged to respect the order of creation, the goodness of which God recognized even before the "sixth day," when

---

[6] In addition to the essay mentioned in note 3 above, I would call attention to the five addresses gathered by Joseph Gremillion in *The Church and Culture since Vatican II* (Notre Dame: University of Notre Dame Press, 1985), 187–222; hereafter abbreviated "Gremillion." Included are John Paul II's address to the UNESCO General Conference at Paris: "Man's Entire Humanity Is Expressed in Culture" (1980); the speeches to the first three of the annual sessions of the Pontifical Council for Culture (1983, 1984, 1985), and the annual Christmas message to the College of Cardinals, "One Church, Many Cultures" (1984).

[7] *Original Unity of Man and Woman: Catechesis on the Book of Genesis* (Boston: St. Paul Editions, 1981).

Adam was formed. People all too easily forget that their power to reshape the world through their own labor is always based "on God's prior and original gift of the things that are" (CA 37). The relationship of men and women to the rest of creation is therefore one of responsible stewardship. Without them there would be no one to till the earth (cf. Gen 2:5–6).[8]

2. *Human Existence and Culture.* What distinguishes humankind from every other kind of creature is culture. Plants and animals live but have no culture. Thomas Aquinas, commenting on Aristotle, affirmed that humanity lives by creativity and intellect ("Genus humanum arte et ratione vivit").[9] John Paul II paraphrases this as meaning that "man lives a really human life thanks to culture. . . . Culture is a specific way of man's 'existing' and 'being'."[10] Culture is that by which man becomes more human, thereby achieving an increase, not necessarily of having, but of being. As a result of culture man *is* to a greater degree. Culture is *of* man, since no other being has culture; it is *from* man, since man creates it; and it is *for* man, since its prime purpose is to develop man as man.[11]

From this follows the basic norm by which any culture is to be evaluated. Human nature, according to the pope, "is itself the measure of culture and the condition ensuring that man does not become the prisoner of any of his cultures, but asserts his personal dignity by living in accordance with the profound truth of his being" (VS 53). Does a given cultural development enhance all the dimensions of human existence, perfecting all the capacities that are distinctively human?

In opposition to the Marxists, John Paul II denies that culture is determined by simply economic factors, such as the conditions of production. Rather, it is the self-expression of the human spirit

---

[8] On the dominion of humankind over nature see John Paul II, *Original Unity,* esp. 20–26, 53–54. For commentary see Kenneth L. Schmitz, *At the Center of the Human Drama: The Philosophical Anthropology of Karol Wojtyla/Pope John Paul II* (Washington, D.C.: Catholic University of America Press, 1993), 96–97.

[9] Thomas Aquinas, commentary on Aristotle, *Post. Analyt.,* n. 1; quoted by John Paul II in UNESCO Address, §6; Gremillion, 189.

[10] Ibid.

[11] Address to Intellectuals and Scientists at Coimbra, Portugal, May 15, 1982, §3; *Origins* 12 (May 27, 1982): 27–29, at 28; hereafter abbreviated Coimbra, followed by paragraph number.

and is essentially related to truth, goodness, and beauty. Although culture is always objectified in products of one kind or another, it is also constitutive of the human subject. Whenever we engage in a truly human action (*actus humanus*), we not only produce an external effect but simultaneously modify ourselves. The essence of praxis consists in the self-realization of the acting subject, who at the same time renders the nonhuman environment in some sort more human. Praxis, in the sense of action that recoils upon the agent, "provides a basis for speaking of culture as a connatural reality in relation to the human being."[12]

Because culture deals with the human in all its dimensions, it transcends politics and economics, which deal only with inner-worldly activities. Culture is inseparable from religion, inasmuch as God is the author, sustainer, and final goal of human existence. "Religion," says the pope, "often represents the transcendent dimension of the culture itself."[13] And elsewhere he declares: "At the heart of every culture lies the attitude a person takes to the greatest mystery: the mystery of God. . . . When this question is eliminated, the culture and moral life of nations are corrupted," as may be illustrated from the decay and collapse of European Communism (CA 24).

3. *The Gospel and Culture*. The link between the Gospel and culture, for John Paul II, comes through humanity, for the Gospel, as we have seen in our discussion of *Gaudium et spes*, "fully discloses humankind to itself and unfolds its noble calling" (GS 22). Jesus Christ is the truth that liberates men and women from the powers of sin and death. They rise to their full stature through increasingly perfect knowledge of, and adherence to, the truth.[14] The Gospel favors the development of culture, and authentic culture, conversely, brings people closer to the Gospel.

In many of his speeches and writings, the pope expatiates on the capacity of the Gospel, with its concern for the primacy of truth and for the authentic well-being of all humanity, to promote and defend human values. In the encyclical *Centesimus Annus*,

---

[12] "Problem," 266–67; quotation from 267.

[13] Apostolic Exhortation *Vita consecrata*, §79; text in *Origins* (Eng.) 25 (April 4, 1996): 681–719, at 708.

[14] UNESCO §17, 196.

for example, he characterizes the Church's special mission toward cultures:

> For an adequate formation of a culture, the involvement of the whole person is required, whereby one exercises one's creativity, intelligence, and knowledge of the world and of people. Furthermore, a person displays his capacity for self-control, personal sacrifice, solidarity, and readiness to promote the common good. Thus the first and most important task is accomplished within the heart. ... It is on this level that the Church's specific and decisive contribution to true culture is to be found. The Church promotes those aspects of human behavior which favor a true culture of peace, as opposed to models in which the individual is lost in the crowd, in which the role of one's initiative and freedom is neglected, and in which one's greatness is posited in the arts of conflict and war. The Church renders this service to human society by preaching the truth about the creation of the world, which God has placed in human hands so that people may make it fruitful and more perfect through their work; and by preaching the truth about the Redemption, whereby the Son of God has saved mankind and at the same time has united all people, making them responsible for one another. (CA 51)

It should be evident, therefore, that human culture can always be renewed in the light of a sound anthropology and the principles of the Gospel.[15] This realization is central for the mandate of the Pontifical Council for Culture, as the pope indicated by declaring: "We must make our contemporaries understand that the Gospel of Christ is a source of progress and enrichment for all human beings."[16]

4. *The Contemporary Crisis of Culture.* John Paul II agrees with those who discern a certain alienation in modern culture. The achievements of technology and politics, which have erected elaborate new instruments intended for the service of humanity, have taken on a life of their own, enslaving and threatening their own producers (RH 15–16). The power to subdue the earth turns against humanity, inducing suffering and anxiety, as may be seen from the massive poverty of the Third World and the persis-

---

[15] Coimbra #7.
[16] Address to Pontifical Council for Culture, January 17, 1987; text in *Origins* (Eng.) 9 February 1987: 11–12.

tent fear of nuclear disaster (RH 16). Speaking to UNESCO in 1980 he declared:

> The future of man and of the world is threatened, radically threatened, in spite of the intentions, certainly noble ones, of men of learning, men of science. It is threatened because the marvelous results of their researches and their discoveries, especially in the field of the sciences of nature, have been and continue to be exploited—to the detriment of the ethical imperative—for purposes that have nothing to do with the requirements of science, and even for purposes of destruction and death, and that to a degree never known hitherto, causing really unimaginable damage. Whereas science is called to be in the service of man's life, it is too often a fact that it is subjected to purposes that destroy the real dignity of man and of human life. That is the case when scientific research itself is directed towards those purposes or when its results are applied to purposes contrary to the good of mankind. That happens in the field of genetic manipulations and biological experimentations as well as in that of chemical, bacteriological, or nuclear armaments.[17]

John Paul II speaks often of the signs of disintegration in contemporary society. The recent loss of cultural influence of the West, he asserts, "seems to have its basis in a crisis of truth." This is at bottom a metaphysical crisis. "An objective vision of the truth is often replaced by a more or less spontaneous subjective view. Objective morality gives way to individual ethics, where each person seems to set himself up as the norm. . . ."[18]

In his encyclical on moral norms, *Veritatis Splendor*, John Paul II contends that in view of today's social and cultural situation it is urgent for the Church to mount a major pastoral effort to clarify the relationship between human freedom and divine law. All around us, "the saving power of truth is contested, and freedom alone, uprooted from any objectivity, is left to decide by itself what is good and what is evil" (VS 84). This moral relativism, in the judgment of the pope, leads to gross violations of human rights and disrespect for human life, especially in the stages before birth and in old age.

In his encyclical on "The Gospel of Life," *Evangelium Vitae*,

---

[17] UNESCO #21, 198.
[18] Coimbra #6.

the pope remarks that the scientific and technical mentality prevalent in contemporary culture often fosters "a practical materialism, which breeds individualism, utilitarianism, and hedonism." All too often, he says, suffering is regarded as a useless burden, sexuality is depersonalized and exploited, and procreation is avoided (EV 23). This mentality breeds a "culture of death" resembling that described by the apostle Paul in the first chapter of his Letter to the Romans. In proclaiming the "gospel of life" the Holy Father calls for a cultural transformation in which the links between freedom, truth, and life are reestablished.

In his critique of Western societies the present pope speaks frequently of the menace of consumerism, which ensnares people in a web of false and superficial gratifications rather than helping them to express their personhood in an authentic way. Advertising and aggressive marketing, intent upon profits, create artificial human needs that hinder the formation of a mature personality. People lose themselves in the quest for affluence, luxury, amusement, and sensory pleasures, neglecting the quest for truth, beauty, goodness, and communion with others (CA 36). In this way people are alienated from their deepest selves, from their fellow human beings, and from God, their final destiny (CA 41).

This critique of contemporary culture is reinforced in the pope's addresses to the Pontifical Council for Culture. He speaks at one point of the growth of an "anti-culture" that manifests itself in growing violence, murderous confrontations, and the exploitation of instincts and selfish interests.[19] He notes that our world is characterized by clashing ideologies.[20] "Social and cultural transformation, political upheaval, ideological fermentations, religious restlessness, ethical research, all show a world in gestation, which is trying to discover its form and direction, its organic synthesis, and its prophetic renewal."[21] This situation constitutes a challenge and an opportunity for the Church to penetrate the soul of living cultures. "The meeting of cultures is nowadays a

---

[19] Address to Pontifical Council for Culture, January 16, 1984, §8; Gremillion, 207–9, at 209.

[20] Address to Pontifical Council for Culture, January 15, 1985, §3; Gremillion, 210–11, at 211.

[21] Address to Pontifical Council for Culture, January 13, 1986; text in *Origins* (Eng.), 27 January 1986: 3.

privileged area of dialogue between men committed to the search for a new humanism for our time" in which the various cultures can overcome their harmful limitations and open themselves "to him who is their source and end" and whose grace alone can heal the wounds of sin.[22]

5. *Reciprocity between the Church and Culture.* The dependence between the Church and culture is mutual. On the one hand, the cultures of the world need the Gospel, which enriches them "by helping them to go beyond the defective or even inhuman features in them, and by communicating to their legitimate values the fullness of Christ."[23] The Gospel "does not spring spontaneously from any cultural soil; it has always been transmitted by means of an apostolic dialogue which inevitably becomes part of a certain dialogue of cultures."[24] A culture that has been impregnated with the Gospel, sincerely received in faith, becomes capable of expressing and living out the truth and of proclaiming the revealed mystery.[25]

From Paul VI the present pope takes over the idea of an evangelization of cultures. The Gospel, he maintains, is creative of culture, as may be seen from the great masterpieces of art, music, and literature that emerged from Christian Europe.[26] The contributions of the Gospel to the cultures of Europe and Latin America in the past are capable of being matched by other regions in the future, as the pope has explained in his pastoral visits to Asia, Africa, and other continents. Their cultures, as the pope seems to view them, could be vastly enriched by the transcendent values that the Gospel can supply.

While human cultures depend on the Gospel for their purification and enrichment, the Gospel, conversely, depends on culture. The Church has need of culture in order for it to manifest the unsearchable riches of Christ and "to progress towards a daily more complete and profound awareness of the truth, which has

---

[22] Casaroli, 19.

[23] Apostolic Exhortation *Catechesi Tradendae* §53 (Boston: St. Paul Books & Media, 1993), 44.

[24] Ibid.

[25] Homily at Cartagena, Colombia, July 6, 1986, §7; text in *Origins* (Eng.) 8 September 1986: 6.

[26] UNESCO §10, 192.

already been given to her in its entirety by the Lord" (FC 10). "The synthesis between culture and faith," writes Pope John Paul II, "is not just a demand of culture, but also of faith. . . . A faith that does not become culture is a faith that has not been fully received, not thoroughly thought through, not faithfully lived out."[27] The Church relies on culture for its ability to express and communicate the truth of the Gospel. It "uses the discoveries of various cultures to spread and explain the message of Christ to all nations, to probe it and more deeply understand it, and give it better expression in liturgical celebrations."[28]

6. *Inculturation.* At various times since the beginning of his pontificate John Paul II has used the term "inculturation," which, though a neologism, "expresses very well one of the elements of the great mystery of the Incarnation."[29] Speaking to the members of the Pontifical Biblical Commission, the pope recalled that in some measure before the Incarnation, "the same divine Word had previously become human language, assuming the ways of expression of the different cultures which, from Abraham to the seer of the Apocalypse, offered the adorable mystery of God's salvific love the possibility of becoming accessible and understandable for successive generations, in spite of the multiple diversity of their historical situations." According to his benevolent condescension God reveals the transcendent and absolute message in the fragility of particular human languages.[30]

John Paul II returns to the theme of inculturation in his encyclical on Cyril and Methodius, *The Apostles of the Slavs.* While incarnating the Gospel in the cultures of Slavic peoples, they introduced these cultures into the life of the Church. Reflecting on this achievement, the pope remarks that for the fullness of catholicity, every culture must play its part in the universal plan of salvation. But in order to play that part, the cultures must remain open and alert to the other churches and traditions, main-

---

[27] Discourse to participants in the National Congress of the Movement of Cultural Commitment, January 18, 1982, *Origins* (Eng.), March 8, 1982; quoted in Casaroli, 19.

[28] Coimbra §5.

[29] Address to Pontifical Biblical Commission, April 26, 1979; *Origins* 9 (May 24, 1979): 15–16, at 15.

[30] Ibid.

taining the universal Catholic communion (SA 26). Recalling the relationship between Byzantium and Rome in the first millennium, John Paul II frequently remarks that the Church then breathed with two lungs, and that it must learn to do so once again (UUS 54).

The principle of inculturation has great significance for missiology, as the pope brings out in his talks to young churches on his visits to Zaire, Kenya, India, and elsewhere. To the aboriginal peoples of Australia he declared in November 1986: "You do not have to be divided into two parts. . . . Jesus calls you to accept his words and his values into your own culture" (UUS 19). His apostolic exhortation on the Church in Africa calls attention to the need to avoid syncretism and mandates study commissions to examine in depth all the cultural aspects of problems concerning marriage, the veneration of ancestors, and the spirit world from the theological, sacramental, and liturgical points of view.[31]

There is of course an inbuilt danger in inculturation: that it may adulterate the Gospel by embracing the ideas, values, and behavioral patterns of people still in need of evangelization. Recognizing this danger, the pope points out that the Gospel can build only on authentic human values, and that it inwardly transforms even these values by integrating them into Christian faith (RM 52). He enunciates two criteria for sound inculturation: compatibility with the Gospel and communion with the universal Church (FC 10). Speaking at Cartegena in Colombia in 1986, he declared: "The closer a particular church is to the universal Church . . . 'the more will this church be able to translate the treasure of faith into the legitimate variety of expressions of the profession of faith'."[32]

In an address to a meeting of cardinals, he cautioned that emphasis on special experiences in different sociocultural contexts must respect the necessity of being "in tune with those which other Christians, in contact with different cultural contexts, feel called to live in order to be faithful to demands arising from the

---

[31] Apostolic exhortation *Ecclesia in Africa*, §64; Eng. trans. in *Origins* 25 (October 5, 1995): 249–76, at 261.

[32] Cartegena §11, quoting Paul VI, *Evangelii Nuntiandi*, 64; text in *Origins* (Eng.) 8 September 1986: 6.

one single and identical mystery of Christ."[33] Catholics all over the world must be able to recognize one another as worshiping the same God and as united by the same Spirit of Christ. The Apostolic See, according to the pope, has a special responsibility to serve the Church's universal unity. The Church must therefore provide commonly shared standards of belief and conduct. Solicitude for unity among all the churches therefore gives rise to a daily tension in the life of every pope.[34] No abstract formula can resolve that tension. Often enough, a balance between conflicting goods must be worked out pragmatically. The bishops of the region, according to John Paul II, have the major responsibility for mediating between the concerns of the universal and the local church.[35]

7. *Applications to the United States.* In his speeches to American bishops on their quinquennial visits to Rome, and on his several trips to the United States, the pope has had occasions to comment on the cultural situation of this nation, as he sees it. He has made it abundantly clear that he supports the fundamental principles of the Declaration of Independence and the ethical and spiritual concerns that influenced the Founding Fathers. He espouses freedom, not as an end in itself but as a means whereby people can exercise their generosity and responsibility to one another as children of God and brothers and sisters in a common humanity.[36]

In his visit to the United States and Canada in the autumn of 1987 the pope spoke frequently of the reconciling power of Christ, which enables people of diverse races and cultures to live together in mutual love and respect. He gave addresses aimed specifically at African American, Native American, and Hispanic Catholics. Then on September 16, in Dodger Stadium, Los Angeles, he spoke at some length of ethnic diversity. After observing that many Catholics in California had imported their faith together with their specific cultural traditions, he went on to say:

---

[33] John Paul II, "One Church, Many Cultures," Annual Christmas address to the College of Cardinals, Vatican City, December 21, 1984, §4; Gremillion, 215.

[34] Ibid. §6; 217–18.

[35] Address to bishops of India, New Delhi, February 1, 1985, §5; in *Origins* 15 (February 20, 1986): 587–91, at 589.

[36] See, for instance, his remarks to President Ronald Reagan on September 10, 1987; *Origins* 17 (September 24, 1987): 238–39.

As a result, the Church in California, and particularly the Church in Los Angeles, is truly catholic in the fullest sense, embracing peoples and cultures of the widest and richest variety.

Today in the Church in Los Angeles, Christ is Anglo and Hispanic, Christ is Vietnamese and Irish, Christ is Korean and Italian, Christ is Japanese and Filipino, Christ is Native American, Croatian, Samoan, and many other ethnic groups. . . . And the Church, with all her different members, remains the one Body of Christ, professing the one faith, united in hope and in love.[37]

Permeating this hymn to diversity was the pope's realization that where diversity is cultivated without mutual love and respect, it could easily lead to the kind of violence that has more than once erupted in Los Angeles itself, both before and after the pope's visit of 1987.

At a later point in the same address John Paul II alluded to the problem of consumerism, which has been one of his major concerns. He stated:

> The Church faces a particularly difficult task in her efforts to preach the word of God in all cultures in which the faithful are constantly challenged by consumerism and a pleasure-seeking mentality, where utility, productivity, and hedonism are exalted while God and his law are forgotten. In these situations, where ideas and behavior directly contradict the truth about God and about humanity itself, the Church's witness must be unpopular. She must take a clear stand on the word of God and proclaim the whole gospel message with great confidence in the Holy Spirit.[38]

Still more sharply focused were the reflections on American culture embodied in the pope's response to Archbishop Rembert Weakland in their dialogue at Los Angeles on September 16, 1987. Archbishop Weakland had stated: "The Church in the United States of America can boast of having the largest number of educated faithful in the world."[39] To this the pope replied that in that case the Church should be in a position to exercise great influence upon American culture. Then he asked:

---

[37] "The Ethnic Universality of the Church," *Origins* 17 (October 15, 1987): 305–9, at 307.

[38] Ibid., 308–09.

[39] "Meeting with United States Bishops," *Origins* 17 (October 1, 1987): 255–67, at 262.

But how is the American culture evolving today? Is this evolution being influenced by the gospel? Does it clearly reflect Christian inspiration? Your music, your poetry and art, your drama, your painting and sculpture, the literature you are producing—are all those things which reflect the soul of a nation being influenced by the spirit of Christ for the perfection of humanity?[40]

The pope went on to assert that it is above all for the laity, once they have been inspired by the Gospel, to bring the Gospel's uplifting and purifying influence into the world of culture. He did not give a judgment about how well the American laity are fulfilling their mission. He left the answers to his own questions open. Perhaps it is for us, as religious guides and educators, to evaluate our own influence as individuals and that of the Society of Jesus in this country. Are we, through our publications, educational institutions, and other apostolates, making a positive contribution toward the synthesis of faith and culture, or are we responsible for perpetuating that unhealthy cleavage, which Paul VI memorably described as "the drama of our time"?

Although I have been able to give only a bare summary of the pope's rich reflections on the relationship between faith and culture, I hope that I have made it apparent that he has given much timely guidance for us as Jesuits as we seek to implement our mandate to bring this theme to the center of our apostolate.

---

[40] Ibid., 263.

8. DEMOGRAPHIC ETHICS
John Paul II on Demographic Ethics

John J. Conley, S.J.

INTERPRETING THE TEACHING of Pope John Paul II on demographic issues is not the simplest affair. There is no one document in which the pope systematically studies the moral issues concerning human population. Typically, the reflections of John Paul II on demography embed themselves as brief passages in longer documents dealing with the family or as brief communiqués submitted to international conferences dealing with population problems. The controversial Cairo Conference on Population (1994) was the occasion for the Vatican and regional episcopates to construct a veritable library of texts on the moral and political dilemmas surrounding population.

Although clearly "acts" of John Paul II's pontificate, these various documents evince different levels of solemnity and authority. They range from the letters that John Paul II himself wrote to formal testimony by the president of the Vatican delegation, Archbishop Renato Martino, to statements of clarification by the Holy See's official spokesman, Dr. Joaquin Navarro-Valls. The richest of the Vatican texts developed in the prelude to the Cairo conference is *Ethical and Pastoral Dimensions of Population Trends*, issued by the Pontifical Council for the Family (May 13, 1994).[1] Carefully citing previous magisterial statements, this document provides a synthesis of Pope John Paul II's teaching on demographic questions.

The various Vatican commissions, however, do not provide a completely coherent overview of population issues. In the heated

---

[1] Pontifical Council for the Family, "Population Trends: Ethical and Pastoral Dimensions" in *Origins* 24 (1994): 173–86.

overture to the Cairo conference, two prominent pontifical academies sparred with each other over the empirical issue of population growth. The Pontifical Academy of Sciences, in the report *Population and Resources* (1994), argued that "it is unthinkable that we can indefinitely sustain a birth rate that goes much above the level of two children per couple, which is enough to guarantee the replacement of generations."[2] (PR 175) The Pontifical Academy for Life, however, argued in its June 21, 1994, statement that dire warnings concerning further population growth were part of an "alarmist campaign" that distorted data in the service of anti-life ideologies.[3]

Despite divergences on the empirical issues of world population growth and hermeneutical problems concerning the magisterial "note" of various Vatican statements, John Paul II's pontificate provides a corpus of texts developing a clearly recognizable position on the moral problems surrounding population.[4] Certain themes constitute the stable axis of his judgments concerning demographics. First, he criticizes certain illicit means touted for limiting population growth: namely, artificial contraception, direct sterilization, abortion, and infanticide. Second, he underscores the pivotal role of the family, especially of the parents, in deciding the number and spacing of their children. Third, he criticizes the increasing tendency of the state to coerce individuals and poorer nations in their family planning decisions. Indeed, as the pontificate progresses, the teaching on demographic issues becomes an increasingly political critique of the pretensions of the state and international organizations to limit the procreative freedom of a couple in decisions regarding children. The intertwining of the prophetic and diplomatic concerns of the Holy See in the documents concerning demography constitutes one of the distinctive traits of this part of John Paul II's discourse in applied ethics.

---

[2] Pontifical Academy of Sciences, "Popolazione e Risorse," text in *Origins* (Eng.) 24 (1994): 175–76.

[3] Pontifical Academy for Life, "Statement of June 21, 1994," text in *Origins* (Eng.) 24 (1994): 176–77, here at 176.

[4] See *Christian Family in the Teaching of John Paul II* (Boston: St. Paul, 1990). See also "Population and Development" in *Origins* 24 (1994): 260–63; "Population Conference Draft Document Criticized" in *Origins* (Eng.) 23 (1993): 716ff.; and Monsignor Diarmuid Martin, "Population Conference Planning Session" in *Origins* 23 (1994): 757–58.

At the beginning of his pontificate, John Paul II sketches certain moral norms regarding demography in the apostolic exhortation *Familiaris Consortio* (1981). Synthesizing the debate and conclusions of the 1980 synod of bishops on the family, the document pinpoints certain of the persistent concerns of the pope in the field of population: the illicit nature of certain means of birth regulation; the moral and practical value of natural family planning; the ideals of responsible parenthood; the interlocked unitive and procreative goods of the marital covenant; the procreative and educational rights of the family; ethical norms of state intervention in the demographic arena. The exhortation also underscores the two key social units, the family and the state, who constitute the major actors in the act of population planning. It is the relationship between these two social principals, often construed in terms of imbalance and antagonism, which will remain one of the pope's preoccupations in the area of demographic discernment.

In elaborating his doctrine concerning population issues, the pope examines the ideological framework in which contemporary demographic questions emerge. He criticizes the rise of an anti-life mentality, which diminishes the value of human life, especially that of those perceived as a burden. This pessimism has affected certain assertions of demographic fact. "An anti-life mentality is born, as can be seen in many current issues: one thinks, for example, of a certain panic deriving from the studies of ecologists and futurologists on population growth, which sometimes exaggerate the danger of demographic increase to the quality of life" (FC 30). The pope not only challenges the accuracy of those who project overpopulation catastrophe. He examines the mentality that nurtures and justifies this apocalyptic discourse.

Typical of the pope's method in applied ethics, the exhortation examines the ideological culture that shapes common perceptions of the moral order before it defends particular moral norms. It is this ideological framework (in this case, a pervasive diminution of the good of human life, fueled by a despairing view of history) that renders the comprehension and acceptance of certain norms difficult in a given society.

Opposed to this apocalyptic culture is the Church's life-affirming culture. It is the Church's unconditional endorsement of the good of human life that undergirds the particular norms of action that it defends in the familial order. "The Church firmly believes that human life, even if weak and suffering, is always a splendid gift of God's goodness. Against the pessimism and selfishness which cast a shadow over the world, the Church stands for life: in each human life she sees the splendor of that 'yes,' that 'Amen,' who is Christ Himself" (FC 30). The pope's contrasting of these two ideological frameworks, which shape conflicting attitudes toward specific demographic issues, anticipates the dialectic between "the culture of death" and "the culture of life," which structures the argumentation of *Evangelium Vitae* (1995).

John Paul II examines the issue of morally proper means in the act of procreation. He excludes artificial contraception, sterilization, and abortion as opposed to the objective moral order. The pope lends particular attention to discerning the moral difference between artificial contraception and natural family planning. The divorce of the procreative from the unitive values of the conjugal embrace constitutes the central evil of contraception.

> When couples, by means of recourse to contraception, separate the two meanings that God the Creator has inscribed in the being of man and woman and in the dynamism of their sexual communion, they act as "arbiters" of the divine plan and they "manipulate" and degrade human sexuality—and with it themselves and their married partner—by altering its value of "total" self-giving. Thus the innate language that expresses the total reciprocal self-giving of husband and wife is overlaid, through contraception, by an objectively contradictory language, namely, that of not giving oneself totally to the other (FC 33).

The pope's distinctive personalist philosophy emerges in this critique of contraception. It is the union between spouses, and not only the procreative potential of intercourse, which is vitiated by contraception. The social category of language replaces the older biological categories of natural finality in this censure of contraception as a contradiction of the total gift of self, body and soul, which distinguishes marital union from other affective bonds.

John Paul II insists upon the moral superiority of the natural methods of family planning. In developing this case, he stresses the various personalist values implicit in the use of family planning that respects rather than suppresses human fertility.

> The choice of the natural rhythm involves accepting the cycle of the person, that is, the woman, and thereby accepting dialogue, reciprocal respect, shared responsibility, and self-control. To accept the cycle and to enter into dialogue means to recognize both the spiritual and corporal character of conjugal communion, and to live personal love with its requirement of fidelity. In this context the couple comes to experience how conjugal communion is enriched with those values of tenderness and affection which constitute the inner soul of human sexuality in its physical dimensions also. In this way sexuality is respected and promoted in its truly and fully human dimension, and it is never "used" as an "object" that, by breaking the personal unity of soul and body, strikes at God's creation itself at the level of the deepest interaction of nature and person (FC 32).

The unitive good defended in this version of the Church's apology for natural family planning is not simply the integral, mutual donation of the couple. It is the union between body and soul that constitutes the human person.

In deliberately destroying the procreative potential of the conjugal act, the couple mutilates the person's integration of physical fertility and affective commitment. Not only does natural family planning avoid the violation of the person's somatic-spiritual integrity. By situating family planning decisions within the framework of respect for the person's cycle of fertility, it opens the couple to the social virtues of affective dialogue and the ascetical virtues of self-control. The freedom of the couple and the individual partner is strengthened in the maturation of personalist values necessary in natural family planning but easily submerged in the recourse to periodic or total sterilization.

Familiaris Consortio also identifies the political dangers surrounding the question of demography. The decision regarding the number and spacing of children resides uniquely with the married couple. Increasingly, however, the state exceeds its authority through direct and indirect pressure on the procreative decisions of the couple.

> The Church condemns as a grave offense against human dignity and justice all those activities of governments or other public authorities which attempt to limit in any way the freedom of couples in deciding about children. Consequently, any violence applied by such authorities in favor of contraception or, still worse, of steriliza-

tion and procured abortion, must be altogether condemned and forcefully rejected. Likewise to be denounced as gravely unjust are cases where, in international relations, economic help given for the advancement of people is made conditional on programs of contraception, sterilization and procured abortion (FC 30).

This critique of the state's intrusion into the procreative domain, brief and secondary in *Familiaris Consortio*, will become increasingly prominent in later documents of John Paul II, as the anti-natalist policies of nation-state and international organizations become more pronounced. This passage also suggests the critique of contraceptive imperialism, engineered by the world's affluent elite against the impoverished formerly colonial populations, which will inform later Church censures of political programs of population control.

In another key document of his early pontificate, the *Charter of the Rights of the Family* (1982), the pope underscores the respective roles of the family and the state in the area of demographic decisions. Pointedly "addressed principally to governments" (CRF, Introduction), the charter uses legal categories to specify the limits of state intervention in family planning.

In article 3, the Holy See specifies the rights of the family vis-à-vis the state in the demographic area. "The spouses have the inalienable right to found a family and to decide on the spacing of births and the number of children to be born, taking into full consideration their duties toward themselves, their children already born, the family and society, in a just hierarchy of values and in accordance with the objective moral order, which excludes recourse to contraception, sterilization and abortion" (CRF 3).

This concept of procreative rights differs sensibly from the view of "reproductive" rights current in Western society. First, the decision to procreate is proper only to a duly married couple ("the spouses"), not to individuals or to cohabiting couples. Second, the right is inalienable—that is, intrinsic to the very structure of the human person. Therefore, it is neither conferred nor capable of abolition or restriction by the state. Third, this procreative right entails several distinct moral responsibilities if it is to be properly exercised by the spouses. On the one hand, the right to procreate involves prudential family planning. The duties toward self, the already born children, and the broader society (including the demographic state of society) must inform the decision to plan family size. On the other hand, this family planning discernment must carefully weigh the moral values inherent in the various methods of family planning. The reduction of family planning to a utilitarian calculus of efficiency is excluded. Wise moral evaluation of these methods will firmly exclude those methods that divorce the unitive and procreative goods of marriage (contraception and sterilization) and those methods that attack human life itself (abortion and infanticide). In this lapidary formula, the pope sketches the salient traits of responsible parenthood.

In the annexes to this article, the charter specifies the contours of proper state action in the procreative domain. First, the state may not limit the procreative rights of spouses. "The activities of public authorities and private organizations which attempt in any way to limit the freedom of couples in deciding about their children constitute a grave offence [sic] against human dignity and justice" (CRF 3.a). Second, international society may not use economic force to curb population through immoral means. "In international relations, economic aid for the advancement of peoples must not be conditioned on acceptance of programs of contraception, sterilization and abortion" (CRF 3.b). Finally, the state must refrain from imposing one model of family size, especially that of the small family, as it fulfills its duty to assist families. "Those married couples who have a large family have a right to adequate aid and should not be subjected to discrimination" (CRF 3.c). It is striking that, in the charter's discernment of family demography, the state emerges primarily as a threatening figure whose power must be strenuously limited.

In the more recent part of his pontificate, John Paul II has continued to emphasize the key tenets of demographic ethics outlined in the earlier documents. The pope continues to underscore the ethical value of particular means of family planning; the procreative rights of the family; the limits of state intervention; skepticism regarding doomsday population scenarios. In these recent texts, however, certain new accents give a different cast to the Church's longstanding positions on demographic problems. The documents surrounding the 1994 United Nations Conference on Population at Cairo clearly manifest these new concerns.

In his *Letter to Families* (February 2, 1994), John Paul II devotes an entire section to the principles of responsible parenthood. While repeating the earlier personalist arguments against contraception, he places a new emphasis upon the nature of "gift" in the marital covenant, specifically in the conjugal act:

> Every man and woman fully realizes himself or herself through the serious gift of self. For spouses, the moment of conjugal union constitutes a very particular expression of this. It is then that a man and woman, in the "truth" of their masculinity and femininity, become a mutual gift to each other. All married life is a gift; but this becomes most evident when the spouses, in giving themselves to each other in love, bring about that encounter which makes them "one flesh" (Gen 2:24) (LF 12).

This emphasis upon the gift of the self as central to an adequate anthropology and to an accurate exploration of the ethics of birth control echoes the earlier contention of *Veritatis Splendor* (1993) that self-sacrificial love, epitomized by the martyr (VS 90–94), constitutes the heart of human dignity. This donatory anthropology, fundamentally opposed to dominant anthropologies, which posit autonomy as the center of human rights, provides a new ground for the critique of contraception and for the call to generosity in bearing and educating children.

The diplomatic documents surrounding the Cairo conference also indicate certain shifts in the papacy's concerns in the controversy over population. The key texts of Archbishop Renato Martino,[5] the special delegate of the Holy See to the conference, underscore the two primary reservations of John Paul II concerning the draft and final documents of the conference. First, under the veil of "reproductive health," the conference clearly intended to endorse abortion as a right or, at least, as a practice that should be universally tolerated. The Vatican coalition's work to restore language from previous conferences that "abortion should be excluded as a means of birth control" effectively blocked this tacit endorsement of abortion under the rubric of population control. Second, the controversial documents tended to remove procreative ("reproductive") decisions from the domain of the family,

---

[5] Archbishop Renato Martino, "Holy See: Partial Association with the Consensus" in *Origins* (Eng.) 24 (1994): 257–58.

especially that of the parents, in favor of a radically individualistic view of human sexuality, where the autonomous individual, even a minor, simply receives value-neutral assistance from the state to ward off disease and unwanted pregnancy. This tendency of the international community to promote abortion and to dissolve family authority under claims of demographic apocalypse assaulted the fundamental goods of life and love which structure human society.

Particularly interesting in the Cairo corpus is the pope's *Letter to President Clinton* (March 19, 1994).[6] John Paul II devotes only one sentence to concern over "a general international recognition of a completely unrestricted right to abortion" (LPC 760). The bulk of the letter criticizes the abolition of the family suggested by the draft document and the ideological imperialism that increasingly dominates the demographic debate.

John Paul II criticizes the diminution of the family operated by the draft document, especially in its treatment of sexuality. An individualistic anthropology has replaced an older anthropology that privileged the family, especially the parents, as the principal actors in sexuality and procreation. "The idea of sexuality underlying the text is totally individualistic, to such an extent that marriage now appears as something outmoded. An institution as natural, fundamental and universal as the family cannot be manipulated by anyone.... Who could give such a mandate to individuals or institutions? The family is part of the heritage of humanity..." (LPC 760). This tacit abolition of the family strikes at the heart of human rights, since the United Nations' Universal Declaration of Human Rights (Art. 16.3) had clearly recognized the rights proper to the family as the fundamental unit of society. The weakening of the family can only destroy the human person, since it crushes the key institution that provides the proper biological, affective, and spiritual resources for the person's maturation.

The issue is no longer the Church's longstanding defense of the rights of the family against the encroachment of the state. It is now the very recognition of the family *as* family, as an irreducible social actor with its own rights and prerogatives. In the pope's

---

[6] *Letter to President Clinton,* text in *Origins* (Eng.) 23 (1994): 760.

perspective, the diminution of familial authority in the demographic realm is only a grave symptom of the increasingly aggressive abolition of the social group from which the person derives fundamental identity and direction.

The pope complements this defense of the family with a critique of the imperialism operative in the Cairo draft and similar national and international population programs. Following a long tradition of the magisterium, well represented by Paul VI's *Progressio Populorum* (1967), John Paul II underscores the duty of economic development suppressed by the affluent West's obsession with contraceptive programs as the solution to demographic problems. "One notes, for example, that the theme of development, on the agenda of the Cairo meeting, including the complex issue of the relationship between population and development, which ought to be at the center of discussion, is almost completely overlooked, so few are the passages devoted to it" (LPC 760). This position, elaborated at greater length in *Population Trends* (1994), argues that it is economic development and education, especially the rise of literacy among women, that will effectively address demographic imbalance. Not only does the single-minded emphasis upon population control prove ineffective. It prevents the affluent minority from examining and condoning the necessary economic reforms to permit such economic and educational development to occur in global solidarity.

More original is the pope's critique of the ideological imperialism that appears in the population program of Cairo. This radical individualism, strongly tinged by sexual hedonism, which dominates the program, represents the imposition of a lifestyle of certain affluent elites upon the more traditional cultures of the world. "Reading this document . . . leaves the troubling impression of something being imposed; namely a lifestyle typical of certain fringes within developed societies, societies which are materially rich and secularized. Are countries sensitive to the values of nature, morality, and religion going to accept such a vision of man and society without protest?" (LPC 760). Not only does this contraceptive imperialism represent a control of the bodies and sexual relations of the poor by the rich, who consider the poor as an intolerable burden. It represents a colonization of the mind, a libertarian apotheosis of the autonomous individual that destroys the natural law and religious codes of morality that have heretofore animated the vast majority of human societies.

In millenniarist language, John Paul II underscores the sterility of the individualistic culture promoted under the cover of population programs. "As we look forward to the year 2000, how can we fail to think of the young? What is being held up to them? A society of 'things' and not of 'persons.' The right to do as they will from their earliest years, without any constraint, provided it is 'safe.' The unreserved gift of self, mastery of one's instincts, the sense of responsibility—these are notions considered as belonging to another age" (LPC 760). The demographic dispute between the Church and its opponents has become a more fundamental anthropological struggle. On the one hand stands the anthropology of the secular world: materialist ("things"), voluntarist ("do as they will"), and utilitarian ("safety," rather than "right," as the moral criterion). On the other hand stands the anthropology of the Gospel and of the world's great religions, an anthropology that is donatory ("gift of self"), ascetical ("mastery of instincts"), and altruistic ("sense of responsibility"). The apocalyptic tone of the pope's discourse, echoed by similar rhetoric in *Evangelium Vitae* (EV 3–4), indicates the depth of this stark anthropological conflict.

John Paul II's teaching on key moral issues in the demographic arena manifests certain characteristic weaknesses and strengths.

The weaknesses often appear to rise from the piecemeal treatment that the pope usually accords these issues. First, the pontificate's statements concerning demographic facts indicate a certain ambiguity, if not confusion. The point of departure for any elaboration of moral judgments concerning population issues is the determination as to whether population growth is, in fact, a serious problem. The pope's personally signed statements tend to express skepticism about alarmist pictures of overpopulation, but avoid extensive analysis of the veracity of the claims of overpopulation by more sober demographers. The statement *Population Trends* offers a regionalist solution: certain nations do suffer from too many births, while others are failing to replenish their population (PT 175–79). The Pontifical Academy of Sciences affirms the existence of a grave population crisis, while the Pontifical Academy of Life squarely denies it. It is difficult to find a coherent posture toward conflicting claims of the relationship between population and resources.

While one might argue that the estimation of demographic facts is an empirical question outside the realm of Church judgment, it is not so easy to sunder fact from value in many of the anguished ethical questions concerning population. John Paul II, like Paul VI (HV 10), argues that spouses must consider the demographic realities of their society, among other criteria, in determining the number and spacing of their children. The hazy image of this reality in papal documents, however, renders this criterion an uncertain one. In *Humanae Vitae* (23), Paul VI recognized the right of the state to conduct prudent educational programs when overpopulation emerges as a social problem. However, the conflicting statements of John Paul II's pontificate on the nature and severity of the population problem place foggy boundaries around the legitimate rights of state intervention in this area.

Second, the argument of John Paul II concerning responsible parenthood, especially the controversial norms in the area of contraception, remains sketchy. The innovative reflections of the pope concerning the unitive good of marriage, conceived as a language of total mutual gift, remains primarily on the level of metaphor and intuition. The pontificate has yet to produce a systematic treatment of the moral problems surrounding family planning, especially the Church's norms concerning contraception, comparable to the precise, elaborate treatment accorded work in *Laborem Exercens* (1983) or development in *Sollicitudo Rei Socialis* (1987). Undoubtedly, many members of the Church would prefer that the norms in this area simply be quietly affirmed or passed over in silence, given the wide non-reception of this ecclesiastical teaching. However, the Church's duty of formation of conscience requires a careful presentation of the logic of the Church's position. It especially requires a detailed apologetic of the decisive moral differences between "artificial" and "natural" methods of family planning. It is the incapacity of many Church members to grasp these differences that has rendered Church doctrine in this area so problematic.

Despite certain fragilities in his argument on demographic issues, John Paul II has already crafted a distinctive voice in the ethical debate over population. Not only has he maintained the traditional positions of the Church in the public forum. He has provided new anthropological and political resources for the elaboration of the ethical contours of responsible parenthood.

One of the central contributions of John Paul II to the dispute on demographic ethics has been his persistent focus upon the moral character of the means, and not only of the consequences, of population-related acts. He has repeatedly underlined the moral disvalues inherent in the very act of contraception, direct sterilization, and procured abortion before a public that habitually poses the debate in terms of the putative benefits of such acts for such social ends as population control. He has identified the destruction of key human goods, such as life, integrity, and love, operated by the practice of such acts. His statements on demographic issues have repeatedly challenged the utilitarian framework in which the population debate is often unconsciously presented. By insisting upon the moral character of particular acts in the demographic area, John Paul II has applied his broader polemic against consequentialist ethics, elaborated in *Veritatis Splendor* (71–81), to the vexed issue of population planning. His identification of intrinsic evils in this area and his critique of circumstantial justifications of such evil acts reflect the broader polemic in fundamental moral theory.

John Paul II also makes a key contribution to the anthropology that undergirds the Church's position on this nexus of demographic issues. He clarifies the nature of personal freedom within population-related decisions. On the one hand, the married couple enjoys an inalienable freedom to decide the number and spacing of their children. The state, in particular, is barred from any coercion in this arena. To be responsible, however, this procreative exercise of freedom must subordinate itself to the objective moral order, especially the relevant goods of love and life. The Church enjoys a preeminent role in this maturation of moral conscience for the authentic exercise of freedom. This linking of freedom and objective good in the field of population echoes the broader concern of the pope, stated in *Veritatis Splendor* (35–53), to articulate the proper link between freedom and truth in the moral order. The pope constructs his theory of rights upon this concept of personal freedom. In this perspective, right does not impose itself as the freedom to do as one wants. Rather, right emerges as the justified claim of the person to pursue and realize an authentic good in the hierarchy of values. The pope's prophetic call to international organizations to reaffirm key rights in the demographic order (such as the right to life, the rights of the family, the rights of the child before and after birth) is an attempt to ground political action upon the objective goods of the human person.

One of the most original of the pope's contributions to the anthropology of the demographic debate is his insistence upon the donatory nature of the human person. Responsible parenthood cannot flourish upon a thin foundation of freedom and right alone. It requires a series of virtues centered upon generosity. Only a magnanimous attitude toward children can welcome procreation and the education of children. Natural family planning can succeed only if the spouses cultivate the art of compassionate dialogue. Sacrificial love on behalf of one's children and spouse is the mark of the mature person shaping the size of one's own family and, as citizen, designing national and international demographic policies. It is heroic self-gift to the other, tinged by the charity of the cross, which is the ultimate framework for the perception and endorsement of the Church's norms concerning childbearing.

Finally, the pope's combat in the province of demographic ethics serves a larger political project. The issue is not simply that of the proper means in the population-related actions of individuals and nations. A central issue is the proper actor in this area: the married couple. The pope criticizes the continuing effacement of the family in a population scenario that reduces social interaction to two principal actors: the individual citizen and the state. The increasing arrogance of the state and international organizations in coercing procreative decisions only reflects a broader assault upon the family as the central cell of society. The educational and diplomatic work of the Church in demographic battles is a defense of the family as the preeminent social actor who enjoys inalienable rights in the domain of procreation and education. John Paul II's statements on demographic policy are an apology for the corporate freedom of the family to design its own destiny and a warning on the grim nature of a society where the very matrix of the person, the family, has vanished in the tumult of demographic engineering.

Response

John M. McDermott, S.J.

IT IS HARD TO DISAGREE with the overall cogency of Father Conley's presentation, especially his emphasis on the centrality of the family in John Paul II's theological *Weltanschauung* and its vulnerability before the attacks of modern libertarian ideologies. Certainly one aspect of the presentation, the demographic, should remain outside the scope of this comment. Not only is the "science" of demographics extremely complex, involving the synthesis of many diverse ways of studying the human reality and dealing with the unpredictable element of human freedom, but also I am not one of that science's initiates. As an outsider looking in, I am amazed at the degree to which renowned "experts" can disagree on the basic elements of their science and at how widely past predictions have gone astray. Not having been trained in that area, I find it prudent to pass on to other things.

Yet, in passing, I should mention that the Pontifical Academy of the Sciences is not an official ministry of the papacy. Wishing to indicate the Church's support for science, the pope established that body to honor great scientists and to provide a means for consulting them on various issues that require a scientific analysis. Many non-Catholics are members in that academy, and others are invited to participate in its sessions. Granted freedom of investigation and expression, the Pontifical Academy of the Sciences publishes the results of the members' discussions. However embarrassing a discrepancy or contradiction between its results and the documents of the Pontifical Council for the Family may be, the authority of the latter far surpasses the former's authority, since the latter stands under the control of the pope, who may intervene directly in its proceedings.

Leaving aside the demographic hypothesis, I pass on to the

more philosophico-theological aspects of Conley's paper. Here my response is nuanced. On some points I agree wholeheartedly with the pope and with Conley, on others I see some difficulties with the papal position, and on others Conley seems to have overlooked some aspects of the pope's thought.

First, it is easy to support the pope's moral critique of the global village managed by technological bureaucrats apparently liberated from traditional moral restraints. These modern, mentally impoverished heirs of the Enlightenment strive to subject humankind to the tyranny of arbitrary rule in the name of freedom. Although the early *illuminati* sought to ground human rights in a universal nature, whose perception by reason would free humanity from the shackles of tradition, their successors have identified rights almost exclusively with freedom, understood as the capacity to decide one's own destiny and, most recently, to create one's own values. Such an understanding places the individual in opposition to nature, understood as the realm of the necessary, and to God, whose omnipotence allegedly limits (if it does not destroy) human freedom.

Human "liberation" from tradition, nature, and religion has been accelerated along the way by various ideologies that contributed to the acceptance of the liberal notion of individual freedom, even while contradicting it. For they undercut the values of traditional society. Marx submitted reality to the necessity of economic laws, and Freud assured people that they were determined by their libido. Thus, the liberated modern was encouraged to deal with reality in terms of its "basics": money and sex. Add to that terrible twosome the reality of power so lauded by Machiavelli, Hobbes, Nietzsche, and Sartre, and we are left with the unholy trinity that makes the world go around: property, pleasure, and power. Not that this trinity is a particularly recent discovery. New is only its intellectual justification. For the Bible knew these forces as the world (property), the flesh (pleasure), and the devil (power for power's sake). These forces strive against God, but in the end they and their worshipers—those who make them absolute—shall be overcome in the victory of God's infinite love.

By accepting the modern notion of freedom as mere self-determination, humanity has fallen into a trap that threatens enslavement. Separated from nature, religion, and tradition, what should modern people choose? With a relativized reason and a deconstructed reality, they find themselves perplexed, and into such a void of meaning the technological bureaucrats eagerly leap, facilitating the pursuit of goals chosen by some elite that somehow consult their feelings to determine what is politically correct. When individuals are placed in direct confrontation with the unrestrained state, despite their alleged freedom, they are doomed to defeat. Their "liberation" had loosened them from all intermediary institutions that might have guaranteed room for free action by restricting the power of Leviathan, the omnipotent State.

Such a view of the human obviously overlooks the roles of the family, rooted in the order of creation, and of the Church, grounded in the order of redemption, to overcome the wounds of sin. We Americans tend to forget that the origin of nationalism is rooted in the family, extended to the clan and the race, a fact that the recent breakdown of the Soviet empire and the rise of nationalistic parties in Europe are again illustrating. No mere idea, not even the contentless notion of freedom as pure self-determination, can long sustain the struggle against the weightier loyalties of blood and race. Indeed, one might argue that only a universal religion, grounded in supernatural revelation and demanding the sacrifice of all for God, can successfully correct the biases of sciences affected by scotosis and overcome the divisions of nationalism and racism that result from a wounded nature.[7]

However perceptive and correct the pope's critique of modern ideologies, his own positive vision of humanity contains several tensions. On the one hand, by his way of discussing human rights and freedom he has revised the traditional idea of the moral law grounded in nature and the common good. In this he seems to wish to adapt the Christian message to the modern age. On the other hand, against the modern age he insists upon objective, universal values and norms. Within the Church he has seen the danger of proportionalism, which exalts the individual subject's intellectual-volitional dynamism over against the objective order of nature. This new morality, the so-called proportionalism or consequentialism, not only stands on a very weak philosophical basis but also contra-

---

[7] Such, of course, is the attempt of Bernard Lonergan, S.J., at the end of his masterpiece, *Insight*. In this book he recapitulates a long tradition of Catholic and Christian apologetics.

dicts the whole tradition of Catholic morality insofar as it denies the possibility of universal, negative moral norms.

Yet when John Paul II himself so stresses the creative freedom of the individual, how can he ground the universal, apparently abstract norms of traditional morality? Why is freedom bound to truth? How is that freedom to be understood? These questions are all the more difficult to answer because the pope, following traditional scholastic doctrine, apparently upholds a double notion of freedom: freedom of indifference, which is the basis of the Enlightenment's self-actuating and self-defining freedom, and the Augustinian engaged freedom, which exists only in choosing the good, a notion of freedom championed by transcendental Thomists and Protestants.[8]

Although these tensions can be picked out in the pope's thought, there are other elements, I believe, that can serve to synthesize them. Their center lies in the pope's vision of marital love and the family. Let me spell that out briefly. As Walter Kasper noted, there is no freedom without an absolute. If all is relativizable, reason can never find any reason for a choice, and a choice that is irrational can be neither human nor free. This absolute cannot be an abstraction, for the real is concrete. Neither can it be the necessary goal of an intellectual-volitional dynamism, for such necessity destroys freedom and a true absolute cannot be restricted to the position of a distant goal.[9]

---

[8] Freedom of indifference designates that understanding of freedom whereby the distinction between intellect and will is clearly maintained in view of their distinct formal objects, the true and the good. In the exercise of freedom, the intellect presents various *species* or intellectually perceived possibilities to the will, which chooses one of them. The will thus follows the intellect's lead, but it is not subordinated to it since, as existentially oriented to the unlimited Good, no finite object presented as good can determine it. The will chooses on its own to make the final *species* presented to it final, and that *species* informs the will in its choice. Engaged freedom designates that understanding whereby intellect and will are joined in a single spiritual dynamism seeking the concrete true as its good. Since this dynamism is natural to the individual, it underlies all choices as their condition of possibility and is implicitly actuated in all of them. Since human nature itself is understood as this striving, it is always engaged. For the difficulties involved in each understanding and their mutual complementarity, see J. McDermott, S.J., "the New Scholastic Analysis of Freedom," *International Philosophical Quarterly* 34 (1994): 149–65.

[9] The notion of a finite absolute was inherent in a conceptualist Thomism that maintained that the mind can grasp reality through an abstraction released (*absolutum*) from the limitations of time and space. Transcendental Thomism adopts another notion of an Absolute, identifying it with the infinite God as the

The true Absolute is given in every true experience of love, for love demands unconditional commitment. A love that says, "I love you for twenty minutes, for twenty years, for as long as the good times last or the money holds out" is not a true love, for all is made to depend upon the alleged lover's determinations, not upon the good of the beloved to whom the lover commits. Yet no human being can by right demand total dedication from another human being. Love is a gift that engenders joy. Lovers know that they do not condescend in their love; they are called out of themselves by the demand of love in the concrete. Moreover, love is not an act of supreme rationality. Were that the case, every rational woman would be obliged to love the same man, and every rational man would be compelled to love the same woman. The resulting, almost universal frustration among unsuccessful suits would argue strongly against such a rationalistic understanding of love.

Love is really directed to the individual, who resists all reduction to a universal, rationalistic schema. Reason can never force anyone to love. For love involves free giving. Yet this giving depends on more than an abstract independence, from whose Olympian heights one condescends. Rather, one falls in love and, according to one's viewpoint, love either gives eyes or blinds them.

The only One who can demand an absolute commitment from humanity is God. That is the mystery of love. Through the finite other the infinite God self-manifests, calling humanity to a total commitment, and upon one's response to God depends one's eternal salvation or damnation. That, I believe, is the sacramental structure of reality and Christian revelation. It is clearly manifested in marriage, the sacrament of creation, with its lifelong commitment of fidelity, that renders man, male and female, the image of God. In its structure are united various apparent opposites:

---

term of human intellectual-volitional striving. Were this Absolute merely the goal of a striving, it could never be attained, since the finite can never of itself reach the Infinite. Were this Absolute already present, as one would expect of a truly infinite, omnipresent God, there would be no need of striving after God. This difficulty especially touches transcendental Thomism, which is built upon the existential judgment, a reflexive act, and implies a self-conscious intellectual soul. But if God is everywhere and the soul is immediately self-conscious, it should be intuiting God in itself. But the intuition of God is the beatific vision.

1. particular and universal, for love must be particular yet acknowledge no inherent bonds (the basis for the unity in love of the human race);
2. subject and object, for the perception of the objective claim of love depends upon the subject's eyes to see, and these eyes are determined by the use of freedom;
3. necessary and free, for it both imposes with a moral necessity and yet allows rejection;
4. freedom of indifference and engaged freedom, for the distance guaranteed by the finite sign through which the infinite God summons us guarantees the possibility of rejection, and the imperative initiative of love allows no neutrality.

After sin destroyed the primordial unity of God and humankind and of human beings among themselves, Christ the God-man is recognized to be necessary as the sacramental structure's recapitulation—that is, its restoration and elevation, granting humanity renewed knowledge of God. God alone could assure humanity of the reality of love, create the conditions of human response, and restore the unity of the whole race. This new unity in Christ results from the total response of love, corporeal as well as spiritual, to his love and so forms the Church, the Body of Christ in space and time.

From such a viewpoint and developing the insights of *Love and Responsibility*, one may defend the Church's position against artificial contraception. The bodily union of spouses is intrinsically open to procreation. Since the body is the symbol of the soul, which both expresses and exercises a true causality upon the soul, it is hardly surprising to find that, as an expression of love, it reflects the nature of love. For whoever tries to restrict love stifles it. Of itself love is expansive, whether among human beings it should move one to write poetry and sing in the rain, or within the Trinity the love of the Father is expressed in the Son, engendering him, or in creation, where God, as it were, goes beyond himself, or in redemption, when God shares the divine life blood with us. The procreative aspect of love's physical expression should not be separated from the unitive aspect, since in God love and life are one in self-communication. This interpretation also permits the refutation of the frequently heard objection that the use of natural methods of birth control intends the same separation of the unitive and procreative aspects of marital love as does the use of artificial methods. For, essential to the goodness or illicitness of a moral act is not primarily the subject's intention but the objective significance of the act given by God. Insofar as the subjective agents correlate their actions with natural rhythms inherent in bodily functions and acts, acknowledging thereby the primacy of an act's objective goodness, they do not frustrate the act itself. They submit themselves to an objective norm of love established by God even in the flesh.

Finally, this view agrees with the pope's view about the person. Although *The Acting Person* starts with an analysis of the person as a self-conscious center of free activity, it later expands its treatment to include the communitarian or relational aspects of the person. Indeed, later articles particularly stress the communitarian aspect. In this Karol Wojtyła maintains the tension in Catholic thought between the diverse, apparently contradictory notions of the person found in Catholic theology. The Christological notion of person, *substantia individualis rationalis naturae*, stresses the "in-itself" or individuality of the subject, whereas the trinitarian notion, *relatio subsistens*, highlights the relative or communitarian aspects of personality. These two notions of the person correspond, respectively, to freedom of indifference, exercised by the individual subject, and engaged freedom, wherein the subject is always oriented to a goal. Insofar as love represents the objective order of reality, the task of freedom is to respond to the gift of love, and the task of intelligence is to recognize the sacramental structure of freedom, apart from which there is no meaning. Thus, an objectivity rooted in God serves as the norm for human subjectivity. There is no longer any opposition between subjectivity, freedom, and objectivity, since love provides the objective structure of reality, which embraces and empowers subjective freedom. "Rights language" can then be understood as an attempt to preserve the minimum necessary conditions of freedom in a world of sin, which tends to objectivize and instrumentalize human beings.[10]

---

[10] This pope's derivation of rights from the primordial covenant love that serves as the ultimate norm of human actions has been worked out by Robert Spitzer, S.J., in his contribution, "Covenant Love: Interpersonal Person, Family, and Work in the Social Theory of John Paul II" (chap. 11).

9. ECONOMIC ETHICS
Neoclassical Economics and the Economic Encyclicals of John Paul II

John J. Piderit, S.J.

INTRODUCTION

John Paul II has used three encyclicals to articulate his concern for the economic development of the modern world: *On Human Work* (*Laborem Exercens*, 1981), *On Social Concern* (*Sollicitudo Rei Socialis*, 1987), and *On the Hundredth Anniversary of Rerum Novarum* (*Centesimus Annus*, 1991). They present increasingly differentiated views of the economic order and the economic problems faced throughout the world.[1]

A number of themes articulated by John Paul II cast light on the neoclassical model of economic behavior, which is the standard reference model in the discipline of economics. Reflecting on these themes suggests ways to qualify or situate the neoclassical model. The model, on the other hand, provides a useful analysis of some important topics covered by Pope John Paul II. Since he focuses on fundamental economic motivation and behavior, the paper concentrates on those aspects of the encyclical and the model that highlight motivation and behavior.

---

[1] These encyclicals also comment about political relationships, either within individual nations, between individual nations, or between blocs of nations. As important as such relationships are, they will not be treated in this paper so as to allow a focus on the specifically economic issues.

Ideology, Theology, and Economic Models

Because John Paul II approaches economic subjects in a theological and philosophical style, and because the vast majority of economists are not schooled in philosophy, much less theology, a useful exercise is to explore the relationship among philosophy, theology, and economics.

John Paul II describes his analysis of economic and social issues as theological. That is, he uses theology to justify the proper economic motives for workers, managers, and entrepreneurs. Much of what he calls theology is in fact a philosophy of the human person as it is articulated in the New Testament. Consonant with scriptural tradition, John Paul II consistently appeals to a transcendent human person, but in so doing he does not rely on any doctrine specific to the Christian faith. By establishing his argument as inclusively as possible and using basic philosophical principles, he wants to persuade all people who believe in God that the Catholic tradition of social ethics is sound and appealing.

One goal of this paper is to explore whether John Paul II's analysis is consistent with that used by neoclassical economists. Before addressing this issue, it is useful to examine the unusual distinction that John Paul II makes between ideology and theology.

Ideology and Theology

In the three social encyclicals treated in this study, John Paul II comments frequently upon evils and shortcomings of the present economic order. He also suggests reasons why such deficiencies are so prevalent in modern society. He is careful, however, to avoid espousing a particular economic system. In fact, he says that promoting a specific economic and social structure would be inappropriate for the Church since the Church's social doctrine is not an ideology:

> Nor is [the Church's social doctrine] an *ideology*, but rather the *accurate foundation* of the results of a careful reflection on the complex realities of human existence, in society and in the international order, in the light of faith and the Church's tradition. Its main aim is to *interpret* these realities, determining their conformity with or divergence from the lines of the Gospel teaching on man and his

vocation, a vocation which is at once earthly and transcendent; its aim is thus *to guide* Christian behavior. It therefore belongs to the field, not of *ideology*, but of *theology* and particularly of moral theology.

The teaching and spreading of her social doctrine are part of the Church's evangelizing mission. And since it is a doctrine aimed at guiding people's behavior, it consequently gives rise to a "commitment to justice," according to each individual's role, vocation, and circumstances. (SRS 41).

The use of the term *ideology* in this context merits attention. Usually, broad social systems such as Marxism, liberalism, and capitalism would be considered ideologies by academics. But when John Paul II explains why the Church's social doctrine is not an ideology, it appears that Marxism, liberalism, and the like, would also qualify as not being ideologies. In terms of John Paul II's thought, each of these systems is an (arguably) "accurate formulation of the results of a careful reflection on the complex realities of human existence, in society, and in the international order." The difference is that they do not conduct their analysis in the light of faith or the Church's tradition.

As used by John Paul II, "ideology" appears to mean a comprehensive social, economic, or philosophical system that does not incorporate the transcendent dimension of human existence. They are ideologies precisely because they neglect a fundamental feature of the human situation. Marxism and capitalism also interpret the realities of human existence, though in each case the transcendent, religious dimension is omitted. Marxism denies the existence of such an order, while capitalism (or one of its variants) chooses not to incorporate it formally into its system, though it acknowledges that many people make economic and personal decisions based on their religious orientation. For John Paul II, an ideology is any comprehensive system that omits theological considerations. In this sense, any ideology is at best a partial synthesis, as seen from the Catholic perspective.[2]

Perhaps influenced by the demise of Marxism in formerly com-

---

[2] John Paul II's desire to complement social analysis with theology is supported by independent scholars, using a general Christian approach. See Mark R. Schwehn, *Exiles from Eden: Religion and the Academic Vocation in America* (Oxford: Oxford University Press, 1993).

munist countries, John Paul II in *Centesimus Annus* cautiously comments concerning social and economic systems as they are viewed by the Church:

> The Church has no models to present; models that are real and truly effective can only arise within the framework of different historical situations, through the efforts of all those who responsibly confront concrete problems in all their social, economic, political, and cultural aspects, as these interact with one another. For such a task the Church offers her social teaching as an *indispensable and ideal orientation*, a teaching which, as already mentioned, recognizes the positive value of the market and of enterprise, which at the same time points out that these need to be oriented towards the common good. (CA 43)

Since part of the mission of the Church is to provide guidance for many different social groups, existing at many different points in time and throughout the world, it is impossible for the Church to develop a model that could generate policies binding on all such societies. As the pope points out, any effective economic model has to apply to a certain historical situation. Interested in the predictive ability of models, economists strive to develop a model that fits reality. Even if they were able to generate such a model for the current form of capitalism, they would readily admit that the model would have to be modified as soon as economic behavior changes, whether it be the behavior of individuals, significant groups, firms, or large agents such as the government.

Absent a model, the social teaching of the Church resorts to pointing people in the approximately correct direction. Orienting people correctly sometimes is best achieved by telling them to avoid approaches that are clearly wrong. At other times, the ideal orientation is determined by describing as best one can the contours of the ideal society. In either instance, the orientation or ideal is understood relative to the present position of society. The danger of not using a model is that the Church's message comes across as vague and exceedingly idealistic. Yes, the Church does present some ideals that will only be attained at the end of time. However, the purpose of writing a social encyclical is to persuade people and institutions to modify their behavior so as to move society closer to a just society, given our present conditions and within a reasonable amount of time.

John Paul II usually speaks of justice as an ideal toward which each society should strive. Although he does not address the issue of changing standards of justice, he implicitly acknowledges that practical standards of justice are constantly being modified. For example, in speaking of just working conditions, he is aware that for many countries—including both developed and less developed countries—the working conditions that currently exist are far superior to those that prevailed one hundred years ago. Nonetheless, he would also point out that the gap between the working conditions in the First World and those in the Third World has probably increased over the past one hundred years. Clear progress has been made, but the improvements have occurred more rapidly in the wealthy than in the poor countries. Because the wealthy countries have been able to improve their working conditions so dramatically, the injustice suffered by the poor is greater and more patent.

In order to know whether a society is close to an ideal of justice or making good progress toward justice, a person such as the pope has to use some sort of economic model, in addition to relying upon the moral and theological principles that he presents in the encyclicals. Note, his use of some implicit model does not contradict John Paul II's earlier statement that the Church does not prescribe models of economic or social structures. One can use a model to give a first approximation to where one stands at the present moment, without necessarily implying that the same model should be used to suggest which changes should be introduced into society. Nonetheless, if one wishes to introduce economic changes and one wants to avoid undoing the good results that have been achieved to date, some economic model—implicit or explicit—is unavoidable.

John Paul II has chosen not to tell us which economic model he has used in analyzing the current state of economic affairs. In so doing, he has committed no egregious error, since, for the most part, only economists walk around with models in their heads, making judgments about the state of the economy and how it can be improved. Some model, however, is important, because without it, even solid moral and theological principles do not provide a sufficient framework to answer some fundamental questions or to address significant issues.

Some clear benefits are associated with the use of an economic model. First, as was indicated earlier, one needs an economic model to know whether one is making progress toward justice, in all its various forms, both at the individual, the firm, and the societal levels. Second, since a model makes certain assumptions and since it is unlikely that all the assumptions will be fulfilled at any point in time, the model indicates areas that require modification if the predictions of the model do not come true. Third, the moral and theological principles enunciated by the pope can be used to challenge, to improve, or simply to modify the model. This last point is particularly significant if the model is widely used among people who are influential in setting economic and social policy.

The Free Market System

In *Centesimus Annus* John Paul II cautiously endorses the free market economy as the preferred path toward economic development, at this point in the stage of economic development:

> Can it perhaps be said that, after the failure of Communism, capitalism is the victorious social system, and that capitalism should be the goal of the countries now making efforts to rebuild their economy and society? Is this the model which ought to be proposed to the countries of the Third World which are searching for the path to true economic and civil progress?
>
> The answer is obviously complex. If by "capitalism" is meant an economic system which recognizes the fundamental and positive role of business, the market, private property, and the resulting responsibility for the means of production, as well as free human creativity in the economic sector, then the answer is certainly in the affirmative, even though it would perhaps be more appropriate to speak of a "business economy," "market economy," or simply "free economy." But if by "capitalism" is meant a system in which freedom in the economic sector is not circumscribed within a strong juridical framework which places it at the service of human freedom in its totality and sees it as a particular aspect of that freedom, the core of which is ethical and religious, then the reply is certainly negative. (CA 42)

John Paul II emphasizes the significance of a strong, juridic structure in which the free market must be embedded if it is to achieve the moral and theological goals that are important for Christians and adherents of other religious denominations. This qualification applies to any economic model that is proposed, and it is a consideration to which we will have to return for closer analysis.

The market economy is so inclusive and prolific that it is sometimes blamed for generating too much variety. Is it socially important that people be able to choose from over sixty shades of pink lipstick? Do consumers really need over one hundred varieties of automobiles from which to choose? Despite the plethora of choices, the market economy also operates under certain constraints. One constraint is that the economy does not embrace sufficient participants. If such participants had purchasing power, it would likely be revealed in a different composition of goods produced:

> It would appear that, on the level of individual nations and of international relations, the *free market* is the most efficient instrument for utilizing resources and effectively responding to needs. But this is true only for those needs which are "solvent," insofar as they are endowed with purchasing power, and for those resources which are "marketable," insofar as they are capable of obtaining a satisfactory price. (CA 34)

John Paul II's concern is that the market is efficient in any meaningful way only for the limited number of people who can fully partake in the market mechanism. The real needs of the vast majority of people—the poor—never get expressed in the marketplace because the people with those needs do not have sufficient assets—financial or educational—to be players in the marketplace. John Paul II notes this reservation even as he acknowledges the overall advantages of the market economy.

Since, all things considered, John Paul II is inclined to give approval to the free economy over competing systems that use a centrally regulated approach, I will present here an economic model that approximates the workings of a free economy, at least as it operates in the United States. The model is called the "neoclassical model," and it has been developed and refined over the past century to such a point that it is the most widely accepted model among practicing economists in the First World. To be sure, its wide acceptance does not guarantee its verisimilitude, but it does suggest that it is the appropriate model to use if one wishes to influence the manner in which people analyze the economy and the actual policies that are proposed to improve performance of the economy. In the next section I present the model as well as its predictions and some of its shortcomings.

The Neoclassical Model—Static and Dynamic

The neoclassical model makes certain assumptions about the economic behavior of individual consumers, laborers, and producers (or capitalists). The model comes in two forms, static and dynamic. Although the dynamic form is the one that should be applied to any actual economy, it has not been as well developed as the static version, which has been carefully refined so that it adheres to the strictest canons of the physical sciences. Whether physical sciences should be the norm against which an economic model is measured has been thoroughly debated by economists. For the past several decades, despite continuing debate on this topic, the norm of the physical sciences has been the guiding hermeneutic for neoclassical economics. Because the static model conforms most closely to this norm, I will present theorems that can be derived from that model.

Significant Theorems of Neoclassical Economics

The power of the neoclassical model is revealed in four theorems, which I will present and discuss informally. Later I will present the assumptions used to arrive at the results.

A. *The First Theorem of Welfare Economics.* For any distribution of initial assets in a free market economy, there exists a set of prices for all goods, services, labor, and capital, which generate full employment of all resources in the economy.

B. *The Second Theorem of Welfare Economics.* Corresponding to any set of prices in a free market economy, there exists an initial endowment of assets such that all resources in the economy are used in the most efficient manner possible. That is, the prices generate full employment of labor and other assets.

The first theorem states that, whatever the initial distribution of wealth is in a static economy, a free market economy generates an efficient use of all resources in the economy. That is, all labor and capital are employed, and there is no rearrangement of activities that will produce a better outcome. If, for example, a social planner were able to establish a priori what the initial distribution of income should be, such an economy would be efficient if it were a free market economy. The second theorem reverses the first and says that for any equilibrium set of prices in the marketplace, one can find an initial distribution of assets that will generate such a price in a static free market economy.

C. *The International Trade Theorem of Comparative Advantage.* Any free market country benefits by trading freely with other countries, even when the country feels that its resources are weak compared to those present in another country.

The third theorem says that, under fairly general conditions, countries always gain by entering into unencumbered international trade. This is true, even when the other country imposes a tariff on goods entering its country. The reason is that each country has a comparative advantage in some good. Suppose that country A produces beer, potatoes, and computers, and in an absolute sense does so much more efficiently than country B, which produces the same products when there is no trade between the countries. Nevertheless, relative to country A, country B will be better at producing one or more of those products, and it will make sense for country B to focus its energies on producing the other products and then trade with country A for the other products. Despite general feelings to the contrary, in a broad variety of circumstances, small countries gain more from trade than large countries.

D. *The Money and Stock Market Theorem.* If the growth rate of money is known and information concerning stocks is publicly available, money improves performance of the economic system and variations in returns on assets vary predictably according to risk characteristics.

The fourth theorem says that one should not worry too much about inflation, as long as it is predictable. If people know how much the pace at which the money supply will increase, they will make the necessary adjustments and the markets will help them to do this. Furthermore, as long as information is equally shared among all participants, the stock market provides predictable returns for a given amount of risk. Some investors will want to assume more risk than others, and they will receive a greater expected return.

Assumptions of the Neoclassical Model

The above theorems are so reassuring that reasonable noneconomists must doubt whether they are really true. These suspicions are indeed justified because, although the theorems as theorems are true, in order to apply them to the real world, the assumptions made in the theorems must be reasonably accurate for the economy to which they are applied.

For the static neoclassical model, the following assumptions are necessary to prove the four theorems presented above:

1. All markets are perfectly competitive—that is, there are no dominant economic agents (such as monopolists, oligopolists, or the federal government) who participate in the market.

2. There are no barriers to entry into a market, such as unknown technology or large capital outlays that cannot be financed through banks or other institutions. Even if there are barriers, markets can be "contested"—that is, other economic agents have the resources to enter the market and deprive the current participants of market share.

3. Consumers strive to maximize their own well-being without regard to others, and all producers seek to maximize profits.

4. There are no public goods, such as silence, clean air, safety, and so forth.

5. There are no externalities, such as pollutants, generated by firms and affecting economic agents outside the sector in which they are generated.

6. There are no bankruptcies.

7. All goods are traded—that is, there are no markets which are incomplete, or emerging.

The above assumptions are stringent, and they are certainly not fulfilled in an absolute sense. For example, assumptions 1 and 2 imply that the methods for producing any good are known within society. However, in the case of new products, this assumption is patently false. Precisely because new products often involve new technology, investors in new technology are able to earn a return on capital that is far above normal. To be sure, such entrepreneurs usually invest in a variety of projects, some of which are successful and many of which fail. In the real world entrepreneurs defend their high return on capital on new ventures by claiming that they were lucky and by noting that consumers benefit from the new product, as is apparent through their willingness to purchase the product.

Since any model is only an approximation to reality, the theorems are still useful when trying to understand how an actual economy, such as that of the United States, functions. Even though any particular economy does not fulfill all the conditions or all agents in the economy do not adhere to the behavior assumptions, the theorems indicate a pattern that one expects to see replicated in the real economy. In cases where some assumptions are known not to apply even approximately, suitable interventions can be undertaken. Unfortunately, however, economists are not able at the current time to gauge to what extent the assumptions are not fulfilled and to what extent this makes a difference.[3] Whenever one of the assumptions is judged not to be true in a particular economy, economists say that a market imperfection exists. Provided that one can remove the imperfection without doing harm to the competitiveness of other markets, it makes sense to remove the imperfection or at least diminish its impact.

Assumption 7 indicates that the four theorems refer to a static economy, one in which all the goods are known and traded. In reality, every economy generates new products and production processes every year, products and processes that were unknown at the beginning of the year. Indeed, one of the attractive features of the free market economy is that it seems to generate more new

---

[3] A particularly disturbing theorem of neoclassical economics is the Theorem of the Second Best. It states that once one knows that two or more of the conditions for efficiency in the economy are not realized, intervening to guarantee that one of the requirements for efficiency is restored does not necessarily improve the performance of the economy as long as the other suboptimal conditions remain suboptimal.

products than occurs in economies that are centrally controlled or operate under various constraints. Recent theoretical work in economics has focused on how new products are developed and the impact that such products have on international trade and welfare. However, the models developed so far are very restrictive, and economists have not been able to generate welfare theorems that apply to dynamic economies.

In short, we do not have a sophisticated dynamic model to know for sure how efficient they are and how they function. However, the static theorems suggest that what is true in a static economy will likely be true in a dynamic economy. If the economic assumptions of a free market economy are broadly true, neoclassical economics makes a secular act of faith that such economies are efficient. Whenever it is suspected that the assumptions are grossly inaccurate, it makes sense to intervene in the market, either through the government or some other entity. However, one should intervene in such a way that one does the least damage in rectifying the market imperfection.

Some ethically sensitive thinkers are inclined to reject neoclassical economics because its assumptions are patently false. People, especially those who are ethically sensitive, should reject this decision for two reasons. First, the model seems to work well in many different areas. At the very least, it works better than other models that have been suggested. Second, whatever model is proposed should generate a theorem saying that it allows an efficient distribution of resources, or that an economy organized according to the contours of the model is more efficient than one conforming more closely to the assumptions of an alternate model. In fact, John Paul II singles this factor out as a reason why the communist regimes of Eastern Europe eventually fell.[4]

---

[4] In *Centesimus Annus* John Paul II states: "The second factor in the crisis was certainly the inefficiency of the economic system, which is not to be considered simply as a technical problem, but rather a consequence of the violation of the human rights to private initiative, ownership of property, and freedom in the economic sector" (CA 24). Later in the same section he emphasizes that the most powerful reason for the fall of the communist system was the "spiritual void brought about by atheism." For a thorough discussion of the merits and shortcomings of "thin" models of consumer behavior, see Michael Walzer, *Thick and Thin: Moral Argument at Home and Abroad* (Notre Dame: University of Notre Dame Press, 1994), and Alan Wolfe, *Whose Keeper? Social Science and Moral Obligation* (Berkeley: University of California Press, 1989).

Not wasting goods in a world where people are in need is an ethical principle of considerable importance. Any ethical person concerned about the welfare of others would like to know that goods are not needlessly being wasted and that all people are receiving a basic minimum so that they can maintain their health, provide for their families, learn about the world, practice their religion, and have a modicum of beauty and play in their lives.

Even with all its shortcomings, the neoclassical model provides a useful framework in which to understand the modern economic and social situation. When the economic assumptions of the model do not fit the real situation, some effort must be made to modify the rules of the game so that the economic outcome is fair. In terms of the issues raised by John Paul II, each issue must be addressed individually to determine what, if any, is the appropriate type of intervention in the marketplace. Alternately, one may have to adjust economic behavior by changing the juridical framework.

In the next section the neoclassical model, with all its shortcomings, is used to help understand some new directions pointed out by John Paul II. Before doing this, it is useful to provide a sympathetic explanation why the neoclassical model has such austere lines.

A Thin Model of Economic Behavior

The neoclassical model explains human behavior in a parsimonious manner, using as few assumptions as possible. Criticizing it because its assumptions are not completely accurate misses the mark, since the intent of the model is to capture the essential characteristics of individual and corporate behavior. In addition, the neoclassical model is thoroughly "liberal" in that it professes not to contain any ethical or moral values. It considers itself "above" all partisan debate concerning different ethical values. The way the model achieves this position, which the neoclassicals view as a position of superiority, is by making the utility function unstructured and available to accept whatever ethical principles a particular consumer might choose to adhere to. That is, very few constraints are placed on the utility function in order to accommodate consumers of all different convictions and beliefs.

Consumers who purchase small amounts of goods in the belief that they thereby adhere more closely to Christ's message are as easily treated in this system as consumers who want to make as much money as they can and spend all of it. Neoclassical economists describe the assumptions pertaining to behavior by consumers and producers as constituting a "thin" model of economic behavior. According to the neoclassicals, a "thin" model does not pack much ethics into the structure, while a "thick" model contains more ethical assumptions.[5] The advantage of a thin model, if it is properly formulated, is that it captures the behavior of all consumers, whatever their individual ethical principles.

Although neoclassical economics would like to allow altruism to enter into a utility function, they have not been able to find a mathematically tractable way that allows them to do this. Neoclassicals understand that some people are indeed motivated by the desire to help others, without calculating whether such actions will benefit themselves. However, so far, attempts to introduce such complications into the utility functions jeopardize the mathematical proof of the first three theorems that were enunciated above.

The neoclassicals strive to accommodate everyone, but they do so by emptying the utility function of moral content. According to the neoclassical model, each consumer desires only his or her utility, which can be interpreted as satisfaction, happiness, or well-being. Nothing else counts. This is what the model says, and this is the way neoclassical economists describe consumer behavior. Understandably, John Paul II takes a different view, and we will examine why specific parts of the neoclassical model require qualifications and reinterpretations to accommodate the broader theological perspective enunciated by the pope.

Neoclassical economists have also studied the distribution of income and wealth, but their results have not been sufficiently clear that they can be incorporated into the usual macroeconomic model. Economists realize that this is an important question and

---

[5] This terminology, though prevalent, disguises the ethical assumptions underlying the neoclassical framework, which is fundamentally a utilitarian system. See Michael J. Sandel, *Liberalism and the Limits of Justice* (Cambridge: Cambridge University Press, 1982), and John Piderit, S.J., *The Ethical Foundations of Economics* (Washington, D.C.: Georgetown University Press, 1993).

that most people will not accept a distribution of income that is skewed heavily toward the rich. Furthermore, economists acknowledge that one of the main purposes of income tax is to redistribute income away from the rich and middle class toward the poor. How much redistribution should take place economists leave to politicians or to ethicians such as John Paul II. Justifying a particular distribution or redistribution is "arbitrary" in the eyes of most economists. That is, it is based on unarticulated estimates of the benefits that accrue to one group and the disadvantages incurred by the group that pays the taxes. In the neoclassical view, stating the importance of solidarity as a principle of distribution does not provide any guidelines about how much should be taken from whom.

In sum, economists are engaged in three activities that warrant review by people with ethical concerns. First, they make assumptions about behavior by economic agents. Second, they assume that markets are "perfectly competitive," that is, that a sufficiently large number of people are engaged in the transactions so that no single individual is able to influence the outcome of any economic transaction. Third, economists are sufficiently concerned about the distribution of wealth and income to examine it, but they have been given no general principles concerning the desired or optimal distribution of income and wealth.[6]

The Economic Teaching of John Paul II

John Paul II's comments concerning the economy and economic behavior are extensive, far too encompassing to treat in this paper. Since an interest of this paper is showing how John Paul II's theological approach influences the types of models that economists use, it is useful to focus on three groups who can be directly influenced by theological considerations: consumers, workers, and producers, including entrepreneurs. In this section I will present actual citations from the three encyclicals pertaining to con-

---

[6] Research has also begun to explore the extent to which the human ethical sense is transmitted biologically. See James Q. Wilson, *The Moral Sense* (New York: Free Press [Macmillan], 1993).

sumers and producers; then I will analyze the meaning and context of these statements. Finally, in light of the analysis, I will make some recommendations and qualifications.

Before undertaking such an analysis, it is important to note a deficiency in John Paul II's presentation as it is viewed by economists and people accustomed to using statistical information to help formulate policies. John Paul II makes many assertions about how people think and act and about how they react to various policies. However, he does not present any statistical information to suggest that his interpretation of the situation is more or less accurate. To be sure, in many places within the encyclicals the pope is stating not what is the case but what he thinks ought to be the case. However, he also makes more specific factual claims. It would be helpful if the pope were able to cite factual data supporting his assertions.

In many instances the type of statistical information that John Paul II would need to substantiate his point of view is not available. In instances where pertinent statistical information is lacking, various laypeople in society could provide an important service by starting to collect the relevant data. Even though some of the most important data require knowledge about the religious outlook of people, polling organizations in the United States have good experience in gathering such data.

An adage frequently heard in business circles and promoted in management courses is this: what gets measured, gets done. The implication is that what is not measured, doesn't get done. If one produces electronic components and the quality of one's product is suspect, one has to measure its quality regularly, rigorously, and at different points in the production process if one wants to improve quality. Only when one has some quantitative indices can the manager know what progress is being made and where.

Unless one is serious enough about a problem to measure what it is and the impact of various remedies, one is unlikely to resolve the difficulty. To the extent that John Paul II mentions problems that he wishes to be addressed, it is important that interested parties begin collecting empirical data on these issues.

Economic Behavior of Consumers

John Paul II frequently points out that modern consumers need principles to guide their choices. Price and culture—what everyone else is doing—are insufficient guides because human beings are expected to adhere to certain principles. Human beings are part of a hierarchy of being and they have goals that God wants them to attain. Consumer goods and services are available to consumers to reach these goals, and consumers should choose wisely among the "superabundance" of goods generated in a free market economy:

> This superdevelopment, which consists in an *excessive* availability of every kind of material good for the benefit of certain social groups, easily makes people slaves of "possession" and of immediate gratification, with no other horizon than the multiplication or continual replacement of the things already owned with others still better.... The evil does not consist in "having" as such, but in possessing without regard for the *quality* and the *ordered hierarchy* of the goods one has. *Quality and hierarchy* arise from the subordination of goods and their availability to man's "being" and true vocation. (SRS 28)

Without specifying what the "ordered hierarchy" of goods is, which may be different in various parts of the world, John Paul II stresses the importance of understanding what this hierarchy is. For example, educational services would be placed on a higher level than entertainment. John Paul II's point is that such a hierarchy exists and that it should be a reference point for consumers.

John Paul II's theological perspective is intentionally broad, applying to all those who believe that human beings are oriented to God. Since all human beings are made in God's image and likeness, each person has a true affinity to God. Therefore, those things that people purchase should help them become more like God:

> However, in trying to achieve true development, we must never lose sight of that *dimension* which is in the *specific nature* of man, who has been created by God in his image and likeness (*cf.* Gen. 1:26).... Thus man comes to have a certain affinity with other creatures: he is called to use them, and to be involved with them. ... But at the same time man must remain subject to the will of God, who imposes limits upon his use and dominion over things (*cf.*, Gen 2:16–17), just as he promises him immortality (*cf.* Gen 2:9, Wis. 2:23). Thus man, being the image of God, has a true affinity with him too. On the basis of this teaching, development cannot consist only in the use, dominion over, and *indiscriminate*

possession of created things and the products of human industry, but rather in *subordinating* the possession, dominion, and use to man's divine likeness and to his vocation to immortality. This is the *transcendent* reality of the human being. (SRS 29)

This transcendent reality of human existence is not captured in the neoclassical model. A reasonable question, however, is whether those who embrace their transcendence to God follow different consumption patterns from those for whom such belief is relatively unimportant. A recent study by Robert Wuthnow shows that believers tend to make the same types of economic decisions that nonbelievers make.[7] This is a disturbing result, suggesting that religious organizations do not project a clear image of expected economic behavior.

John Paul II has spoken of consumerism in many different contexts, as have many other commentators in the United States and elsewhere:

> The historical experience of the West, for its part, shows that even if the Marxist analysis and its foundation of alienation are false, nevertheless alienation—and the loss of the authentic meaning of life—is a reality in Western societies too. This happens in consumerism, when people are ensnared in a web of false and superficial gratifications rather than being helped to experience their personhood in an authentic and concrete way. (CA 41)

> A given culture reveals its overall understanding of life through the choices it makes in production and consumption. It is here that *the phenomenon of consumerism arises*.... Of itself, an economic system does not possess criteria for correctly distinguishing new and higher forms of satisfying human needs from artificial new needs which hinder the formation of a mature personality. *Thus a great deal of educational and cultural work* is urgently needed, including the education of consumers in the responsible use of their power of choice, the formation of a strong sense of responsibility among producers and among people in the mass media in particular, as well as the necessary intervention by public authorities. (CA 36)

John Paul II notes the need for education concerning the correct pattern of consumption and savings in modern society. Some

---

[7] Robert Wuthnow, *God and Mammon in America* (New York: Free Press, 1994).

groups, such as the Amish, are known for their desire to live simply in modern society. John Paul II suggests that all believers have to think more consequentially about their consumption patterns. In this area both statistical data and economic analysis would be helpful. As a first step, articulating the structured hierarchy of goods and their relationship to valid human goals should be a priority. An appropriate place where such study could be conducted would be in Catholic universities, although it is important to emphasize that there is nothing specifically Catholic in the principles enunciated by the pope. Whatever guidelines are developed through research should in principle apply to all who believe that they are made in the image and likeness of God.

John Paul II also notes the limited relevance of the market mechanism. Many important human goods exist that cannot or should not be purchased and sold: "Here we find a new limit on the market: there are collective and qualitative needs which cannot be satisfied by market mechanisms. There are important human needs which escape its logic. There are goods which by their very nature cannot and must not be bought or sold" (CA 40). Collective needs such as peace, security, clean air and water, and historical awareness cannot be purchased. Although a nation can commit services to help to bring these goods about, the goods require cooperation by the majority of people in the economy if they are to be realized. Personal goods that are not traded in modern economies (though not mentioned explicitly by John Paul II) include personal honor, political votes, prison terms, people (slavery), marriage, commitment, and self-confidence. Items that should not be purchased and sold include sexual services, parental services, babies, and addictive drugs.[8] A detailed analysis of the characteristics of such goods and a presentation of the reasons why they ought not to be traded would help to clarify the limitations of the neoclassical model.

John Paul II has spoken against consumerism consistently throughout his term as pope. His pointed comments on this topic suggest his frustration in getting even committed Catholics to ad-

---

[8] For a discussion of "prohibited goods" and why they are deemed inappropriate in the marketplace, see Michael Walzer, *Spheres of Justice: A Defense of Pluralism and Equality* (New York: Basic Books, 1983).

dress the issue in a deliberate and substantive manner. Consumerism appears to be as ingrained in Western culture as the various gods were when the Celtic missionaries worked among the Franks, Visigoths, Saxons, and Nordic peoples in the seventh through the tenth centuries.[9] Remnants of the gods appeared in superstitions and beliefs of Western Europeans for hundreds of years after the people had accepted Christianity; eradicating consumerism is likely to be a project requiring sustained effort over many generations.

Economic Behavior of Workers

John Paul II reacts negatively to the use of categories such as labor and capital because he believes that such objectification runs the risk of disembodying labor of its personal content. People can too easily forget that labor, although it is a quantity that is appropriately measured and analyzed, also consists of human beings who should never be considered solely as means to an end or as cogs in a larger process. John Paul II speaks of the subjectivity of work as the primary locus for its meaning. It is a reminder that a human person is always the subject of our analysis:

> As a person, man is therefore the subject of work. As a person he works, he performs various actions belonging to the work process; independently of their objective content, these actions must all serve to realize his humanity, to fulfill the calling to be a person that is his by reason of his very humanity. . . . Christianity brought about a fundamental change of ideas in this field, taking the whole content of the Gospel message as its point of departure, especially the fact that the one who, while *being God*, became like us in all things devoted most of the years of His life on earth to *manual work* at the carpenter's bench. This circumstance constitutes in itself the most eloquent "Gospel of work," showing that the basis for determining the value of human work is not primarily the kind of work being done but the fact that the one who is doing it is a person. The sources of the dignity of work are to be sought primarily in the subjective dimension, not in the objective one. (LE 6)

---

[9] See Peter Brown, *The Rise of Western Christendom: Triumph and Diversity, AD 200–1000* (New York: Blackwell, 1996), 276–321.

Economists refer to skilled and unskilled labor in their models and also refer to human capital. According to John Paul II, such uses of the terms "labor" and "capital" are always secondary. The primary meaning is the person who works. As a person made in the image and likeness of God, the worker should be treated in a certain way and has legitimate expectations as a human being.

Most economists will listen politely to such comments and then ask how these observations should influence their activities as economists.[10] After all, economists find the variable they call "labor" to be helpful, and they will still use the category of labor as one of the inputs into a production function. They do not believe that they act unethically or in a misguided way by using the concept in this manner. Two responses to economists, consistent with John Paul II's approach, are possible. One is that as long as economists consider their economic model as only a distant but useful approximation of reality, the technical use of the word "labor" referring to disembodied work is legitimate. However, once the model is applied to an actual firm, the analysis may not be appropriate when one analyzes the actual workers present in the firm.

A second response addresses the presumed competitiveness of the market for labor services. Economists assume that laborers and management have symmetrical and reasonably complete information when they address labor issues. If workers are dissatisfied with some aspect of their job, they can seek employment elsewhere. In many instances the mobility of workers is restricted, limiting the extent to which they compete in a competitive market for labor services. Also, much recent work has shown that salary structures in firms do not follow the pattern predicted by a perfectly competitive market. Perceived ranking according to ability also plays an important role.[11] Thus, even the economics profession itself has begun to acknowledge specifically human factors in the job market.

---

[10] Recent work by some economists incorporates the personal dimension into neoclassical models. See Horst Siebert, ed., *The Ethical Foundations of the Market Economy: International Workshop* (Tübingen: J.C.B. Mohr, 1994), especially the article by Amartya Sen, "Markets and the Freedom to Choose," 123–38.

[11] See Robert H. Frank, *Choosing the Right Pond: Human Behavior and the Quest for Status* (Oxford: Oxford University Press, 1985).

Unions The importance of unions in securing the rights of workers was first highlighted in *Quadragesimo Anno* (1931) by Pope Pius XI. In subsequent encyclicals on economic conditions, the popes have asserted the right of workers to join unions. In his various encyclicals John Paul II has also reaffirmed this right, while pointing out that the right to strike should be restricted to achieve legitimate economic goals: "In this connection workers should be assured the right to strike, without being subjected to personal penal sanctions for taking part in a strike. While admitting that it is a legitimate means, we must at the same time emphasize that a strike remains, in a sense, an extreme means. *It must not be abused*; it must not be abused especially for political purposes" (LE 20). Work in a firm is done with co-workers who collaborate to produce a product that is valued in the economy. Because of the many shared experiences at work, work itself is a social phenomenon, and socialization of workers usually extends beyond the workplace. Providing opportunities for such socialization is one of the functions of unions:

> [Unions'] task is to defend the existential interests of workers in all sectors in which their rights are concerned. The experience of history teaches that organizations of this type are an indispensable *element of social life*, especially in modern industrialized societies. (LE 20)
>
> Finally, "human" working hours and adequate free-time need to be guaranteed, as well as the right to express one's own personality at the workplace without suffering any affront to one's conscience or personal dignity. This is the place to mention once more the role of trade unions, not only in negotiating contracts, but also as "places" where workers can express themselves. They serve the development of an authentic culture of work and help workers to share in a fully human way in the life of their place of employment. (CA 15)

While unions may be an indispensable element of social life, at least in the United States they perform their critical function with an ever-decreasing percentage of the workforce as members. For the past thirty years an increasing number of workers believe that they can function well in the workplace without unions. This reality may only indicate that "unions" as conceived in the papal encyclical should be understood more broadly. Unions might include groupings of laborers within an industry which do not have a formal structure or system of representation. Alternately, they may include the community of workers in an individual firm which has an informal structure for communicating concerns and satisfactions. These could be classified as "informal unions" to contrast them with unions that have formal organizational structures.

A difficulty with many formal unions, given their current orientation, is that their focus is quite narrow. They concern themselves primarily with those workers currently employed or laid off in a particular industry. As revealed by their actions, the purview of such unions does not extend to other industries in any effective sense, nor are they particularly concerned about unemployed workers who would like to secure a job in the industry in which their union operates. While individual unions of this type accord nicely with the principle of subsidiarity, the narrowness of their focus conflicts with the requirements of solidarity, an important principle of justice repeatedly invoked by John Paul II in the encyclicals under study.

The Catholic Church in the United States has a distinguished history for the past sixty years of supporting unions. More and more members of the Catholic Church, however, have chosen not to join unions or are antagonistic to them. As noted earlier, this may be due to poor communication. On the other hand, their message may be quite clear, but the rigidity of the message might be excessively confining for modern workers and consumers. It is strange that an institution so consistently promoted by the Catholic Church receives so little grassroots support from lay people in and outside the Catholic Church.

A particular policy advocated by most U.S. unions is "buy American." Such a policy is anachronistic and contrary to the interests of most countries, including Third World countries. The International Trade Theorem of Comparative Advantage shows that countries are better off as a group when they engage in trade. If one invokes a related theorem of international trade as it applies to the United States, it predicts that the United States will tend to import goods that are labor intensive, because labor, compared with capital, is in comparatively short supply in the United

States.[12] In fact, the United States tends to import labor intensive goods and, because many unions produce labor intensive goods, unions would like to avoid international competition. As a result, they promote tariffs and quotas when they expect that their industry will be adversely affected.

The narrow focus of unions also leads them to protect jobs in their union, no matter what the consequences. Various unions have insisted on maintaining positions, even when the positions are no longer necessary. In addition to being inefficient, such forms of featherbedding infuriate managers and consumers. Since such practices violate the principle of solidarity, the pope in future statements could usefully condemn such activities.

From the perspective of self-interest, the protectionist approach of unions is understandable. However, significant benefits accrue to both the United States and its trading partners, many of whom are Third or Fourth World countries, by participating in the structure of international trade. By being protectionist, unions risk being viewed as out-of-date or irrelevant. At least in terms of the U.S. situation, future treatment of unions in papal documents should be more nuanced.

Gains from International Trade John Paul II has given cautious endorsement to the market economy. He is concerned, however, that so many people, especially those in the Third and Fourth Worlds, lack the ability to participate in the market economy. Sometimes the reason for their inability to participate is the political structure in their own country, a topic that John Paul II addresses. Another reason why they cannot participate is that they lack the education and attendant skills required for modern, sophisticated methods of production:

> The fact is that many people, perhaps the majority today, do not have the means which would enable them to take their place in an effective and humanly dignified way within a productive system in which work is truly central. They have no possibility of acquiring

---

[12] A country, such as the United States, can have a relatively short supply of labor, compared with capital, and still experience regular or cyclical levels of unemployment. The theorem referred to in the text is the Heckscher-Ohlin Theorem. For an explanation, see Dominick Salvatore, *International Economics*, 5th edition (New York: Macmillan, 1995).

the basic knowledge which would enable them to express their creativity and develop their potential. They have no way of entering the network of knowledge and intercommunication which would enable them to see their qualities appreciated and utilized. Thus, if not actually exploited, they are to a great extent marginalized; economic development takes place over their heads, so to speak, when it does not actually reduce the already narrow scope of their old subsistence economies. (CA 33)

While not denying that many people in this world are marginalized, both as workers and consumers, it is important to identify the primary reason for their marginalization. Since many poor countries have benefitted significantly from international trade during the past thirty years, international trade is not likely to have caused the marginalization. In this context, John Paul II may not appreciate the economic power even of countries whose populations are not well educated.

A frequent comment made in the media is that the United States needs protection because it cannot compete with cheap labor around the world. In fact, workers in the United States mistakenly complain when a production plant, not requiring skilled workers, is shut down in the United States and moved to a Third World country. On the other hand, workers in a Third World country, equally misguided, complain that they cannot possibly compete with the United States because U.S. workers have so much capital equipment at their disposal.

These complaints undermine one another. What counts is not the absolute number of workers in a country or the absolute amount of capital, but the ratio of capital to labor in one country compared with another country. Furthermore, whatever the ratio of capital to labor is in a particular country, that country can profitably trade with another country. A commitment to the principle of solidarity means that one should support international trade.[13] A more resolute papal statement promoting international trade would be more consistent with ethical principles enunciated by the Church for the past sixty years.

---

[13] Economists always have exceptions arising out of the suppositions of their models. There are some minor exceptions to the advantages arising out of international trade. However, the benefits flowing from international trade are robust in many different circumstances.

When one combines a theoretical analysis and statistical evidence, the case for opening up markets to trade is overwhelming. Free trade policies frequently allow some people in the economy to earn considerable wealth in a short period of time. However, the growth experienced by such countries benefits all the citizens. One reason why Africa is among the poorest of the continents is that countries there have not embraced a free market economy and international trade. Asia was once considered the poorest section of the world. Free market policies have enabled some countries to move out of poverty into a middle tier of countries. The pope could help the poor throughout the world by noting and supporting these trends.

Despite the previous comments, workers everywhere, not just in developed countries, should have the opportunity to acquire skills and to educate themselves. John Paul II is correct in implying that workers who do not receive such training will be restricted in the types of labor markets that they can enter. In addition, their remuneration will be less than if they were well trained. Increasing the amount of training in First World countries while limiting the amount occurring in Third World countries increases the gap between earnings for workers in the respective groups. The best way to make such training available is by generating jobs within the economy. No policy does this better than removing the barriers to ownership, development, and trade—that is, promoting the free market economy. The free market economy is not a panacea, but it has undeniable strengths. The pope's nuanced support for free market economies is excessively qualified. Experience teaches that the best way for countries to overcome poverty is to introduce free market policies.

Civility and Friendship in the Workplace In earlier centuries agricultural work was the usual activity for males and for females, who also assumed the additional burden of caring for the home. Outside the Third World, most people now work in offices or factories, in close cooperation with other workers. Such people spend most of their time during the working week with colleagues at work. This is their primary community, one in which they seek satisfaction and fulfillment. Because they are engaged in work and because work is usually arduous, their activity is not always pleasant. However, it should have the natural rewards that accrue from associating with friends and acquaintances. In addition, someone at work should have the satisfaction of knowing that he or she is contributing to society through the production of socially useful goods or services. Only in such a context can a person appreciate the transcendent dimension to human existence:

> As a person, one can give oneself to another person or to other persons, and ultimately to God, who is the author of our being and who alone can fully accept our gift. A person is alienated if he refuses to transcend himself and to live the experience of self-giving and of the formation of an authentic human community oriented towards his final destiny, which is God. A society is alienated if its form of social organization, production, and consumption make it more difficult to offer this gift of self and to establish this solidarity between people. (CA 41)

Goods or services are socially useful if they help other people to achieve their proximate and ultimate ends. The ultimate end is God and proximate ends are those activities that enable them to pursue deeply human activities oriented toward God.[14] Each worker may have to struggle to maintain such a focus, especially at times when he or she is occupied by troubles at home. However, it is just such an orientation that should make workers willing to assist their co-workers during times of family stress. Personal troubles are more easily overcome with the help of friends and supporters, and those who lend support generously adhere to the principle of solidarity.

Economic Behavior of Producers

In the standard neoclassical model neither management nor technology receive much attention, because the model focuses on competition with a level playing field. Each firm is assumed to have the same technology and talent available; all products and

---

[14] "It is therefore necessary to create lifestyles in which the quest for truth, beauty, goodness, and communion with others for the sake of common growth are the factors which determine consumer choices, savings, and investments." (CA 36)

production processes are known and available. It is important to recall that these assumptions are part of an ideal model, one that abstracts from reality, not a precise description of the world.

Neoclassical economists understand that managers differ from one firm to another, some being kinder or more perspicacious than others. Given large numbers of managers and firms, however, such differences are assumed to cancel one another out. The neoclassical economist is not usually interested in a single firm, but rather in an entire industry or economy.

With the tacit presumption in the neoclassical model that management in all firms is the same, managers adhere to three types of rules: profit maximization, the laws of the land, and socially enforced mores. Each of these constrains the actions of the manager. Economists focus exclusively on profit maximization and relegate laws of the land and socially binding mores to the background of their model. For good reasons John Paul II is interested in the background and highlights some important issues concerning working conditions and relationships: "The attainment of the worker's rights cannot, however, be doomed to be merely a result of economic systems which on a larger or smaller scale are guided chiefly by the criterion of maximum profit. On the contrary, it is respect for the objective rights of the worker—every kind of worker: manual or intellectual, industrial or agricultural, *etc.*— that must constitute *the adequate and fundamental criterion* for shaping the whole economy" (LE 17). Rights of the worker are determined in part by the socioeconomic status attained by a particular society. In a society with especially strong mores that constrain the activities of most of the managers in the economy, it is sufficient for such rights to subsist as part of the social fabric. In many instances, however, such mores are insufficient constraints on human activity, and it is necessary that the rights of the worker be legislated. Indeed, the process of legislating proposed rights is a useful exercise in clarifying the boundaries to such rights.

The neoclassical economic model is given a benign interpretation in this essay, following the principles of St. Ignatius Loyola, first, to interpret positively things that people say, and, second, to advance God's greater glory by making good use of all available human constructs. Such optimism should not deteriorate, however, into the unreal work of a Pollyanna. The neoclassical model is only a model, and adjustments must be made in applying it to reality. Some people are careless in making the application. From the explicit assumption that managers are interested only in profit maximization, and seeing no mention of social mores or the laws of the land, some people conclude that the *only* things that should interest managers is profit maximization:

> This general analysis, which is religious in nature, can be supplemented by a number of particular considerations to demonstrate that among the actions and attitudes opposed to the will of God, the good of neighbor and the "structures" created by them, two are very typical: on the one hand, the all-consuming desire for profit, and on the other, the thirst for power, with the intention of imposing one's will upon others. In order to characterize better each of these attitudes, one can add the expression "at any price." In other words, we are faced with the absolutizing of human attitudes with all its possible consequences. (SRS 3)

Neoclassical economists insist that their model contains no ethical prescriptions. Although in my opinion the neoclassical model is built on a utilitarian foundation and to this extent promotes an ethical point of view, the model, by emphasizing profit maximization, should not offer a justification for violating the law or acting contrary to binding social mores.[15]

Labor Mobility When discussing workers in the previous section, we noted the importance of the community of workers at any particular firm. This is a vital group for a variety of reasons. Workers rely upon one another not only to accomplish their goals at work but also to help one another in times of difficulty. On a work day, workers spend more time with one another than they do with their own families; one therefore expects that the work environment will at a minimum maintain civility—that is, adhere to the binding social mores:

> The Church acknowledges the legitimate *role of profit* as an indication that a business is functioning well. When a firm makes a profit,

---

[15] Some economists recognize the need for ethical principles among managers, especially when the "agency problem" exists and employers have to trust managers. See Thomas H. Noe and Michael J. Rebello, "The Dynamics of Business Ethics and Economic Activity," *American Economic Review* 84.3 (1994): 531–47.

> this means that productive factors have been properly employed and corresponding human needs have been duly satisfied. But profitability is not the only indicator of a firm's condition. It is possible for the financial accounts to be in order and yet for the people—who make up the firm's most valuable asset—to be humiliated and their dignity offended. Besides being morally inadmissible, this will eventually have negative repercussions on the firm's economic efficiency. In fact, the purpose of a business firm is not simply to make a profit, but it is to be found in its very existence as a *community of persons* who in various ways are endeavoring to satisfy their basic needs, and who form a particular group at the service of the whole society. Profit is a regulator of the life of a business, but it is not the only one; *other human and moral factors* must also be considered which, in the long term, are at least equally important for the life of a business. (CA 35)

Citing neoclassical models of economics, some people are inclined not to legislate various behaviors in the workplace. The primary justification is that the laws are unnecessary. Workers can migrate to another job if they are dissatisfied with the working conditions at their current place of employment. Even if a worker has an array of work options (in many instances workers lack this vital mobility), a manager is not permitted to abuse—physically, verbally, or emotionally—a worker. This prohibition against abuse is not contained in the neoclassical model, but in order for a God-fearing person to be able to use the model, this restriction must be present somewhere, if only in the hinter ground. If correct treatment of workers by management is prone to be overlooked, instituting such moral factors in the juridical framework of society is necessary. Especially in American society, law educates and provides common standards for the manner in which people interact with one another.

Law should not insert itself into all manner of personal interaction. Nonetheless, because one's job is so important to securing the goods required to pursue one's overall goals in life, job-related legislation serves a moral end, provided the legislation is formulated in such a manner as to provide managers with broad freedom to handle individual situations in an appropriate manner.

Profit Sharing and the Just Wage   Both managers and laborers are workers. The traditional difference between management and labor is that management assumes responsibility for the overall performance of the firm, while the laborer agrees to perform particular services, without regard to larger concerns of the corporation. Based on this distinction, workers are traditionally paid on an hourly basis while managers are paid fixed salaries, independent of the hours worked. Senior management may be offered financial incentives, based on the economic performance of the firm.

This traditional distinction is undergoing modification. In many firms workers have been asked to consider the overall operation of the firm. In return for their commitment to the successful performance of the firm, workers and managers are offered participation in the economic livelihood of the firm through employee stock ownership plans (ESOP):

> A labor system can be right, in the sense of being in conformity with the very essence of the issue, and in the sense of being intrinsically true and also morally legitimate, if in its very basis *it overcomes the opposition between labor and capital* through an effort at being shaped in accordance with the principle put forward above: the principle of the substantial and real priority of labor, of the subjectivity of human labor and its effective participation in the whole production process, independently of the nature of the services provided by the worker. (LE 13)

ESOPs are a welcome innovation, and they certainly demonstrate in an effective manner the common interests of worker and manager. Granting participation in the very ownership of the corporation overcomes the opposition between labor and capital. Joint ownership is not the only method for overcoming this tension. For many years Germany has adhered to a system of *Mitbestimmung*, which allocates seats for labor at the directorship level (governing body) of the firm. This is an alternate approach, which has worked well in Germany. A few U.S. firms have imitated it. For a variety of reasons *Mitbestimmung* is not as popular in Germany as it once was, but it provides a structure for cooperation on a human level between labor and capital.

One implication of the priority of the person in human work is that a worker should be able to earn a wage that enables him or her to provide sufficiently for those people who are one's dependents: "In many cases [the 'poor'] appear as a *result of the violation of the dignity of human work*: either because the opportunities for human work are limited as a result of the scourge of unemployment, or because a low value is put on work and the rights that flow from it, especially the right to a just wage and to the personal security of the worker and his or her family" (LE 8). The "just wage," which is a central part of Catholic social teaching in this century, has performed different functions at various times. Especially at a time when capital markets were less developed than they are today in the United States and when the just wage was interpreted as the living wage, it set a moral boundary on the amount of profits that capitalists could secure through their enterprise. It also set a level of expectation for government intervention when the market economy did not generate sufficient jobs or jobs paying wages at or above the "just wage." Today, capital markets for goods that have been in existence for some time are well developed. However, the just wage is no longer just the living wage. Rather, the just wage should be at a level that allows even the lowest paid workers to pursue the fundamental activities in life—that is, those that lead eventually to God. Other than pointing to the demands of justice, John Paul II and other popes have not indicated how such a wage should be calculated, on a scale that can be continually adjusted for modern circumstances.

A reasonable challenge for economists is to determine the parameters of a just wage. To date there has not been much interest on the part of economists, even Christian economists, for undertaking this task because economists claim that the wage is determined by the forces of supply and demand in the labor market. While it is true that in a market economy any wage, corresponding to a particular skill class of labor, is determined by the market, the market clearing process occurs within a social setting. As was indicated earlier, both the legal structure and socially binding mores determine in part the wage that is paid to workers. In recent years management has experienced little pressure to increase the wage because the United States and the rest of the developed world has experienced a considerable restructuring, prompted by efficiencies in other countries that are making themselves felt in the marketplace. Once such restructuring has been accomplished,

American society might be ready to entertain suggestions concerning the proper level for the minimum wage.[16]

Human behavior, even when it is consistently well intentioned, is subject to the allure of sin. Personal sin means that a person violates the divine law, which may or may not be part of the juridical framework of society. Personal sin is usually acknowledged, at least implicitly, by the person who committed the sin. Especially in an economic setting, the effects of sin have an adverse impact on the lives of others:

> A part of this divine plan, which begins from eternity in Christ, the perfect "image" of the Father, and which culminates in him, "the first-born from the dead" (Col. 1:18), is our own history, marked by our personal and collective effort to raise up the human condition and to overcome the obstacles which are continually arising along our way. It thus prepares us to share in the fullness which "dwells in the Lord" and which he communicates "to his body, which is the Church" (Col. 1:18, Eph. 1:22–23). At the same time sin, which is always attempting to trap us and which jeopardizes our human achievements, is conquered and redeemed by the "reconciliation" accomplished by Christ (*cf.* Col. 1:20). (SRS 31)

Sin continues to occur because we are human. However, faith in Christ and membership in his Church give people a strength they would not otherwise have. The usual path for that increased strength is personal prayer and the community of the faithful, but especially the latter. One way to improve the Church's contribution to society is to provide a more cohesive community for workers and managers, a community that is publicly committed to working and managing in a just environment. If the Church wishes to excel in this area, structures will have to be created that promote the common, and not merely the personal, pursuit of justice. Justice involves consensus concerning shared goals. Achieving such agreement is more likely among Church members than outside the Church.

---

[16] The usual objection to raising the minimum wage is that it causes unemployment. In recent years this claim has been contested by a certain group of economists. At the worst, increasing the minimum wage causes short-term unemployment. A healthy economy will discover new opportunities for the use of available labor and capital, whatever the wage level is in the economy.

Entrepreneurs Entrepreneurs perform a vital service to workers and managers alike. They use their God-given imagination to structure an enterprise that offers new products to the economy. Without entrepreneurs society would not be able to pursue as effectively the goals God has set for them: "Organizing such a productive effort, planning its duration in time, making sure that it corresponds in a positive way to the demands which it must satisfy, and taking the necessary risks—all this too is a source of wealth in today's society. In this way, the *role* of disciplined and creative *human work* and, as an essential part of that work, *initiative and entrepreneurial ability* become increasingly evident and decisive" (CA 32). Entrepreneurial ability is part of the dynamic economy, about which neoclassical economists have little to say, though much to recommend. The faith of economists is that the freedom provided within a market economy will elicit more entrepreneurial activity from people who have the talent. Economists presume that the main reason why entrepreneurs undertake their activity is to secure an above-average rate of return on their capital. Much more study of human motivation is required to determine whether profit is indeed the primary motive, or whether the main motive is simply to make an important difference in society. Whatever the motivation, entrepreneurial activity has always been important and will continue to be so in the future.[17]

Single-minded focus on economic performance can produce devastating results in the human psyche. Managers who forget the primacy of the human run the risk of undermining the self-worth and self-confidence of workers:

> Alienation is found also in work, when it is organized so as to ensure maximum returns and profits with no concern whether the worker, through his own labor, grows or diminishes as a person, either through increased sharing in a genuinely supportive community or through increased isolation in a maze of relationships marked by destructive competitiveness and estrangement, in which he is considered only a means and not an end. (CA 41)

The destructive capability of management is not captured in the neoclassical model. It is, however, a real possibility for managers

---

[17] See Peter H. Werhan, *The Entrepreneur: His Economic Function and Social Responsibility*, Ordo Socialis no. 4 (Trier: Paulinus-Verlag, 1990).

who underestimate the fragility of the human psyche or are blind to essential aspects of their own humanity. By placing such important human concerns in the background, the model implicitly assumes that all managers attend to these human concerns in a "satisfactory" manner. Within the framework of the model, "satisfactory" means that the managers do not jeopardize the existence of the firm by violating such codes. Since going out of existence is bankruptcy, which is assumed not to exist in the model, the model implicitly assumes that managers act in a human manner, though it never specifies violations of humane, ethical conduct.

Managers who neglect the human dimension suffer reversals and loss of profits that are not captured in the neoclassical model. Such an omission is not serious if the concern is with an entire industry and one can assume that most managers adhere to the moral code embedded in social mores. If either of these assumptions is not correct, the neoclassical model requires modification.

Conclusion

John Paul II's encyclicals provide a rich source of material that both relies upon and challenges the standard neoclassical model. The pope's cautious endorsement of the market economy relies upon previous work by economists that suggests but does not prove that the dynamic version of the neoclassical model is efficient in the narrow sense that no resources are wasted. To be sure, in addition to efficiency a fair distribution of wealth and income is also an important value for an economic system. However, because the communist system was not efficient, it could not compete.[18] Though by no means the only principle of justice, efficiency is certainly an important one.

John Paul II gives strong support to unions, which continue to diminish in popularity in the United States. A suggested reason for decreased interest on the part of workers is the narrow per-

---

[18] As John Paul II points out, because the communist economy also did not respect personhood, it lacked a juridical framework and social binding mores that would permit it to engage the allegiance of workers.

spective taken by unions. Unions strive to improve the situation of their own members, without proper regard for workers who would like to work in their industry and without proper consideration for other countries in the world economy. Union members should be encouraged to implement more consistently the ethical principle of solidarity.

Analysis by neoclassical economists also indicates the power of international trade to improve the economic situation in countries, no matter what their stage of development and no matter how poorly educated their populace is. Advanced nations fear the labor power of less-developed nations, and the less-developed nations can take market share away from developed nations. Future papal pronouncements would be strengthened by incorporating these results from neoclassical analysis. In particular, strong papal support for free-market economics is warranted by a combination of theoretical and statistical analysis.

Clear statements by John Paul II concerning the proper motivation and behavior of economic agents suggests caveats in two areas. First, the neoclassical model by itself should never be used to justify behavioral activity by various economic agents. Pursuing profits at any price will not improve the economy, nor does the neoclassical model predict that it will. John Paul II's observations highlight the importance of socially binding mores and the juridical framework, aspects of the neoclassical model that are implicit rather than explicit. Both the mores and the legal system should reflect the moral principles that John Paul II enunciates.

The laws of a democracy reflect the ethical principles of the majority of people in the country. The most important moral obligations of committed Catholics in the United States is to persuade a majority of our compatriots that the ethical principles enunciated by John Paul II should be adopted. Because of our training, commitment, and tradition in higher education, Jesuits have a special responsibility to help inform and form people about reasonable ways of proceeding.

10. MARITAL ETHICS
The Prophetic Mission of Marriage: John Paul II's Vision of Human Sexuality

Martin X. Moleski, S.J.

Introduction

I shall not attempt a comprehensive overview of the whole of John Paul II's teaching on marriage. Richard M. Horgan and John M. LeVoir have provided a detailed summary of his work in the second edition of *Covenant of Love: Pope John Paul II on Sexuality, Marriage, and Family in the Modern World, with a Commentary on Familiaris Consortio*.[1] Ramón García de Haro provides abundant background material for understanding John Paul II in the second edition of *Marriage and the Family in the Documents of the Magisterium: A Course in the Theology of Marriage*.[2] My purpose here is to highlight the revelatory power of sacramental sexuality. In the collection of his Wednesday addresses entitled *The Theology of Marriage and Celibacy*, John Paul II gives a compact account of his vision of human sexuality: ". . . On the basis of the 'prophetism of the body' the ministers of the Sacrament of Marriage perform an act of prophetic character. They confirm in this way their participation in the prophetic mission of the Church received from Christ. A prophet is one who expresses in human words the truth coming from God, one who speaks this truth in the place of God, in His name and in a certain sense with His authority."[3] This

---
[1] San Francisco: Ignatius Press, 1992 [1985].
[2] San Francisco: Ignatius Press, 1993 [1989].
[3] *The Theology of Marriage and Celibacy: Catechesis on Marriage and Celibacy in the Light of the Resurrection of the Body* (Boston: Daughters of St. Paul, 1986), 318–19. Hereafter TMC.

passage proposes four themes for reflection: 1) the revelatory character of the body; 2) the prophetic message of the Church; 3) the crisis of truth in our culture; and 4) an exploration of how to speak the truth in an age of unbelief.

The Revelatory Character of the Body

We have often heard it said that actions speak louder than words, but for John Paul II, the existential substructures underlying human action themselves speak in every action that is undertaken. John Paul II preserves the ancient worldview as described by Thomas Howard, in which "everything means something," as opposed to "the reductionistic modern worldview, in which nothing means anything."[4] In *Original Unity of Man and Woman: Catechesis on the Book of Genesis*, John Paul II views the whole of created reality, and especially the creation of humans, as outward signs of hidden divinity: "The sacrament of the world, and the sacrament of man in the world, comes from the divine source of holiness, and at the same time is instituted for holiness" (OU 145). As a creature of God, the body speaks of God and for God, even before it is used in any human actions; since we are not the authors of our own bodies, we do not control the deepest meanings of our bodily nature:

> In the prophetic texts of the Covenant, on the basis of the analogy of the spousal union of the married couple, it is the body itself which "speaks"; it speaks by means of its masculinity and femininity, it speaks in the mysterious language of the personal gift, it speaks ultimately—and this happens more frequently—both in the language of fidelity, that is, of love, and also in the language of conjugal infidelity, that is, of "adultery."[5]

I do not think that we can provide a complete definition of all the meanings hidden in what John Paul II calls "the language of the body."[6] As a word spoken by God in creation and as a sign pointing toward God, the body is defined by and oriented toward

---

[4] Thomas Howard, *Chance or the Dance?* (San Francisco: Ignatius Press), 23.
[5] TMC, 311.
[6] TMC, 301.

a reality that can never be adequately expressed—to paraphrase the first line of the *Tao Te Ching*, the God that can be put into words is not the real God. Nevertheless, John Paul II invites us to meditate on the body as a revelation from God and a revelation of God:

> Thus, in this dimension, there is constituted a primordial sacrament, understood as a sign that transmits effectively in the visible world the invisible mystery hidden in God from time immemorial. And this is the mystery of truth and love, the mystery of divine life, in which man really participates. . . . The body, in fact, and it alone, is capable of making visible what is invisible: the spiritual and the divine. It was created to transfer into the visible reality of the world the mystery hidden since time immemorial in God, and thus be a sign of it.[7]

In John Paul II's reflections, the body is primarily a sacrament of the divine. It is also a sacrament of the person. The inward reality of the person is effectively given to others through the outward sign of the body. "Therefore, in some way, even if in the most general way, the body enters the definition of a sacrament, being 'a visible sign of an invisible reality,' that is, of the spiritual, transcendent, divine reality."[8] "The body, in fact, and only it, is capable of making visible what is invisible: the spiritual and the divine."[9]

The sacrament of marriage depends upon body language to fulfill in action what is promised in the vows: the total gift of self to the other. John Paul II portrays marriage as "the central point of 'the sacrament of creation' " and calls it "the primordial sacrament."[10] The language of the body is seen as "the substratum and content of the sacramental sign of spousal communion."[11] To eyes trained by the book of Genesis, all marriages have the same sacramental orientation, pointing to the Creator whose image is reflected in the union of male and female. The marital union of Christians has an added revelatory and sacramental dimension

---

[7] Ibid.
[8] TMC, 175.
[9] TMC, 252.
[10] TMC, 253.
[11] TMC, 301.

over and above the natural sacramentality of marital union; each Christian marriage tells of the "marriage between Christ and the Church (cf. Eph 5:21–33)" and therefore is a special example of "the prophetism of the body."[12]

In silence, in the deepest privacy of their sexual union, even when they are not conscious of the deepest meanings of their embrace, "the ministers of the Sacrament of Marriage perform an act of prophetic character."[13] The union of man with woman silently speaks of the glory of God and the goodness of creation; each taste of ecstasy here on earth is a foretaste of heaven's own bliss. In the union of two God-like creatures, God speaks to us about our union with God.

The Prophetic Message of the Church

By its very nature, marriage speaks of God; but in the revelation given to the Church, God speaks of marriage. Paul VI courageously preserved the message entrusted to us by tradition: ". . . the Church, which interprets natural law through its unchanging doctrine, reminds men and women that the teachings based on natural law must be obeyed and teaches that it is necessary that each conjugal act remain ordered in itself [*per se destinatus*] to the procreating of human life" (HV 11). As Pope Paul VI himself predicted, many did indeed "think this teaching difficult, if not impossible to keep" (HV 20). John Paul II calls *Humanae Vitae* the key to a "pedagogy of the body" located in "the full context of a correct vision of the values of life and of the family."[14]

Seen as a word spoken by God, the body is always a sacrament of the spiritual and the divine. Seen as the sacrament of the human person, however, the body becomes capable of expressing the rejection of the spiritual and the divine: "the body speaks the truth through fidelity and conjugal love, and when it commits 'adul-

---

[12] TMC, 308.
[13] TMC, 318–19.
[14] *Reflections on* Humanae Vitae: *Conjugal Morality and Spirituality* (Boston: Daughters of St. Paul, [1984] 1993), 37. Hereafter RHV.

tery,' it speaks lies, it is guilty of falsity."[15] John Paul II calls us to make the "biblical distinction between 'true' and 'false' prophets."[16]

This is perhaps the most painful, difficult, and divisive element of John Paul II's vision of the mission of marriage. Up to this point, many people might find his theology of the body very attractive. John Paul II takes a consistently positive view of the body and especially of marital sexuality. Like Matthew Fox, John Paul II celebrates the glory and goodness of creation: "Procreation is rooted in creation, and every time, in a sense, reproduces its mystery" (OU 83). But John Paul II reads the whole of Genesis and the biblical tradition as Fox does not. It is not enough to say that the body reveals the divine, that sexual union recapitulates the original innocence of the first couple, or that sexuality abounds with the goodness that fills the whole earth; the new pagans might say as much. For John Paul II, as for the unbroken tradition before him, the language of the body "is subject to the demands of truth, . . . to objective moral norms . . . [and] should be judged according to the criterion of truth."[17]

It is painful, difficult, and divisive to tell married couples that they are misusing the gift of their sexuality, especially if their own bodily experience tells them that there is great pleasure in the way that they have chosen. I find it very hard to stand in judgment of my family members, colleagues, and friends who have chosen artificial methods of birth control or sterilization. Of course, I know nothing of their true condition before God. As John Paul II says, "Conscience makes its witness known only to the person himself. And, in turn, only the person himself knows what his own response is to the voice of conscience" (VS 57). Objectively, however, they are at odds with the prophetic voice of the Church and, to the extent that they teach others to betray the language of the body, my family members, colleagues, and friends are false prophets. They are guilty of turning the God-given language of the body against itself, so that they say one thing in the act of intercourse ("I give you myself totally and I receive you totally")

---

[15] TMC, 314.
[16] TMC, 327.
[17] RHV, 32–33.

but do another, refusing to give fully of their own fertility or to receive fully that of their partner.

John Paul II is uncompromising on this point: "*The two dimensions of conjugal union, the unitive and the procreative, cannot be artificially separated* without damaging the deepest truth of the conjugal act itself (HV #12)."[18] In *Love and Responsibility*, first published in 1960, he identified the decision to contracept with hedonism because "the very fact of deliberately excluding the possibility of parenthood from marital intercourse makes 'enjoyment' the intention of the act" (LR 234–35). In his later reflections, John Paul II treats this distortion as hypocrisy: "the innate language that expresses the total reciprocal self-giving of husband and wife is overlaid, through contraception, by an objectively contradictory language, namely, that of not giving oneself totally to the other" (FC 32).

The Crisis of Truth

Humanae Vitae sparked a firestorm of dissent. It is not congenial to the culture at large. The voice of this age counsels hedonism, narcissism, and relativism: "If it feels good, do it. No one knows anything for sure. Let your conscience be your guide. If you think it's OK, it's OK. You can have sex with anyone or anything you want, as long as you're sincere about it and wear two condoms. The system is corrupt. We don't need institutional religion or institutional marriage. Marriage is supposed to make us happy; if it doesn't, it's dead, and the sooner we move on, the better off we'll be. You can't tell me anything different, because it's just your opinion—you've got your opinion and I've got mine."

"A little leaven leavens the whole dough."[19] The contraceptive mentality is only one example of a much larger pattern of rejection of the natural law tradition of the Church and of the Church's claim to be the definitive interpreter of divine law.[20] "Doubt or error in the field of marriage or the family involves

---

[18] LF #12.
[19] 1 Cor. 5:6 and Gal. 5:9.
[20] RHV 20, GS #50.

obscuring to a serious extent the integral truth about the human person, in a cultural situation that is already so often confused and contradictory" (FC 31). The leaven of doubt has spread through the whole of our culture, so that "our age is one marked by a great crisis, which appears above all as a profound "crisis of truth" (LF 13). At the core of the crisis of truth is a deep disagreement about the nature of conscience. John Paul II's insistence that we tell the truth at all times in our sexual nature is a special case of a larger moral principle. The Church's teaching on the nature of human sexuality cannot be isolated from its teaching on the whole of human nature; to attack the Church's authority in the sexual arena is to destroy its voice in every other area:

> Once the idea of a universal truth about the good, knowable by human reason, is lost, inevitably the notion of conscience also changes. Conscience is no longer considered in its primordial reality as an act of a person's intelligence, the function of which is to apply the universal knowledge of the good in a specific situation and thus to express a judgment about the right conduct to be chosen here and now. Instead, there is a tendency to grant to the individual conscience the prerogative of independently determining the criteria of good and evil and then acting accordingly. Such an outlook is quite congenial to an individualistic ethic, wherein each individual is faced with his own truth, different from the truth of others. Taken to its extreme consequences, this individualism leads to a denial of the very idea of human nature. (VS 32)

Millions of Catholic families are spreading the leaven of individualism and hedonism to their children. John Paul II calls the family "the first school of how to be human" and believes that "the primary current of the civilization of love" flows through the family (LF 15). In contracepting families, that current is checked by the refusal to love God with the whole of our natural sexuality. Instead of teaching children to surrender to the Author of their human nature, the parents tacitly teach them how "to 'soothe' [their] consciences by creating a 'moral alibi' " (LF 14). Actions speak louder than words—and the actions of contracepting parents teach their children to think of their bodies as desacralized objects:

> ... the human family is facing the challenge of a *new Manichaeism*, in which body and spirit are put in radical opposition; the body

does not receive life from the spirit, and the spirit does not give life to the body. Man thus *ceases to live as a person and a subject*. Regardless of all intentions and declarations to the contrary, he becomes merely an *object*. This neo-Manichaean culture has led, for example, to human sexuality being regarded more as an area *for manipulation and exploitation* than as a basis of that *primordial wonder* which led Adam on the morning of creation to exclaim before Eve: "This at last is bone of my bones and flesh of my flesh" (Gen 2:23). (LF 19)

Once the self is wrongly turned into an object for manipulation, the door is open to many other desecrations. The very same mentality that grounds contraception also can act as a rationalization for any and every sexual aberration. In and of itself, contraception may not lead to adultery or other sexual misconduct; but all sexual sins come from the same root conviction that the body is totally at our disposal for our own pleasure and that good intentions are all that are required to make actions morally good. If there is no intrinsic moral structure to the human sexual act, then we can do whatever we feel like doing with our bodies. In this case, we reject the body as a word spoken by our Creator and act as though our intentions are the sole determinant of the meaning of the language of the body.

Speaking of Visions in an Age of Unbelief

When I was a freshman at Boston College, my best friend from my high school days tried to persuade me to do drugs with him. He was a year older than I and had become established as a drug dealer by the time I moved from Buffalo to Boston. Jim was (and is) very bright and aggressive, and he had trained as a debater both in high school and college. He would not take "no" for an answer. He wanted to know why I would not join him in his new-found pleasures.

I can't remember the whole of our dialogue, which lasted most of the fall of 1970. At some point, I said I would not do drugs because I thought God did not want me to. In some inchoate fashion, I sensed that "the rights of the Creator over the creature are very extensive" (LR 249) and that since I was not my own author, I was not free to abuse the gift of life. This led directly to the question of whether I could prove to Jim that there was a God, and even if there were, whether that God had any concern about our personal choices, and even if God did have a concern, whether God had any right to limit our freedom.

Jim's questions stayed with me. One day, I realized that what I really wanted was to be able to send a camera crew from "60 Minutes" to quiz God and the Virgin Mary about the claims of Christianity—and at the same moment, I realized that no video could withstand Jim's withering skepticism. I also saw that I had no independent access to God or to Our Lady. If there be any truth to the claims of Christianity, the only way for me to know that truth is by accepting what other people tell me is the truth. If I will not take the word of witnesses, I cannot know any historical reality, especially that of God-become-human.

This insight into the witness-based structure of Christianity is so strong that I have not wavered in my commitment to accept whatever the Church teaches me to believe, but it is so weak as a logical argument for the faith that I rarely bring it into the light of dialogue with others. For me, the recognition that I could have no evidence other than the testimony of witnesses was decisive. It was the last straw in an almost unnoticed series of insights that broke the back of my own unbelief and opened my eyes to a whole new dimension of the tradition within which I had been raised.

In this experience, I felt not only the power of my own reason to command me to assent, but the powerlessness of my reason to compel my friend to assent to the same truths. I could not force him to see things as I saw them, no matter how hard I tried. I experienced the strange reality that I could see far more than I could say and that no amount of argument with my friend could make him see what he did not want to see.

John Henry Newman explored the mystery of the strength and weakness of reason in his *Essay in Aid of a Grammar of Assent* (1870). He shows that certitude is an act of the whole person and that formal reason depends upon informal reasoning. His epistemology is strikingly similar to that of Michael Polanyi, who approached the issue from his experience as a scientist. Polanyi, born a year after Newman died, was a Hungarian Jew who was baptized a Catholic in 1919, largely for social reasons, and who gravitated toward liberal Protestantism in his latter years. He trained in medicine as an *entrée* to a career in science, then entered the field of physical chemistry shortly afterward, where he worked on the interaction of gases and solids, explored the molecular structure of crystals, and traced the energy exchanges that take place in chemical reactions. Polanyi's theory of personal knowledge and Newman's view of informal reasoning sustain and enrich each other, even though their theologies diverge sharply. My purpose here is to show that their common approach to integrating the subjective and objective poles of knowledge may be helpful in defending John Paul II's understanding that couples must tell the truth, the whole truth, and nothing but the truth in their married lives.

The epistemology common to Newman and Polanyi grasps both the strength and weakness of human reason. In his *Apologia Pro Vita Sua*, Newman outlined how the convergence of logically incomplete arguments contribute to the judgment by the intellectual conscience that one must give full assent to an unproved proposition:

> My argument is in outline as follows: that that absolute certitude which we were able to possess, whether as to the truths of natural theology, or as to the fact of a revelation, was the result of an *assemblage* of concurring and converging possibilities, and that, both according to the constitution of the human mind and the will of its Maker; that certitude was a habit of mind, that certainty was a quality of propositions; that probabilities which did not lead to logical certainty, might suffice for a mental certitude; that the certitude thus brought about might equal in measure and strength the certitude which was created by the strictest scientific demonstrations; and that to possess such certitude might in given cases and to given individuals be a plain duty, though not to others in other circumstances. . . . This was the region of Private Judgment in religion; that is, of a Private Judgment, not formed arbitrarily and according to one's fancy or liking, but conscientiously, and under a sense of duty.[21]

---

[21] *Apologia pro Vita Sua: Being a History of His Religious Opinions*, edited and with introduction by Martin J. Svaglic (Oxford: Clarendon Press, [1864] 1967), 29–30.

What Newman calls "private judgment" is very much what Polanyi means by "personal knowledge": a conscientious commitment to accept as true what one knows might conceivably be false.[22] Polanyi showed that such personal commitments are at the core of objectivity in science. Scientific judgments, like "private judgment in religion," must not be "formed arbitrarily and according to one's fancy or liking, but conscientiously, and under a sense of duty."

This is precisely the understanding of conscience that John Paul II uses to uphold the Church's teaching on the nature of human sexuality:

> The responsible parenthood of which we speak here . . . is rooted in the objective moral order established by God—and only an upright conscience can be a true interpreter of this order. . . . For this reason, in regard to the mission of transmitting human life, it is not right for spouses to act in accord with their own arbitrary judgment, as if it were permissible for them to define altogether subjectively and willfully what is right for them to do. (HV 10)

In *Love and Responsibility*, then-Archbishop Wojtyla proposed the need for a subjective and personal commitment to objectivity: "Love is always a subjective and inter-subjective fact, it has a subjectivity peculiar to itself. At the same time it must be protected from subjectivist distortion, or else the tendency to disintegrate will insinuate itself, and various forms of egoism supervene. Therefore both persons involved, while cultivating as intensely as they can the subjective aspect of their love, must also endeavor to achieve objectivity" (LR 158). Polanyi has shown that subjectivity and objectivity are not opposites in science, but complement each other. Where Polanyi calls for scientists to recognize the subjective element in objectivity, John Paul II calls for Christians to recognize the objective element in their religious subjectivity: "The rightful autonomy of the practical reason means that man possesses in himself his own law, received from the Creator. Nevertheless, *the autonomy of reason* cannot mean that reason itself *creates values and moral norms*" (VS 41). The objectivity of the moral

---

[22] *Personal Knowledge: Towards a Post-Critical Philosophy* (Chicago: University of Chicago Press, (1958) 1962; "Torchbook Edition," with unique preface (New York: Harper and Row, [1962] 1974), 109. Hereafter PK.

order does not detract in any way from the need for personal commitment: "The acting subject personally assimilates the truth contained in the law. He appropriates this truth of his being and makes it his own by his acts and corresponding virtues" (VS 70).

Both Polanyi and Newman agree that formal reasoning depends upon informal reason. Both stand against the Cartesian theory that knowledge consists of clear and distinct ideas established by strict proof. Ian Ker brought together three images that Newman used to illustrate how formally incomplete arguments bound together by an informal, personal assessment take on a strength that no single strand of thought possesses alone: a load-bearing structure in which "the weight is ingeniously thrown in a variety of directions, upon supports which are distinct from, or independent of each other"; a cable woven of many strands, no one of which is sufficient to bear the load carried by the whole; and a "bundle of sticks, each of which . . . you could snap in two, if taken separately from the rest."[23]

Other "grammars of assent" begin with clear and distinct ideas and attempt to create "chains" of argument; in such formal systems, the argument is never any stronger than the weakest link in the chain. Newman begins with ideas that cannot be completely expressed in words and supposes that even those trains of thought that stop short of the goal nevertheless make a definite contribution to the final act of judgment:

> It is plain that formal logical sequence is not in fact the method by which we are enabled to become certain of what is concrete; and it is equally plain, from what has been already suggested, what the real and necessary method is. It is the cumulation of probabilities, independent of each other, arising out of the nature and circumstances of the particular case which is under review; probabilities too fine to avail separately, too subtle and circuitous to be convertible into syllogisms, too numerous and various for such conversion, even were they convertible.[24]

---

[23] *The Achievement of John Henry Newman* (Notre Dame: University of Notre Dame Press, 1990), 50–51.

[24] *An Essay in Aid of a Grammar of Assent*, edited and with introduction by Nicholas Lash (Notre Dame: University of Notre Dame Press, [1870] 1979), 230.

When the pieces of the intellectual mechanism are assembled, or the strands of thought woven into a cable, or the branches of probability gathered into a bundle, one can no longer see each component separately and cannot directly inspect its contribution to the function of the whole.

Where Newman appeals to images like the braided cable, Polanyi uses the findings of Gestalt psychology as a guide for reflection. In a Gestalt switch, the pieces of a mental puzzle fall into place in a flash of insight and the parts take on an entirely new meaning because of the newly perceived relationship to a previously unrecognized whole. The perception of the whole transforms the meaning of the parts. Discoveries in science depend upon this transformation of perception:

> To say that a discovery of objective truth in science consists in the apprehension of a rationality which commands our respect and arouses our contemplative admiration; that such discovery, while using the experience of our senses as clues, transcends this experience by embracing the vision of a reality beyond the impressions of our senses, a vision which speaks for itself in guiding us to an ever deeper understanding of reality—such an account of scientific procedure would be generally shrugged aside as out-dated Platonism; a piece of mystery-mongering unworthy of an enlightened age. Yet it is precisely on this conception of objectivity that I wish to insist. . . .[25]

In a scientific discovery, "the vision of a reality beyond our senses" is a Gestalt that organizes and interprets the data of the senses. This vision or Gestalt is a form of tacit knowledge. The Gestalt that can be put into words is not the real Gestalt, and yet it "speaks for itself in guiding us to an ever deeper understanding of reality."

Gestalts compete with each other to succeed as the interpretive framework that we use as our guide to understanding experience. False and inadequate science depends as much upon Gestalts as does authentic science. As Lonergan suggested in *Insight*, simply looking at nature with an "empty head" does not automatically yield a correct interpretive framework. A Gestalt is a patterned perception, not just a blank stare. The mind does not operate on

---
[25] PK 5–6.

raw data, but on a formulation that reveals how to read the data. To free oneself from inadequate images, another, better Gestalt must drive out the earlier interpretive structures.

In the Catholic tradition of natural law, we need a fundamental insight to structure our perception of human nature. Human nature is evident to the eye of reason only when the eye of reason has been opened by a careful and appropriate education. We must learn how to see who we really are. Humans raised in isolation from other humans do not become preternaturally gifted innocents like Burroughs's Tarzan, lord of the apes; instead, they become wolf children, permanently injured by the lack of training in humanity at critical stages of development.[26]

The vision of human nature that can be put into words is not the real vision, and yet without words, the vision of human nature as the foundation of all ethics cannot be communicated to others. The tendency of the Enlightenment epistemology is to say, "If you can't put it into words, it's not real." Lao Tzu, Newman, and Polanyi, respond, "If you can put it into words, it's not real." The only things that can be perfectly expressed in words are abstractions and other constructs of the mind.

The different observations made about human nature and the moral principles drawn from or sustained by those observations form a whole, a *tao*. The insight that human nature is the ground of all morality is a reservoir from which any number of propositions can be drawn. The fact that it is difficult, if not impossible, to put "human nature" into words does not mean there is no human nature, nor does it mean that human nature is unknowable. It simply means that we are at one of the limits of language, a perfectly normal experience. When interpreted correctly, such an experience of hitting limits reveals the nature of the mind. As Polanyi says, we can see more than we can say, we know more than we can tell, and our words always mean more than we consciously intend them to.

---

[26] Lucien Malson, *Wolf Children and the Problem of Human Nature*, with the complete text of *The Wild Boy of Aveyron* by Jean-Marc-Gaspard Itard (New York: Monthly Review Press, 1972). These sad cases do not prove that there is no such thing as human nature by which we may judge right and wrong. Instead, they reveal that one of the principles of the law based on human nature is that we must be educated in order to be whole.

The argument based on Gestalt psychology is holistic. It requires a tacit grasp of many subsidiaries, each of which sustains the others. This is a process that Newman calls "reasoning from wholes to wholes" or the "cumulation of probabilities." Where formal logic moves from one proposition to other propositions, informal logic moves from thing to thing. However, to express the whole insight to another person, it must pass through the medium of language, which means taking the whole part-by-part. Disassembling the insight to put it into language means it is no longer self-sustaining. A car in pieces is not a real car. No single piece of the Brooklyn Bridge spans the river by itself; the parts become a bridge only when they are properly combined into the whole. Similarly, an insight broken into pieces—deconstructed—will not function as an insight. Viewed in isolation, every part becomes dubious and appears extremely weak. Only when integrated with other elements of the Gestalt do the fragments become what Newman called a "living idea."

In sacramental sexuality, the body reveals the person, and the person reflects the glory of God. In the debate over the proper reading—John Paul II calls it the "rereading" of the body[27]—there is a contest of Gestalts. If the body is a word of God, whose meaning is determined more by God's creative activity than by the scope of human freedom, then sharp limits are imposed on the use of the body in sexual activity. If the body is not a sacrament of God, then it is wholly at our disposal to do with as we please.

Conclusion

Our age is an age that values feelings and personal experience perhaps more than any other era in history. Married couples who put the teaching of the Church into practice have a special authority to teach others the gospel of life and the civilization of love. In *Humanae Vitae*, Paul VI called for a special ministry of like to like so that couples who personally experienced the fruits of sacramental sexuality would become "guides" for other married couples (HV 26). I am grateful for the many apostolic couples who have testified to the joy they have found by accepting the principles of *Humanae Vitae*.

---

[27] TMC 325–26.

Response

Edmund W. Majewski, S.J.

I WOULD LIKE TO THANK Father Moleski for his fine presentation. I will make a number of general observations and then comment upon some of his major points.

First, I highly recommend *Love and Responsibility*, written by Karol Wojtyła while still archbishop of Krakow, as a fine introduction to his thoughts on marriage and human sexuality. I was surprised by the candor with which he treats various sexual and psychological difficulties in the final chapter. This was especially surprising if one remembers that the first edition appeared in 1960 when few people discussed human sexuality with much openness. Secondly, the pope is uncompromising in his vision of marriage. He is hard, yet he denies that he is a rigorist. Couples must express the whole truth about the beauty of marriage and God through their actions and lives. The question arises whether the pope is offering an ideal or an absolute norm for all.

We now turn to Moleski's presentation. First, let us look at the Holy Father's theology of the body. The human person is a unity of body and soul. Through its actions and gestures the body reveals the person and the truth about itself and God. The human being is symbolic and all our gestures intend meaning. Through the body, even through sexual actions, I utter gestures, words, and actions that reveal who I am. All this is very incarnational since in the Incarnation God the Son became a man. Jesus is the unity of the human and the divine and is the visible image of the invisible God. The person is also a "who" and not simply a "what." Therefore, my actions reveal a reality that is far deeper than superficial knowledge about who I am. Furthermore, human nature exists concretely not as a genderless or neuter abstraction but as either masculine or feminine. John Paul II's understanding of the human person and human sexuality is based upon the complementarity of the sexes. God made us male and female. Each sex is unique, different, distinct, and irreducible, yet in this diversity there is an equality. This is so because man and woman are each incomplete without the other. Each comes to fulfillment and completion only through their relations and love for each other. We often reduce nature to a simple abstraction and hence neglect the complementarity of the sexes.

Furthermore, the body and creation as such are gifts by God. There is a certain givenness to creation and human nature. We use the grammar given to us by our nature to reveal who we are. We must conform to the demands of nature, yet as persons we always transcend nature without contradicting it. Human sexuality has a positive value in John Paul II's thought. Marriage is the sacrament of the human and the divine. The pope is very critical of Manichean tendencies which devalue the importance, the goodness, and the value of human sexuality. The sexual act plays a positive role since it possesses a revelatory character about God who is the author of life and the Creator of man and woman, about the person in his or her depths, and about human marriage and love. Vowed or covenantal love is important because this love must be faithful and irrevocable, and it expresses the gift of self that occurs in marriage. Although human love is free and personal, it must be objective. All subjective human actions must conform to the demands of truth and objective moral norms, which are absolute. Subjectivity and objectivity are oriented to each other. It is here that real difficulties and controversies begin to arise. Many theologians and ordinary persons who find much value and beauty in the Holy Father's vision maintain that these teachings are impossible for many people.

However, the pope has insisted that although these teachings are often difficult, they are not impossible to keep. One must admit that there is much in life that is difficult but which can be embraced. One might also question whether the truth about *Humanae Vitae* has really been taught in most seminaries and universities in the past twenty-five years. Certainly, we must admit that many sincere Catholics have difficulties with *Humanae Vitae*. Moleski is correct that we must avoid becoming judgmental about the actions of others and their motives. A proper pastoral approach must show compassion toward those who experience obstacles and failures in their marital relationships. Nevertheless, the truth must be proclaimed in this as in every other area. Teaching truth should not be seen as a condemnation of people but as a means of inviting them to new life, to a consistent ethic of the sanctity of life and the meaning of marriage. Humanity does not simply create objective moral norms but must submit to them. Has an excessively subjectivist approach to marital and sexual issues led to a lack of objectivity in so many other issues of moral behavior?

We now turn to a consideration of the Holy Father's rationale for such a high ideal for marriage. Why does he maintain that the two dimensions of the conjugal union, the procreative aspect and the unitive aspect, cannot be artificially separated without damaging the truth of the act itself? Such a separation contradicts the very symbolic nature of the act and the sacramentality of the marriage. According to the pope, by precluding the possibility of procreation in the marital act, man and woman shift the focus of their experience from a personal encounter in the direction of sexual pleasure as such, thereby making enjoyment alone or sexual pleasure alone the intention of the act. Why is this wrong? John Paul II does not deny the goodness of human sexuality or hold that procreation must take place without any enjoyment. Far from it.

According to the pope, the problem is that a focus on sexual pleasure alone without any openness to new life reduces the "other" person to an object, an object that I need to fulfill my needs and desires. I am reducing another person (a person is always to be an end-as-such) to a means to an end, something necessary for the satisfaction of my desire for enjoyment. Thus, the person is no longer treated as a person but as an object, and personalism is thereby reduced to utilitarianism. Love of the person includes a desire for the person, but it also goes beyond desire and includes my affirmation of the good of the other person in himself or herself, no matter what I receive in return. Love does not say, "I love you as a good for me" but rather, "I long for your good, for what is really good for you" even if I am required to sacrifice something for you.

Even when two persons agree to affirm each other equally as sources of pleasure, to use each other in mutual enjoyment, they are involved in mutual sexual pleasure and not true love. One danger is that as soon as one person is no longer desirable, the reason for their erotic love no longer exists and the love will grow cold. Love of husband and wife are not two loves, but one love and one reality. It exists as a reality between them. The pope uses the preposition "between" to underline this reality that they share. Furthermore, this bilateral love of the two persons allows a single "we" to arise from the two "I's." The pope speaks about a betrothed love between husband and wife. Such a love is based on the mutual gift of the self and the surrender of the self to the other. The "I" that is essentially mysterious and incommunicable is given totally and freely. In true love nothing is held back by either partner. Of course, the pope is aware that this is a gradual process, and hence their union becomes more profound over time.

We should note that a theology of the Trinity is needed to shed light on the theology of marriage. The Father and the Son love each other fully and without reservation. Husband and wife are also called to love each other completely and unconditionally. From the love of the Father and the Son for each other proceeds the Holy Spirit, a third person, who is neither Father nor Son, but the union and personal love between them. In some writings John Paul II refers to the Holy Spirit as "person-love since he is a love that is so fully personal that it is person." Likewise, in marriage perfect love between husband and wife gives rise to a new reality and can open itself to the birth of a third person, who is the result and fruit of their love. Marriage can become a participation in the Trinity's life since the love of two persons can give rise to something new, something greater than either person, a child, to a third person. Marital love becomes less egotistic because it is open to new possibilities; the circle of love is no longer closed but open to other persons.

The pope sees the mutual self-surrender of the two spouses as a reflection of the summons of the Gospel paradox about life and death. Jesus proclaimed that whoever loses oneself finds oneself. One must die to oneself in order to find new life. Only if love goes out of the self and discovers a fuller existence in others does the lover really find himself or herself and experience genuine fulfillment. Betrothed love requires the virtue of chastity, lest love degenerate into egoism. Sensuality has a positive value in the pope's vision of marriage and betrothed love. However, the danger arises that the lover may seek to possess sexual values for their sake alone; sensuality may lead to a spontaneous sensual concupiscence and from there to carnal desire or lust. The pope notes:

> "Carnal love" born of carnal concupiscence alone lacks the value which love for the person must contain. It substitutes for what should be the object of love, the person, a different object, namely, "the body and sex" of a person. The sensual reaction, as we know, does not relate to the person *qua* person, but only to "the body and sex" of a concrete person, and to these specifically as "a possible object of enjoyment." This means that a person of the other sex is discerned by active desire resulting from carnal concupiscence not as a person but as "body and sex." The sexual value as such usurps the place of the personal value which is essential to love, and becomes the core around which the whole experience crystalizes. (LR 150)

Sensuality must serve true love, but it should not dominate it.

Moleski mentions that much controversy has arisen over Pope Paul VI's condemnation of artificial means of birth control as contrary to the natural law. According to Pope John Paul II, marital love involves the union of two orders: the order of nature, which is concerned with reproduction, and the personal order, which deals with the love of persons. The pope does not intend to reduce the order of nature to a biological order, but simply points out that the human sexual act is naturally oriented to and affected by its purpose, which is procreation. The two orders are ordered to each other, mutually condition each other, and cannot be separated since human sexual relations involve a synthesis of both orders.

In the animal world, procreation occurs on the level of instinct. For human persons procreation is related to love, and both involve the free and conscious commitment of persons. The free acceptance of the possibility of parenthood elevates a sexual union into a union of persons. Objections are often made that the Church's insistence upon the priority of nature and natural law subordinates a person to the realm of mere nature. However, the pope disagrees:

> Some people might say that this ruling subordinates man, who is a person, to "nature," whereas in so many fields he triumphs over nature and dominates it. This, however, is a specious argument, for wherever man dominates "nature," it is by adapting himself to its immanent dynamism. *Nature cannot be conquered by violating its laws.* Mastery over nature can only result from a more thorough knowledge of the purposes and regularities which govern it. Man masters "nature" by exploiting more and more effectively the possibilities latent in it. (LR 229)

The pope stresses that love has a natural, inner logic and that spouses must open themselves to its logic if their interpersonal love is to be true to its nature:

> Since the sexual relationship is grounded in the sexual urge, and since it draws another person into a whole complex of acts and experiences, the attitude to that person and that person's moral value is indirectly determined by the way in which gratification of the sexual urge is geared into the relationship. In the order of love a man can remain true to the person in so far as he is true to nature. If he does violence to "nature," he also "violates" the person by making it an object of enjoyment rather than an object of love. Acceptance of the possibility of procreation in the marital relationship safeguards love and is an indispensable condition of a truly personal union. The union of persons in love does not necessarily have to be realized by way of sexual relations. But when it does take this form, the personalistic values of the sexual relationship cannot be assured without willingness for parenthood. Thanks to this, both persons in the union act *in accordance with the inner logic of love*, respect its inner dynamic, and prepare themselves to accept a new good, an expression of the creative power of love. Willing acceptance of parenthood serves to break down the reciprocal egoism—(or the egoism of one party at which the other connives)—behind which lurks the will to exploit the person. (LR 229–30)

Hence, love remains personal only when it acknowledges the demands that nature places upon persons. However, many contemporary philosophers and theologians have questioned this view of the relationship of the natural and personal order.

We now turn to Moleski's assertion that a crisis of truth exists today. Yes, there certainly is a crisis of truth. Popular culture proclaims that if it feels good, it is good. All truth is relative; there are no absolute truths; there are no absolute moral truths, obligations, or laws. Yet, if all is relative, how can we make any assertions about reality? Moleski speaks about the process of conversion to truth. Most of us were trained in a type of neo-scholasticism that tends to analyze statements by breaking them down into parts and then to build them up again, step by step. The danger is that the entire structure falls as soon as the weakest part of the foundation grows weak or defective.

Truth is also a totality. Theologians such as Cardinal Newman, Water Kasper, and Hans Urs von Balthasar have come to a realization that truth must be approached as a totality. Newman speaks about a theory of convergent probabilities. A series of pieces of evidence emerge, and they point in the direction of a certain conclusion, toward some particular truth. However, to arrive at the conclusion, one must make a leap, perhaps even a leap of faith. Kasper speaks about the importance of trust and faith, even in scientific research. The scientist must trust his instruments, his colleagues, his methodology. Most detective work involves following possibilities in the hope of convergence. There is no hard, indisputable proof in a mathematical sense in their work.

Kasper and von Balthasar note that the person who sees with the eyes of faith actually sees more, not less. And thinkers such as Polanyi talk about the intellectual process in which the parts begin to fit into a previously unrecognized whole. Von Balthasar maintains that Catholicism is fullness; it is the fullness of truth and revelation. The Church is Catholic because it proclaims the truth of Jesus, who is Catholic since he reveals the fullness of the truth and love of the Father. This approach can be applied both to the method and process of approaching truth and also to our understanding of truth as a totality.

This process is very intuitive rather than logical in an analytical sense, and it closely resembles some of the thinking of the Holy Father. With regard to birth control and human sexuality, various questions can be raised. How do the Church's teachings on birth control and sexuality relate to the totality, to the primacy of persons and the goodness of creation? If one element of Catholic doctrine, even a minor point, is denied, does this have consequences in other areas? Does dissent not chip away at the fullness of Catholicity? The use of birth control pills may seem a small issue to many people, but does it not lead to a subtle bias against procreation and an anti-life attitude, which may lead to a culture of death? The use of birth control and abortion are distinct issues, but is there a link between them? Does the acceptance of one lead to a greater openness to the greater evil? What happens to relations between man and woman when the woman is reduced to a sexual object that the man can dominate freely and without any constraints through technology? Does the pill not lead to a new form of male domination and manipulation? Has greater use of the pill led to greater personal intimacy and dialogue between spouses or prevented genuine dialogue?

Moleski spoke about his experiences with couples who use natural forms of family planning. Perhaps not all couples are able to practice it, but some are. This process has its difficulties, but it can also be a means of growth and liberation for many couples. Both partners must cooperate; not only the woman must exercise responsibility. It works only if both partners really communicate and speak to each other on a profound level. And the husband must become more sensitive to the rhythms of nature in his wife and to her physical and emotional needs. If the Church is to deal with some of these issues, then we must begin to listen to the laity, not only to those who disagree with its teachings on sexuality, but also to couples who are trying to live what the Church teaches about marriage. This will require some humility for theologians.

What successes have these couples had? What are some of their difficulties? How do they deal with failure? How has natural family planning helped their marriages become more solid and loving? Even here in discussing all sorts of problems and solutions, we should not lose sight of the totality, of a vision of marriage and sexuality as something beautiful and good since it leads to interpersonal intimacy and the gift of the self to others. They flow from gratitude to the One who gives life and who is Life and Goodness, Truth and Mercy.

11. RELATIONAL ETHICS

Covenant Love: Interpersonal Person, Family, and Work in the Social Theory of John Paul II

Robert J. Spitzer, S.J.

Introduction

I will limit my investigation to three works of Pope John Paul II: *Laborem Exercens*, *Familiaris Consortio*, and *Sollicitudo Rei Socialis*.

In *Sollicitudo Rei Socialis*, an encyclical celebrating the twentieth anniversary of *Populorum Progressio* (1967), John Paul II shows himself to be squarely in line with the social teaching of the Church embodied in the works of Leo XIII,[1] John XXIII,[2] the Second Vatican Council,[3] and Paul VI.[4] In the midst of his affirmation of Paul VI's socio-economic assessment of the good and just society, John Paul II inserts an uncharacteristically vehement statement about the proper end of society: "When individuals and communities do not have a rigorous respect for the moral,

---

[1] Pope Leo XIII, *Rerum Novarum*, 15 May 1891, encyclical letter *On the Condition of the Working Classes*.

[2] Pope John XXIII, *Pacem in Terris*, 11 April 1963, encyclical letter *Peace on Earth*.

[3] Second Vatican Council, *Gaudium et Spes*, 17 December 1965, Pastoral Constitution on the Church.

[4] Pope Paul VI, *Populorum Progressio*, 26 March 1967, encyclical letter *On the Progress of Peoples*.

cultural, and spiritual requirements, based on the dignity of the *person* and on the proper identity of each community, beginning with the *family* and *religious communities*, then all the rest—availability of goods, abundance of technical resources applied to daily life, a certain level of material well-being—will prove unsatisfying and in the end, contemptible" (SRS 33). Material well-being and the socio-economic apparatus required to bring it about, cannot be ends in themselves. If they are treated as ultimate or sufficient ends of human society, they will emerge not only as unsatisfying but contemptible. For John Paul II, the higher ends of the human person and society (moral, cultural, and spiritual ends) must be respected and cultivated alongside and ahead of the socio-economic apparatus giving rise to material well-being. If these higher ends slip into a subordinate role, leaving the material end to become dominant, the resultant materialistic society will eventually undermine human identity, achievement, development, and progress. The society will engender a momentum toward mediocre and even base objectives of human creativity and striving. The result would be both unsatisfying and contemptible.

Hence, John Paul II does not take a Maslowian approach to social theory (a hierarchy of needs). The material must be pursued along with the ideal, the tangible with the intangible, the work of human hands with the work of human hearts.

These moral, cultural, and spiritual ends are more than thoughts, ideals, or systems. They arise out of, are animated by, and give purpose through real interpersonal persons, families, religious and cultural communities. Great ideals cannot endow human striving and creativity with "rigorous respect" unless these ideals be infused with an awareness of and contact with the intrinsic dignity of every person, family, and community. This rigorous respect for the intrinsic dignity and value of persons, families, and religious communities transforms moral, cultural, and spiritual ideals into inalienable rights, as the pope notes in *Sollicitudo Rei Socialis*:

> On the internal level of every nation, respect for all rights takes on great importance, especially the right to life at every stage of its existence; the rights of the family, as the basic social community, or

"cell of society"; justice in employment relationships; the rights inherent in the life of the political community as such; the rights based on the transcendent vocation of the human being, beginning with the right of freedom to profess and practice one's own religious belief. (SRS 33)

In sum, the material aspects of social justice, the systems of distributing material goods, and the environment in which human work gives rise to these goods must be animated by an attitude seated within the individual and collective human heart, an attitude of awareness of and respect for moral, cultural, and spiritual ideals woven through the intrinsic dignity of persons, families, and communities. Inasmuch as this vast complexus comes fully alive through love, one might conclude that the central ideal of John Paul II's social theory and the true alpha and omega of human society is covenant love, long-term committed love, which in the light of faith is seen to originate from the covenant initiated by the Lord who is Love itself.

The following investigation will focus on the interpersonal person in the family and at work, for this interrelated reality will reveal the dignity, ideals, higher ends, and love that must ground our material and socio-economic strivings—indeed, our very lives. I will first look into the relationship between person and family, then into the relationship between person and work, and finally between family and work. I will conclude with some observations concerning John Paul II's view of the relationship between covenant love, our moral, cultural, and spiritual ideals, and our interpersonal personhood.

Society, Person, and Family

In light of the above, it is clear that committed covenant love is for John Paul II the proper aim and vocation of every human being and society. Love is the unity of our higher moral, cultural, and spiritual ends. It is the bond of unity between persons, and the unity between persons and their higher ends. It is therefore the proper end of culture and society, and it must be attended to as actively as material and economic concerns. In *Familiaris Consortio*, he reinforces and advances this philosophical approach to society by appealing to the key tenet of Christian faith: " 'God is love,' and in himself he lives a mystery of personal loving communion. Creating the human race in his own image and continually keeping it in being, God inscribed in the humanity of man and woman the vocation, and thus the capacity and responsibility, of love and communion. Love is therefore the fundamental and innate vocation of every human being" (FC 11). Again, the Holy Father emphasizes that love is not only the proper end of the human person but the proper end of society—indeed, the whole human family. God's creation of human beings in God's own image is not merely the creation of individual loving beings, but the creation of a community, a community that emulates the Trinity's interior life of loving communion. From a philosophical point of view, committed love is the aim of human society. Through the eyes of faith, the Trinity's absolutely loving interpersonal communion is the model and example for human society.

Committed love, particularly that which aims toward the interpersonal love of the Trinity, requires a continuous conversion toward detachment from evil and adherence toward good. Without this conversion, the conditions necessary for love (true respect for the intrinsic dignity of others, freedom for commitment, and reflection unobscured by self-deception) would be unrealizable:

> What is needed is a continuous, permanent conversion which, while requiring an interior detachment from every evil and an adherence to good in its fullness, is brought about concretely in steps which lead us gradually with the progressive integration of the gifts of God and the demands of his definitive and absolute love in the entire personal and social life of man. Therefore, an educational growth process is necessary in order that individual believers, families, and peoples, even civilization itself, by beginning from what they have already received of the mystery of Christ, may patiently be led forward, arriving at a richer understanding and a fuller integration of this mystery in their lives. (FC 9)

Love is not only the proper end of the individual and society, but the means through which it must occur. If love is to be the proper means to its own perfection, it will require a concrete, step-by-step unfolding within a relationship where the commitment to love can outlast and even grow through hardship, misunderstanding, and failure. It will be a commitment whose "staying power" and resolve will allow imperfections in love to become occasions for learning and pursuing love's deeper dimensions: "Christian revelation recognizes two specific ways of realizing the vocation of the human person, in its entirety, to love: marriage and virginity or celibacy. Either one is, in its proper form, an actuation of the most profound truth of man, of being 'created in the image of God.' " (FC 11).

I will restrict my comments in this paper to the way of marriage and family, for marriage is the intimate community through which all of us are brought into society and are called to the love that is the proper end of every individual, community, and society. The family is the community through which the proper end of the individual and the society (and the means to that end) originates and gradually unfolds. *If the family declines, then society and all individuals within it must also decline.* If the family loses the sense of its proper vocation or the means to that vocation, it will fail to foster and guide individuals and society to their proper end. All the material prosperity and technological benefits that human creativity can muster will not be able to overcome this decline, for they cannot lead the individual or society toward their highest end, an end which is worthy of them, which can truly satisfy, which can motivate toward a generosity and unity truly worthy of human beings, which is, by its very nature, eternal.

Within the context of Christian faith, the strength of the family and its sense of its own vocation are paramount, for it not only initiates the above-mentioned process of conversion toward love, but it infuses this process with the faith, revelation, prayer, and grace, which bring covenant love to perfection within the communion of the Trinity: "The Christian family, in fact, is the first community called to announce the Gospel to the human person during growth and to bring him or her, through a progressive education and catechesis, to full human and Christian maturity" (FC 2).

John Paul II believes that this foundation of human community and society is experiencing a serious decline, which threatens the spiritual, cultural, moral, political, and sociological life of humankind. Ironically, this is happening at a time when technology has achieved remarkable feats, when the world seems to have a greater appreciation for rights, freedom, and equality. Indeed, it is this very appreciation of freedom that seems to be at the root of the decline. The Holy Father begins his assessment by enumerating many of the benefits of the current age:

> On the one hand, in fact, there is a more lively awareness of personal freedom and greater attention to the quality of interpersonal relationships in marriage, in promoting the dignity of women, to responsible procreation, to the education of children. There is also an awareness of the need for the development of interfamily relationships, for reciprocal spiritual and material assistance, the rediscovery of the ecclesial mission proper to the family, and its responsibility for the building of a more just society. On the other hand, however, signs are not lacking of a disturbing degradation of some fundamental values: a mistaken theoretical and practical concept of the independence of the spouses in relation to each other; serious misconceptions regarding the relationship of authority between parents and children; the concrete difficulties that the family itself experiences in the transmission of values; the growing number of divorces; the scourge of abortion; the ever more frequent recourse to sterilization; the appearance of a truly contraceptive mentality. At the root of these negative phenomena there frequently lies a corruption of the idea and the experience of *freedom*, conceived not as a capacity for realizing the truth of God's plan for marriage and the family, but as an autonomous power of self-affirmation, often against others, for one's own selfish well-being. (FC 6)

The autonomous view of freedom (freedom from others and from constraint) has undermined the interpersonal view of freedom (freedom for others, which entails commitment to those others and their good). In the autonomous view, one feels free when one is unfettered from extrinsic demands. But this view is necessarily antithetical to commitment, for commitment means self-constraint for self-determination toward a higher goal, identity, purpose, or ideal. One cannot have it both ways. If one wishes to be free for others or the good, one will have to commit oneself, which entails acceptance of external constraint.

This false view of freedom has led many to a gigantic scotoma toward the beauty and efficacy of commitment. In so doing, it has undermined the family, which is utterly dependent on spouses' mutual intention toward such commitment.

This false view of freedom has also undermined authority. When children appropriate a false view of freedom, they unconsciously feel stifled by just and good parental demands. Instead of seeing these demands as part of their commitment to their families and the good beyond themselves, which engenders a fuller manifestation of their interpersonal personhood and capacity for love, they feel that their parents are devilishly attempting to eradicate their very being!

Again, one can see this false view of freedom behind resistance to revealed truth and religious authority. Rather than seeing this truth as a guide and grace toward greater commitment, love, and interpersonal freedom, it is seen as an imposition, as somebody else "telling me what to do."

This attitude spills over into one's view of tradition. Once societal and religious traditions have been relegated to the domain of impositions and "self-extinguishings," all wisdom that has stood the test of time and has survived the winnowing of generations of virtuous lives seems to be an anachronism, which does not fit into the contemporary enlightened era. But it is much harder to do without wisdom than one at first might think. Children have lost their trust and respect for adult wisdom, adolescents have no right of passage, and adults have no instincts for dealing with hardship and marital crises. In a desperate attempt to find our way out of these problems, we look toward new, empirically based, "value free," scientific and socio-scientific surrogates. But impressive and precise as it is, science is not equipped to provide wisdom, virtue, and morals, to plumb the depths of love, or to spark our need for commitment and self-transcendence. Science needs wisdom. It is not a replacement for it:

> It becomes necessary, therefore, on the part of all to recover an awareness of the primacy of moral values, which are the values of the human person as such. The great task that has to be faced today for the renewal of society is that of recapturing the ultimate meaning of life and its fundamental values. Only an awareness of the primacy of these values enables man to use the immense possibilities given him by science in such a way as to bring about the true advancement of the human person in his or her whole truth, in his or her freedom and dignity. Science is called to ally itself with wisdom. The following words of the Second Vatican Council can

therefore be applied to the problems of the family: "Our era needs such wisdom more than bygone ages if the discoveries made by man are to be further humanized. For the future of the world stands in peril unless wiser people are forthcoming." (GS 15) (FC 8)

The wisdom of which the Second Vatican Council speaks must include a correction of contemporary misimpressions about freedom.

Finally, this false view of freedom has encouraged an unrestrained venting of passion. Curbing one's passions feels like a stifling of one's freedom, expression, and being. Self-discipline feels like slavery instead of the path to freedom and virtue. This elevation of passion over discipline has led to a series of cultural problems, not the least of which is an undisciplined and unhealthy outlook on sexuality and fertility. As a consequence, sexuality is being divorced from commitment, marriage, children, family, and therefore covenant love. It is biological, but not spiritual. This has far-reaching consequences for our views of love, commitment, and marriage:

> Sexuality, by means of which man and woman give themselves to one another through the acts which are proper and exclusive to spouses, is by no means something purely biological, but concerns the innermost being of the human person as such. It is realized in a truly human way only if it is an integral part of the love by which a man and a woman commit themselves totally to one another until death. The total physical self-giving would be a lie if it were not the sign and fruit of a total personal self-giving, in which the whole person, including the temporal dimension, is present: If the person were to withhold something or reserve the possibility of deciding otherwise in the future, by this very fact he or she would not be giving totally. This totality which is required by conjugal love also corresponds to the demands of responsible fertility. This fertility is directed to the generation of a human being, and so by its nature it surpasses the purely biological order and involves a whole series of personal values. For the harmonious growth of these values a persevering and unified contribution by both parents is necessary. (FC 11)

There are many consequences of this erroneous view, such as the undervaluation of sexual fidelity, the valuing of wealth and job advancement over familial love, and the ambiguities and difficult choices of "women who want and need it all."

Society and culture seem to be unraveling. As we move toward a more radical desire for autonomy and "freedom from," many seem to be losing their sense of direction and meaning in life. Children feel ignored and unloved. Shared values and community-unity seem to be overshadowed by discontent and disrespect.

What can be done to extricate ourselves from this downward momentum? The Holy Father would recommend starting our social theory in the right place. We must begin not only with a consideration of socio-economic justice, but with a deep appreciation and dedication to covenant love, that love without which material socio-economic welfare would be unsatisfying and even contemptible. This covenant love must be fostered within the family, which is the fundamental and primary community within society. The commitment and intimacy of the family is capable of embracing love as the means to its own perfection, is capable of weathering mistakes through forgiveness, and encouraging growth through mutual trust and faith in God. A responsible social theory must also call the culture (that formulates and transmits social values) to its proper end. This would include not only the call to covenant love, but a call to a view of freedom that is consistent with that love, a view of commitment, of interpersonal freedom, of "freedom for," which recognizes the need for self-discipline, revelation, tradition, wisdom, and responsibility, particularly the responsibility for connecting sexuality with total self-giving that supports both family and covenant love.

Co-Responsibility, Work, and Society

Part one of *Familiaris Consortio* constitutes the framework through which the Holy Father approaches social theory. This framework, in which covenant love is both ends and means, is actualized through a gradual conversion of the person in a family and a particular community. This love can come alive only through a proper understanding and appropriation of freedom (commitment/"freedom for"), which the pope terms "covenant love." Certain moral standards govern and guide a proper understanding and actualization of all the above in their interrelationship with one another. This covenant love comes more fully alive through faith in God, Jesus Christ, and the Gospel, and comes even more fully alive through the universal Church.

Were I to relate this complex, interdependent reality to a philosophical concept, I believe that it might be best characterized by what Scheler and Marcel termed "co-responsibility." This concept stands in stark contrast to autonomous responsibility, which holds basically that "I take responsibility for myself; therefore, you should too." Co-responsibility overcomes the abandonment of the less strong, powerful, and self-sufficient by pointing to the stark truth of human interdependence, the interpersonal nature of the human person, and committed love as the highest end of human life. In so doing, the concept of co-responsibility also overcomes the flaws of autonomous rights theories and theories that subordinate the dignity of the individual to particular economic or political systems.

This concept, and the way in which John Paul II hopes to make it a reality, is much more profound than I can discuss in this paper. I will therefore restrict my discussion of it to three topics that are germane to the Holy Father's approach to social theory and social analysis: (1) the place of work and the worker in social theory, (2) the place of rights and systems analysis in social theory, and (3) the implicit priorities in social theory as they form a hermeneutical key to the approach to social theory and social policy.

Before proceeding, we may do well to refer to the diagram that accompanies this essay. It is designed to present "the big picture" by sketching the pope's implicit ranking of the elements involved in social theory, analysis, and policy. In addition to the above textual references to this implicit ranking in *Sollicitudo Rei Socialis* and *Familiaris Consortio*, the pope's order of presentation in *Laborem Exercens* is particularly revealing. The order of the encyclical corresponds to the six major levels of diagram 1:

1. Part two, section 7. John Paul II begins with a definition of work. He then turns to the ideal of co-responsibility and the problem of the reversal of the right order of socio-economic theory:

> A systematic opportunity for thinking and evaluating in this way, and in a certain sense, a stimulus for doing so, is provided by the quickening process of the development of a one-sidedly materialis-

tic civilization, which gives prime importance to the objective dimension of work, while the subjective dimension—everything in direct or indirect relationship with the subject of work—remains on a secondary level. In all cases of this sort, in every social situation of this type, there is a confusion or even a reversal of the order laid down from the beginning by the words of the Book of Genesis: Man is treated as an instrument of production, where he—alone, independent of the work he does—ought to be treated as the effective subject of work and its true maker and creator. (LE 30)

2. He then shows how work receives its meaning from the three domains in which covenant love (co-responsibility) is actualized:

(a) the person (section 9):

Remaining within the context of man as the subject of work, it is now appropriate to touch upon, at least in a summary way, certain problems that more closely define the dignity of human work in that they make it possible to characterize more fully its specific moral value. In doing this we must always keep in mind the biblical calling to "subdue the earth," in which is expressed the will of the Creator that work should enable man to achieve that "dominion" in the visible world that is proper to him." (LE 38)

(b) the family (section 10):

It must be remembered and affirmed that the family constitutes one of the most important terms of reference for shaping the social and ethical order of human work. The teaching of the Church has always devoted special attention to this question, and in the present document we shall have to return to it. In fact, the family is simultaneously a community made possible by work and the first school of work, within the home, for every person. (LE 42)

(c) the larger community (section 11):

The third sphere of values that emerges from this point of view—that of the subject of work—concerns the great society to which man belongs on the basis of particular cultural and historical links. This society—even when it has not yet taken on the mature form of a nation—is not only the great "educator" of every man, even though an indirect one (because each individual absorbs within the family the contents and values that go to make up the culture of a given nation); it is also a great historical and social incarnation of the work of all generations. (LE 44)

3. The whole encyclical is concerned with work as a primary mediator between the domain of co-responsibility through which work is directed toward its proper objective and subjective *ends* (the common good and the good of the worker as manifested through covenant love) and the domain of socio-economic systems, which are the *means* through which work is accomplished. The end and dignity of work must be related to the good of each worker and the common good. If work is viewed outside the context of co-responsibility, it would eventually destroy the person, the dignity of the person, the society, and, in the end, itself. The Holy Father defines work in both an objective and subjective way. Without losing ourselves in the distinction, it can be said that work produces two fruits: it provides for the necessities of life (objective)[5] and it allows human beings to "subdue the earth," that is, to use our creativity and energy to achieve our highest ends and the common good (subjective).[6] This subjective purpose of work is intrinsically satisfying and produces a kind of elation amid work's toil. Were work viewed outside the context of co-responsibility, the goal of "subduing the earth" might be seen as a justification for using the earth's resources in any way one pleases. This could result in unparalleled irresponsibility. Perhaps worse, the toil necessary to produce the necessities of life might be seen as "necessarily limitless" for some in order to provide a lap of luxury for others.

4. In part three of *Laborem Exercens*, the Holy Father first turns his attention to human rights, especially those manifest in the workplace. He sets out his major operating principle on rights through his view of work: work is a positive phenomenon "on condition that the objective dimension of work does not gain the upper hand over the subjective dimension, depriving man of his dignity and inalienable rights" (LE 45).

He then develops his theory of rights through an extensive discussion of the struggle between labor and capital, where he tries

---

[5] See part one, section 6, LE 16–21.
[6] See part one, section 6, LE 22–27.

to rise above the inadequacies of Marxist and pure Capitalist social theories. Both theories result in substantial rights abuses and (as noted above) cannot be treated as ends in themselves without undermining co-responsibility, the person's higher ends, human dignity, and unity (see LE 46–64). The pope makes two important contributions to the theory of socio-economic rights: (a) his demonstration of the priority of labor over capital[7] through his personalist (co-responsibility) argument,[8] and (b) setting out the parameters for the relationship between work and ownership[9] through the same personalist approach.

5. Part three is concerned with many elements on the fifth level of the diagram (the means of production, ownership, distribution, and technology). It should be noted that the pope derives his view of these systemic elements from his theory of worker's rights, which he, in turn, derives from his overriding principle about work within the context of co-responsibility: "the objective dimension of work should not override the subjective one."

Part four is devoted to specific issues in the relationship between labor and owners, a relationship that involves systemic issues of production and distribution. Special attention is given to employment issues (LE 77–87), social benefits (LE 88–93), unions (LE 94–100), agricultural work (LE 101–3), and disabled persons (LE 104–6). As the pope moves through these issues, he dialectically pieces together a theory of production, distribution, and technology. It must be noted that he does *not* derive his theory from an economic theory or model of any kind. He is not concerned with ideal (or equilibrium) prices in classical economic theory, nor does he resort to Marxist principles of distribution arising out of the "propensity toward the production of inelastic goods." *He derives his view of production and distribution through a superstructure formed out of the rights of the laborer derived from the personalist approach (co-responsibility) and the proper balance between subject and objective work.*

6. By now it must be clear that the Holy Father will not devote a section of *Laborem Exercens* to theoretical models of economics

---
[7] Part three, section 12, LE 52–57.
[8] Part three, section 15, LE 70–71.
[9] Part three, section 14, LE 63–69.

and economic systems. His approach to theoretical economics is much like St. Ignatius's approach to certain recommendations in the *Spiritual Exercises*: it is a matter of *tantum quantum*. Insofar as certain theoretical frameworks will help to achieve the ends of rights, work, and co-responsibility set out above, they should be used. Insofar as they are not useful, they should be set aside. Certainly, no theoretical model or system should be treated as an end-in-itself and no theoretical model should be used as a basis to derive the rights of workers or to set out the dignity of work, the person, or the family.

Diagram 1: Implicit Priorities in John Paul II's Social Theory

Co-Responsibility

Telos = Covenant Love = Love ⟷ Freedom for/commitment
and the moral standards consistent with them
↓
Comes more fully alive through Gospel faith
↓
Comes even more fully alive through the Church

| INTERPERSONAL PERSON | FAMILY, including Sexual responsibility Fertility responsibility | PARTICULAR COMMUNITY |

Mediation

WORK/WORKER
Subdue/Respect/Toil
Experience the fruit of
creativity and energy

RIGHTS
Political rights
Economic Rights

| End and Means of Production | End and Means of Technology | End and Means of Distribution | End and Means of Consumption |

ECONOMIC SYSTEM
View of Free Market,
Credit, Taxation, Trade,
Government Regulation
(labor, securities, money, monopoly, etc.)

12. MORALITY AND GENDER
Letter to Women and *Ordinatio Sacerdotalis*

John M. McDermott, S.J.

MANY AMERICANS both in the Church and outside it find a tension, if not a contradiction, between the pope's *Letter to Women*, in which he praises and encourages the movement for the liberation of women, and *Ordinatio Sacerdotalis*, in which he affirms that the Church has no authority to ordain women to the priesthood. After the publication of *Ordinatio Sacerdotalis* some Catholic theologians questioned the binding authority of the apostolic letter. Their questions and complaints were not silenced by the subsequent response of the Congregation for the Doctrine of the Faith to a *dubium* (doubt) proposed to it. Given the heated debate in the American Church and its potential for dividing the Church further, the underlying issues of authority, ecclesial order, and theological grounding have to be studied, clarified, and explained to the faithful.

During our meetings four basic areas of discussion were proposed: the role of authority, the theological arguments in favor of the prohibition or opposed to it, the larger role of women in the Church and in society, and the philosophical meaning of equality (sameness) in an age of nominalism that stresses the uniqueness of each human being, especially when faced with the universality of the moral law. Due to the limitations of time, attention was directed principally to the first two areas.

THE ROLE OF AUTHORITY

Although all agreed that if the limitation of sacerdotal ordination to male believers is of divine law (*jure divino*), pertaining to the very constitution of the Church, and both the pope and the Church are bound definitively to follow Christ's will in this matter, the question of the definitiveness of the papal decision was raised. Because the apostolic letter was not promulgated as an infallible decision *ex cathedra*, the pope's decision, it was argued, need not be definitive and could be changed. According to this view, the question of women's ordination, like the question of slavery, permitted further development; with time, ordination could be and would be extended to women. The pope's use of authority, moreover, was considered monarchical in this case, not taking into account the collegiality of his fellow bishops.

Against this, those defending the papal position argued that any reversal of *Ordinatio Sacerdotalis* would be contrary to the normal process for the development of doctrine, since the possibility of women's ordination had often been considered in the past and always rejected. The increasing weight of magisterial decisions makes it unthinkable that a clear reversal of the traditional and current papal position would ever take place. Admittedly, the response of the Congregation for the Doctrine of the Faith does not of itself add any authority to the pope's apostolic letter, but, issued as it was with the pope's approval, it clarified the intent of the apostolic letter. Although the apostolic letter's claim to be definitive as authoritatively and legitimately interpreting the infallible ordinary magisterium does not fit easily into the categories previously elaborated by theologians, the papal magisterium certainly employed a very high degree of authority in promulgating its decision and demanding that it "be definitively held by all the Church's faithful."

Just as it took time for the Church to become aware of the supreme authority exercised at the Council of Nicaea in rejecting the Arian heresy, so also it may take more time for the Church to come to greater clarity about the degree of authority employed in *Ordinatio Sacerdotalis*, but without doubt this apostolic letter marked a very significant exercise of papal authority, culminating a long tradition that prohibited the extension of sacerdotal ordination to women. Surely the burden of proof rests upon the shoulders of those arguing for a change in the tradition that restricts the ordination of priests to males.

The Theological Argument

Those favoring women's ordination argue mainly on the ground that to deprive women as a group of the possibility of ordination is to perpetuate traditional, unjust prejudices against women, which the pope opposed in his *Letter to Women* and which is a scandal for many in the modern world. The traditional prohibition is based on cultural biases that undervalue women and implicitly reaffirm their submission to antiquated patriarchal authorities. Although Scripture does not mention the election of women to the hierarchical priesthood, it does not explicitly forbid their selection. Various aspects of the New Testament's moral message seem rather to demand it.

In response to that position, one person mentioned that, while many demands raised by feminist theologians derive from and easily fit into the modern mentality, the underlying presuppositions of their argument would overturn the whole understanding of traditional Catholicism. Their radical bias in favor of egalitarianism often rejects the hierarchical structure of the Church as contrary to the mind of Jesus. Their biblical exegesis restricts our knowledge of the historical Jesus and refuses the authority of any sacred text deemed patriarchal, insofar as it runs counter to their own presuppositions. Moreover, their dogmatic speculations tend to be strongly agnostic in their doctrine of God, preferring to allow the divine mystery to be designated by various names according to the needs of contemporary cultures.

Positive arguments favoring the traditional position embraced by John Paul II relied upon arguments included in *Ordinatio Sacerdotalis* as well as his other writings and added some novel points. In favor of the obligatory nature of biblical revelation and in order to show that prohibition of women's ordination could not be dismissed under the universal rubric of cultural conditioning, it was mentioned that, contrary to all the surrounding nations, the Jews persisted in accepting only a male priesthood and rejecting every type of priestess. Jesus' restriction of ordination to the twelve apostles, who were males, did not represent a blind submission to the cultural restraints of Jewish culture. For in other ways he resisted and changed the norms governing the relations between men and women that obligated pious Jews. This is illustrated, for example, by his freedom in addressing the Samaritan woman, a public sinner, at the well (John 4) and by his accompaniment by women on his missionary journeys (Mark 15:41; Luke 8:2f.; 23:49, 55; Matthew 27:55f.).

That the election of males as those who were to celebrate the Eucharist in his memory in no way implies the superiority of men over women becomes clear when one realizes that Jesus passed over his mother Mary, the holiest and most favored of creatures. Certainly the office of the priesthood does not presuppose or imply a necessarily corresponding degree of sanctity that is assured its holder. Yet it is sanctity, the following of Jesus, that is decisive in the Christian life. In service all enjoy a full equality, and Petrine authority makes sense only if it is seen as in the service of sanctity. Not power, but the apparent powerlessness of the universal service of Christ and his Church stands at the center of the Christian message and life. However essential the hierarchical structure, linked to sacerdotal service and Petrine authority, may be for the Church, through the ages the real power in the Church has been exercised charismatically by the saints who dedicated their lives to service. To confound the latter with the former would not only involve a theological error but also do great damage to the Church, reducing its effective power in the Spirit. Charity, the full self-emptying accomplished on the Cross in the service of God and one's fellows, remains the ultimate meaning and goal of the Christian life.

Since the Church's deposit of faith derives not from Scripture alone, but from Scripture in its living unity with tradition and the magisterium, its legitimate interpreter, theological reason, has to be employed for the proper interpretation of Scripture and tradition. Here various insights were offered to illuminate and defend the traditional position.

The strongest argument concentrated on the implications of sexual complementarity and the iconic role of the priest as the representative of Christ. Sexuality is not an indifferent, merely physical matter in the supernatural order. For the Church has never recognized the cohabitation of homosexuals as a true marriage nor as a legitimate way of expressing love. Moreover, the analogy between marriage and God's love for the chosen people, already developed in the Old Testament, found a further expansion in the New Testament, where Jesus compared himself to the bridegroom (Mark 2:19f.). St. Paul developed that image into a whole theology of Jesus' union with his Body, the Church, with whom he is one yet different (1 Cor. 6:12–20; 2 Cor. 11:2; Eph. 5:21–33), and the Apocalypse employed it to describe the eschatological salvific union of Christ with his bride, the Church (21:2).

Regarding the names of God, it was observed that the Old Testament, despite and apparently in deliberate rejection of the feminine deities and consorts prominent in the surrounding nature religions, consistently applied masculine nouns and pronouns to Yahweh. This usage was not only accepted but also intensified by Jesus, who called God *Abba*. Since this represents the culmination of revelation, showing God as a Father of tremendous, loving intimacy, of a love so great that even the cross could not destroy it but manifested its profundity, Christians must take seriously the implications of the masculinity involved in the title.

Were *Abba* merely a culturally conditioned appellation, no other name of God could claim any revelatory authority. Jesus' consciousness as the final revealer of God would be relativized, and the very divinity of Jesus would be imperiled. For at the time of the Arian controversy, the great orthodox Fathers of the Church—Athanasius, Hilary, and Gregory of Nyssa—all agreed that since God has been revealed to be Father, he always had a Son. Because in both Greek and Latin the word for "nature" (*physis, natura*) stems from the verbal form "to be born" (*phyesthai, nasci*), the One eternally begotten of the Father must possess the same nature as the Father.

More recent study has also indicated how novel was Jesus' appellation of God as *Abba*, an Aramaic caritative, which a child or grown son would employ in addressing his father. As such it might even be translated as "daddy" or "dad." Out of reverence, Jesus' Jewish contemporaries habitually avoid naming the all-holy Yahweh. It is therefore not surprising that, as far as current knowledge goes, Jesus is the first Jew ever to call God *Abba* in prayer. Were Jesus' claim as "the Son" to have a unique knowledge of his Father (Matthew 11:25–27) to be relativized, the foundations of Christian faith would be undermined.

Granted the masculinity of God, the masculinity of the humanity of Jesus, who is the "image (*icon*) of the invisible God," "the effulgence of His glory," and "the impression of His subsistence" (Col. 1:15; 2 Cor. 4:4; Heb. 1:3), cannot be dismissed as irrelevant to the question. It reveals something about God, about the Father as well as the Son. For since the soul expresses itself through the body and the free person through his or her human nature, the eternal Son chose for himself the humanity that might serve as his best human self-expression. If the masculinity of Jesus manifests in a sacramental symbol the masculinity of the Son and of the Father, then the masculinity of the priests who represent Jesus in the celebration of the Eucharist and in the sacramental structure of the Church pertains to the reality of the ordained priesthood.

These insights were offered to support the papal position, yet it was recognized that as rational arguments they were not thoroughly convincing. Their acceptance presupposes faith and an obedient adherence to tradition and the magisterium. Other presuppositions from outside tradition will lead to different conclusions. For that reason, one participant declared, Christ established Peter and his successors: they were to decide questions pertaining to the faith when divisions arose that threatened to divide the Church. Surely the weight of evidence is on the side of the pope, especially in view of the unbroken tradition and the witness of the ordinary magisterium, which is infallible.

Another pointed out that the matter may become clearer with time. In the past the Arian heresy marked a crisis of the previously dominant Logos Christology, which tended to see Jesus as the mediator of creation and left a certain ambiguity about his divinity. In response to it, the orthodox Fathers developed a Son Christology, which in turn opened the way to a greater appreciation of love as the essential reality of the God who exists as three personal relations as well as to the clearer defense of his freedom in creation and redemption. Similarly the present crisis of feminist theology may open the way to a more adequate understanding of human nature.

Neo-scholastic thought viewed nature as the undifferentiated common element achieved by abstraction and resulting in a universal concept. More recently, transcendental Thomism has come to see nature as an individual intellectual-volitional dynamism transcending concepts but essentially the same in all human beings. In both interpretations something of the richness of the original notion of nature, which is linked to generation as the continuation of the species, is lost. Since among human beings the cooperation of male and female is required for procreation in love, the complementarity of the sexes would seem to pertain to the proper understanding of nature. Perhaps with time and reflection this view will be generally accepted as a more adequate understanding of human nature. That would help to strengthen the papal position and make it more intelligible to believers and nonbelievers alike.

The suggestion was made that something might be learned about women's ordination from others, especially from the Episcopalians, who have a similar understanding of priesthood. If, after all, there is a contradiction between the ordination of women and the Christian message, one would expect that contradiction to manifest itself in a decline in the Church's life. Another participant agreed, pointing to the decline in morality that resulted from the rejection of *Humanae Vitae*, a result predicted by Paul VI but summarily dismissed by many of his opponents. Yet another held that those churches that had accepted female priests were experiencing a disintegration of doctrine and a hemorrhage of membership. Their example should warn the Catholic Church against ordaining women. But others were not so ready to accept the argument from consequences since many of the norms employed to judge results seem to be vague. Over how long a time must the experiment be pursued before a definitive judgment can be reached? Is this not giving in to proportionalism or consequentialism? Is not the matter of Church life so complex that one issue alone cannot be totally determining? Should there not be clearer norms within the tradition that derives from Christ, so that the Church might avoid experiments that make it appear that Christ's will is not clear and that shake the faith of the simple? In short, however helpful some results may be in indicating the correctness of a decision, the results do not contain in themselves the norm of their judgment and are subject to varying interpretations.

Much of the debate about women's ordination is framed in terms of authority as power to oppress. Although the Christian understanding of authority means power in serving others and helping them to grow to the fullness of Christ's stature, the misuse of authority in the past probably contributed to the fervor of many feminists who interpret reality, even Church life, as a contest for power. In his *Letter to Women*, after admitting the difficulty of assigning blame for cultural conditions that contributed to the oppression of women, John Paul II wrote, "And if objective blame, especially in particular historical contexts, has belonged to not just a few members of the Church, for this I am truly sorry. May this regret be transformed, on the part of the whole Church, into a renewed commitment of fidelity to the gospel vision."

One participant suggested that if this desire is to become a reality, the image of the marital covenant has to be taken more seriously than in the past. For marriage involves dialogue among free partners. Much can be done in consulting women and letting them take a more active part in the decision-making process of the Church. Thus it will become clear, another participant remarked, that the pope's position in both *Ordinatio Sacerdotalis* and in his *Letter to Women* relies upon a theology of marital covenant that defends and preserves both femininity and masculinity as the essential difference in the community of a single nature.

13. MORALITY AND FAMILY RIGHTS
Familiaris Consortio, Fifteen Years Since

Christopher M. Cullen, S.J.

Introduction

In 1981, on the feast of Christ the King, just over thirteen years after *Humanae Vitae,* Pope John Paul II addressed many of the same moral issues in his apostolic exhortation *Familiaris Consortio.* The latter document was the result of the synod of bishops that had met the previous fall to discuss the Christian family. People interested in seeing what this pope would do with the teachings of *Humanae Vitae* eagerly awaited this document. Drawing on his collaborative work with the synod, the pope reaffirmed the teaching of *Humanae Vitae,* to the chagrin of some.

But he did more than simply repeat its words; he incorporated the teaching of *Humanae Vitae* on sexuality and the teachings of the Second Vatican Council on the family found in *Gaudium et Spes* #47–52 (chapter entitled "The Dignity of Marriage and the Family") into the Christology and personalism that he first presented in the encyclical so foundational to his papacy, *Redemptor Hominis.* Like the *Catechism,* therefore, *Familiaris Consortio* is a work of synthesis and incorporation, continuing to define the meaning of the council's teaching.

Fifteen years later, John Paul II has turned out to be arguably the world's leading defender of Christian teaching on marriage, sexuality, and the family in the late twentieth century. *Familiaris Consortio* has been, if you will, the charter for this papacy's ceaseless and frenetic work on family issues. John Paul II has taken its teachings to every corner of the globe in order to communicate the Christian vision of family life. He is uniquely qualified for this task. For he spent much of his life working on these issues in one way or another, whether as a young parish priest in rural Poland, as moral philosophy professor in Lublin, as the archbishop of Krakow, or as a close advisor to Paul VI. He comes to these issues as a theologian, philosopher, and pastor. He is ready as a result of these experiences to discuss them from a theoretical or a practical standpoint. His is a voice that is accustomed to discussing these matters that so intimately touch human life. After a pontificate that has been long by papal standards, it is worthwhile to return to the document that has been so vital to the work of this pontificate. Certain key issues in it are worthy of renewed attention. This is, in part, the purpose of this essay.

In 1994 this "charter" was amended, not because it was in error, but because it had to respond to distressing developments in the world that required a more vigorous critique from the Church. This amending was carried out in a *Letter to Families*. It was issued as the papacy was preparing for the United Nations Conference on Population and Development to be held in Cairo, Egypt. The 1994 *Letter to Families* is compelling reading—the pope at his most eloquent. But what is more important for our purposes, *Familiaris Consortio* must now really be read in conjunction with this letter in order to understand the pope's current thinking on the family in today's world.

First, let us take an overview of *Familiaris Consortio*. It is a document with four major parts. The first part gives the context to the exhortation. The second part is a presentation of the plan of God for marriage and the Christian family. The third is about the role of the Christian family. And the final part is on the pastoral care of the family.

The first part, labeled "Bright Spots and Shadows for the Family Today," lists some of the good things about the situation in which the family finds itself, such as a more lively awareness of personal freedom, greater attention to the quality of interpersonal relationships in marriage, and greater attention to the dignity of women, among other things. But it also lists some of the bad things such as the number of divorces, the scourge of abortion, and the appearance of the contraceptive mentality. The document goes on to call for a "new humanism" and a renewal of society by recapturing the meaning of life and its fundamental values.

In the second part of the document on the plan of God for marriage, John Paul II appeals, not surprisingly, to Genesis and the original plan of God. Humanity is created in love and is made for love. The human being cannot live without love. Sexuality, by which a man and a woman give themselves to each other, is not simply a biological phenomenon but a part of the love for which humankind is made. It is directed to the generation of a human being, to the child, who is to be seen as a gift of God. The truth about marriage has been revealed by Christ. Finally, the family is a communion of persons.

In the third part, the document speaks of the role of the Christian family. It is precisely because of what it is, that it has a particular mission: what it must do is rooted in its identity. What is the family in God's plan? It is an intimate community of life and love. It has a mission to become more and more what it is. It has a mission to guard, reveal, and communicate love. This identity of the family as a community of persons, as a community of life and love, gives it four general tasks:

1. to form a community of persons;
2. to serve life;
3. to participate in the development of society;
4. to share in the life and mission of the Church.

In the fourth part of the document, the pope outlines the pastoral care of family, discussing the stages, structures, and agents of care to families.

Certain key issues are worthy of special consideration in *Familiaris Consortio*. First, it is important to see *Familiaris Consortio* in various ways as a commentary on chapters 1 and 2 of the second part of *Gaudium et Spes* dealing respectively with "The Dignity of Marriage and the Family," and "Proper Development of Culture." The pope is not only dealing with the same issues, he develops many of the same themes. In this regard, he is both commenting on the conciliar text and helping to define the meaning of the text. One sees this very clearly in the first part of *Familiaris Consortio* where the pope is assessing the positive and negative phenomena currently facing the family. This section of the exhortation closely resembles the chapter of *Gaudium et Spes* on "The Dignity of Marriage and the Family," which even points to some of the same positive and negative phenomena.

But whereas *Gaudium et Spes* remains silent on the source of the problems facing the family, *Familiaris Consortio* attempts to expose error. It traces the evils threatening the family to a corruption of the idea and experience of freedom in which freedom is seen, not as a capacity for realizing the truth of God's plan for marriage and the family, but as the autonomous power of self-affirmation for one's own selfish well-being. There is, the pope explains, a false understanding of freedom, which lies behind many of the problems the family faces.

This is no small point. First, it shows a pope more willing to refute error than was the council (Vatican II). Secondly, it shows an awareness of one of modernity's key problems—namely, its understanding of freedom. The pope is dealing with one of the contradictions at the heart of modernity. Modernity demands freedom from external restraint for individuals, while at the same time maintaining that there is no true internal freedom. Modernity tends not to believe that "man in himself" is truly free—he is a slave to varying degrees of the various factors that shape him, whether these factors are found in his environment, or in his psychological background, or in his emotions. In short, free will is an illusion. Modern society tends to accept a radical determinism with regard to the interior life of the human being, while demanding a radical autonomy with respect to external restraint. This combination is deadly. It leads to an understanding of freedom as autonomy without responsibility.

John Paul II is defending the position that a human person is a free being; that is, a person with a free will. He is calling human beings to accept their freedom as persons and the responsibility that goes with it. Freedom and responsibility cannot be rightfully separated, according to the pope.

Furthermore, the pope clearly believes that ideas matter. One's views shape the concrete choices of life. Freedom as autonomy combined with a psychological determinism ends as a destructive force undermining the society of persons which is the family.

Another element of *Familiaris Consortio* worthy of recalling is the Christological context in which the pope has placed the

Church's teaching on the family. *Gaudium et Spes* #22 says that Christ reveals man to himself. This understanding of Christ has been central to John Paul II's own thinking. He quotes at length this section of *Gaudium et Spes* in chapter 8 of his first encyclical, *Redemptor Hominis*.

The pope returns to this theme in chapter 11 of the encyclical: "in Christ and through Christ man has acquired full awareness of his dignity, of the heights to which he is raised, of the surpassing worth of his own humanity, and of the meaning of his existence." This Christological foundation of John Paul II's anthropology is evident in *Familiaris Consortio*: "He [Christ] reveals the original truth of marriage, the truth of the 'beginning,' and, freeing man from his hardness of heart, He makes man capable of realizing this truth in its entirety" (*Familiaris Consortio* 13). One can see this same foundation at work again in the document as the pope discusses the way in which parents share in the threefold mission of Christ, as priest, prophet, and king.

A Christological context also implies an anthropological one. In *Familiaris Consortio* the pope has placed the Church's teaching on the family in a very clear anthropological context, which involves a definite philosophical standpoint. Each person is a unified and integrated being; in short, an incarnate spirit. In this understanding, the body exists for the sake of the soul. The soul is not a separate substance dwelling in the body, let alone one that has been imprisoned in the body; rather, the human person is a composite, a psychosomatic whole.

The pope is drawing on an understanding of the unity of the human being that was first formulated in the writings of St. Thomas Aquinas; and it is this Thomistic personalism that provides the basis for the pope's understanding of the human being and of human sexuality. Thomistic personalism has provided the pope with a profound philosophical foundation from which to affirm and defend the Christian teachings on sexuality in the post-Enlightenment world. One may not agree with the position, but the position cannot be lightly dismissed with intellectual honesty. Is this not the sort of defense of Christian doctrine that Leo XIII envisioned in his program for the renewal of Christian philosophy in *Aeterni Patris*? Indeed, it seems so; *Familiaris Consortio* is an intellectual fruit of *Aeterni Patris* (1879).

Given this Thomistic personalism, it is not surprising then that the document argues that an adequate doctrine of the family and of sexuality must take account of the human being as a whole, as a unity of body and soul. The pope presents a personalist view of marriage. Marriage is a covenant between persons—indeed, a communion of persons. Sexuality, then, can never be isolated from this understanding of human beings as persons. Human sexuality cannot be treated as animal copulation. It is always the physical union of persons, of a husband and wife who give expression to their communion as persons in the physical union. Artificial birth control fails to respect the personhood of the other human being. As *Humanae Vitae* gave us the natural law arguments against artificial birth control, so *Familiaris Consortio* gives us the personalist arguments against artificial birth control.

It is this personalism that is so important when the pope outlines the responsibilities or "tasks" of the family. It is the family's very identity as a community of persons that gives it four general tasks. The first task is that the family must form a community of persons. The pope speaks of the family as a community founded on a communion of persons; first, a communion of the husband and wife, and this communion of persons is the foundation for a broader communion—that of the communion of persons, parents and children, which is the family. Thus, the first task of the family is to be what it is—a community founded on the communion of persons.

It is in this context that the pope calls the Christian family the specific realization of ecclesial communion, the "domestic church." The family is the school of deeper humanity and of being a Christian.

The second task of the family is to serve life. And this task of serving life is twofold: the family is to transmit life and to educate. Both of these aspects of the task to serve life is rooted in the vocation of the married couples to participate in God's creative activity. In the transmission of life married couples must be on their guard against the culture that would separate sexuality from personhood. Sexuality must preserve the full meaning of the mutual self-giving that marriage involves, and human procreation must respect the nature of the human person.

In education parents must understand that they are responsible for helping the child (a new person) to live a fully human life. The family is the first fundamental school of humanity. It is where we learn to be human. But the family is also where the child learns to be a Christian, and the Lord entrusts this task first and primarily to the parents. The parents are "the first heralds" of the Gospel.

A third task of the family is to participate in the development of society. The family is the foundation of society, the vital cell of society. It is where society must first be humanized and personalized. What is more, the family is a society in its own right. But our current culture has attacked the inviolable rights of the family and thereby violated the principle of subsidiarity.

The fourth task of the family is to share in the life and mission of church. This is the ecclesial task. The parents share in the threefold mission of Christ. They share in the prophetic mission in their educating their children in the faith; they share in the priestly mission by living the sacramental life, for the family is called to be sanctified and to sanctify.

Finally, it is important to note that *Familiaris Consortio* is a pastoral document in that it is clearly meant to help pastors and all those engaged in work with married couples and families in the church. The pastoral aspect is especially clear in the fourth part of the document, where the pope explains the implications of the church's teaching for the stages, structures, and agents of the pastoral care of the family as well as for difficult cases in the church. The pope is definitely concerned with the concrete and specific problems that face both pastors (and their assistants) and married couples. He exhorts pastors and those involved in ministry to couples and families to realize that there are stages to the care of the family and all are important: marriage preparation, the celebration of marriage, and the time after marriage.

Perhaps, the most discussed issue of this section is his reaffirmation that the divorced and remarried are not to be admitted to communion. Nevertheless, he goes out of his way to exhort pastors and all the faithful to help the divorced realize that they are still part of the Church and are not separated from it. The divorced are still called to share in the life of the church by attending the Sacrifice of the Mass, by persevering in prayer, by contributing to works of charity, and by bringing their children up in the faith.

John Paul II has provided a profound theological and philosophical context for the Church's teaching. But he is deeply aware of the catechesis required to implement this teaching. And so, if there is an underlying message of this section, it is that the truth must be spoken in love. In the eyes of the pope truth and love are inseparable. Love without the truth is not true love; and the truth without love does not persuade.

1994 Letter to Families

Familiaris Consortio should really now be read in conjunction with John Paul II's 1994 *Letter to Families*. Why? First, because much has happened in the Church and in the world since 1981. The West has traveled much farther down the path of secularism. The 1994 *Letter to Families* reflects a significantly more pessimistic view of developments in society. Indeed, the letter came out in the very year that the Vatican was preparing for the United Nations Conference on Population and Development, the now famous "Cairo Conference," in which it took a full diplomatic offensive on the part of the Vatican to avoid the declaration of abortion as a fundamental right. The letter was no doubt in preparation for the Cairo Conference. In this context, it is no wonder then that the *Letter to Families* sees civilization itself at stake in the battle over the modern issues surrounding the family.

But the main reason to read *Familiaris Consortio* in conjunction with the 1994 *Letter to Families* is because of the theological and philosophical developments within the papal position. There are at least five key ones. First, there is a significant change in tone in the 1994 letter. Second, this letter, while presenting many of the same ideas and themes as *Familiaris Consortio*, presents the Church's teaching in an even more explicitly Christological and Trinitarian perspective. Third, this letter develops certain key insights of the personalist view of marriage and sexuality. It then applies these insights to a strong critique of artificial birth control. Fourth, this letter ties more explicitly the life of the family to the civilization of love; indeed, the case is made that the whole of civilization is at stake in the family. And finally, John Paul II gives one of his most striking and withering critiques of a society constructed along the lines of the sexual revolution. In this regard the letter attempts to define the meaning and significance of *Gaudium et Spes*, #53–62, which is the chapter on "The Proper Development of Culture."

One of the most striking points about the *Letter to Families* is its tone. It is very different in tone from both the documents of Vatican II and the pope's earlier writings. The tone of the 1994 letter is pessimistic about developments in the secular world; it is defiant and countercultural. One is reminded of Gregory IX's *Mirari vos* or Pius XII's *Summi pontificatus*.

The letter presents a Christological and Trinitarian view of the family similar to *Familiaris Consortio*, but one now even more extensively explicated, especially with regard to the Trinitarian view. The primordial mode of the person is Christ, and it is Christ who reveals what it is to be human and to be a person. Furthermore, the primordial model of family is the Trinitarian mystery of God's life. Human fatherhood and motherhood contain an essential likeness to God as a community of persons united in love. The family is founded on a communion of persons—that is, the husband and wife.

This letter develops in at least two significant ways the personalist view. First, it argues forcefully that the human being as a person is willed for his or her own sake, because God is present in human begetting and in all instances of begetting: for a person is created. Thus, what the pope calls "the genealogy of the person" is inscribed in the biology of generation. Because the human being is willed for his or her own sake, he or she cannot be treated as a means to an end. This, in turn, means that the other—the other human being—cannot be treated as an object, but must be treated as a subject, as a person. Human persons are necessarily then involved in "I-Thou" relationships. The other is never to be treated as an "It," but only as a "Thou." On this point the pope develops an insight also found in the Jewish existentialist philosopher, Martin Buber, who wrote extensively on the "I-Thou" relationship.

Second, John Paul II expounds and makes even more explicit a teaching found in *Familiaris Consortio*—namely, that people cannot find themselves except through the gift of self. Here again the pope is attacking the view of freedom as autonomy.

This personalism is then applied to a critique of artificial birth control, in which the pope argues that the conjugal union can only be adequately understood in the context of the person's full gift of self to the other. Artificial birth control falsifies this gift. The logic of total gift of self to the other involves potential openness to procreation. The person cannot be treated as a means, especially not as a means to pleasure. Artificial birth control falsifies the "I-Thou" relationship: the other who is always a "Thou" is treated as an object, an "It." Hence, artificial birth control interferes with the communion of persons; it thereby attacks the foundation of family, and thus also the foundation of society. In short, artificial birth control is an attack on the civilization of love.

The family is the first human society. This is a crucial point that this document makes clear. The pope clearly sees the family as a society in its own right. Society in general ought not to be seen as just made up of individuals and the Leviathan state. The state must respect the sovereignty of the family, because it is a legitimate society that rightfully exists on a level between the individual and the state. The pope makes even clearer in this latter document that the failure to respect the sovereignty of the family is a violation of the principle of subsidiarity. And because the family is the first human society, it is thus organically linked to civilization. There can be no civilization of love without an understanding of the family as the first society in which the human person becomes aware of self as a creature willed for his or her own sake.

Finally, John Paul II presents a striking critique of modern society. He speaks of a crisis—a crisis of truth, a crisis of concepts. And the truth involved is the truth about freedom and the communion of persons. The pope says that modern society is profoundly positivistic and that positivism ends in agnosticism in theory and utilitarianism in practice. Our current society is building a civilization of production and use: of things, not persons. In a civilization of things, the woman is an object for man, children are a hindrance to parents, and the family is an institution inhibiting freedom. In such a civilization of things, there is no safe sex. Indeed, he says, it is extremely dangerous because there is a loss of truth about the self and the family, and thus a loss of freedom and a loss of love. The family's search for "fairest love" is exchanged for concupiscence in which the man and woman use each other, and persons become slaves to their weaknesses.

In a civilization of things, individualism reigns supreme, and freedom comes to mean that the subject does what he or she wants and establishes the truth of whatever he or she finds pleasing or useful. Such a utilitarian happiness identifies happiness with pleasure.

At the basis of this civilization of things is a rationalism that makes metaphysical errors about humanity. Human nature is seen in a dualistic fashion, and the body is considered to be simply a body like other bodies. The human body is not seen as a spiritualized body and is not seen as an aspect of the person who has been made in the image and likeness of God.

Furthermore, the pope says that the current society is filled with a "new Manichaeism" in which the body has no life from the spirit. Hence the human being ceases to live as a person and as a subject but lives only as an object. Rationalism cannot tolerate the mystery of the human as male and female. As evidence of this the pope could have pointed to the rapidly developing androgyny in modern society, which resembles that found in ancient Manichaeism and gnosticism. In short, the pope says we live in a society that is sick. It is sick because it has broken away from the full truth about man.

The 1994 letter is an historic document. For it makes clear that *aggiornamento* cannot mean the blind acceptance of modern culture with its rationalism and its concomitant errors about man and society. The human being cannot be remade. Human nature must be respected.

In this regard the letter attempts to define the meaning and significance of *Gaudium et Spes*, #53–62, which is the chapter on "The Proper Development of Culture." This chapter of Vatican II takes a very positive and optimistic view of modern culture and even calls for the collaboration of Christians in the life of that culture. But the pope's letter precludes a use of this chapter of Vatican II as a means of embracing the values and principles of the sexual revolution, as well as the practices associated with that revolution, such as abortion, artificial birth control, and free sex.

In this regard the pope's letter is profoundly countercultural. The pope, in effect, is saying that Vatican II's program of *aggiornamento* with regard to culture cannot be used to condone a society built on the principles of the sexual revolution, which deny the truth about man. Vatican II's openness in respect to culture cannot be interpreted to mean that the Church must abandon its ancient truth. The Church will stand in such a culture as a prophetic witness to the truth.

Five key documents now constitute that prophetic witness since the beginning of the sexual revolution in the 1960s: *Gaudium et Spes* #51–52, 87(1965), *Humanae Vitae* (1968), *Familiaris Consortio* (1981), *The Catechism of the Catholic Church* #2331–2400 (1992), and the *Letter to Families* (1994). But it is primarily in the last document that the reader finds an extensive critique of the errors currently eroding family life.

It is important to see that the pope is a man who profoundly understands the link between ideas and actions, and so he is not only concerned with safeguarding doctrines. He is a pastor deeply concerned with the care of souls. But he understands the organic link between what people believe and who they become as human beings through their actions. Furthermore, there is a direct link between religious belief and culture, because culture is a human product. And it is this point one must keep in mind when considering the pope's vigorous critique of our brave new world. True love demands the truth. And the pope clearly believes that true compassion means calling people to the best in themselves. He calls married couples, for example, not merely to love but to "fairest love." He is not indifferent to the problems and difficulties that beset the family. But these cannot be overcome by false answers that deny the truth about human beings. As he wrote in his book *Crossing the Threshold of Hope*, also released in 1994, "Moving away from this truth [the truth about humanity] does not represent a step forward, and cannot be considered a measure of 'ethical progress.' "[1]

In the same book, the pope wrote: "Generations come and go which have distanced themselves from Christ and the Church,

---

[1] John Paul II, *Crossing the Threshold of Hope* (New York: Alfred A. Knopf, 1994), 174.

which have accepted a secular model of thinking and living or upon which such a model has been imposed. Meanwhile, the Church is always looking toward the future. She constantly goes out to meet new generations."[2] The pope seems clearly aware that his teaching may not meet with acceptance among many of his contemporaries. The pope now sees his pontificate as a preparation for the year 2000 and the upcoming millennium. He has said as much. He calls the Church to a new evangelization in its third millennium. In *Familiaris Consortio* and his 1994 *Letter to Families,* the pope has gone out to meet the new generations in the approaching millennium.

---

[2] Ibid., 113.

14. COMPREHENSIVE ETHIC OF LIFE

Some Observations on *Evangelium Vitae*

Arthur R. Madigan, S.J.

Permit me to begin with a feature of the encyclical *Evangelium Vitae* that I find extremely helpful. Instead of simply restating a series of categorical prohibitions (of abortion, suicide, euthanasia, and so on), and arguing for these prohibitions one by one, the encyclical situates these prohibitions within the larger positive context of the gospel of life. I find this helpful. Helpful in what sense? Arguments for categorical moral prohibitions have a way of being less than cogent. However self-evident the premises, however rigorous the logic, arguments for categorical prohibitions have a way of leaving some of the audience unconvinced.

There are always people who say "I just don't see it. You haven't proved it to me." The encyclical speaks to this problem. In effect, it says: "Stand back for just a moment from the individual issues and arguments. They all really come down to one basic issue: Are you for life, or are you against life? Search your mind and your heart: which side are you on? Surely you see that deep down you want to be on the side of life. Once you get a grip on that fact, on the deep affirmation of your own heart and mind, you can start to appreciate what the gospel of life means in the details of your life."

This is the right move to make, both theologically and pastorally. The culture that Pope John Paul II terms a "culture of death" has, however, a subtlety and complexity that chapter 1 of the encyclical only begins to explore, but that we will have to explore and understand if we expect to promote the gospel of life. I will try to articulate that culture—the culture in which abortion, suicide, and euthanasia are at home—in its strongest, most consistent, most attractive form, so that we can understand why the culture of death is so tenacious and why the gospel of life sometimes meets with incomprehension and resistance. My account of the culture of death is, of course, an amalgam, drawn from books that I have read, from the print media, television, radio, and bumper stickers, and from people I know.

Thesis 1: *The culture of death is not the same thing as moral relativism, moral skepticism, or nihilism.*

In *Natural Law and Natural Rights* (Oxford: Clarendon Press, 1980), John Finnis maintains that there are seven basic forms of human good: (1) life, (2) knowledge, (3) play, (4) aesthetic experience, (5) sociability or friendship, (6) practical reasonableness, and (7) religion. Finnis contends that the seven forms of good are all equally fundamental, and that every one of our actions ought to respect each and every one of the seven goods. We do not need to argue about these claims here. I use Finnis's list simply as a framework to articulate the culture of death.

(1) Life. This is the good that *Evangelium Vitae* is primarily concerned to defend. The culture of death distinguishes sharply between merely biological life and any other sense of the term "life." Merely biological life has no value in itself. It has instrumental value inasmuch as it is the necessary condition for goods (2) through (6). "Life" in any other sense than merely biological life is really another way of talking about goods (2) through (6). When people say things like "that's really living" or "that's what makes life worth living," they are talking about goods (2) through (6). And the culture of death is happy to affirm the goods of (2) knowledge, (3) play, (4) aesthetic experience, and (5) sociability and friendship. But when there is no prospect of goods (2) through (6)—when life is merely biological life—then it has no value and may be ended.

(6) Practical reasonableness. It is not necessary to go into the details of what Finnis means by practical reasonableness. In place of practical reasonableness the culture of death substitutes what Charles Taylor in *Sources of the Self* (Cambridge: Harvard University Press, 1989) calls "self-responsible freedom." There is a famil-

iar line of thought that runs something like this: freedom in itself is neither good nor bad; what makes freedom good or bad is how you use your freedom. The modern notion of self-responsible freedom turns this around: freedom is a good in and of itself, and how it is used is a secondary question.

The culture of death embraces the modern notion of self-responsible freedom. Think, for example, of all the conversations about abortion—not just about public policy on abortion, but about abortion itself—that go nowhere because one party supposes that the central issue in abortion is human life, while the other party supposes that the central issue in abortion is human freedom. It was suggested in the discussion at Georgetown that the culture of death takes self-responsible freedom to be the highest of goods, and I am inclined to agree.

(7) Religion. The culture of death is insulated against religion. Not that it necessarily presupposes atheism or that it always rejects religious observance. But even when it affirms God, it affirms God at a distance, God not impinging on human life. Even when it affirms a life beyond the grave, it insists that our current life ought to make sense inside its temporal bounds. The culture of death cannot make sense of the notion that one might sacrifice important goods in this present life with a view to a future life. God, religion, transcendence are domesticated or marginalized.

The culture of death, in the version that I have just sketched, is not nihilism, for it affirms numerous human goods under headings (2) through (6). Nor is it across-the-board moral skepticism, even if it denies the good of biological life as such. Nor is it across-the-board moral relativism, for it insists on the disvalue of causing or permitting pain, and on the value of self-responsible freedom. Typically it admits a high degree of relativity in how the goods of knowledge, play, aesthetic experience, and sociality are realized, but so do most ethical systems. In any case, the standard objections against nihilism, moral skepticism, and relativism are not by themselves sufficient to refute the claims that biological life is a good subordinate to other goods.

Is the culture of death a hedonism? It does not have to be a crude hedonism. If someone enjoys eating too much or drinking too much or abusing women, there are plenty of people in the culture of death who will condemn these forms of hedonism as barbaric. But if it is hedonism to work hard in a satisfying profession, make a lot of money, enjoy good food and drink, carry on enlightened conversation with articulate and sensitive companions in beautiful surroundings, then, my friends in the culture would say, What is wrong with that?

Is the culture of death alienating or depersonalizing? Its proponents would reply that it is not. Further—and it is important for us to take account of this—proponents of the culture of death tend to view the position of *Evangelium Vitae*, and the stance of the pope generally, as depersonalizing, and this on two counts. First, they tend to find papal talk about life abstract—removed from concrete circumstances and complexities of life. I can picture some of my friends replying: "What the pope says about life may be true. But it if be true, it is true in the way that plane geometry is true: it is true in Flatland. But we don't live in Flatland." Second, they tend to view the pope's insistence that the claims of biological life override the good of self-responsible freedom as itself grossly depersonalizing. My hunch is that this second count lies at the root of much of the hostility toward papal teaching and toward the person of the pope himself.

Thesis 2: *The culture of death is strongly rooted in certain tendencies of modernity.*

We have already spoken about two typical features of Western modernity: the embrace of self-responsible freedom and the marginalization of the transcendent. Let me now mention a third such feature, the stress on the evil of pain. Charles Taylor, again in *Sources of the Self,* cites as a pervasive and typical feature of modernity the view that pain is, if not the worst of all evils, close to the worst. To cause pain, or even to permit it to continue when one could stop it, is among the worst if not the worst of moral evils.

Modernity takes the evil of pain as a basic axiom: pain is evil, to cause pain is evil, and even to permit pain is evil. Given this axiom, the evil of intense pain can easily outweigh the good of life as such. Thus suicide and euthanasia can be justified as relieving pain. Abortion can be justified as relieving the pain of the mother. (I suspect that the axiom of the evil of pain is what enables people to slide so easily from the formula "protecting the health of the mother" to "sparing the mother pain.") Abortion can even be justified as protecting the child in the womb from pain that is foreseen as the result of deformity, congenital disease, or even from the child's not being wanted by the parents.

Where *Evangelium Vitae* would say that the basic issue in a case of suicide or assisted suicide or abortion is whether you are for or against life, Western modernity tends to say that the issue is whether you are for or against pain. The axiom of the evil of pain is also one ground for the insistence on privacy, for having one's decisions and actions known to others can be painful in itself and can lead to questions and challenges that inflict additional pain.

In the culture of death, the axiom that life is good is replaced by the axiom that pain is evil. But this axiom, like the embrace of self-responsible freedom and the marginalization of the transcendent, is part and parcel of Western modernity. In its affirmation of self-responsible freedom, its insulation of human life from transcendence, and its estimate of pain as among the worst of evils, the culture of death is typically modern. Anyone who tries to counter the culture of death is going to run up against these entrenched features of modernity, and had better have something worth saying about them. And, at least in my opinion, he or she should not waste time arguing that we can or should attempt to return to a premodern ethos. The work of the contemporary German philosopher Robert Spaemann is helpful in this respect. Spaemann is not trying to restore the premodern world, but to sort out the positive from the negative features of modernity. It would be good if Spaemann's approach to modernity could be transposed from a Germanic into an American idiom (*Basic Moral Concepts*, tr. T. J. Armstrong [New York: Routledge, 1989]).

Thesis 3: *The culture of death looks on itself as a culture of life and not as a culture of death.*

There is a famous passage in the *Wisdom of Solomon*: "Ungodly men by their words and deeds summon death; considering him a friend, they pined away, and they made a covenant with him, because they are fit to belong to his party" (1:16, RSV). The chapter that follows is the nearest thing I know of in scripture to an inside view of the culture of death.

As I read *Evangelium Vitae*, I was thinking all the while, how could anyone even think of embracing the culture of death? The more I have thought about it, I think that the answer is this: what the Holy Father terms the culture of death understands itself not as a culture of death but as a culture of life: life in the sense of delight in the senses, delight in beauty, delight in companionship, delight in activities, knowledge, work, sport, eating and drinking, and conversation. So, if we are going to put the teaching of *Evangelium Vitae* across to the men and women of our time and place, we will have to do more than simply contrast the gospel of life and the culture of death. We will have to find ways of leading people beyond what they recognize as life and are tempted to settle for, to a more abundant life.

The culture of death experiences itself as a culture of life. At the risk of irreverence, I can imagine some of my friends from the culture of death commenting on *Evangelium Vitae*: "There's all this talk about life, life, life, but it's not all that lively." Now that is rhetoric, not theology or philosophy, and one cannot expect an encyclical to have the same kind of emotional impact as a drama or as a powerful photo. But talk about life, life, life can have the unintended effect of making life seem to be an abstraction. To put the point aggressively: we do not have obligations to life, we have obligations to living beings. The struggle with the culture of death is not carried out on the plane of ideas alone. When the issue is personal conversion, rhetoric and image and affect are not irrelevant. Perhaps we need to find livelier ways of presenting the gospel of life, ways of transposing the language of life into more concrete terms.

In the discussion at Georgetown, the question was raised about how best to work with people in the culture of death. I would suggest two avenues of approach. One is to start with the modern commitment to not causing pain, and even to lessening or eliminating pain, to intimate that this commitment sets limits on the good of self-responsible freedom, and from there to work toward recognition of other limits and toward a more adequate conception of justice. The other is to start with the readiness for self-examination and therapy that is so common in contemporary culture, and to try to devise forms of therapy that lead a person away from narcissism and toward the recognition of a broader range of goods and claims.

Let me close with a remark about sections 68–74 and 90 of

Evangelium Vitae. These sections are concerned with the politics of the gospel of life. They challenge us as Americans to reflect on our place in the American political process. My own sense is that many American Catholics, including Jesuits, are in an anomalous position. We are committed to the American system of government with its distinctive procedures and procedural constraints, and we are committed, at least in theory, to promoting the gospel of life in the context of the American system. Some participants in the system, however, contend that some of the goods and arguments that are most important to us are not legitimate matters of public political discourse, but matters of private choice that should be protected against intrusion. These fellow citizens are trying to dictate the terms on which we may participate in the American system, and we tend in practice to accept their terms. Instead of articulating the good of life in the political forum, we (or many of us, myself included) practice a greater or lesser degree of self-censorship. We act as though our commitment to these procedures and procedural constraints of American democracy entail a further commitment not to challenge or disturb the current moral and political culture.

The notion that Catholics ought to be wholeheartedly committed to the American political system is often associated with the name of John Courtney Murray. I do not pretend to know how Father Murray, who died in 1967, would analyze the current politics of human life; but I am confident that he would have seen the difference between commitment to the American political system and allegiance to the current American ethos. If the pope is right about the political dimension of the gospel of life, and if American political culture has been seriously infiltrated by the culture of death, then we may have to be more countercultural than we have been in recent years. In any event, we will have to do some serious thinking about the terms on which we take part in the American political system.

III.
Postscript: John Paul II's Vision

15

Homily

Preached by Stephen M. Fields, S.J., at the Eucharist in Dahlgren Chapel of the Sacred Heart, Georgetown University, August 4, 1996

"For I am certain," St. Paul tells us today in the Epistle to the Romans, "that neither death nor life, neither angels nor principalities, neither the present nor the future, nor powers, neither height nor depth nor any other creature, will be able to separate us from the love of God" (Romans 8:38–39).

Looking out over contemporary culture with John Paul II, we probably do not carry around with us the consistent sense of consolation that these words of St. Paul express. I doubt that John Paul II himself does. In fact, his experiences as the universal pastor are probably all too similar to our own more modest ones in the classroom, the confessional, the pulpit, or, for that matter, the haustus room. At times they can provoke in us a sensation quite opposite to consolation. They can fill us with that Ignatian sense of "desolation," which manifests itself in turmoil of spirit, in restlessness, in self-feeding doubts, and in thoughts that we are becoming ever more separated from the love of God.[1] Indeed, as we look out over our world, we might again view it through the lens offered by the meditation on the Incarnation in the *Spiritual Exercises*. There we are told to wonder at the ingenuity of human beings applying their energy to a vast panoply of dark banalities: to swearing, blaspheming, wounding, killing; to the deeds that lead down to hell, as Ignatius himself says.[2]

---

[1] Ignatius Loyola, *The Spiritual Exercises*, ed. Louis J. Puhl, S.J. (Chicago: Loyola University Press, 1951), s. 317.

[2] Ibid., ss. 107–08.

As our conference has made us more aware, John Paul II's vision of contemporary culture sees us living through a crisis that arises from the fragmentation of Christianity's moral and religious heritage. This crisis is caused by forceful pressure from the secular, whose dominance of Western mores means that our common cultural conscience is losing, not only its sense of God manifesting his abundant and life-giving presence, but also its ability to distinguish clearly between the holy and the hellish.[3] The secular attitude, now strident and aggressive, has lost the civility it once possessed just a century ago. The liberally educated person, John Henry Newman writes in *The Idea of a University*, will cultivate the virtue of respect for religion, even though no longer believing in it.[4] But, by contrast, the secular person of today is finding it increasingly difficult to co-exist in a tolerant way with the Judeo-Christian values that have made the West viable. And, for our part, we Christians are discovering that, the harder we try to persuade our fellow citizens of our positions, the fewer we seem to find listening. Many have rejected not only the faith but the vestiges of its moral, ethical, and civilizing legacy as well.[5]

No wonder it has been remarked that our times are strikingly similar to those of St. Augustine, the great Father of the West, who lived to see the violence of invasions destroy his life's work in Africa.[6] Like Augustine, we are facing an upheaval caused by our culture's apathy or hostility to many cherished values. Like Augustine, we are being confronted with the apparent un-doing of decades of religious labor that has formed our society. And, like Augustine, living through this carnage at times evokes in us the odd mixture of confusion, grief, and anger, because, at times, the

---

[3] See Louis Dupré, *The Other Dimension* (New York: Seabury, 1979), 14–17.

[4] John Henry Newman, *The Idea of a University*, ed. I. T. Ker (Oxford: Clarendon Press, 1976), 180.

[5] See Stanley Hauerwas, *Dispatches from the Front: Theological Engagements with the Secular* (Durham: Duke University Press, 1994), 7, 197–98, citing Leszek Kolakowski, *Modernity on Endless Trial* (Chicago: University of Chicago Press, 1990), 30.

[6] This remark was made by David Tracy of the University of Chicago in the fall of 1987 at Yale Divinity School, where he was a visiting professor. He ascribed the remark to Joseph Komonchak of the Catholic University of America. See also Peter Brown, *Augustine of Hippo* (Berkeley: University of California Press, 1969), 425.

City of Man seems to have grown so great that, like some giant Leviathan, it threatens to consume the City of God.

To take but one instance, in America secular culture has been setting up its own idols that, ironically, are filling the vacuum created by the absence of God. The "right" of choice is assuming prominence among these idols. Diametrically opposed to John Paul II's understanding of the person, this right seeks to maximize the person's freedom to act on the basis of one's own preference. Those who advocate it seem to be demanding an ever-growing range of rights—the right to commit suicide; the right to abort a fetus even in its late term; the right to have one's unmarried companion, whether male or female (depending on preference), subsidized by co-workers and fellow citizens; the right to say what one desires when and where one desires, so long as it does not hurt anybody.[7] When Christians challenge these "rights" in the name of an authentic understanding of the human person, as John Paul II did recently in Berlin, they are often rebuffed as intolerant and "mean-spirited busybodies."[8]

In the face of this crisis of culture that mistakes the bad for the good because it has lost its sense of the Source of the Good, it would be all too easy for us to surrender in a host of subtle ways to the activity of the desolating spirit that wants to discourage us. Surely, if our limited experiences give us reasons to doubt the consoling words that St. Paul brings us today, then John Paul II has many more. He has been heckled in as many languages as the apostles spoke on Pentecost. He has lived through the *Blitzkrieg*, the Holocaust, the hammer and sickle, and his own assassination attempt. He has seen Armageddon come—and go. But like Ignatius, when he speaks, he turns our attention away from ourselves, always back to the image of the Lord.

As he reminded the crowd gathered at Paderborn in June during his visit to Germany, the Lord is seated here with us in the boat as it is flailed about in the storm threatening to be overwhelmed. It is Christ who will save his people. It is Christ who will steer his Church. The fears, the complaints, the doubts, the

---

[7] William J. Stuntz, "When Rights Are Wrong," *First Things* 62 (April 1996): 14–18 at 16–17.

[8] John Paul II spoke in Berlin as part of his third pastoral visit to Germany, June 21–23, 1996. See also Stuntz, 17.

sloths, and the tepidities raised by our "little faith," he tells us, must not be allowed to gain sway over our hearts. Christ has mastery over the wind and the waves.[9] He will put down the petty idols of the City of Man, just as surely as he will come to quell the desolations that disturb our peace of soul. And he will come especially when he appears to be asleep and the boat seems to be sinking.

Let us today then ask, as Ignatius would have us do, for what we desire. Let us ask the Lord who stills the storm to keep us confident, trusting, warmly compassionate, and joyful in our zeal, so that we might do what John Paul II continues to ask of bishops and priests: to guide the young, to encourage the fainthearted, to comfort the sad, and to preach the love of God from which "neither death nor life, . . . neither height nor depth, nor any other creature" can ever separate us.[10]

---

[9] John Paul II, "Remember Your Long History of Faith" (Homily at Senne Military Airport, June 22, 1996), *L'Osservatore Romano*, Weekly English Edition (July 3, 1996), 3, cc. 1–2.

[10] Ibid., c. 4.

About the Contributors

John J. Conley, S.J., is Associate Professor of Philosophy at Fordham University in New York City.

Christopher M. Cullen, S.J., is Campion Fellow in Philosophy at Fordham University in New York City.

Avery Dulles, S.J., is McGinley Professor of Religion and Culture at Fordham University in New York City.

Steven M. Fields, S.J., is Assistant Professor of Theology at Georgetown University in Washington, D.C.

Benjamin Fiore, S.J., is Professor of New Testament in the Religious Studies Department at Canisius College in Buffalo, New York.

Joseph W. Koterski, S.J., is Associate Professor of Philosophy at Fordham University in New York City.

Patrick J. Lynch, S.J., is Associate Professor of Religious Studies at Canisius College in Buffalo, New York.

Arthur R. Madigan, S.J., is Associate Professor of Philosophy at Boston College in Chestnut Hill, Massachusetts.

Edmund W. Majewski, S.J., is Associate Professor of Theology at St. Peter's College in Jersey City, New Jersey.

J. Michael McDermott, S.J., holds the Pio Laghi Chair as Research Professor at the Pontifical Seminary Josephinum in Columbus, Ohio.

Ronald A. Mercier, S.J., is Dean and Professor of Moral Theology at Regis College in Toronto, Ontario.

Martin X. Moleski, S.J., is Associate Professor of Religious Studies at Canisius College in Buffalo, New York.

John M. Piderit, S.J., is President of Loyola University in Chicago, Illinois.

The Most Rev. Terrence Prendergast, S.J., is Archbishop of Halifax, Nova Scotia.

James V. Schall, S.J., is Professor of Government at Georgetown University in Washington, D.C.

Robert J. Spitzer, S.J., is President of Gonzaga University in Spokane, Washington.

INDEX

Abbott, W., 26, 31, 156, 179, 254
abortion, 21, 25, 72, 81, 95, 97, 131, 156, 164, 191–98, 201, 269, 275, 294, 300, 303, 306–10, 317
Adam, 156, 179, 254
Aleu, J., 127
Allers, R., 4
Allsop, M., 171
Altaner, B., 138
Ambrose, 108
Anselm, 112
anthropology, 48, 84–85, 89, 111, 178–81, 197–202, 297
Aquinas, T., 6, 8, 10–17, 47, 86, 107, 116–20, 123, 127–28, 170–72, 179, 297
Arianism, 286, 289–90
Aristotle, 4–5, 10, 13–15, 17, 86, 90, 120, 170–71, 179
Arkes, H., 15
asceticism, 134, 165, 194, 200
assisted suicide, 310
Athanasius, 289
Auer, A., 149
Augustine, 4, 43–44, 94, 107, 147, 207, 316
Aumann, J., 134–36
authority, 41, 70, 79, 84, 95–96, 105, 109–10, 122–23, 132–40, 144–45, 151–56, 162, 165, 168–69, 190, 194–99, 204, 228, 247, 253, 261, 275–76, 286–89, 291–92
autonomy, 19, 33, 149, 197–99, 257, 275, 278–79, 296, 302

Barnabas, letter of, 95
Barrett, T., 129
Baum, G., 24, 140, 175
beatific vision, 119, 124, 126, 134, 158–59, 161, 208
beatitudes, 85–86, 91, 114

Berger, P., 94
Bernanos, G., 103
Bickel, A., 95
Billot, L., 123
Binns, E., 150
birth control. *See* contraception
Bloch, E., 114
Bloom, A., 20
body, 7, 18, 28, 56, 89, 132, 134, 139, 142, 157, 166–67, 193–94, 209–10, 248–54, 261–63, 266, 290, 297–98, 303; Body of Christ, 22–23, 135, 138, 188, 209, 289; language of the body, 248, 251–52, 254; theology of the body, 251, 262
Boethius, 18
Bouscaren, L., 133
Boyer, C., 118
Boyle, J., 100–101, 149
Brown, P., 316
Buber, M., 301
Burns, J., 118
Burrell, D., 160
Butler, C., 149

Cahill, L., 108, 160
Cajetan, T., 120–23
Callahan, D., 139
Callahan, S., 139, 166
Campion, D., 176
canon law, 128, 133
capitalism, 11, 24, 37–38, 213–14, 216, 282
capital punishment, 131
Carey, G., 7
Carlin, C., 52
Carlin, D., 97
Carmody, J., 35
Carrier, H., 176
Cartechini, S., 137
Carter, S., 35

Casaroli, A., 177
casuistry, 131, 133
catechism/catechist, 44, 83–85, 88, 90, 97–113, 300
Catechism of the Catholic Church, 10, 38, 42, 82–115, 293, 304
Catherine of Siena, 96
Catholicism, 10–13, 21, 28, 30, 41–42, 79, 81, 117, 158, 169, 172, 186–87, 207, 210, 212, 233, 242, 246, 268, 287, 291, 312
Chesterton, G., 4, 9
Christology, 42, 47, 52–54, 69–70, 73, 77, 114, 126, 170, 210, 290, 293, 296–97, 300–301
Church, 11, 15, 23–26, 33, 37–38, 42–47, 53–54, 60, 64, 68, 76, 79, 103, 105–7, 115, 122, 132–39, 148–52, 156, 160, 169, 177–78, 181–88, 193, 198–206, 209, 213–14, 239, 243–44, 247, 250–55, 268, 279, 286–92, 298–300, 304–5
Cicero, 4, 98
class struggle, 29
Claver, P., 33
Clement, first letter of, 95, 110
Clement V, Pope, 47
Cole, E., 89
Coles, R., 88
collectivism, 94
commandments, 25, 47, 61–62, 74–76, 83, 91, 103–5, 108, 111, 135, 143
common good, 11, 25, 32–33, 37, 95, 97, 133, 176–77, 181, 229, 281
communion of persons, 22, 33, 240, 273, 295, 298, 301–2
communism, 27, 31, 38, 177, 180, 216, 222, 245
community, 17–19, 78–79, 82, 94–98, 142, 144, 169, 178, 210, 236, 243, 271–72, 280
conceptualism, 116, 120–21, 123–28, 134, 140–41, 163–70, 207, 290
conceptualist morality, 128–40, 147, 168
confession, 128, 135
Congar, Y., 137
Conley, J., 47, 49–51, 203–4
conscience, 42–53, 62, 64, 68, 77–79, 84–90, 95, 107, 113, 129, 132–33, 144, 156, 160–62, 167, 202, 251–52, 256–57, 316; doubtful conscience, 93; erroneous judgment, 45, 88, 129, 145; formation of conscience, 47, 73, 77–78, 88, 129, 144–45, 156, 161, 201; judgment of conscience, 78
consequentialism, 87, 202, 206, 291
conservatism, 8–9, 11–12
consumers/consumerism, 38, 183, 188, 224–30
contraception, 40, 100, 105, 138–39, 152, 163, 191–97, 199, 201–2, 209–10, 251–54, 266, 268–69, 275, 294, 298, 300, 302–3
co-responsibility, 278–82
Cousins, E., 72
covenant, 23, 31, 57, 61, 102, 248, 292, 298
covenant love, 210, 263, 270–72, 277–78, 280–81
Cozzi, A., 123
creation, 24–30, 34–38, 44, 54–55, 63–64, 72, 109, 150, 178–79, 208–9, 248–51, 254, 263, 268, 290
Crespi, F., 149
Crowe, M., 100
culture, 12, 34, 45, 72, 175–89, 295, 301–4
culture of life/culture of death, 56, 61, 71–73, 183, 193, 269, 306–12
Curran, C., 35, 41, 139, 143–45, 149, 163–64

Darlap, A., 126, 140
Davis, C., 140
Davis, H., 129–34
Dawson, C., 109–10
Decalogue, 50, 61, 91, 103, 132
deconstructionism, 4
de Grandmaison, L., 160
de Guibert, J., 135–36
de Haro, R., 247
de Lubac, H., 124, 127
democracy, 24, 35, 53, 246, 312
demography, 190–204
Denzinger, H., 84, 119, 137
Descartes, R., 12, 257
determinism, 18, 86

Didache, 92
Dieter, T., 59
diplomacy, 191, 197, 203, 300
discernment of spirits, 136, 314–15
Dolan, J., 164
double effect, 131, 145–47
Dubay, W., 140
Dulles, A., 27, 47, 152
Dupré, L., 316
Duquoc, C., 152–53

ecclesiology, 33, 78, 125–26, 148
ecology, 28, 192
economic development, 26, 30, 34, 36, 39, 149, 199, 211, 216, 235, 246
economics, 11, 26–29, 34, 45, 97, 176, 179–80, 195–96, 205, 211–46, 282
Ellis, A., 133
Ellsberg, R., 24
emotions. *See* passions
emotivism, 90
entrepreneurs, 244–45
epikeia, 133
equality, 33, 96, 148, 160, 229, 263, 275, 287–88
essence and existence, 120–23, 127, 151, 170, 172, 179
ethics (moral theory), 13–16, 42, 111, 113, 183, 191–92, 197, 201, 203, 260, 264, 308
euthanasia, 306–9
evangelical counsels, 135, 167
evangelization, 25, 33, 177, 184, 186, 213, 305
evil, 10, 16, 19, 27, 32, 50, 76, 85–86, 91, 131, 134, 159, 182, 227, 269, 273, 309; doing evil that good may come, 16, 87–88, 130, 145, 147, 168; intrinsic evil, 15–16, 41, 47, 87, 130, 168, 201; moral evil, 10, 87, 101, 143–46, 309; ontic (premoral) evil, 145–46, 169; physical evil, 146–47; toleration of evil, 76, 147, 197, 316–17
evolution, 150
existential judgment, 120, 123–25, 127, 140, 142, 170, 208

Fagothey, A., 44
faith, 11, 45, 57–58, 66, 69, 83, 103–6, 109, 115–19, 122, 125, 134, 137, 140, 153–55, 163, 167, 175, 177, 184–86, 212, 255, 274, 299
family, 22, 27, 94–95, 176, 190–99, 203–7, 247, 250–53, 268–73, 280, 288–89, 293–305
Faricy, R., 149–51
Farraher, J., 129
feminism, 89–90, 287, 290–92
fertility, 193–94
Filograssi, J., 138
Finnis, J., 100–101, 307
Fisichella, R., 124
Fitzmyer, J., 93
Flanagan, J., 97
Foot, P., 90
Fox, M., 251
Francis of Assisi, 165
Frank, R., 231
freedom, 11, 15, 21, 25–28, 31, 35, 43–46, 50, 53, 57, 60–63, 75, 84–88, 92, 97, 99, 112–23, 129, 134, 137, 144, 147, 150, 156–59, 165–68, 170–72, 178, 181–82, 187, 191, 194–96, 202, 204–10, 254, 261, 272–78, 294, 296, 302–3, 308–11
free market, 216–19, 227, 236, 246
Freud, S., 205
Fries, H., 153
Fuchs, J., 68–69, 141–47, 149, 161
fundamental option theory, 41, 69, 92–93, 143, 152–53, 156–59, 162, 168

Gallagher, J., 26
Gardeil, A., 137
Garrigou-Lagrange, 137
General Catechetical Directory, 83
Giddes, L., 129
Gilligan, C., 89
Gilson, E., 123
Glaser, J., 142, 145, 155
Glendon, M., 97
gnosticism, 12, 109–10, 303
God, 6, 9, 17, 21–22, 25–34, 43–44, 50–63, 66, 72, 78, 86, 90, 95, 104–5, 108, 112–20, 124–25, 131, 134, 154–61, 171–72, 176, 180, 183–87, 205, 208–10, 227, 237, 247, 249, 254–55, 261–65, 279,

287, 289–90, 295, 301, 308, 315–17
golden rule, 88, 99
Gonzales-Ruiz, J., 149
government, 34, 38, 95, 195, 214, 312
grace, 43, 47, 71, 82, 84–85, 90, 98–107, 109–11, 117–22, 125–26, 134–38, 140, 144, 147, 149–50, 157–58, 167–68, 171, 184, 274
Graf, E., 104
Gregory IX, Pope, 301
Gregory of Nyssa, 289
Gremillion, J., 178, 183, 187
Grisez, G., 62, 100–101
guilt, 88, 118, 164–65, 168

Hanigan, J., 154
Hankey, W., 117
happiness, 22, 85–86, 111, 114, 119, 148, 165–66, 224, 252, 303
Harrington, D., 93
Harvanek, R., 42
Hauerwas, S., 72, 316
Haughton, R., 105
heaven, 23, 31, 85, 148, 151
Hehir, J., 29
Heidegger, M., 12, 70
Heinzel, G., 129
hell, 92, 118, 157
Herbermann, C., 129
hermeneutics, 108, 110, 191, 218
Higgins, T., 100
Hilary, 289
Himmelfarb, G., 4, 8
historico-critical method, 107–10
Hittinger, R., 42, 100–101
Hobbes, T., 205
Holy Spirit, 50, 53–54, 57, 64, 72–73, 78–79, 93, 99, 132, 148, 153, 156, 188, 265, 288; fruits of the Holy Spirit, 90; gifts of the Holy Spirit, 66, 88, 90, 140
homosexuality, 163, 166, 169, 288
Honoré, J., 91, 94, 103
Horgan, R., 247
Howard, T., 248
Hughes, G., 154–55, 163
Hugon, E., 118
human being: as the image of God, 27–32, 38, 43, 54–55, 84–85, 96, 111–13, 118, 129, 146, 171, 178, 209, 227–29, 231, 249, 273, 303; human dignity, 13, 16, 25–29, 31–35, 39, 46–48, 55, 60, 62, 68, 77, 84–86, 96–97, 111–14, 178–79, 182, 194, 196–97, 230, 240, 242, 271–72, 279, 281; human nature, 11–12, 15, 18, 22, 27, 43, 46, 62, 65–67, 98, 111, 154, 162, 170, 179, 244, 253, 259–60, 262, 290, 303
Hutcheson, F., 44
Hütter, R., 59

ideology, 183, 191–93, 198–99, 204–5, 212–16
imperialism, 33, 195, 198–99
inculturation, 185–86
individualism, 29, 33, 78, 183, 198–200, 205, 253, 303
infallibility, 40, 106, 115, 139, 144, 152, 154–55, 162, 287, 290
infanticide, 191, 196
insemination, 163
intellect, 13, 43–44, 66, 89–90, 113–14, 119, 121, 124–25, 133–34, 141–42, 146, 159, 161, 179, 207
intention, 86, 91, 131, 143, 145, 154–60, 165, 254, 264
international trade, 234–36, 246
in vitro fertilization, 162
Irenaeus, 107
Isaac, 131
Israel, 23, 85, 99, 101–2, 288
Itard, J., 260

Jans, J., 171
Janssens, L., 145–48
Jedin, H., 104
Jesus Christ, 25, 30–34, 43–50, 52–65, 67–69, 72, 74–75, 77, 79, 81, 85, 91, 93, 96, 101–2, 107–8, 114, 121–22, 126, 132, 134–35, 138, 141, 143–44, 153, 165, 167–68, 172, 178, 180, 184, 186–89, 193, 209, 230, 243, 262, 265, 268, 279, 287–91, 297, 299, 301, 304, 317–18
Joan of Arc, 104
John XXIII, Pope, 69; *Pacem in Terris*, 94–95, 270; *Mater et Magistra*, 94
John of St. Thomas, 122

John Paul II, writings of: *The Acting Person*, 53, 66, 170–71, 210; *Catechesi Tradendae*, 184; *Catechesis on the Book of Genesis*, 178–79; *Centesimus Annus*, 9, 24–34, 69, 94–95, 180, 183, 211, 214, 216–17, 222, 228–29, 232–33, 237, 240, 244; *Charter of the Rights of the Family*, 195–96; *Crossing the Threshold of Hope*, 304; *Dives in Misericordia*, 57; *Dominus et Vivificantem*, 91; *Evangelium Vitae*, 54, 60, 64, 68, 70–73, 166–72, 182–83, 193, 200, 306–12; *Faith according to St. John of the Cross*, 53, 65–66; *Familiaris Consortio*, 185, 192–95, 247, 252, 270–79, 295–305; *Fidei Depositum*, 83; *Fides et Ratio*, 70; *Laborem Exercens*, 24, 26, 28–33, 38, 69, 73, 113, 201, 211, 232, 238, 242, 270, 279–82; *Letter to Families*, 197, 252–54, 294, 300–305; *Letter to Women* 286–87, 292; *Love and Responsibility*, 171, 209, 252, 254, 257, 262, 266, 267; *Ordinatio Sacerdotalis*, 286–87, 292; *Original Unity of Man and Woman*, 248, 251; *Person and Community*, 3–4, 10, 13–14, 17–19, 177, 180; *Reconciliatio et Paenitentia*, 93; *Redemptoris Mater*, 73; *Redemptoris Missio*, 186; *Redemptor Hominis*, 35, 48, 52–75, 79, 178, 181–82, 293, 297; *Reflections on Humanae Vitae*, 250–52; *Slavorum Apostoli*, 185; *Sollicitudo Rei Socialis*, 24–37, 69, 94, 201, 211, 227–28, 239, 243; speeches, 178–89, 318; *Theology of Marriage and Celibacy*, 247–50, 261; *Ut Unum Sint*, 186; *Veritatis Splendor*, 7, 15–16, 27, 35, 38, 40–57, 60–75, 77, 79, 81–82, 87, 91–92, 99, 101, 109, 115–16, 140, 151, 166–71, 179, 182, 197, 202, 251, 253, 257; *Vita Consecrata*, 80
Johnson, P., 12
Johnson, S., 4
justice, 25, 27, 29, 32, 33–37, 50, 55, 80, 93, 95, 118, 130, 148, 196, 213–15, 233, 242–43, 246, 272, 278, 311
justification, 84, 102–4
just wage, 240–42

Kant, I., and Kantianism, 14–15, 59, 61, 66, 69, 124, 127, 147–48
Kasper, W., 72, 153, 207, 268
Kavanaugh, J., 140
Ker, I., 258
Kiely, B., 160
Kirk, R., 12
Knauer, P., 145–47
Kohlberg, L., 88
Kolakowski, L., 316
Kolbe, M., 33
Komonchak, J., 316
Korth, F., 133
Kosnik, A., 163, 166
Kossel, C., 4, 7–8
Küng, H., 36, 152, 154

Lao Tzu, 260
Lash, N., 258
Latourelle, R., 176
law, 21, 87, 90, 96, 98, 101–2, 131, 133, 139, 240; divine law, 87, 99, 132, 142–43, 182, 188, 243, 252, 286; eternal law, 98, 129; law of the Gospel, 98; old law and new law, 98–99, 101, 108, 132, 143. *See also* natural law
Lehmkuhl, A., 128
Leo the Great, Pope, 84
Leo XIII, Pope, 5, 117, 123; *Aeterni Patris*, 116, 123, 297; *Rerum Novarum*, 24, 270
LeVoir, J., 247
Lewis, C .S., 5
liberalism, 8–9, 11–12, 213, 223
libertarianism, 204
Liguori, A., 47
Lindsnaes, B., 94
Lonergan, B., 61, 118, 124, 127, 143, 160, 206, 259
love, 92, 99, 115, 132, 139, 141–43, 158, 162, 166–67, 171, 202, 208–10, 248, 257, 264–67, 272–74, 277, 279, 290, 295, 300, 304
Loyola, I., 238, 283, 315, 317–18

Machiavelli, N., 12, 16, 205
MacIntyre, A., 90, 98
Macmurray, J., 90
Madigan, A., 111–14

Magisterium, 43–44, 46–48, 50, 104–9, 126, 139, 152–56, 161–63, 168–69, 191, 199, 247, 287–88, 290
Maguire, D., 149, 164–65
Mally, E., 93
Malson, L., 260
Manicheeism, 253, 263, 303
Marcel, G., 279
Marechal, J., 127, 161
Marin-Sola, F., 137
Maritain, J., 122, 129, 131, 132
marriage, 22, 65, 81, 136, 138, 140, 166, 176, 186, 192–98, 201, 203, 207–10, 229, 247–52, 261–65, 269, 274–75, 277, 288, 292–300
Martin, D., 191
Martino, R., 190, 197
martyrdom, 57, 65, 75–76, 197
Marxism, 8–10, 37, 148, 179, 205, 213, 228, 281
Mary, Blessed Virgin, 75, 78, 80, 137–38, 255, 288
Mass, 135, 299
masturbation, 163
May, W., 100, 171
McCool, G., 92, 122, 168
McCormick, R., 41, 144–45, 147, 149, 162, 171
McCoy, Charles N. R., 47
McDermott, J., 42, 117, 119, 124–27, 129, 141, 147, 154, 160–61, 170, 207
McDonald, W., 129
McInerny, R., 100–101
Melina, L., 78–79
Mercier, R., 74–77
mercy, 55, 91, 93, 132
Merkelbach, B., 129–34
metaphysics, 6, 13–18, 22, 111, 121, 125, 128, 133, 182, 210, 303
Metz, J., 149–51
Micou, A., 94
Milhaven, G., 145
Miller, J., 176
Minkiel, S., 119
missiology, 186
modernity, 10, 12–14, 16, 21, 117, 296, 309–10
Moleski, M., 262–69
Molina, L., 123

Monden, L., 92
Moore, M., 139
morality/the moral life, 15, 37, 41, 44, 52, 55, 58, 60–64, 69–75, 77–78, 80–81, 83, 86, 88, 92, 95, 98, 105–8, 111, 115–16, 128, 139, 142–44, 147, 151, 154, 167–68, 171, 182, 199; act-centered morality, 14, 16, 19, 41, 43, 45, 65, 68, 71, 84, 86–89, 92, 129, 146, 156, 168, 180, 201, 210, 248; moral judgment, 5, 88, 105, 154, 163, 200, 253, 258; moral law, 43, 57, 76, 84, 95, 98–102, 118, 122, 131–32, 153, 161–62, 167–68, 206 (*see also* natural law); moral theology, 41–42, 49, 77, 80–81, 104–5, 116, 127–28, 131, 140, 143, 154, 167–68, 171, 213
Mouroux, J., 141
Muhlen, H., 150
Murdoch, I., 90
Murphy, F., 129
Murray, J., 101, 312

natural family planning, 192–96, 201, 203, 269
natural law, 13, 35, 42–44, 61–62, 77, 98–101, 103, 106–8, 111–12, 118–19, 130–32, 139, 143, 154, 161–63, 165, 167–70, 199, 250, 252, 259, 266–67, 298, 307
natural rights, 86, 99
nature, 17–18, 28, 30, 112–13, 117–19, 121–22, 125–26, 129–30, 132, 134, 137, 141, 143, 149–50, 156, 160, 170–71, 194, 205–6, 263, 266, 289–91
Navarro-Valls, J., 190
Neuhaus, R., 94
Newman, J., 108, 255–58, 260–61, 268, 316
Nietzsche, F., 12, 205
nihilism, 307–8
Noe, T., 239
Nolan, M., 145
Noldin, H., 129–33
nominalism, 121, 153–54, 160–62, 172, 286
Norland, R., 40
Novak, M., 139

O'Connell, T., 154
O'Keefe, J., 171
O'Malley, J., 109
ordination, 286–87, 290–91

pain, 309–11
participation, 95, 97, 120, 130, 217, 234, 249, 298–99
Pascal, B., 90
passions, 87–89, 113, 133, 161, 277, 296
Paul VI, 69, 138–39, 184, 189, 266, 294; *Evangelii Nuntiandi*, 176–77, 186; *Humanae Vitae*, 138–40, 152, 162, 164, 201, 250–52, 257, 261, 263, 291, 293, 298, 304; *Progressio Populorum*, 69, 199, 270
peace and war, 35–36, 69, 80, 95, 148, 164, 176, 181, 229
Perry, M., 35–36
person, 3, 7, 14–21, 23, 26–27, 34, 38, 50, 59–64, 67–68, 71–72, 78–82, 84–86, 89, 94–98, 111–13, 137, 142, 167, 170–71, 176–78, 181, 183, 194–95, 198–200, 203, 210, 212, 230, 237, 241, 249, 251, 255, 261–62, 264, 266–67, 270–80, 290, 296–99, 301–2
personalism, 99, 111–12, 115, 152, 193, 197, 264, 267, 282, 293, 297–98, 300–303, 317
pharisaism, 102
Piderit, J., 97, 214
Pieper, J., 4
Pinto de Oliveria, C., 149
Pius XI, Pope: *Casti Connubii*, 138; *Quadragesimo Anno*, 232
Pius XII, Pope, 94–95, 137; *Summi Pontificatus*, 96, 301
Plato, 4, 7, 13, 170, 259
Plesants, J., 139
pluralism, 96, 126–27, 148, 168–70, 229
Polanyi, Michael, 255–60, 268
politics, 11, 13, 16, 35, 97, 176, 180–81, 183, 191, 211, 272, 312
Pontifical Academy for Life, 191, 200
Pontifical Academy of Sciences, 191, 200, 204
Pontifical Biblical Commission, 185

Pontifical Council for Culture, 177–78, 181, 183
Pontifical Council for the Family, 190, 199–200, 204
population, 25, 36 190–203, 294, 300
private property, 28, 97, 130, 282
profit-sharing, 240
prophecy, 54, 58–60, 66, 107, 121, 149, 191, 247, 250–52, 299, 304
proportionalism, 40–42, 67, 76, 87, 146, 164, 171, 206, 291
Pseudo-Dionysius, 119–20
public theology, 24, 26–27, 32–36

Rahner, K., 57, 63, 68, 92, 124–27, 139–41, 143, 147, 149, 151–52, 155–60, 170
Ramsey, P., 147
rationalism, 117
reason, 13, 117, 128, 130–31, 137, 146, 155, 161, 171, 206, 208, 253, 255–56, 259, 307
Rebello, Michael J., 239
reconciliation, 55, 57
redemption, 24–25, 30, 34, 36, 38, 44–47, 54–55, 59, 62, 178, 181, 206, 209, 290
relations/relational, 4, 7, 15, 17–19, 22–23, 60, 71–72, 80, 142, 210, 270, 290
relativism, 13, 61, 66–67, 69–71, 76, 90, 99, 108, 182, 206–7, 252, 307–8
responsibility, 11, 86, 95, 195, 200–201, 228, 278, 296
revelation, 12–17, 47, 55, 59–71, 77, 83, 106, 108, 117–22, 126, 128, 132, 137–38, 140, 151, 154, 161–63, 165, 170, 208, 249–50, 256, 268, 274, 276, 287, 289–91
Ricoeur, P., 72
right to life, 203, 271
rights, 26–29, 32, 35, 63, 68–69, 86, 96–98, 112, 114, 182, 192, 195–98, 200–203, 205–6, 210, 222, 232, 238, 271, 275, 279, 281–82, 299–302, 317
Rommen, H., 4, 7
Rondet, H., 138
Rousselot, P., 124, 127, 160
Royo, A., 134–36

INDEX

Rush, V., 154
Ryan, J., 139

Saarinen, R., 59
Sabetti, A., 129–34
sacraments, 25–26, 31, 33, 55, 83, 105, 132, 135, 137–38, 150, 153, 186, 208–10, 247–50, 261, 263–64, 290
salvation, 23–25, 36, 43, 46–48, 54, 57, 86, 103, 106, 108, 114, 119, 126, 138, 144, 149–51, 158, 185, 208
Salvatore, D., 234
Sandel, M., 224
Sartre, J., 205
Saul, J., 70
Schall, J., 6–7, 10, 21–23
Scheler, M., 14, 279
Schillebeeckx, E., 141, 148–51, 153
Schlette, H., 149
Schmaus, M., 138
Schmitz, K., 179
Schoonenberg, P., 157–59
Schrems, John J., 8
Schuller, B., 129, 131, 139, 141–47, 156, 158, 162
Schuster, J., 155–56, 163
Schwehn, M., 213
science, 11–12, 45, 143, 164, 176, 182–83, 204, 206, 218, 255–57, 259, 276
Scola, A., 75
Scotus, J., 104
Scripture: Genesis, 26–34, 179, 197, 227, 249, 251, 254, 280, 295; Deuteronomy, 92; Psalms, 45; Wisdom, 227, 310; Matthew, 34, 47, 49, 56, 61, 85–86, 92–93, 101–2, 107, 288–89; Mark, 37, 49, 93, 102, 119, 288–89; Luke, 25, 33, 93, 102, 288; John, 50, 99, 288; Acts, 119; Romans, 46, 50, 91, 95, 99, 102, 183, 315; Galatians, 50, 91, 102, 252; 1 Corinthians, 31, 46, 91, 99, 252, 289; 2 Corinthians, 289–90; Ephesians, 57, 91, 99, 243, 250, 289; Colossians, 91, 99, 243, 290; Philippians, 51, 57; 1 Timothy, 95; 1 Peter, 95; Hebrews, 290; James, 102; Revelation, 289

Selling, J., 171
Sen, A., 231
sexual conduct, 99, 139–40, 142, 163, 166, 169, 193, 197, 250
sexuality, 81, 162–63, 171, 183, 193–94, 198, 247–69, 277, 288, 291, 293, 295, 297–98, 300, 303–4
Shaftesbury, A., 44
Shannon, T., 164
Shehan, L., 26
Siebert, H., 231
sin, 29–34, 44–45, 56–59, 61–62, 80, 91–94, 99, 122, 180, 184, 206, 209, 243; gravity of sin (mortal/venial), 91–92, 118, 157–58, 168; original sin, 55, 118, 132–34, 166; personal sin, 30, 38, 93, 135, 243; remission of sin, 104, 128; sins crying to heaven, 93; sinful social structures, 30, 38, 45, 93, 95
situationalism/situation ethics, 87, 160–62
skepticism, 4–5, 45, 71, 90, 196, 200, 255, 307–8
Slater, T., 129–34
Smith, M., 134–36
social charity and justice, 96
social ethics, 11, 19, 24–25, 35, 53–54, 65, 68–69, 212–14, 242, 270–72, 278
Socias, J., 91
society, 9–11, 15, 18, 22–25, 27, 34, 56, 60–61, 63, 68, 94–98, 176, 178, 183, 196, 198, 203, 212, 232, 237, 270–78, 299–302
Society of Jesus, 104, 122–23, 134, 175, 189, 246, 312
solidarity, 24–25, 30–36, 96–98, 149, 181, 199, 225, 233–35, 237, 246
Solzhenitsyn, A., 9
soul, 17, 65–66, 85, 89, 132–34, 157, 167, 193–94, 208–9, 262, 290, 297–98, 304
Spaemann, R., 310
spirituality, 133, 135
Spitzer, R., 210
state, 11, 27, 38, 131, 191–95, 198, 201, 203, 206, 302
Stein, G., 83
Steinfels, P., 40

sterilization, 163, 191, 193–95, 201, 251, 275
Strauss, L., 4, 12–13, 16
Stuntz, W., 317
Suarez, F., 123
subjectivity, 14, 19, 29, 40, 76, 99, 112–13, 117, 124–25, 129, 131, 143–44, 153, 156–60, 168, 179, 182, 209–10, 230, 241, 257, 263–64, 281–82
subsidiarity, 94, 233, 299, 302
substance, 3, 15–19, 22–23
suicide, 164–65, 306–10, 317
Sullivan, F., 106, 152, 162–63
supernatural, 117, 199, 121–22, 124, 132, 134, 136–38, 141, 149–51, 157, 163, 171, 206

Tanqueray, A., 134–36
Taylor, C., 84, 308–9
Teilhard de Chardin, P., 141, 148–51
Tettamanzi, D., 144
Thatcher, M., 9, 11
Thomism, 11, 14, 44, 50, 119, 121–24, 127, 140, 170, 297–98
Tiberghien, P., 160
Tierney, B., 154
torture, 47
Tracy, D., 316
transcendental moral theology, 140–52, 165
transcendental Thomism, 116, 123–28, 137–52, 160, 163, 165, 167–72, 207–8, 290
Trent, Council of, 82, 103–4, 136
truth, 11, 16, 27–28, 31, 43–45, 48, 50, 53, 56–67, 74, 76, 78, 80, 113–117, 122, 126, 137, 144, 152–54, 163, 170–71, 178–84, 197, 202, 207, 247–48, 250–54, 262–64, 267–68, 276, 300, 302–4
Tucci, R., 176

unions, 29, 38, 232–34, 245–46, 282
universal and unchanging norms, 15, 21, 43–46, 50, 54, 65, 70, 75–78, 80–81, 99, 111, 128, 130–31, 135, 142, 148, 152–53, 161–62, 165, 167–69, 182, 206–7, 210, 251, 257, 262–64, 286

utilitarianism, 45, 67, 76, 183, 188, 196, 200–202, 224, 239, 264, 302

Valsecchi, A., 139
Van Noort, G., 137
Varga, A., 44
Vatican Council I, 115
Vatican Council II, 10, 17, 33, 54, 58, 80, 115–16, 136–38, 151, 175–76, 277, 296, 301, 304; *Dei Verbum,* 107, 138; *Dignitatis Humanae,* 53, 106; *Gaudium et Spes,* 31, 56, 59, 85, 87, 93–95, 138, 175–78, 180, 252, 270, 277, 293, 295–97, 301, 303–4; *Lumen Gentium,* 26, 33, 106, 138; *Optatam Totius,* 42
Vereecke, L., 129
Vermeersch, A.,129–34
vice, 93
Vienne, Council of, 47
virtue ethics, 90, 111
virtues, 13, 32, 34, 84, 87, 90–91, 118, 128, 136, 143, 147, 203, 257, 276–77, 316
Voegelin, E., 12–14, 16
von Balthasar, H., 74–75, 79, 268

Waldenfels, H., 153
Walzer, M., 222, 229
Weakland, R., 188
welfare economics, 218
Werhan, P., 244
will, 15, 17, 33, 89, 101, 113–14, 118, 124–25, 134, 141–42, 146, 159, 161, 207, 296
Williams, G., 65–66
Wills, G., 139
Wilson, J., 225
Wojty(a, K. *See* John Paul II
Wolfe, A., 222
Wolter, A., 143
women, 21, 166, 194, 199, 269, 286–92, 294, 302
work/workers, 24, 27–29, 31–32, 38, 179, 214, 225, 230–34, 237–42, 244–46, 272, 278–82
Wuthnow, R., 228
Wyschogrod, E., 54, 70–71

Zalba, M., 139